Grosset's **UNIVER**

A distinguishe~~d~~ ~~of~~ fine books
in attractive paperbound editions

W9-BCN-497

OSCAR WILDE

HIS LIFE AND WIT

By HESKETH PEARSON

"A fellow of infinite jest, of most excellent fancy."

Grosset's UNIVERSAL *Library*

GROSSET & DUNLAP · NEW YORK

OSCAR WILDE

His Life and Wit

CONTENTS

ACKNOWLEDGMENTS

I wish to express my sincere thanks to Mr. Hugh Kingsmill, who gave me material and helped me greatly with his advice both before and after this book was written; to Sir Bernard Partridge, for the vivid reminiscences of Wilde with which he has enriched my biography; and to the following for their valuable assistance: Mr. Allan Aynesworth, Mrs. Belloc-Lowndes, Mr. David Cross, Mr. Franklin Dyall, Mr. Francis Gribble, Mr. Laurence Housman, Mr. Douglas Jeffries, Mr. A. E. W. Mason, Miss Eleanor O'Connell, Mr. Conal O'Riordan, Mr. Eden Phillpotts, Mr. Bernard Shaw, Mrs. Robert Sherard, Mrs. Joan Thornton, Dame Irene Vanbrugh, Mr. John Wardrop, Mr. Alan White, and Dr. G. T. Wilson.

Lord Alfred Douglas and Sir William Rothenstein, both of whom died while the book was in progress, gave me useful information.

For permission to quote, I am grateful to the authors (or their representatives) and the publishers of these works:

As We Were, by E. F. Benson (Longmans, Green & Co.)
Echo de Paris, by Laurence Housman (D. Appleton-Century Co. Inc.)
The Romantic '90's, by Richard LeGallienne (Doubleday, Doran & Co.)
Aspects of Wilde, by Vincent O'Sullivan (Constable & Co. Ltd.)
Recollections of Oscar Wilde, by Charles Ricketts (Random House)
Life Was Worth Living, by W. Graham Robertson (Harper & Brothers)
I Have Been Young, by H. M. Swanwick (Victor Gollancz Ltd.)

Letters addressed to Mr. Vincent O'Sullivan and Mrs. H. M. Swanwick have been returned; but I trust that they or their representatives will forgive my presumption in taking their permission for granted.

The extracts from the works and letters of Oscar Wilde which will be found in these pages are reprinted by permission of Mr. Vyvyan Holland, the owner of the copyright. For leave to quote from *The Soul of Man Under Socialism*, I have to thank Mr. A. L. Humphreys, who owns the copyright.

CHAPTER ONE

THE PROLOGUE

EARLY in January 1943, I mentioned to Bernard Shaw that I wished to write a Life of Oscar Wilde.

"My advice is, very decidedly, Don't," was Shaw's reply. "The re-issue of Frank Harris's book, revised by Lord Alfred Douglas (who improved it) and with a full dress preface by me, had no great success as far as I know: certainly not enough to encourage any publisher to venture on another biography. Harris, Ransome and Sherard have gleaned that field. Sherard has done the hero-worshipping, Ransome the respectable, and Harris the vivid portraiture. There is nothing more to be said that is of any interest, for Wilde was incomparably great as a *raconteur*, conversationalist, and a personality; and those points cannot be reproduced. I could repeat one of Wilde's anecdotes for you, but not his way of telling it, without which it would be nothing; and it would be dismissed as a paraphrase of a story by Mark Twain. His plays are already in print. His poems made a great impression on the Germans, but that was because they had not read Rossetti or Swinburne or Morris and supposed that Wilde had created their school. I quite agree that some day, when the Queensberry business is forgotten, the Encyclopaedias will give an account of him in which it will be dismissed in half a line, like Verlaine's similar misadventure; but that will not be in my time, and hardly in yours. So much has been written since his conviction on the subject of his inverted sexual instinct that the subject is stale. The last acquaintance of mine who was prosecuted for it got five months instead of Wilde's two years; and the case was not mentioned in the press."

I answered Shaw's objections by saying that no one had yet attempted to reconstruct Wilde as a great character; that far too much attention had been paid to his tragic story and nothing like enough to his delightful personality; that my intention was to take him out of the fog of pathology into the light of comedy, to restore the true perspective of his career, to revive the conversationalist, not the convict; that not one word of Harris's book in particular could be accepted as true without corroborative evidence; that Wilde's genius

1

as a talker was by no means dependent on his manner, and had been pre-served in numerous specimens which were not only original but of a kind that could be recorded without essential loss; that to compare Mark Twain's humour with Wilde's was like comparing a giraffe with a gazelle; and that, anyhow, as I wanted to write the work, I would have to go ahead.

From the age of nineteen I have been attracted to Oscar Wilde. Just after leaving school I came across *The Soul of Man Under Socialism*, and it per-formed the vital operation of making me think for myself. Before that I had accepted, as became my station in life, the Conservative Party and the Church of England as the sole channels of political and religious truth. I dare say I should have been emancipated in time from the beliefs of my class without the help of Wilde's *Soul of Man*, but I doubt if any other work could have shaken me up so quickly and successfully, because a social philosophy has never been expressed so entertainingly, and the gravity with which such themes are generally treated would have had no effect on me but a sopor-ific one. For ridiculing all the beliefs in which I had been brought up, for laughing my mind out of its rut and so enabling me to think freely with the aid of what inner light God had given me, I have always been grateful to Oscar Wilde.

But I am indebted to him for more than that. Wit, humour, good nature and invincible gaiety of spirit are the qualities in people that make the strong-est appeal to me, and with the exception of Sydney Smith, and in a different way Bernard Shaw, no one who spoke our language was so consistently, light-heartedly and unmaliciously amusing as Wilde. It is my desire to re-create him first and foremost as a genial wit and humorist, because in my view the essential Wilde was expressed in spontaneous laughter, not in the pose of a martyr. I shall not dismiss the trial and its aftermath as matters of no importance, but the final phase must not be allowed to overshadow the rest: it lasted for five years in a life of forty-six years: that is, one-fifth of his manhood. His sexual peculiarity must also be dealt with, though briefly. It is not as interesting as some people have tried to make out. Unfortunately it has been used by those who are similarly addicted as a sort of advertisement, the implication being that as Wilde was a genius and a pederast it is quite on the cards that every other pederast is also a genius. The normal man might just as well claim to be a great novelist on the ground that Fielding too was normal.

Having been interested in Wilde's personality for close on forty years, I have picked up a good deal of information about him that has not yet been published. It did not occur to me in my early days of enthusiasm that I would ever tackle his biography; but as I always intended to write something about him sooner or later, I made a point of discussing his personality with everyone I met who had known him. By a stroke of good fortune I started my stage career under Sir Herbert Tree, who told me a lot, and continued it under Sir George Alexander, who told me more. Tree enjoyed talking, and as he had admired Wilde more than anyone he had ever known I had no difficulty in getting him on to the subject, though it was not always easy to distinguish between what was Wilde's and what was Tree's. On the other hand, Alexander was usually busy and seldom in a reminiscent mood. Yet when at last I got him to recall the past one evening in his home at Chorley Wood, he gave me some of my best material; and as he had a first-rate memory and not much imagination, I could rely on everything he said. Both Tree and Alexander saw and approved the notes I made of what they had told me about Wilde, my own memory before the 1914 war being good enough to reproduce conversations almost verbatim. Two other actors, Lewis Waller and H. B. Irving, though I only knew them slightly, were also helpful.

Of Wilde's intimate friends, I have known and corresponded with Alfred Douglas, Robert Ross, Adela Schuster and Robert Sherard, from each of whom I received something valuable; and I was on friendly terms with Frank Harris, whose reminiscences I have since discovered to be suspect. It was Robert Ross who gave me the original conversational versions of several witticisms by Wilde which were slightly altered when he put them into his stories and plays. The source of everything of importance that appears here for the first time is mentioned in the text.

A wealth of Wildeana has lain for some years untouched by a biographer in certain works, chief among them being: *Echo de Paris* by Laurence Housman, *The Romantic '90s* by Richard Le Gallienne, *Oscar Wilde Discovers America* by Lloyd Lewis and Henry Justin Smith, *Bibliography of Oscar Wilde* by Stuart Mason, *Aspects of Wilde* by Vincent O'Sullivan, *Recollections of Oscar Wilde* by Charles Ricketts, *Time Was* by Graham Robertson. I have done more than touch this material: I have grabbed it.

CHAPTER TWO

THE PARENTS

A MAN'S myriad ancestors probably have more influence on his mental and physical being than his two parents, whose effect on his upbringing can only qualify the main traits of a character produced by innumerable forebears. But sometimes a man's nature seems to owe a great deal to his parents; and as this was especially so in the case of Oscar Wilde, we must pay some attention to his father and mother, both of whom achieved considerable distinction in their way.

Towards the end of the seventeenth century an Englishman named Ralph Wilde left Walsingham near Durham and settled down in Dublin as a builder. One of his sons became a land agent in Connaught and married into the ancient family of O'Flyn. A child of this union became a doctor, and improved the social status of the family by marrying Emily Fynne, who was related to some of the chief people in Connaught, and whose family has been described as 'very unstable mentally.' Thus their son, William Wilde, had a good deal more native Irish blood in him than most of the Anglo-Irish could claim, and this will account for his keen interest in the country of his birth and for not a little of his personal oddity.

He was born in 1815; and as he showed skill and aptitude in dressing the wounds of his father's patients, inflicted in the course of those free fights with which Irishmen so often terminate a day's fun, he was sent to Dublin at the age of 17 to become a surgeon. His appearance was peculiar. Short and slender in build, he had a pale face, fine forehead, long nose, and shrewd prominent eyes. The other features were not so pleasant to look at: a wide mouth, sensual lips and receding chin. We shall later have to notice that his son Oscar suffered from the same dissimilarity between the upper and lower portions of his face, and in both cases the features were an index to character.

William Wilde's experiences as a medical student were of the usual kind in those days: much low humour and horseplay in the dissecting-room, much laughing, singing, drinking, smoking and fornicating elsewhere. One of his fellow-students was Charles Lever, an industrious practical joker, who later forsook the knife for the pen, with which he dissected many of his early contemporaries. But life was grim as well as comic, and in his first year as a student Wilde showed that he possessed both courage and ability. Cholera broke out in Dublin, and his parents insisted on his returning home. Reluctantly he did so, but while staying with some relations in Connaught, he was asked to visit a man who was seriously ill in a neighboring village. He arrived to find the man dead of cholera and the owner of the house down with the same disease. No help was to be got from the villagers, who were too frightened to come near the place, so Wilde nursed his patient alone. The cholera left the man exhausted, in which state he passed out, and though Wilde managed to get a coffin from the villagers he had to do everything else himself, burning what was necessary, fumigating the house, and (helped by a man who was too drunk to care) removing the coffin on a donkey-cart, digging the grave, and burying the remains in quicklime. It was probably due to Wilde's action that no other case of cholera occurred in the village. Soon afterwards his quickness and ingenuity were manifested when a piece of potato got lodged in a child's windpipe, which he promptly opened with a pair of scissors. This operation, which saved the child's life, was performed *coram populo*.

Back in Dublin he worked hard, and, though ill with fever, acquitted himself brilliantly in an examination; after which he collapsed and was on the point of death when an unorthodox doctor prescribed strong ale, which, taken hourly, saved him, and inspired him with a lifelong belief in the health-giving qualities of alcohol. His recovery was hastened by a sea-voyage in the Mediterranean as doctor to a wealthy patient. This trip was a godsend, not only on account of his health, but because of his keen interest in diseases and ancient monuments, Egypt and Palestine supplying him with a varied assortment of both. The number of people in Egypt who were either blind or half-blind from trachoma first aroused his interest in eye-diseases; while the tombs, pyramids and mummy-pits he was able to explore sharpened his appetite for archaeological research. On his return he passed on the knowledge he had gained by writing a book describing his travels and by lecturing before several scientific societies. The excavations he undertook in Ireland shortly after this brought him membership of the Royal Irish Academy at the early age of 24. As time went on he became very popular as a lecturer, dealing in a fluent and forthright manner with such topics as the interiors of monkeys and fish, which entertained the audiences of those days as much as the exteriors of film "stars" excite them nowadays. He was taken up by society and especially liked by women, which pleased him well. His success with them was not won by any outward physical advantage. He was none too clean in appearance, and plain enough to be included, at a later date, in a series of caricatures of celebrated ugly men. Clearly he possessed charms of another sort, for the patronage of the older women, such as Maria Edgeworth, helped him in his profession, while the favours of the younger ones were an important part of his recreation. But accidents will happen, even to doctors, and in due course several children appeared without the advantage of their father's name.

That name was soon to become famous. Having devoted the royalties on his travel-book to a course of study in London and Vienna, he converted a Dublin stable into a hospital for diseases of the eye and ear, and quickly obtained a large practice among rich and poor alike, being forced to move in a few years to more commodious quarters, where students from all parts of the world came to learn aural surgery. A book on his continental tour, containing much statistical information, obtained for him the appointment of Medical Census Commissioner; and this, with the kudos his antiquarian researches brought him, his editorship of the *Dublin Quarterly Journal of Medical Science,* and his unrivalled position as an ear surgeon, made Wilde a leading figure in Ireland, among his friends being Charles Lever, Sheridan Le Fanu, and the more prominent scientists and politicians of his day. His reputation as a writer was sealed by his work on *The Closing Years of Dean Swift's Life,* and by his book describing *The Beauties of the Boyne and Blackwater*, which was the outcome of his fondness for fishing coupled with his passion for ancient ruins and remains. When Macaulay visited Ireland to get material for his History, he was shown the battlefield of the Boyne and many other places by Dr. Wilde.

The failure of the potato crop brought the terrible Irish famine of 1845-9, with its attendant pestilence, and Wilde slaved away at his statistics, his reports and his surgical work. It also brought the Young Ireland party into great prominence, and thereby introduced Wilde to his future wife.

The Young Ireland party was started by Gavan Duffy, Thomas Davis and John Blake Dillon. At first they had worked with Daniel O'Connell for the Repeal of the Union, but soon they went further than he was prepared to go, advocated complete national independence, to be achieved by force of arms if necessary, and in 1842 founded a paper, *The Nation*, to forward their views. They were quickly joined by most of their gifted young contemporaries, and the sale of the paper rose to some 250,000 copies. Davis died in the autumn of '45, and John Mitchel took his place as editor of *The Nation*. The driving-force behind Davis had been a love of Ireland, but that behind Mitchel was a loathing of England, and the political atmosphere began to warm up. The contributions to the paper became highly inflammatory, some of the more sensational ones, written in a florid style, appearing under the name of "John Fenshaw Ellis." Verses were also printed, signed "Speranza," the enthusiasm of which was more obvious than their inspiration; and it was whispered that "Ellis" and "Speranza" hid the name of the same person, and, more surprising still in view of such vigorous exhortations as "to arms! to arms! for truth, fame, freedom, vengeance, victory!", that the writer was a woman. At length, Mitchel, whose fanaticism had led to a break with *The Nation* and who had started a periodical called *The United Irishman*, boiled over. "Let the man among you who has no gun sell his garment and buy one," he wrote. Giving his countrymen no time to profit by this advice, the authorities arrested every leader of the movement they could lay hands on, and the two papers were left without their staffs. Gavan Duffy's sister-in-law and "Speranza" promptly took charge of *The Nation*, and the latter produced an article headed *Jacta Alea Est*, which was printed in the number for July 29th, 1848, calling upon the people to rise in their might and die for Ireland. "Oh! for a hundred thousand muskets glittering brightly in the light of heaven," she cried, "and the monumental barricades stretching across each of our noble streets made desolate by England—circling round that doomed Castle, where the foreign tyrant has held his council of treason and iniquity against our people and our country for seven hundred years.... One bold, one decisive move. One instant to take breath, and then a rising; a rush, a charge from north, south, east and west upon the English garrison, and *the land is ours*."

Unfortunately the rush came from the wrong quarter: the foreign tyrant suppressed the paper, seized the entire issue in which this article appeared, and prosecuted Duffy for sedition, high treason, and so forth. "Speranza" was not one to sit quietly and watch others take the blame for her actions; and when the Attorney-General had read passages from two of her articles to the jury and demanded the conviction of Duffy on the strength of them, she broke the silence which followed by calling out "I alone am the culprit. I wrote the offending articles." As a result of her confession the jury disagreed. But state trials followed several abortive risings, the leaders were packed off to Van Diemen's Land, and the Young Ireland movement was next to be known as Fenianism, then as Sinn Fein, finally achieving its aim by the foundation of the Republic.

William Wilde, though in secret sympathy with the movement, was too cautious to make his feelings widely known. Nevertheless, some three years after the exile of Mitchel and company, he became engaged to the poetess of the revolt, and they were married on November 12th, 1851.

Her name was Jane Francesca Elgee. Her great-grandfather, an Italian, had come to Ireland in the eighteenth century, and her grandfather, Archdeacon Elgee, was rector of Wexford. She was born, according to her own statement, in 1826, but as her father had died two years earlier it is probable that she under-estimated her age, a habit that her son Oscar was later to copy. She was a precocious child, her early years at Wexford being spent in learning Latin, French, German and Italian for pleasure, and soon after she came to Dublin at about the age of 20 she translated works from the French and one book, *Sidonia the Sorceress*, from the German. Having accidentally witnessed the funeral procession of Thomas Davis, of whom she had never heard, she became interested in the Young Ireland movement, and enrolled herself as a fighter and writer for the cause, with the result we know.

William and Jane made a strange pair. He was short, eager, restless, excitable, easily moved to anger, and ugly enough to be instantaneously recognised as the original of "Dr. Quilp," the leading character in a pamphlet written to expose him by a woman with whom he had been intimate. His wife was tall, stately, aloof, dignified, handsome, and in full command of her emotions, though her rich vibrating voice and dark lustrous eyes suggested an enthusiastic nature rather at variance with her physical poise. Like so many small men, Wilde was greatly attracted by women of imposing presence, and some years before his marriage he had fallen in love with the famous actress, Helen Faucit, on whom his charm had failed to operate.

The Wildes were living at No. 21 Westland Row when their two sons were born: Willie towards the end of 1852, and Oscar on October 16, 1856. Both were burdened with four christian names, the younger's being Oscar Fingal O'Flahertie Wills, though the last three names were abandoned by their owner, one at a time, as he grew up. On reaching the age of 30 he told a friend why: "My name has two O's, two F's, and two W's. A name which is destined to be in everybody's mouth must not be too long. It comes so expensive in the advertisements. When one is unknown, a number of christian names are useful, perhaps needful. As one becomes famous, one sheds some of them, just as a balloonist, when rising higher, sheds unnecessary ballast . . . All but two of my five names have already been thrown overboard. Soon I shall discard another and be known simply as "The Wilde" or "The Oscar." ' But his destiny was not apparent to him in childhood, and when asked his names he gave full value to every syllable in all of them.

Twelve years of increasing fame and fortune followed the marriage of William Wilde. The success of his hospital had been so great that he had fitted out a much larger building, which became world-famous and attracted specialists as well as students from the leading cities of Europe and America. He was, says his biographer, Dr. T. G. Wilson, "the first and, in many ways, the greatest of English-speaking ear surgeons." His work on *Aural Surgery* (1853), for many years the standard textbook on the subject, crowned his reputation, and the same year he was given the post of Surgeon Oculist in Ordinary to the Queen in Ireland, a post that had apparently been created in order that he might occupy it. His energy seemed inexhaustible. Single-handed he prepared a medical report on the 1851 census, a huge undertaking of some 600 folio pages, published in '54; and three years later he was ready with the first part of a catalogue of the antiquities in the Royal Irish Academy museum, the preparation of which had already baffled a committee.

Meanwhile he had moved his family to No. 1 Merrion Square, where the leading doctors and lawyers of the city were his neighbours and where he and his wife could entertain in style. His success went to his head, and he was less eager to please than he had once been: he began to make enemies by showing his impatience with less efficient co-workers, and by losing his temper with those who did not agree with him: an acid quality crept into his conversation, and he developed the habit of ridiculing people who had not realised that they were legitimate objects for ridicule. Naturally they returned the compliment; his personal appearance gave them the cue; and before long Dublin society was amusing itself with the question "Why are Dr. Wilde's nails so black?" the answer to which ran "Because he has scratched himself." His wife's rather slapdash methods as a hostess also did not escape censure, and it was said that she had once admonished a servant with "Why do you put the plates in the coalscuttle? What are the chairs meant for?" Undoubtedly the Wilde household was queer. It was of the kind that Charles Lever revelled in: dirty and daring, disorderly and picturesque. If the doctor was conscious of his importance, garrulous, quick-tempered, and addicted to alcohol, his wife was certain of her genius, majestic, self-contained, and addicted to poetical recitations. The dress, habits and manners of both were out of the ordinary, and they were probably the most talked-of people in Dublin.

Both as doctor and as archaeologist Wilde was now known to his fellow-workers in those fields all over the continent, and he received the attentions of royal folk. Napoleon III sent a Commissioner to consult him; the Emperor Maximilian, en route for Mexico, visited him; the King of Sweden decorated him with the Order of the Polar Star; and the Prince of Wales, afterwards Edward VII, inspected the exhibits of the Museum in his company. Degrees, diplomas, dinners, were given to him; and in 1864 he was knighted at Dublin Castle, not for his surgical or archaeological achievements, but for his services to "Statistical Science, especially in connection with the Irish Census." This was not exactly the kind of "rush" upon the "doomed Castle" which his wife had once envisaged, but there is no evidence that she protested against it. Indeed she seems to have enjoyed the recognition of "the foreign tyrant." And in any case life was flowing along very pleasantly just then. She had longed for a daughter, her prayers had been answered, and Isola Francesca was born some three years after Oscar. They were now very well off, Wilde being so busy that he sent many of his cases to his natural son, Henry Wilson, who was his assistant in private practice; they entertained everyone of note who visited Ireland; and their assemblies were among the events of the season. They also had a delightful country residence, at Moytura on the shores of Lough Corrib in Connemara, where Wilde had bought some land and built a house, and where, usually with his family, he spent his holidays for the rest of his life, fishing or exploring the caves of the district. And so things might have continued to the end, if only an attractive girl of 19 had not called to consult the doctor one summer day back in 1854.

She was the daughter of a professor at Trinity College, and her name was Mary Travers. The medical consultation led to a friendship between doctor and patient, which quickly ripened to physical intimacy. They went about together and he spent a good deal of money on her. His wife got to know of the affair, but, accustomed to the doctor's habits, treated it as a normal occurrence. Mary, however, though well aware that her lover had done his full share in raising the birth-rate of Ireland, felt that hers was a special case and determined to monopolise his affections. After the early excitement had worn off, her exigence began to grate upon him, especially when her intention to become a permanent member of his household took the form of a visit to his wife's bedroom, when she was expelled with some heat by "Speranza"; and he decided to get rid of her. But that was a decision more easy to reach than to accomplish: Mary's views for the future did not harmonise with his. He tried to buy her acquiescence with money, with clothes, with anything that took her fancy. She accepted these gifts as the thank-offerings of a loving heart. His cooling passion became more apparent when he entreated her to join her brothers in Australia. Accepting his offer of the passage-money, she enjoyed a trip to Liverpool, and enjoyed still more the return trip to Dublin. Again he begged her to go to Australia, offering to see her boat off at Liverpool. Rejecting the offer, she again took the passage-money, went to Liverpool, saw the boat off herself, and returned home. By this time it was perfectly clear to her that Wilde was sick of her, and she determined to make him pay for his loss of interest. For a while she was content with the pleasure of watching him squirm whenever she demanded money and of harassing him with unexpected visits in private and awkward appearances in public. But at last, galled by his ill-concealed distaste for her society and infuriated by the snubs of his wife, she thought out a scheme of revenge.

Starting with anonymous letters and poems, each more scurrilous than the last, she soon produced and printed a pamphlet, copies of which, and sometimes bundles, arrived by nearly every post at 1 Merrion Square for several weeks. Wilde's friends, acquaintances, enemies and patients were also supplied with the work; and as the contents were of a startling nature it was not long before everyone in Dublin society knew the story, which, spiced with much dramatic detail, told how a certain "Dr. Quilp" had first chloroformed and then violated a girl in his consulting-room. As a final touch, the writer's pseudonym was given as "Speranza." Wilde ignored the pamphlet, which enraged Mary Travers, and a short while after it had been going the rounds he was knighted, which drove her mad. Certainly her next move was not that of a sane woman. Wilde was billed to lecture on Ireland for the Young Men's Christian Association in the spring of '64, and Dublin society flocked to hear him at the Metropolitan Hall. In the street outside several urchins were vociferously selling "Speranza's" pamphlet and distributing free of charge printed copies of Sir William Wilde's private letters to the girl he had "wronged." Not to leave any reader in doubt as to who was meant by "Dr. Quilp," a statement accompanied the pamphlet giving Wilde's name and address, together with the address where the originals of his printed letters could be inspected.

In the hope that the scandal created by this episode would blow over, Lady Wilde took her children to Bray. But she was allowed no peace. Small boys called at her house on the sea front offering the pamphlet for sale, and at last her patience gave out: she wrote an angry letter to Dr. Travers complaining of his daughter in terms which made that daughter's heart jump for joy when she accidentally came across the letter in the professor's cupboard a few weeks later:

TOWER, BRAY,
May 6

Sir,
    You may not be aware of the disreputable conduct of your daughter at Bray, where she consorts with all the low newspaper boys in the place, employing them to disseminate offensive placards, in which my name is given, and also

tracts, in which she makes it appear that she has had an intrigue with Sir William Wilde. If she chooses to disgrace herself that is not my affair; but as her object in insulting me is in the hope of extorting money, for which she has several times applied to Sir William Wilde, with threats of more annoyance if not given, I think it right to inform you that no threat or additional insult shall ever extort money for her from our hands. The wages of disgrace she has so loosely treated for and demanded shall never be given her.

JANE F. WILDE

To Dr. Travers.

Sir William Wilde knew nothing of this letter, and would undoubtedly have prevented its despatch if his advice had been asked; but he was in Dublin when it was written, and his wife did not mention it on her return, thinking no doubt that they would hear no more of the matter. But there was nothing in her own nature to warn her of the hatred, jealousy and ferocity in Mary's, and when she was sued for libel it was a shock for her no less than for her husband. Two thousand pounds damages were claimed, and Sir William was joined in the action "for conformity" as her husband, though everybody knew perfectly well that he was the real villain of the piece.

The case was tried in December '64. Their son Oscar, aged 10, had just gone to Portora Royal School, Enniskillen, where, boys being boys, he must have heard more about his father's doings than if he had been at home. Dublin society thrilled with agreeable sensations, smacked its lips, and settled down to the delightful occupation of hearing unsavoury stories and passing moral judgments. After stating that nothing but the sternest sense of public duty would have induced him to touch such a case, and leaving it to be understood that the question of fees had not influenced him in the smallest degree, counsel for Mary Travers unfolded the sad story which, such is the nature of human beings with a grievance, Mary herself had probably come to believe. To make the incident of her violation more picturesque, the chloroform was dropped, and Wilde was now accused of having half-throttled her before performing what Shakespeare called "the deed of darkness."

Then began the series of lies, half-lies, contradictions and prevarications which are the main feature of courts of justice, for people who in ordinary life are honest enough become hopelessly untrustworthy the moment they enter the witness-box and give evidence on oath. Mary Travers lied because the truth would not have served her turn; Lady Wilde lied because the truth would have been awkward for her husband; and Sir William refused to give evidence because he knew that neither lies nor truth would leave his character spotless. It is clear that Wilde had been very provoking, for he had told Mary that she was mad. "No one but a person that was mad would wear such a bonnet!" he had once screamed at her. But it is equally clear that most of the provocation had come from her, and when her counsel described her as a "bleeding, broken-hearted woman" the jury were not greatly impressed by the picture. The judge's summing-up was fair: he pointed out that a woman who is being violated usually objects to the process at the time and does not remain on calling terms with her ravisher. But he implied that as Wilde had not gone into the box to refute her story of "guilty intimacy," the jury would be justified in assuming that he had seduced her. The jury took about two hours to make up their minds, and then brought in a verdict for the plaintiff, assessing the damages at one farthing. As this meant that Wilde had to pay the costs of the case, it appears to a layman that the jury charged Wilde from two to three thousand pounds for seducing a girl whose virtue they valued at a farthing. In any profession but that of the law this would be called profiteering.

The publicity given to the case had an unfortunate effect on Wilde, who rapidly deteriorated. He dropped out of public life, took no further interest in his profession, left his son Wilson to run the hospital, was careless with his patients, rude to his colleagues, and spent as much time as possible at Moytura, where he seemed to be more at home with what Carlyle called "the venerable rocks" than with the human species. He became dirtier than ever and more pithecoid in appearance; his consumption of drink increased; and old friends began to draw away from him. He was not wholly unproductive in his last years, for he wrote his most popular book, *Lough Corrib*, started several others, and was awarded the Cunningham Gold Medal by the Royal Irish Academy for his work on the catalogue of antiquities. But his energies had been exhausted too early in life, and the Travers case was a knock-out blow to an already spent man.

Domestic tragedy deepened his gloom. His little girl Isola died in '67, and a few years later two of his natural daughters, aged 21 and 22, were burnt to death at a dance, when the crinoline of one caught fire and ignited that of the other who tried to save her. Wilde followed them in the spring of '76. Though the technical cause of death is unknown, it is almost certain that he died because he did not wish to live. In after years Oscar Wilde paid this tribute to his mother:

"She was a wonderful woman, and such a feeling as vulgar jealousy could take no hold on her. She was well aware of my father's constant

infidelities, but simply ignored them. Before my father died, in 1876, he lay
ill in bed for many days. And every morning a woman dressed in black and
closely veiled used to come to our house in Merrion Square, and unhindered
either by my mother or anyone else used to walk straight upstairs to Sir
William's bedroom and sit down at the head of his bed, and so sit there all
day, without ever speaking a word or once raising her veil. She took no
notice of anybody in the room, and nobody paid any attention to her. Not
one woman in a thousand would have tolerated her presence, but my
mother allowed it, because she knew that my father loved this woman and
felt that it must be a joy and a comfort to have her there by his dying
bed. And I am sure that she did right not to grudge that last happiness
to a man who was about to die, and I am sure that my father understood
her apparent indifference, understood that it was not because she did not
love him that she permitted her rival's presence, but because she loved
him very much, and died with his heart full of gratitude and affection for
her."

CHAPTER THREE

THE BOY

IT HAS been said that Oscar Wilde's mother, anxious to have a daughter, was so deeply disappointed when her second son appeared that she dressed him as a girl long after the age when the clothes of male and female children become distinctive; and that, in some queer way known to pathology but obscure to common sense, this fashion gravely affected his sexual nature. But as his sister was born about three years after himself, when presumably his mother's desire for a daughter was appeased, it is reasonable to conclude that Oscar's appearances in girlish attire thereafter were limited to special occasions, and that we cannot explain his later fancies by insisting on his early frocks. Undoubtedly his mother spoilt, petted and exhibited him, and visitors to the house in Merrion Square were compelled to view him and to hear stories about him; but other mothers have been known to subject their friends and acquaintances to the same sort of boredom without gravely imperilling the character of their offspring. Nevertheless it is probable that the mother's wish for a girl before his birth had an effect on his nature.

When a writer's early years have been miserable he seldom fails to let his readers into the secret; and as Oscar Wilde hardly ever spoke of his youth, we may infer that it was happy. Two disagreeable incidents have been recorded. Playing in the nursery with his elder brother Willie, of whom he was fond, his arm was broken. "It was my first introduction to the horrors of pain, the lurking tragedies of life," he afterwards said. And one night he was awakened by a series of wails and shrieks. "Why are they beating that dog?" he cried, "Tell them to stop beating the dog." He was told that it was the Banshee, and, supernaturally, someone in the neighbourhood had to die the following day. At an age when most boys were fast asleep in bed Willie and Oscar were allowed to stay up for dinner, no matter how large or distinguished the company; and as the liquor flowed as freely as the conversation, the two youngsters were educated in the ways of the world long before such knowledge was helpful.

In his tenth year Oscar joined his brother at Portora Royal School, and evidence concerning his nature began to accumulate. He was unlike the other boys in all his tastes and habits. On the negative side, he disliked exercise, detested games ("I never liked to kick or be kicked"), loathed fighting, refused to climb trees, had no desire to collect or possess the usual things boys hanker after, and was wholly deficient in the spirit of adventure. On the positive side, he read a great deal, was careful about his clothes, wore his top hat on weekdays, loved flowers, admired sunsets, enjoyed solitude, and often mooned about in a state of abstraction. By the age of thirteen he had become clumsy, ponderous and over-large, loutish in fact, and the unpopularity gained by his lack of sportsmanship had been increased by his facility in inventing nicknames for other boys, nicknames which were so effective that they pleased everyone except the victims, to whom they stuck; but as he exercised this faculty over a wide field, a good deal of the pleasure he gave was cancelled out. Indeed he was only able to minister to the unmixed joy of his schoolfellows by twisting his limbs into curious shapes and giving faithful representations of the saints in stained-glass windows, a performance which almost persuaded the onlookers that there was something human in him after all. Now and then he took part in a boyish rough-and-tumble, in one of which his arm was broken for the second time, but he did not blame anyone for the accident. Occasionally he was to be seen swimming in the lake, and even rowing a boat, which he did awkwardly; but as he spent most of the time so employed in contemplating the sky or musing over the shells he had picked up on the shore, no one thought any the better of him for such diversions.

He had no special friends during his schooldays, and his brother took little notice of him. Willie was popular: he could play games and use his fists and tell amusing stories and do all the other things that boys liked. Also he was considered much cleverer than Oscar, who at first was just as lazy at work as he was hostile to play. The incompetence of the masters may have been partly responsible for his lack of interest, but no power on earth could have made mathematics attractive to him. Like all purely artistic natures he remained a complete dunce on that subject all his life; and Science generally left him cold. He could appreciate a sunset without wanting to know whether the earth went round the sun or the other way about, and his own indifferent attitude to all knowledge that did not enrich the soul was summed up in a remark he was later to put into the mouth of Dorian Gray: "Alan, you are scientific. You know about chemistry and things of that kind. You have made experiments."

School-education of any sort he thought valueless. "Nothing that is worth knowing can be taught," he once said, and "We teach people how to remember, we never teach them how to grow." His opinion of school-masters was not flattering: "Everybody who is incapable of learning has taken to teaching—that is really what our enthusiasm for education has come to." And it was with a feeling not far removed from horror that he once described the experience of sitting at dinner next to a man who had spent his life trying to educate others: "How appalling is that ignorance which is the inevitable result of the fatal habit of imparting opinions! How limited in range the creature's mind proves to be! How it wearies us, and must weary himself with its endless repetitions and sickly reiteration! How lacking it is in any element of intellectual growth! In what a vicious circle it always moves!" Even the reminder of some slight effort to do well at Portora was distasteful to him, for when a History of English Literature in two volumes, won by him as a prize, turned up in some second-hand bookseller's and was bought by a friend and presented to him after his release from prison, he cried "Do take those dreadful things away! Don't keep them yourself. Give them to the cab-driver."

He certainly did his best while at school to prevent the masters from boring him with facts and figures, though they did not guess that his apparent desire for information was simply an attempt to make the time pass more easily. Sitting in form, with his long hair brushed straight back from his forehead, his large sagacious eyes widely opened, his lips parted as if in eager expectation of valuable knowledge, he would gradually, by cunningly put questions, lead the unsuspecting master away from the subject of the lesson and make him expand on more interesting themes. And when the master, suffering from a spasm of conscience, returned abruptly to the curriculum, Oscar would retire into himself and think out new methods of side-tracking the topic and lessening the tedium of learning. According to the masters, his conduct was "good," though a boy who was at school with him related that he once "cheeked" the headmaster and "got into an awful row."

His favourite romantic reading as a child was his mother's translation of *Sidonia the Sorceress*, but in his early 'teens he read the novels of Dickens, which he did not like, and those of Disraeli, which he did. Then came poetry and the classics, which were his natural sustenance, and it was observed that the only possessions in which he took a pride were large-paper editions of his favourite Greek authors, his fondness for whom enabled him to leave the rest of the school far behind in his last year and win the Gold Medal.

Those of his schoolmates who did not think that the main object in life was to kick or hit a ball about a field liked Oscar. Apart from his unpleasant knack of distributing nicknames, he was a gentle, kindly, affectionate, dreamy youth, who never quarrelled if he could help it, was easily pleased, would give advice to any one for the asking, and possessed in a remarkable degree the gift of lying in a humorous and picturesque manner. A meeting with a dwarf became in his description a combat with a giant, a frisky dog was converted into a snorting charger, a sparrow into an eagle, and an eel into a sea-serpent. One day his love of romancing took a queer turn. An ecclesiastical prosecution had caused a minor sensation, and Oscar was enlarging on the strange constitution and mysterious doings of the Court of Arches. It was all very weird and very wonderful, and carried away on the wings of his fancy he suddenly exclaimed that nothing would please him more than to be the leading figure in a great trial and to achieve fame as the defendant in a case of Regina v Wilde. His wish was to be granted, but not in the form that he had pictured it.

Willie and Oscar spent their summer holidays either with their mother on the continent or with their parents at Moytura, sometimes exploring the caves and ancient remains with their father, sometimes swimming or fishing in the lake. Oscar's fishing was perfunctory. In later life, as already remarked, he seldom referred to his youth; but for several days after his release from prison he continually reverted to it. Unfortunately his companions, Robert Ross and Reginald Turner, were anxious to hear all about his recent experiences, and kept interrupting his reminiscences of boyhood with questions about his treatment in gaol. In conversation with me, Ross could only recall two slight details. The first was that Oscar once ran away from home and hid in a cave, the second that he and Willie used to fish in Lough Corrib. "It was full," said he, "of large melancholy salmon, which lay at the bottom of the lake, and paid no attention to our bait."

An event during his school life had such an effect on him that some years afterwards he wrote a poem on it. His sister Isola died at Edgeworthstown at the age of nine, and the doctor recorded that Oscar's "lonely and inconsolable grief found its outward expression in long and frequent visits to his sister's grave in the village cemetery." He had probably longed for the day when Isola would be the sympathetic and affectionate companion he had failed to find in Willie.

In October 1871, he received an "exhibition" from Portora and won an entrance scholarship at Trinity College, Dublin, where he remained for three years, his love of the classics gaining him many prizes, a "Foundation" scholarship, and eventually the Berkeley Gold Medal for Greek, which turned out to be his most useful and expensive academic distinction, for he pawned it when hard-up and redeemed it when in funds at frequent intervals all through his life. Academic honours are won by grinding or a good memory, not by genius, and Oscar's successes in that field were not due to hard work, for he remained lazy, but simply to the fact that he revelled in the classics and could not help remembering every word he read, his memory being prodigious. It happened also that one of his tutors at Trinity College was the Rev. John Pentland Mahaffy, then Professor of Ancient History, later Provost of the College, whose passion for Hellenic culture and ideals was only equalled by his passion for British titles and dinners.

Mahaffy influenced Oscar considerably, though in a later chapter we shall find that the pupil spotted his old tutor's main weakness and censured it. The Anglo-Irish are a curiously snobbish people, and Mahaffy was a prime specimen of his kind. He was an out-and-out social snob: that is, he would rather have sat down to a bad meal with a stupid aristocrat than to a good meal with an intelligent tradesman. However, the choice was never forced upon him, as the Dublin aristocrats of those days fed themselves very well. He loved a lord, adored a duke, and would have worshipped a prince. To attain social position and prestige was the ambition of his life, and to that end he studied the art of conversation, the mastery of which would, he believed, give him complete ascendancy wherever the well-born were gathered together. How to speak with familiarity, how to speak with authority, when to pause, when to change the conversation, what manner to adopt towards women, what towards men, how to talk to one's social superiors, how to one's equals, how to condescend, how to be charming, witty, humble, arrogant, affecting, affected: all this could be taught, learnt and practised. And in course of time Mahaffy became a remarkable talker. But the governing class and the leading families were not to be subdued wholly by tact, brilliance and rhetoric at dinner parties and receptions. They liked a man to be a sportsman, and here too the professor was able to oblige them: he developed into an excellent cricketer, a first-class shot and an expert fly-fisherman. Add that he was a walking encyclopaedia on certain matters liable to arise whenever the conversation took a historical turn, also that, though a parson, he was a complete sceptic, and his popularity in the circles he wished to impress need not be questioned.

Oscar responded eagerly to the Mahaffy treatment. Already a humorous and vivacious talker, under his tutor he realised the possibilities of the gift. Already a lover of the Greek poets and historians, he quickly became a lover of everything Greek. Not disinclined by nature and upbringing to accept worldly values, he was soon initiated by Mahaffy into the mysteries of snobbery and taught that superciliousness was a sign of good-breeding. But worse remained behind. For the first and only time in his life Oscar sinned against his nature during his Varsity days by shooting, fishing and playing tennis with some approach to gusto; though in his favour it may be urged that he showed no aptitude for any of them, and, as an exercise, preferred eating and drinking to all three. In return for these benefits Oscar gave Mahaffy admiration, emulation, and the companionship of a quick-witted, high-spirited and eloquent disciple; so that in retrospect the professor was able to say that his pupil, one of the few students he had known who could write a really good Greek composition, was "all verve and *joie de vivre*" throughout the period of their association.

The average student at Trinity College was more interested in fighting, gambling, drinking, football, whoring, and obscene stories, than in Greek culture and the art of conversation, so we are not surprised to learn that Oscar did not mingle with his contemporaries more than was necessary. His rooms were on the north side of an old square called Botany Bay; they were dirty and untidy, and he seldom entertained in them. The attention of his few visitors was drawn to the floral decorations and to a landscape in oils which he always pretended to be improving but which never seemed to alter. Occasionally he went to the meetings of the University Philosophical Society, though he hardly ever spoke, leaving it to his brother Willie to uphold the family reputation in such matters. Once their father was guest-chairman at a debate on social evils, and brother Willie distinguished himself by a fervid outburst in defence of prostitutes. It was a subject on which Sir William and his first-born were authorities and in hearty agreement with one another, though the similarity of their names and natures sometimes led to misunderstandings. One morning the father opened a letter that was meant for the son, in which a girl accused Willie of being responsible for her pregnancy, and when he came down to breakfast his father handed it to him with the words "Here is a most disgraceful letter." Having read it Willie looked at his father and gravely asked "Well, sir, what are you going to do about it?"

Two episodes in Oscar's life at T. C. D. have been preserved, and each displays a permanent trait in his nature. The first was told against him and was supposed to illustrate his effeminacy, though in fact it shows his sensitiveness. One night a tremendous row was heard coming from his room.

Two fellows rushed in to see what was happening, and found him jumping about the floor in a half-dressed condition. "What on earth is the matter?" they asked in amazement. "There's a huge fly in my room, a great buzzing fly," he explained: "I can't sleep till I drive it out." They thought him crazy, their way of getting rid of a fly being simple: "Why not kill the damned thing?" The second incident was advanced in his favour by a fellow-student named Horace Wilkins, who, living in Salt Lake City during Oscar's visit to America in 1882, was astonished to read the descriptions of the affected poet, the weak-kneed poseur who rhapsodised over sun-flowers, the languid aesthete, which were then appearing in the press. Horace recalled Oscar as an ungainly, overgrown, moping, awkward lad who was continually knocking things over when he moved about and at whom everybody laughed, but also as a kind-hearted, good-humoured fellow who never did a mean or underhand thing and whose last shilling was at anyone's disposal. "One day," reported Horace, "a thing happened which seemed, as it were, to change the current of Wilde's life. He wrote a poem which he read at one of the class symposiums. It struck me as a beautiful thing, but when he had finished reading the bully of the class laughed sneeringly. I never saw a man's face light up with such savagery of hate as Wilde's. He strode across the room and standing in front of the man asked him by what right he sneered at his poetry. The man laughed again and Wilde slapped him across the face. The class interfered, but inside of an hour the crowd was out behind the college arranging for a fight. Wilde, in a towering rage, was ready to fight with howitzers if necessary, but the bully wanted to fight with nature's weapons. No one supposed that Wilde had a ghost of a show, but when he led out with his right it was like a pile-driver. He followed the surprised bully up with half a dozen crushers and that ended it. Talk about that chap being a "pallid young man"! When I see these allusions in the newspapers I always think of his fighting qualities. I think he would make an ox shake his head and blink. Well, after that, Wilde's stock was high at Trinity. It seemed to put new ambition into him and the next term found him at the head of all his classes. He seemed to be able to master everything he tackled."

To lay a man out is not perhaps the best way to make him respect poetry, but it is sometimes the only way to teach him good manners. Oscar was to repeat the lesson at Oxford a year or two later. We must, by the way, discount the suggestion that a physical combat caused Oscar to excel in the classics during his last year. Precisely the same thing had happened at Portora, where a sluggish beginning was followed by a sprint at the close.

If he had wished it, his memory was such that he could have walked away
with every obtainable prize at school and college from start to finish. But
he was indolent, refusing to work until it became necessary; and the
moment his father said he might go to Oxford he showed what he could do,
winning within twelve months a "Foundation" scholarship at Trinity, the
Berkeley Gold Medal for Greek, and a demyship, worth £95 a year, at
Magdalen College, Oxford.

Both father and mother were in fact very proud of him. Many years
earlier the mother had prophesied a great future for Oscar, and it now seemed
that she was going to be justified. He was constantly in and out of the
Merrion Square house, astonishing the strange collection of guests there with
his stories and assertions. "I want to introduce you to my mother," he said to
a college friend: "We have founded a Society for the Suppression of Virtue."
Doubtless they had many applications for membership. Lady Wilde's receptions were extraordinary. She never appeared before five in the afternoon,
and she suppressed daylight as well as virtue, her callers being received in
rooms lit with pink-shaded lamps, the windows shuttered and curtained,
though the sun was shining brightly outside. In this dim if irreligious light
the hostess looked a giant, her husband a monkey, her clothes being as elaborate as his were shabby. One observer guessed that she must have worn
two crinolines, for as she walked there was "a peculiar swaying, swelling
movement, like that of a vessel at sea, the sails full with wind." Over the
long silk gown which swept the floor were "flounces of Limerick lace," and
an oriental scarf was wound round her waist. Her blue-black hair was
crowned with a laurel wreath; a quantity of brooches were attached to her
dress; she wore white kid gloves, carried a bottle of scent, a lace handkerchief and a fan; and the addition of paint to her face emphasised the theatrical effect of her attire. She who had started as a political agitator had ended
as a literary enthusiast, which was perhaps more satisfactory than the reverse
procedure, too many good poets having degenerated into bad prophets; and
the conversation at her receptions was chiefly about books, though in defer-
ence to her husband, science was sometimes allowed to intrude, and as a sop
to her son Willie the law was occasionally given its head.

In due time Willie was called to the bar, and in October, 1876, at the age
of twenty, Oscar went to Oxford, where he spent four happy years.

CHAPTER FOUR

THE OXONIAN

NEVER did Oxford University turn out a less typical Oxonian than Oscar Wilde; and yet it will be seen that the man who graduated there remained in one important respect a typical undergraduate all his life.

At that time Oxford was a lovely city, unblighted by commerce, industrialism and motor cars, and he loved everything about the place except its professors. "One cannot live at Oxford because of the dons," he used to say. We have first-hand evidence of his failure to please some of them. At "Collections" in 1877, reports G. T. Atkinson, "we were all assembled in the college hall and the high table was well filled. The President, Dr. Bulley, called up Wilde and myself." Their History tutor was a keen sportsman who took no interest in his job and did it in a perfunctory manner. "How do you find Mr. Wilde's work?" asked the President. "Mr. Wilde absents himself without apology from my lectures; his work is most unsatisfactory," replied the tutor. "That is hardly the way to treat a gentleman, Mr. Wilde," said the President in his usual courtly manner. "But, Mr. President, he is *not* a gentleman," answered Wilde, who was thereupon ordered to leave the hall. Atkinson also tells us that just before "Moderations" he and Wilde had to atone for past slackness, being the only undergraduates in college throughout the Easter vacation.

But Wilde's lack of sympathy with the authorities was most clearly shown on the subject of religion. Once it was his duty to read the first lesson in chapel, which was from the book of Deuteronomy. His own preference lay elsewhere, and he calmly announced a chapter in the Song of Solomon; but Dean Bramley pulled him up before he had warmed to the theme. He made it clear that the Church of England was not one of his main interests in life when asked by the Proctor what he was taking in the Divinity exam. "Oh, the Forty-nine Articles." "The Thirty-nine, you mean, Mr. Wilde." "Oh, is it really?" Douglas Sladen, who was present on the occasion, is our authority for what happened at the *viva voce* examinations in Divinity. Wilde arrived half an hour late, and one of the examiners, Canon Spooner, Warden of New College, wanted to know why. "You must excuse me; I have no experience of these pass examinations," Wilde explained. As the order of examination was alphabetical his lateness did not matter, but the examiners were so much annoyed by his casual manner that they handed him a Bible and told him to copy out the 27th chapter of the Acts of the Apostles. After he had been writing industriously for some time they relented and said that he had done enough; but observing half an hour later that he was still at it they called him up. "Didn't you hear us tell you, Mr. Wilde, that you needn't copy out any more?" Spooner asked. "Oh, yes, I heard you," he answered, "but I was so interested in what I was copying that I could not leave off. It was all about a man named Paul, who went on a voyage and was caught in a terrible storm, and I was afraid that he would be drowned; but, do you know, Mr. Spooner, he was saved; and when I found that he was saved, I thought of coming to tell you." As Spooner was not only a Canon but a nephew of the Archbishop of Canterbury, he was excessively irritated and ploughed the impertinent fellow on the spot.

For two of the dons, however, Oscar had nothing but praise, and both of them had an effect on his future career. The first was John Ruskin, Slade Professor of Art, to many young men of those days an inspired teacher, who proclaimed the necessity of beauty, the nobility of labour, and the nastiness of machinery, which had already fouled whole districts of England's green and pleasant land and converted them into a wilderness of hideous streets, unsightly slag-heaps, and loathsome factories. His appeal to youth was not only due to his eloquence and idealism, but to the fact that he practised what he preached: his money and his time were at the service of the causes he upheld; his denunciation of materialism was backed by his personal generosity. In the year 1874 this tall, lean, absent-minded, other-worldly man, whose blue eyes sometimes flashed with the fire of fanaticism, and who spoke as one of the prophets, made a curious experiment, which Oscar Wilde described to American audiences eight years later:

"One summer afternoon in Oxford we were coming down the High Street—a troop of young men, some of them like myself only nineteen, going to river or tennis-court or cricket-field—when Ruskin, going up to lecture in cap and gown, met us. He seemed troubled, and prayed us to go back with him to his lecture, which a few of us did; and there he spoke to us, not on art this time, but on life, saying that it seemed to him to be wrong that all the best physique and strength of the young men in England should be spent aimlessly on cricket-ground or river, without any result at all except that if one rowed well one got a pewter pot, and if one made a good score a cane-handled bat. He thought, he said, that we should be working at something that would do good to other people, at something by which we might show that in all labour there was something noble. Well, we were a good deal moved, and said we would do anything he wished. So we went out round Oxford and found two villages, Upper and Lower Hinksey, and between them there lay a great swamp, so that the villagers could not pass from one to the other without many miles of a round. And when we came back in winter, he asked us to help him to make a road across this morass for these village people to use. So out we went, day after day, and learned how to lay levels, and to break stones, and to wheel barrows along a plank—a very difficult thing to do. And Ruskin worked with us in the mist and rain and mud of an Oxford winter, and our friends and our enemies came out and mocked us from the bank. We did not mind it much then, and we did not mind it afterwards at all, but worked away for two months at our road. And what became of the road? Well, like a bad lecture it ended abruptly— in the middle of the swamp. Ruskin going away to Venice, when we came back for the next term there was no leader, and the "diggers," as they called us, fell asunder. And I felt that if there was enough spirit amongst the young men to go out to such work as road-making for the sake of a noble ideal of life, I could from them create an artistic movement that might change, as it has changed, the face of England."

The only drawback to this picturesque tale from a biographical point of view is that the teller was not amongst those present in High Street when Ruskin deflected them from their normal pursuits, though he had probably heard the story from several who were and touched it up on his journey across the Atlantic. The spade-work had been done by the time Oscar arrived, and he took part in the stone-breaking during his first term. The road which resulted from these labours was about the worst in the country, Ruskin's own gardener being responsible for the only level places in it; but the workers had their reward, not in the pride of doing a good job, but in the pleasure of breakfasting and talking with Ruskin in his rooms at Corpus. From that rather futile episode, and from the master's lectures and talks on art and economics, sprang the interest in social questions which became a feature of Oxford after Ruskin's departure, and two of his pupils, Arthur Toynbee and Oscar Wilde, carried his message, in a radically dissimilar fashion, to the outer world. Unfortunately Ruskin did not appreciate the missionary zeal of Wilde.

In considering the influence of a person's work or character on another we must always remember that no one can be impelled for long in a direction he does not wish to take; and it is broadly true to say that any influence which a book or a human being is supposed to have had on a man is nothing more than a disclosure of what is latent in the man himself. Wilde recognised this when he said, towards the end of his life, "The only writers who have influenced me are Keats, Flaubert and Walter Pater, and before I came across them I had already gone more than half way to meet them." Ruskin, then, merely awoke what was dormant in Wilde, a more important part of whose nature was revealed to himself by another Oxford don.

Walter Pater was one of those timid, old-maidish, scholarly recluses who, fearing even the uncertainties of matrimony, preach the gospel of living dangerously. In Germany he would have sung the glories of the sword and the superman. In England he hinted at forbidden fruit. As a young man his ugliness was so remarkable that his fellow-undergraduates were moved to sympathetic action, forming themselves into a Committee to Consider what could be Done for the Improvement of Pater's Personal Appearance. The proposal that he should buy a new hat was rejected on the ground that he could hardly be expected to sleep in it. Whereupon it was agreed that the only possible improvement would be the addition of a feature that should become an integral part of his face, and a resolution was passed in favour of a moustache; which he accordingly grew. He went to Oxford with the intention of taking holy orders, and though he became a complete sceptic he did not consider this a deterrent and asked the Bishop of London to ordain him. A squeamish friend, however, felt it his duty to enlighten the Bishop, who then refused to perform the ceremony.

Pater left Queen's College, where he had been a scholar, and went as a fellow to Brasenose, where he lived austerely in cramped quarters. No one would have noticed this short solid man with his heavy white Dutch face, square chin, thick moustache, small cautious eyes and soft voice, if he had not caused a sensation in 1873 by publishing his *Studies in the History of the Renaissance*, which so many respectable people took for the gospel according to Saint Satan. "Not the fruit of experience, but experience itself is the end," he wrote. " . . . To burn always with this hard gemlike flame, to maintain this ecstasy, is success in life . . . While all melts under our feet, we may well catch at any exquisite passion, or any contribution to knowledge that seems by a lifted horizon to set the spirit free for a moment, or any stirring of the senses, strange dyes, strange colours, and curious odours, or work of the artist's hands, or the face of one's friend. What we have to do is to be for ever curiously testing new opinions and courting new impressions." The teaching that man, who lived but for a "short day of frost and sun," must endeavor to make every moment of his existence significant, went to the heads of the youngsters who had been brought up to believe in duty, self-sacrifice, and what Oscar Wilde called the seven deadly virtues. They over-looked the more spiritual implications in the new doctrine—"the desire of beauty, the love of art for art's own sake"—and were able to extract from it an incitement to debauchery. Here, as it seemed to them, was one of their own professors actually telling them that it was their duty to run riot; and whenever duty is a pleasure it is always performed.

The older people were horrified. Benjamin Jowett, Master of Balliol, ex-pressed disapprobation, and of course those who had not read the essays were unanimous in their condemnation. The opposition he had aroused invaded Pater's private life, and at one of his dinner-parties he was heckled on the subject of Christianity by the High Church wife of a well-known professor. Pressed beyond the point of controversial good manners, he said abruptly that no reasonable person could govern his life by the opinions and actions of a man who had died eighteen centuries ago. The professor and his wife rose in agitation and left hurriedly. Pater was alarmed by the sorrowful disapproval of his seniors, and possibly even more alarmed by the joyful approval of his juniors, and the *Conclusion*, wherein his philosophy was underlined, did not appear in the second edition of the book. He became more of a recluse than ever, and twelve years elapsed before the publication of his next work.

At their first meeting Pater said to Oscar Wilde: "Why do you always write poetry? Why do you not write prose? Prose is so much more difficult." Oscar did not realise what Pater meant until he read the *Renaissance* studies, the self-conscious style of which made an instant and enduring appeal to him. Fifteen years later he was to say that "Carlyle's stormy rhetoric, Ruskin's winged and passionate eloquence, had seemed to me to spring from en-thusiasm rather than from art. I do not think I knew then that even prophets correct their proofs . . . But Mr. Pater's essays became to me "the golden book of spirit and sense, the holy writ of beauty." They are still this to me. It is possible, of course, that I may exaggerate about them. I certainly hope that I do; for where there is no exaggeration there is no love, and where there is no love there is no understanding. It is only about the things that do not interest one that one can give an unbiassed opinion; and this is no doubt the reason why an unbiassed opinion is always valueless." In con-versation he frequently spoke of his "golden book," adding on one occasion, "I never travel anywhere without it. But it is the very flower of decadence: the last trumpet should have sounded the moment it was written."

"But would you not have given us time to read it?" asked some prosaic person.

"Oh no! there would have been plenty of time afterwards—in either world."

On the other hand he had not a very high opinion of its author, whose timid and anxious temperament was in strong contrast to his own, and he was amazed when Pater showed serious concern over an article in which his essay on Charles Lamb had been ridiculed. "Just imagine! Pater!" exclaimed Wilde when recounting the incident. "I could not conceive how one could be Pater and yet susceptible to the insults of the lowest kind of journalism." He used to tell a story, probably invented by himself, in which he delineated Pater's character and fondness for picturesque words. One morning, before beginning his lecture, Pater asked a young man named Sanctuary to remain behind at the end. As Pater was a proctor, Sanctuary felt uncomfortable, but when they were left alone together it was the professor who looked nervous. After a period of embarrassment the young man said: "You asked me to stay behind, sir, did you not?" Pater pulled himself together: "Oh yes, Mr. Sanctuary. I . . . I wanted to say to you . . . what a very beautiful name you have got." Better still was another of Wilde's fancies. "So you are going to see Pater!" he said to Richard Le Gallienne. "That will be delightful. But I must tell you one thing about him to save you from disappointment. You must not expect him to talk about his prose. Of course no true artist ever does that. But Pater never talks about anything that interests him. He will not breathe one golden word about the Renaissance. No! he will probably say something like this: 'So you wear cork soles in your shoes? Is that really true? And do you find them comfortable? . . . How extremely interesting!'"

Pater's lecture on Prosper Mérimée at the London Institution was delivered in a low monotonous voice, as if he were reading to himself, and when he enquired of a few friends "I hope you all heard me?" Oscar Wilde replied for the rest "We overheard you," upon which Pater muttered "You have a phrase for everything." Though he could not help admiring such conversational readiness, Pater never warmed towards Wilde, did not much care for his writings, and in the years to come said some very nasty things about him in private. We can guess why. The sins of the Renaissance were pleasant to dream about in the study, but not to read about in a modern novel. "Yes, poor dear Pater has lived to disprove everything that he has written," summarised Wilde; and it may have distressed Pater that the pupil had dared to do what the professor had only imagined.

It did not content Oscar Wilde merely to display his love of Pater's prose

and Ruskin's rhetoric. His nature was protean: he wanted to be everything
and do everything. And so we find him at Oxford touching life at as many
points as possible, but only touching it, and preferably observing it. He was
once discovered sparring with a friend in his rooms; he was even seen climbing, at considerable danger to himself, from one box to another in a music-
hall, and so on to several other boxes, in order to invite the occupants to a
party he was giving after the performance, his brother having suddenly arrived from Dublin; he was often to be met on the cricket-field, though he
never played; he regularly watched the boat races from his college barge, but
never stepped into a boat if he could help it; he rode on horseback a good
deal, but drew the line at hunting; and he occasionally remembered Mahaffy's
injunctions to shoot and fish. These things were done by him merely because
they were the things to do. He took no pleasure in physical exercise; nor
could he work up the least interest in games, then or thereafter.

The real Oscar was to be seen in his rooms at Magdalen, which were on
the kitchen staircase, the best position in college, looking over the river
Cherwell, the lovely walks and bridge. All three rooms were panelled, and
between the two sitting-rooms was an arch where once had been folding
doors. Old engravings, mostly of naked women, adorned the walls in the
first year or two of Oscar's tenancy; the furniture was pleasant but nothing
out of the common; and two large vases of blue china, bought locally, were
prominently displayed on the mantelpiece. The craze for china had not then
set in, and Oscar's taste was considered peculiar, especially when it got about
that at one of his parties he had exclaimed "Oh, would that I could live up
to my blue china!" This remark was taken quite seriously by people who
took themselves seriously, and Dean Burgon, vicar of St. Mary's, Oxford,
made one of his famous pronouncements. Years before he had protested
against the Darwinian heresy from the same pulpit, crying with clasped
hands "O ye men of science! leave me my ancestors in Paradise, and I will
willingly leave you yours in the Zoological Gardens." In his delirium he now
saw something more awful than apes, and a few years later Oscar told the
Americans what it was:

The first time that the absolute stupidity of the English people was ever
revealed to me was one Sunday at the Oxford University Church when the
preacher opened his sermon in something this way: " 'When a young man says,
not in polished banter but in sober earnestness, that he finds it difficult to
live up to the level of his blue china, there has crept into the cloistered shades
a form of heathenism which it is our bounden duty to fight against and to
crush out if possible.' I need hardly say that we were delighted and amused

at the typical English way in which our ideas were misunderstood. They took our epigrams as earnest, and our parodies as prose."

If the Dean had dropped in on a Sunday evening when Oscar was entertaining his guests, he might have modified his views. On the other hand, such is the nature of preachers, he might not. Before the end of his first year Oscar's parties were famous, his high spirits, good nature, cheerful conversation and generous hospitality (which was always getting him into debt) having attracted all sorts and made him popular outside the circle of his fellow scholars. Everybody who was not too combative and enjoyed talk and laughter and music and punch was made welcome. Walter Parratt, then the college organist, used to accompany the singers, and sometimes a fiddler helped to keep things going. Cigars, churchwarden pipes and tobacco were provided by the host, and when the bowls of gin and whisky punch ran out there was always brandy and soda. The evenings were usually hilarious, and sometimes ended in a friendly skirmish, but never degenerated into a brawl. Wilde could have kept the rest in order by force if it had been necessary, but he preferred to turn every disagreement into laughter.

There was something odd about his personal appearance even in those days. His long rich-brown hair surmounted a big colourless face, made up of a noticeably fine forehead, a prominent nose, full lips, and magnificent eyes which constantly changed colour under their heavy lids: so at least the biographer must write of them, for people who knew him well have described the colour of his eyes as blue, green-yellow, hazel, brown-and-gold, and pretty well every hue except pink, the majority favouring blue flecked with gold, and all agreeing that they were large and luminous.[1] Imperturbable good humour was the dominant expression of his face and the constant note of his conversation. He was over six feet in height, had outgrown his clumsiness, and carried himself with an air of complete self-assurance. The bold check suits that were then the fashion looked bolder on him than on another.

But any peculiarity in his clothes or appearance was forgotten as soon as he began to speak. Rennell Rodd, who was at Balliol when Wilde was at Magdalen, and who afterwards quarrelled with him, wrote that "there was an immediate fascination in the unconventional freedom of his brilliant

[1] Two of his most intimate friends disagree on this point. Alfred Douglas says that Wilde's eyes were green, Robert Ross that they were a light china blue, such as children often have but lose later, Oscar's remaining like that to the end of his life. Anna Comtesse de Brémont reconciles these contradictory impressions by describing his eyes as pale blue, with golden flecks around the iris, that changed strangely until the light within them seemed to turn to green.

conversation and his sureness of himself." David Hunter Blair, another contemporary, said that Wilde was always the leader, whatever the topic under discussion, letting off a stream of paradoxes, quaint comments on men and things, untenable propositions and preposterous theories, laughing as heartily as anyone else at his own absurdities, and in graver moments spouting yards of verse, his own and other people's, uncommonly well. Sixty years later Blair could vividly recall the charm of those intimate talks round the fire between Wilde, himself, and one or two close friends, "when the punch had been drunk, and the pipes smoked out, the lights extinguished, the piano closed, and the merry guests dispersed." In particular he recalled how Wilde, asked what was his real ambition in life, replied: "God knows! I won't be a dried-up Oxford don, anyhow. I'll be a poet, a writer, a dramatist. Somehow or other I'll be famous, and if not famous I'll be notorious. Or perhaps . . . I'll rest and do nothing . . . These things are on the knees of the gods. What will be, will be."

After Wilde had left Oxford, and *Punch* and *Patience* between them had made him notorious as an insipid poseur, with, it must be admitted, some help from himself, it amused his more sporting college contemporaries to invent stories which illustrated their masculinity and his effeminacy; and as most people will believe anything that tells against someone they dislike or flatters their self-esteem, two of these stories, with pleasing variations, became the classical chestnuts of the Oscar saga and even found their way into reputable biographies. The first describes how a party of sportsmen fell upon him, bound him with cords, and dragged him to the top of a hill. "Yes," said he when released, flicking the dust from his coat in the well-known manner of French aristocrats about to be guillotined, "the view from this hill is really very charming." The second describes how another gang of sportsmen (it is always sportsmen who do these things) broke into his rooms, smashed his blue china, and held his head under the college pump for an appreciable period. There is not a modicum of truth in either story so far as Wilde was concerned, though one of his disciples at Magdalen was subjected to the china-smashing and pump-sousing remedy following Oscar's departure from Oxford. It took a real sportsman who was also a "blue" to discredit these yarns half a century after they had gained currency and credence. "So far from being a flabby aesthete," wrote Sir Frank Benson, "there was only one man in the college, and he rowed seven in the Varsity Eight, who had the ghost of a chance in a tussle with Wilde." Sir Frank then described a scene which would completely dispose of the pump, the binding and (one rather regrets) the French aristocrat, even if all the other evidence were not dead against them. The Junior Common Room of Magdalen decided one evening that the time had come to beat up Wilde and smash his furniture. An advance guard of four intoxicated heroes burst into his rooms; the rest watched the proceedings from the stairs, preparatory to joining in if all went according to plan. The first intruder promptly rejoined his companions outside with the aid of Wilde's boot, the second got a punch that doubled him up on to the first, the third made his return journey through the air, and the fourth, a beefy customer of Wilde's own height and weight, reappeared struggling vainly in the arms of his intended victim. Handling him as easily as a nurse handles a baby, Wilde carried him to his rooms and having ceremoniously buried him beneath a pile of his own luxurious furniture invited the spectators, now pro-Oscar to a man, to sample the fellow's wines and spirits, an invitation that was accepted with peculiar pleasure on account of the owner's present plight and past stinginess. That was the first and last attempt to rag Wilde.

There were other kinds of gatherings in his rooms besides those already mentioned, and in the last three years of his residence at Magdalen he gave "beauty parties," when young women came to tea with their chaperons. By that time the engravings on the walls had given way to pictures of a more decorous order. He was always popular with women, for reasons which will become apparent, and for a while he toyed with the idea of marriage, carrying the idea far enough in one case to correspond with a friend of the chosen one, and even further in another case by kissing and fondling the object of his affection and drawing upon himself the wrath of an indignant mother who had discovered her daughter on his knee.

But he also started flirting with something more imposing if less substantial than a girl: with Mother Church in fact. It probably began with a visit he made to Italy during a vacation in 1875, when he was so deeply impressed by the buildings and pictures that he could not remain untouched by the faith which had inspired them. The letters he wrote to his mother and father dealt with the art but ignored the religion, to which they were hostile. Florence, Milan, Padua and Verona drew pages of enthusiasm from him, while Venice, which he said was "beyond description," he described in greater detail than the rest. On his return he had long talks with his friend Blair, a recent convert to the Faith, who took him to Catholic functions and to Sunday morning services at the old chapel on the other side of Magdalen bridge. Here Oscar had several interviews with the priest, who discerned in him a strong attraction to the Church but saw that he was in earnest about nothing except his ambition to do well in the university exam-

inations. "The finger of God," reported the priest, "has not yet touched him."
Oscar's less mystical explanation of his inability to enter the Church just
then was that if he became a Catholic his father would cut him off with
a shilling. All the same his warm feelings for the ancient religion were expressed in sonnets, and as these appeared in Irish publications it became
known that he was wavering in his allegiance to the faith wherein he had
been reared, as a result of which a relation who died at that time left him
£100 instead of the two or three thousand he had expected. "Fancy a man
going before God and the eternal silences with his wretched Protestant
prejudices and bigotry clinging to him still," commented Oscar. Poetry did
not exhaust his interest in the subject. The engravings on his walls were
removed, and pictures of another sort took their place. In June '76, Lord
Ronald Gower was taken by his friend Frank Miles to see Oscar, whom he
described as "a pleasant cheery fellow, but with his long-haired head full of
nonsense regarding the Church of Rome. His room filled with photographs
of the Pope and Cardinal Manning." The odd thing is that Oscar, in the
belief that everything should be given a trial, had only the previous month
become a Freemason.

Blair did his best to counteract such influences, and early in '76 proposed
that his friend should accompany him to Rome. The idea delighted Wilde,
though he had to confess that he was "absolutely and irretrievably 'broke.' "
As Blair was going to stay with his people at Mentone on the way he had
an inspiration: "I will stake a couple of pounds for you at Monte Carlo, and if
it is predestined that you are to come to Rome I shall certainly win the
money." Apparently Destiny favoured the trip: he won £60 and telegraphed
to Wilde, who joined him at Genoa, and they went on to Rome together.
Wilde was enchanted by everything he saw, and it almost seemed as if
Blair's flutter had gained a convert when, at an audience with Pope Pius IX,
the Holy Father blessed Wilde and expressed the hope that he would follow
his friend into the City of God, for the young man was strangely silent as
they drove back to the hotel and locked himself into his bedroom when they
got there. Emerging later in the day he handed Blair the manuscript of
a poem he had written with the impression of the Vatican fresh upon him.
Blair could have dispensed with the poem in return for a little more faith.
In the evening they drove to the basilica of St. Paul's Without the Walls,
and on the way, against the wish of his friend, Oscar stopped at the Protestant Cemetery in order to throw himself on the turf in reverence at the
grave of Keats.

Though he never ceased to feel attracted to the Roman ritual, Wilde could not narrow his life to a creed, and nothing came of Blair's efforts. Indeed the momentary agitation of Rome was soon eclipsed by the thrill of Greece, which he visited with Mahaffy and two other fellows a year later. Rather perturbed by his one-time pupil's Romish inclinations, Mahaffy said "I am going to make an honest pagan out of you." Oscar was not so sure about it, writing to a friend "I wish I could look into the seeds of time and see what is coming." At any rate his nature responded to the Grecian tour far more completely than to the Italian ones.

The four travelers left Brindisi on Easter Sunday, 1877. They could hardly sleep for excitement, knowing that their eyes would see Greece in a few hours, and, probably for the only time in his life, Oscar voluntarily rose at daybreak. In the eighteen-seventies Greece was a hazardous country to ramble in: brigandage, kidnapping and murder were the order of the day, and their journey on horseback through Arcadia was attended with peril as well as discomfort. But the only serious danger they encountered was from the owner of their horses, who, being on foot himself, was enraged when they broke into a trot, becoming homicidal when they galloped. Seizing Oscar's bridle, he drew his knife, and trouble might have ensued if Oscar had not produced a revolver and made it clear that he had the better of the argument.

Athens in reality was more wonderful than the Athens of his imagination, and Oscar was enraptured. He saw everything, and perceived with joy and relief that the Roman Church had not a monopoly of architectural inspiration, and that the beauty produced by paganism was quite as wonderful as the beauty produced by Christianity. Travelling can no more broaden a man's outlook or influence his life than reading: it can but clarify or enkindle what is already innate; and all that the Grecian trip did for Oscar was to "make assurance double sure," to emphasise what he had always known in his heart: that he could never accept the creed of an institution, however lovely its pictures, its buildings and its poems; and that beauty, in itself and for itself, apart from any belief that may have inspired it, was all-sufficient for him. His altered, or rather rearranged, attitude, which he felt had better be explained as due to weakness and want of principle, soon became known to his Catholic friends on his return, and one of them wrote angrily to him, ending the letter: "Do not send me your sonnets; I do not care to see them." Oscar had a childlike and rather touching belief that sonnets describing the emotions aroused in him by the thought of Rome would be acceptable to Catholics in lieu of his conversion. He felt that they ought to be satisfied by the fact that he had been deeply impressed by their religion.

Anyhow the Grecian holiday was a great success for everyone except Mother Church, and the travelers overstayed their leave by a month. Mahaffy got into trouble with the Provost on his return to Trinity, and Wilde was fined £45, which however was returned to him a year later when he did so well in his examinations.

In picturing Wilde at Oxford it is sometimes difficult to remember that he must occasionally have worked. Yet there can be no doubt of it, for in 1876 he took a First Class in "Moderations" in the Honours School, and in 1878 a First Class in the Honour Finals, and both were regarded by his examiners as the most brilliant of their respective years. In spite of these achievements he never seemed to be reading anything but poetry. Keats, Swinburne, Rossetti, Arnold, Browning, Milton, Wordsworth, Shelley: he read them continually, and the works of the first two he almost knew by heart. In his circle the discussions on poets and poetry were endless, and when they did not talk poetry they wrote it, or tried to. "Days of lyrical ardour and of studious sonnet-writing," as he afterwards recalled; "days when one loved the exquisite intricacy and musical repetitions of the ballade, and the villanelle with its linked long-drawn echoes and its curious completeness; days when one solemnly sought to discover the proper temper in which a triolet should be written; delightful days, in which, I am glad to say, there was far more rhyme than reason." Several of his own poems appeared in Irish magazines; and in 1877 the *Dublin University Magazine* published his first essay in journalism: an account of the Grosvenor Gallery Exhibition. He always managed to stay a few days in London on his way to and from Dublin or the Continent during his vacations, and he never failed to visit the theatres and picture galleries while there.

His father died in 1876 and left him a small property worth about £4000. Willie received the same, Henry Wilson the same, and Lady Wilde about £7000. Sir William had pretty well lived up to his large income, and his family now had to face the world on a relative pittance. Needless to say Oscar at once began to raise money on his property, and he must have felt rather aggrieved when Wilson, who died a year after his father, left his share to the hospital. His father's death may have prompted him at times "to scorn delights and live laborious days." At any rate he began to hope for a fellowship and set about writing a long article on *The Rise of Historical Criticism* for the Chancellor's English Essay Prize. He failed to get the fellowship, and the prize was not awarded, but he must have guessed that such things were hardly in his line of life. Walking with a friend one day in the grounds of Magdalen, he confessed "I want to eat of the fruit of all the trees in the garden of the world." He had a large appetite, unsuited to a fellowship or the production of dull theses.

He left Oxford in a blaze of glory. The subject for the Newdigate Prize Poem that year was Ravenna, and it so happened that he had visited the place on his way to Greece, noting it as a theme for poetic treatment. He could therefore put in bits of local colour which the other competitors had to glean from books. He won the prize, as Ruskin and Matthew Arnold had done before him, and declaimed the poem in the Sheldonian Theatre on June 26th 1878. "I understand that some young man wins this prize every year," said W. S. Gilbert when informed of Wilde's poetic achievements. But few young men have recited their prize-poems so well, Oscar's performance winning high praise from everyone who heard it. He had taken a fancy to certain lines in his earlier poems, which he lazily repeated in *Ravenna*; and when the Professor of Poetry, J. C. Shairp, whose duty it was to suggest textual improvements to the winner of the Newdigate, advised certain alterations, Wilde listened with due courtesy, took careful notes of every suggestion, but went away and printed the poem exactly as he had written it.

Perhaps, as he lounged for the last time in Magdalen walks, the most genuinely felt couplet in *Ravenna* was running in his head:

Who can foretell what joys the day shall bring,
Or why before the dawn the linnets sing?

CHAPTER FIVE

THE ACTOR

HAVING celebrated his arrival in London from Oxford by a visit to Brompton Oratory, where he confessed his sins to a priest with so much apparent contrition that the priest thought him ripe for conversion, Oscar started rehearsing another kind of part. And at this point we must try to get an inkling of his peculiar nature, or we shall wholly misjudge his strange actions all through his life.

The main oddity in his composition can be described in a sentence: half of him, the emotional half, never developed beyond adolescence; the other half, the intellectual half, was well developed at an age when those about him had hardly begun to think for themselves, and reached maturity at an age when his talented contemporaries were still trying to find their feet. Thus we shall always see him as an exceptionally brilliant undergraduate, half boy, half genius, which he remained to the end of his days, the curious contrast becoming more and more marked with the continued development of his intellectual powers. How this came about no one can say. Psychologists may attempt an explanation by talking of complexes, physiologists by insisting on glands, but they get us no nearer the truth: the mystery of human personality remains, and the biographer can only note the facts and make his inferences therefrom.[1]

The boy in Oscar accounts for his numerous poses, above all for his love of showing-off, whereat the man in him was sometimes amused and sometimes bored. These two selves, the immature emotional self and the overmature intellectual self, were clearly discernible at every stage of his career, and the opposition marred most of his work, though in one instance the perfect fusion of the two produced a masterpiece. Here it is only necessary to stress the boyish side of his nature, as it explains the singularity of his first appearance in public life, and indeed all his later errors and absurdities.

There is a certain type of boy who is never happy unles he is acting a part

---

[1] Psychology is in its infancy as a science. I hope, in the interests of art, it will always remain so." (O. W.)

or dressing-up or startling people by some form of exhibition or shocking them by some kind of behaviour. Oscar belonged to this type and never outgrew the desire to amaze or discompose his seniors. He also retained the characteristics of the more common run of boys: a romantic view of life coupled with a love of anti-climax, a consciousness of sin with the thrill of sinning, a strong attraction to the joys of over-eating and over-drinking, a sense of the miraculous and a love of fun. Much of his charm lay in the unabashed pleasure he took in the mere act of living, and the youthful high spirits he brought to it; though the parts he played, his love of acting and masquerading, which irritated so many people, were to some extent the outcome of this exuberance.

His first appearance on the public stage—for so one must describe it—was as an aesthete. It is largely due to Gilbert and Sullivan's *Patience* that many people believe Wilde to have been the founder, or at any rate the chief exponent, of what is known as the Aesthetic Movement. But he was neither the one nor the other, for the simple reason that there was no such thing as the Aesthetic Movement. In other words, the aesthetes were not a group of men banded together to pursue a common object, which is the usual meaning of the word "Movement": e.g. the Pre-Raphaelite, the Impressionist, the Socialist Movements. All one can say is that there were a number of people who, each in his own way, had brought about a certain result. The so-called Movement was in the air, never in committee. The poet, the painter, the architect, the sculptor, the dress-designer, the house-decorator, the furniture-maker, the printer: these had reacted against the stereotyped art and craft of the period, and their general tendency was called aesthetic, the work of each being in some way related to the rest, though the relationship was never clearly defined and few of the artists would have claimed kinship with others working along the same lines. Such diverse characters as Ruskin, Morris, Pater, Swinburne, Whistler, Woolner, Rossetti, Burne-Jones, Henry Irving, and even those satirists of the "Movement" Gilbert and Sullivan, were part of the tendency; but it may be doubted if any of them would have cared to be called aesthetes, and the last two would have rejected the appellation with scorn. Each of these artists was playing his own game; and though some might have recognised that the others were on their side, none would have called it a team. In a sense Keats was the unconscious parent of aestheticism: his pictorial poems inspired the Pre-Raphaelites, who were the forerunners of the aesthetes, one of whose first principles was that all the arts were intimately related to one another. Architecturally the aesthetes sought their inspiration in the period of Queen Anne, and the

Bedford Park Estate, where the houses were built in that style, became their model suburb. Roughly summarised, aestheticism, which grew out of pre-Raphaelitism, was an attitude to life as well as art: it rebelled against the hideous conditions and tastes of the majority, as well as the conventional art of the time.

Such a tendency appealed greatly to Wilde, who was nothing if not artistic and thoroughly unorthodox in his attitude to everything, and the part he took was dictated firstly by a love of masquerade and secondly by the fact that, from poetry to wall-paper, all the arts had their recognised high priests except that of dress. But in making his decision to specialise in dress-reform he was careful to cover all the arts and add them to his aesthetic creed, describing himself on leaving Oxford as an art critic and Professor of Aesthetics. In his last term at Oxford he had made something of a hit by appearing as Prince Rupert at a fancy dress ball, and had gone about declaring that a reformation in dress was of far greater importance than a reformation in religion, adding that Luther's neckties must have been quite shocking; so his future line of action had been clarified before settling in London, where he was occasionally to be seen at evening parties dressed in a velvet coat edged with braid, knee-breeches, black silk stockings, a soft loose shirt with wide low turn-down collar, and a large flowing pale green tie. Several followers outdid his extravagances of dress and behaviour and even appeared in daytime curiously garbed, but Wilde himself did not "walk down Piccadilly with a poppy or a lily in his mediaeval hand," as Gilbert suggested in *Patience*. "Anyone could have done that," said Wilde long afterwards. "The great and difficult thing was what *I* achieved —to make the whole world believe that I had done it." All the same his buttonholes were remarkable and he adopted the sunflower and the lily as badges or symbols of his cult, no doubt because they were too large to be overlooked. Nothing could draw attention to him so surely as strange flowers and strange clothes, for notoriety can be obtained by what one wears more easily than by what one says or does. In this way he became publicly identified with "the Aesthetic Movement" and was soon regarded as the leader of it merely because he dressed the part. The other aesthetes were not so fortunate. After all one cannot walk about draped in the latest pattern of wall-paper or carry a table of the most up-to-date design on one's back or hang a picture of the modern school round one's neck. But the dress-reformer is his own publicity agent, and to the rage of many artists who were producing good work in other fields Oscar gained the kudos which should have been theirs and got them laughed at into the bargain. His

desire for immediate fame has been shared by many whose vanity could
only so be appeased or whose financial security could only thus be attained,
but his method of winning it was peculiar to himself and satisfied one half
of his nature.

Now and henceforth he was helped and admired by women, mocked and
disliked by the men who did not know him and by some who did. Quite
early in life he realised how important it was to propitiate women in order
to get on in the world. He found this simple, because his amiable nature
delighted in flattery, his interest in dresses made conversation easy, and
the strain of femininity in his boyishness appealed to women, who could
talk to him almost as to one of themselves, unembarrassed by the awkward-
ness of sex attraction or repulsion. "To get into the best society nowadays,"
he was later to say, "one has either to feed people, amuse people, or shock
people—that is all." As he could not afford to feed them, he amused
and shocked them. To be in society was, he thought, a bore, but to be out
of it was a tragedy. "No man has any real success in this world unless he
has got women to back him, and women rule society." He started well,
being made much of by the Duchess of Westminster, sister of his Oxford
acquaintance Ronald Gower, and through her he soon got to know the
other aristocratic families which then ran society. But he demanded more
than they could give, and the artist in him turned for comfort to the leaders
of another social sphere which was about to attract more public attention
than all the rest put together: the theatre, where he was always emotionally
at home.

Henry Irving had made the Lyceum Theatre famous by the time Oscar
came to town and was steadily raising the social status of the actor to a point
which would have been unthinkable in the time of Macready only a
generation before. Princes, peers, cabinet ministers, judges and even bishops
were constantly to be seen at the Lyceum, and they treated Irving as an
equal, whatever their private feelings may have been. Opinions on his
acting differed, but everyone agreed that he was a remarkable personality;
and Oscar Wilde, unlike his fellow-Irishman, Shaw, thought that Irving
was quite right to produce third-rate melodramas, because they displayed
far better than dramatic masterpieces would have done a personality that
was itself, in every rôle, a masterpiece of histrionic art. Oscar could not
afford expensive seats in those days and was frequently to be seen in the
pit and gallery of the Lyceum. Soon he was on friendly terms with Irving,
whom he addressed in a sonnet "Thou trumpet set for Shakespeare's lips
to blow!" His admiration for Irving's leading lady, Ellen Terry, overflowed

into three sonnets; and although Ellen was in the habit of receiving verses on her beauty, her acting and her incomparable self by nearly every post, she treasured Oscar's lines more than the rest.

> She stands with eyes marred by the mists of pain,
> Like some wan lily overdrenched with rain,

he wrote on seeing her as Queen Henrietta Maria in *Charles I*. "That phrase 'wan lily' represented perfectly what I had tried to convey, not only in this part but in Ophelia," she declared more than twenty years after: "I hope I thanked Oscar enough at the time." She probably did, for she shared with him that rarest of virtues: an unqualified joy in making people happy. When we remember that she had met pretty well every famous man of her time, not a few of whom had fallen in love with her, we shall not underestimate her final tribute: "The most remarkable men I have known were Whistler and Oscar Wilde. This does not imply that I liked them better or admired them more than others, but there was something about both of them more instantaneously individual and audacious than it is possible to describe."

Another leading actress who inspired Oscar with a sonnet was Sarah Bernhardt, whom he met in Paris and flattered in a manner that seemed to her, and indeed was, very un-English; but as he never made love to her they remained on excellent terms. When she came to act in England she was astonished to hear the cry *"Vive Sarah Bernhardt!"* as she stepped ashore at Folkestone. Though she was to be greeted with it often enough in the time to come, this was the first time she had ever heard it, and Oscar, who was the first man to shout it, flung an armful of lilies at her feet and forced the crowd to cheer her as she passed from the boat to the train. In London she found him very helpful in countless ways, with the press, with the acting profession, as an interpreter, adviser, and so on. She did not show the same solicitude for him when, years later, a single decent action on her part would have saved him much distress; but she was not an Ellen Terry.

Like many stage-enthusiasts, Wilde was a collector of photographs, and we find him writing from St. Stephen's Club in 1880 to thank Mrs. Bancroft for hers, which had given him "more pleasure than any quill pen can possibly express, and will be a delightful souvenir of one whose brilliant genius I have always admired." His admiration pleased those who called it forth, and many visits were exchanged. "If you are not too busy to stop and drink tea with a great admirer of yours," he wrote to Geneviève

Ward, "please come on Friday, at half past five, to 13 Salisbury Street. The two beauties, Lady Lonsdale and Mrs. Langtry, and Mamma and a few friends are coming." Madame Modjeska was another friend gained by admiration, and he translated a poem of hers from the Polish, no doubt making a far better job of it than if he had known a word of the original.

Salisbury Street was a turning off the Strand, and Wilde had chambers on the first floor of the house at the bottom of the street overlooking the river. The long room in which he received visitors was panelled, mostly in white, and a number of theatrical stars had scrawled their signatures on the panels, Ellen Terry, Henry Irving and Sarah Bernhardt amongst them. On an easel at one end of the room was Edward Poynter's large yellow portrait of Lily Langtry; there were rugs on the floor, flowers in china pots, and here and there tapestries relieved the monotony of white. The floor above was occupied by an Oxford friend, Frank Miles, who was quickly becoming known for his pencil drawings of beautiful women which appeared in the windows of nearly every stationer's shop and were reproduced in *Life*. His great "find" was Lily Langtry, whom he sketched in every possible attitude from every possible angle, and soon made her the most talked-of beauty of the day. "I with my pencil, Oscar with his pen, will make her the Joconde and the Laura of this century," he once cried in a sort of ecstasy. They shared in the weekly gatherings of celebrities that took place in Wilde's room, and Mrs. Langtry was a constant visitor.

One rather suspects that the main inspiration behind Oscar's poems to the beauty of the hour, to say nothing of his passion for her, was a love of notoriety, an adolescent desire to have his name linked with a woman who had aroused the admiration of the Prince of Wales, the curiosity of society, and the interest of the outside world. No poet has a chance of being taken seriously until he has indulged in a passion, preferably a hopeless one; so Oscar went through all the appropriate emotions and struck all the necessary attitudes. A poem he had already written to a youth was slightly altered to fit her. A more ambitious effort called *The New Helen* was directly attributable to her, and when he gave her a volume of his poems he wrote on the flyleaf "To Helen, formerly of Troy, now of London." She was much flattered by his attentions, which she encouraged. He was an agreeable change from her husband, who preferred racing and gambling to poetry and flowers. Besides, he was becoming famous or at least notorious, as the Great Aesthete, and *Punch* was busy inventing jokes about him. It was very pleasant to be adored by a man who possessed what she described as "one of the most alluring voices that I have ever listened to"; and it soothed her vanity to record in later life that he used to wander round the streets in the neighbourhood of her house and once even went to sleep on her doorstep; but one knows enough about his love of comfort to dismiss the latter incident as a Trojan daydream on the lady's part. He tried hard to make her interested in art, but she remained chiefly interested in herself as a work of art; he introduced Ruskin to her, but without effect; he constantly advised her about the clothes she should wear, but she would not live up to his ideal.

"The Lily is so tiresome," he sighed; "she *won't* do what I tell her."

"Indeed?"

"Yes. I assure her that she owes it to herself and to us to drive daily through the Park dressed entirely in black, in a black victoria drawn by black horses, and with 'Venus Annodomini' emblazoned on her black bonnet in dull sapphires. But she won't."

His own clothes, when not got up in the evening as an aesthete, were fashionable, and we have in Mrs. Langtry's word for it that he wore a black frock coat, only the lower button of which was fastened, light coloured trousers, a brightly flowered waistcoat, and a white silk cravat; also that he carried pale lavender gloves. Thus attired he paid visits to aristocrats and actresses, distributing well-pondered witticisms whenever he did not feel quite at home. It amused him to catch the look of amazement on people's faces whenever he said something unexpected; and he found endless entertainment in dismissing as of no concern the things that others took seriously, and in treating with the utmost gravity such matters as they considered trivial, for only so could his sense of values, his critical sense, harmonise with his boyishness, his sense of fun. "Nothing succeeds like excess," was one of his sayings at this time, while another ran "Give me the luxuries and I can dispense with the necessities." Arriving late at a luncheon party, his hostess mildly remonstrated, pointing to the clock. "And how, madam, can that little clock know what the great golden sun is doing?" he asked. He had timed his arrival for the sake of this rejoinder, having probably turned up late at different places on several occasions before getting the right cue. "I have come to dine with you; I thought you would like to have me," he said as he walked uninvited into William Spottiswoode's drawing-room at Grosvenor Place. He did not know Spottiswoode but had met his wife once or twice. As he was very amusing, they did like to have him. Henry Irving's peculiar gait being mentioned at some dinner, a serious discussion took place as to whether it detracted from his skill as an actor. Wilde's contribution was "Both Irving's legs are delicately intellectual, but his *left* leg is a poem."

Some of his most obvious bits of nonsense were quoted by those who did not like him as evidence of a nauseating affectation. A characteristic specimen was his grave statement, on being asked how he had spent the day, "I was working on the proof of one of my poems all the morning, and took out a comma. In the afternoon I put it back again." Another was "When I had to fill in a census paper I gave my age as 19, my profession as genius, my infirmity as talent." Staying at a country house, he came down to breakfast one morning looking worn out and harassed. Asked if he was ill, he replied "No, not ill, but very very weary. The fact is that I picked a primrose in the wood yesterday, and it was so ill that I have been sitting up with it all night." Apparently primroses called forth all his compassion. Going into a florist's shop in Jermyn Street, he asked the attendant to remove several bunches of them from the window. "With pleasure, sir. How many would you like to have?" "Oh, I don't want any, thank you. I only asked to have them removed from the window because I thought that they looked tired." He knew quite well the effect that such absurdities would have on the average man, and when he heard a passer-by say "There goes that bloody fool, Oscar Wilde," he remarked to his companion "It's extraordinary how soon one gets known in London."

Wilde was determined to be talked about, because fame meant money and money meant freedom, and most of his nonsense had the double effect of amusing himself and making people chatter. His reward followed. In February 1880, George Du Maurier began to caricature him in *Punch*, either as Maudle the painter or as Jeleaby Postlewaite the poet. A year later a play called *The Colonel* by the editor of *Punch*, F. C. Burnand, was produced at the Prince of Wales' Theatre, with Beerbohm Tree as Lambert Streyke, a character which satirised Wilde as an aesthete, portraying him as a charlatan and a swindler. It had a long run. Later he appeared, thinly disguised, as Scott Ramsey (also played by Tree) in *Where's the Cat* at the Criterion, and in *The Charlatan* at the Haymarket.

But the most famous skit provoked by him was Gilbert and Sullivan's *Patience*, produced at the Opéra Comique in April 1881, and transferred in the course of its huge success to the Savoy Theatre. It has been assumed by writers on the subject that the character of Archibald Grosvenor was meant for Wilde, and that he became identified with the character of Reginald Bunthorne (originally meant for Swinburne) owing to his increasing corpulence in the years ahead. But a glance at the libretto will show that Gilbert was much too intelligent to hit directly at Wilde in either part. It was a satire on aestheticism, not on any particular aesthete, though naturally Wilde's

well-advertised oddities of behaviour and costume were ridiculed throughout. It is, however, Bunthorne, not Grosvenor, who sings

> Though the Philistines may jostle, you will rank as an apostle in the high
> aesthetic band,
> If you walk down Piccadilly with a poppy or a lily in your mediaeval
> hand.

And it is Bunthorne who is

> Such a judge of blue-and-white and other kinds of pottery—
> From early oriental down to modern terr-cotta-ry—

both of which peculiarities were associated in the public mind with Wilde.
Equally, but not more so, Grosvenor displays certain characteristics which
readers of *Punch* had been led to regard as Wilde's:

> I am aesthetic
> And poetic!

says he, and admiring himself in a glass, "I am a very narcissus." All the
women fall in love with him, Wilde's popularity with women being one
of the reasons why he was not so popular with men; he has curly hair,
like Wilde's on special occasions; is insipid, as Wilde was supposed to be;
and has a mission, as Wilde half pretended to have. But the tastes of the *Pre-
Raphaelite,* Whistler's love of Japanese pictures, the catch-words of the elite
—"intense," "precious," "consummately utter," "too all-but," etc.—are all
satirised by Gilbert, who was clever enough to spot that Wilde, like Bunthorne, had "more innocent fun within me than a casual spectator would
imagine," and was enjoying his own performance while chuckling at the
spectators. Wilde justified Gilbert's opinion of him by laughing heartily
at *Patience*.

Notwithstanding all this publicity, no money was coming in, and the
estate left him by his father was mortgaged beyond redemption; he even had
to borrow from his mother. There was only one thing to be done and he did
it: *Poems*, by Oscar Wilde, appeared in July 1881. Henry Labouchere reported that he had heard Wilde give as a reason for his aesthetic phase
that he had written a book of poems and believed in their excellence, but
had tried publisher after publisher in vain, until, having hit on the notion
of obtaining notoriety through knee-breeches, he had become lionised and had
instantly got his poems accepted. It is more than probable that Wilde told
this story in the days to come, but it can only be partly true because his

poems were published at his own expense, David Bogue, who brought them
out in a luxurious edition, receiving ten per cent commission, the author
paying the total cost of production. In spite of unfavourable reviews, five
editions were sold off fairly quickly.

The general feeling about the volume at the time was most pithily
expressed by Oliver Elton at the Oxford Union Debating Society, when it
was announced by the Librarian to a crowded house that Mr. Oscar Wilde,
late of Magdalen College, had presented a copy of his *Poems* to the Union.
The usual acceptance and vote of thanks being proposed, Elton rose to
object. "It is not that these poems are thin—and they *are* thin," he said:
"it is not that they are immoral—and they *are* immoral: it is not that they
are this or that—and they *are* all this and all that: it is that they are for
the most part not by their putative father at all, but by a number of better-
known and more deservedly reputed authors. They are in fact by William
Shakespeare, by Philip Sidney, by John Donne, by Lord Byron, by William
Morris, by Algernon Swinburne, and by sixty more, whose works have
furnished the list of passages which I hold in my hand at this moment. The
Union Library already contains better and fuller editions of all these poets:
the volume which we are offered is theirs, not Mr. Wilde's: and I move that
it be not accepted." And for the first time in the history of the Society a presentation copy of a book was returned to its author.

Possibly Elton was a little harsh, but there can be no doubt that Wilde had
read the poets with care, and as he possessed a photographic memory more
of their work appeared in his than perhaps he was aware. The biographer
who knew nothing about Wilde except what could be gleaned from these
poems would have to admit that, but for an obvious taste for physical
beauty, and a tendency to dwell on the bodily grace of boys, nothing could
be deduced from them beyond the fact that the author's favourite poet was
Keats. While writing one of his longer poems Rennell Rodd discovered
him with a book on botany "from which he was selecting the names of
flowers most pleasing to the ear to plant in his garden of verse." If there
is nothing much to be said against this method, there is also nothing much to
be said for it.

The book starts off with a sonnet called *Hélas!*, which Wilde once
described as his most characteristic poem. It has a prophetic quality, especially
perhaps in the last two and a half lines:

> To drift with every passion till my soul
> Is a stringed lute on which all winds can play,
> Is it for this that I have given away

Mine ancient wisdom, and austere control?

.   .   .   .

               lo! with a little rod
I did but touch the honey of romance—
And must I lose a soul's inheritance?

In *Magdalen Walks* he again touches a vatic note:

And even the light of the sun will fade at the last,
And the leaves will fall, and the birds will hasten away,
And I will be left in the snow of a flowerless day
To think of the glories of Spring, and the joys of a youth
    long past.

And again in *Humanitad*:

Being ourselves the sowers and the seeds,
  The night that covers and the lights that fade,
The spear that pierces and the side that bleeds,
  The lips betraying and the life betrayed;
The deep hath calm: the moon hath rest: but we
Lords of the natural world are yet our own dread enemy.

These are the two best verses in the 1881 volume, and each expresses a re-current, if slightly histrionic, emotion concerning himself. The wish was father to the thought: he liked to see himself as a symbolic figure, a charac-ter in a drama, climbing to the heights and dropping to the depths, a great success, a great failure, running through the gamut of comedy and tragedy; and he liked to think it was all foreordained, that he was driven by Fate, that something inherent within himself would inevitably cause his rise and fall.

Wilde was not so foolish as to believe that he could make a fortune out of a volume of verse, and early in 1880 he wrote a play, *Vera*, a small edi-tion of which was printed for private circulation at his own expense in the autumn. Nihilism in Russia had been a favourite topic among book and news-paper readers for some time, and Wilde showed where his sympathies lay, though he was careful to point out that the play dealt with men and women, not with political theories. "The modern Nihilistic Russia," he said, "with all the terror of its tyranny and the marvel of its martyrdoms, is merely the fiery and fervent background in front of which the persons of my dream live and love." In March '81 the Czar, Alexander II, was assassinated, the interest in Russian Nihilism may be said to have soared, and the chance of discovering a gold-mine in *Vera* was too good to be missed. It was announced for production at the Adelphi Theatre in December, with Mrs. Bernard Beere in the leading part. Then something happened to prevent it. It has been said that Wilde was dissatisfied with the casting of the play, and so withdrew it; but this explanation may be dismissed as highly improbable, for Wilde wanted money more than anything else just then. *The World*, in which brother Willie frequently puffed Oscar, announced that the production had been temporarily postponed by the author owing to "the present state of political feeling in England." But it would be nearer the truth to attribute the withdrawal to "the present state of the Prince of Wales' feelings." The Czar's wife was sister-in-law of the Prince, who had met Wilde several times and liked him very much; and Oscar was too kindly a man to distress someone who liked him very much, especially when that someone was the leader of society.

Critics and biographers of Wilde have dismissed *Vera* as an immature and worthless melodrama, showing nothing of the quality which eventually made its author famous as a dramatist. We may grant at once that the serious passages are stilted and lifeless, and that the serious characters speak like no one on earth; but exactly the same thing may be said of the serious parts in the comedies with which he made his name, the explanation being that he never developed emotionally. What the critics have missed is that the intellectual Wilde, the author of *The Soul of Man* and the dramatist who was to criticise manners and morals, is already present in *Vera*, though the chances to display his comedic gift are few.

The Czar's Prime Minister, Prince Paul, is Wilde's mouthpiece in the play, and he actually coins an epigram which was later to appear in *Lady Windermere's Fan*: "Experience, the name men give to their mistakes." Paul, who is bored on the rare occasions when he has to listen to others, also says "It is so exhausting not to talk," a typical Wildeism; and when the President of the Nihilists tells the Prince "We speak the truth to one another here," he replies "How misleading you must find it!" Eleven years later Wilde was to write in *The Soul of Man* "To the wickedness of the Papacy humanity owes much. The goodness of the Papacy owes a terrible debt to humanity." Prince Paul says "Good kings are the only dangerous enemies that modern democracy has."

And it is not only as a revelation of the future wit and critic that *Vera* is interesting. There is nothing in Wilde's work or conversation to show that he had ever read or admired the letters and sayings of Sydney Smith; yet the parson is his closest affinity as man and wit in the world of letters. They were both good-natured, self-indulgent, fond of the table and society;

their humour was by turns affected, rich and nonsensical; their wit was free
from malice; they were eccentric in outlook, behaviour and appearance; they
were as high-spirited as they were kind-hearted; and one may add that each
of them became decidedly fat. If anyone else in history could have written
The Importance of being Earnest it would have been Sydney Smith. Only
in *Vera*, however, is there evidence that Wilde had studied Smith. "If I had
a son who was an idiot, by Jove, I'd make him a parson," said a country
squire to Sydney. "Very probably, but I see that your father was of a
different mind," rejoined the cleric, whose interest in salads and sauces
lends interest to this passage in *Vera*:

> *Prince Paul:* To make a good salad is to be a brilliant diplomatist—the problem
> is entirely the same in both cases. To know exactly how much oil one must
> put with one's vinegar.
> *Baron Raff:* A cook and a diplomatist! an excellent parallel. If I had a son
> who was a fool I'd make him one or the other.
> *Prince Paul:* I see your father did not hold the same opinion, Baron...For
> myself, the only immortality I desire is to invent a new sauce...

Early in 1881 lack of means forced Oscar to quit his elegant quarters
off the Strand and settle in Keats House, No. 3 Tite Street, Chelsea. Frank
Miles accompanied him and they shared rooms. The few accounts of Miles
vary so greatly that it is impossible to separate fact from fiction. For example,
one writer says that he died in a lunatic asylum, another that he committed
suicide. He certainly got into trouble, and Robert Sherard gave me the
reason: "Miles had a predilection for Exhibition natural enough in a
struggling artist but reprehensible, *parait-il*, where only small girls in single
spies are invited to contemplation. Wilde told me how he had saved Miles's
bacon, but never referred to him again. Poor Miles could have shaken hands
on a common taste with Victor Hugo." Everyone seems to be agreed that
Miles was a pleasant good-looking fellow, and as he was also a popular
artist the social gatherings in Tite Street included as many celebrities as had
visited Oscar's rooms in Salisbury Street. The Prince of Wales frequently
called, and the tea-parties given by the two friends became the rage, a
little girl named Sally presiding over them. Miles had discovered her on the
pavement outside Victoria Station, where her mother sold flowers, and
promptly engaged her as his model. Being very beautiful, she was soon in
great demand. Lord Leighton painted a well-known picture of her called
"Daydreams," and Marcus Stone put her into some of his garden scenes.
But behind the façade of gaiety and tea-parties at Keats House there was

an odd happening or two. Once Miles was "wanted by the police," and Oscar repeated his Trinity and Magdalen performances by holding the door while his friend disappeared over the roof to a neighbouring studio. If the authorities at Scotland Yard had known anything about the man who was keeping their representatives at bay, they would have sent a squad armed with a battering-ram; as it was Oscar had no difficulty in securing the door against three other six-footers expert in the removal of obstacles but armed with nothing more lethal than a warrant. Having given Miles sufficient time to get away he allowed them in, receiving them at first with amazement and then with apologies. They threatened to arrest him for re-sisting them in the execution of their duty. He explained that as Miles had left England he thought their attempts to break in, with their well-assumed cries of "police" and "the law," could be nothing but a practical joke played upon himself by some friends. Artists, he declared, were like children, always up to some prank. He was so frank, so amiable, and so obviously well-disposed towards themselves, that they left in a frame of mind almost as pleasing as if they had effected a capture.

Not long after this episode Wilde and Miles quarrelled: we do not know why, and the story told by one chronicler that their separation was due to the disapproval of Oscar's *Poems* by Frank's father, Canon Miles, can-not be taken seriously. In due course the artist's drawings went out of fashion, and the end of Miles, whether by suicide or in an asylum, was unfortunate.

Already Wilde's personality was impressing the young men of his own generation, just as later it was to impress and almost overwhelm his juniors. Rennell Rodd tells us that "association with this daring and gifted person-ality brought me nearer to emancipation from convention" and that "the attraction of his dominant personality took a strong hold upon me...My friends criticised the ascendancy which he began to exercise, and being young I took a certain defiant pride in their criticism." Rodd noted his idol's chief qualities, which were never to vary through life: a keen perception of beauty, almost over-shadowed by a tremendous sense of humour and love of paradox; a laugh that was genuine, spontaneous and infectious; a vivid quickness of apprehension coupled with an absorbent memory; a really genial and kindly nature, which seemed to be at variance with his egotism, self-assertion and love of notoriety, for he took an eager interest in others, encouraging and applauding them; a temperament that was reckless, generous and extremely indolent.

Rodd gives us an instance of his friend's endearing qualities. Following

an unusually high tide one year the Thames overflowed and there was a
disastrous flood in Lambeth, many houses of the poor becoming unin-
habitable, the wretched families camping in the streets. Wilde and Rodd
crossed the river to see what they could do to help, and in the course of
their investigations Wilde discovered an old bedridden Irishwoman in a
miserable tenement. He remained with her for some time, joking and
laughing and cheering her up, attending to her wants and leaving her in
high spirits. As her one ideal in life was a comfortable bed, Wilde told
Rodd as they came away that he had been more than compensated for
everything he had been able to do by her prayer that the Lord would give
him "a bed in glory."

CHAPTER SIX

THE STAGE

PATIENCE had played to record houses in New York; pirated versions were being given in all the leading cities of the United States; and it occurred to D'Oyly Carte that his American Bureau, established to protect his interests in Gilbert and Sullivan opera and to manage his affairs over there, ought to run a possibly lucrative side-line. Having enjoyed the skit on aestheticism, the American public would surely like to see the most famous aesthete, who with a little persuasion might consent to carry a sunflower or a lily down Broadway and wear his curious clothes at lectures and receptions, thus making it clear that he was the original of Bunthorne in the opera. The notion was soon transformed into action, and at the beginning of October '81 Wilde, who was then living with his mother at 1 Ovington Square, received a cable from the Carte Bureau asking if he would consider an offer for fifty readings beginning on November 1st. "Yes, if offer good," replied Wilde. After some negotiation it was agreed that a lecture should be given by Wilde in New York, to be followed by a tour if it proved successful, and that he should have all his expenses paid together with one-third of the box office receipts. It seemed at last as if he were about to make money; and he sailed on the *Arizona* from Liverpool on Christmas Eve, arriving at New York on January 2nd, 1882.

Just before leaving home he heard from an enterprising American publisher, who wanted him to write a poem of twenty lines, at five dollars a line, on the sunflower or the lily. The general impression in the States was that he ate flowers, and they expected to see a man rather resembling a tropical plant; so the reporters who mobbed him on the boat were a little downcast by his appearance, which was more like that of an athlete than an aesthete. True he had long hair, and he wore a bottle-green fur-lined overcoat, with a round sealskin cap on his head, but he was a giant in stature and his fists looked formidable. He naturally expected them to question him concerning his mission; instead they asked him how he liked his eggs fried, what he slept in, how he trimmed his finger-nails, and what temperature he liked his bath to be. His answers displayed a lack of interest in the questions, and they button-holed the passengers for something of a livelier nature. The passengers rose to the occasion: they had heard him complain that the trip was tame, "deucedly stupid" in fact, that the roaring ocean did not roar, and that nothing less than a storm which swept the bridge from the ship would give him any pleasure. That was enough for the reporters, who told their readers that Wilde was "disappointed with the Atlantic Ocean," a phrase which got him far more publicity than his views on aestheticism would have done, or even a sparkling riposte on the theme of fried eggs. Wilde realised that he had not done himself justice on the boat, so made up for it the moment he stepped ashore. "Have you anything to declare?" asked the customs official. "No. I have nothing to declare"; he paused: "except my genius." Few remarks in history have travelled as widely and quickly as that one.

He stayed at the Grand Hotel on 31st Street and Broadway, and had a look round New York before settling down to the serious business of being entertained. Six aspects of American life caught his immediate attention: (1) "Everybody seems in a hurry to catch a train. This is a state of things which is not favourable to poetry or romance." (2) "It is the noisiest country that ever existed. Such continual turmoil must ultimately be destructive of the musical faculty." (3) "There are no trappings, no pageants, and no gorgeous ceremonies. I saw only two processions: one was the Fire Brigade preceded by the Police, the other was the Police preceded by the Fire Brigade." (4) "In America life is one long expectoration." (5) "Why does not science, instead of troubling itself about sunspots, which nobody ever saw, or, if they did, ought not to speak about; why does not science busy itself with drainage and sanitary engineering? Why does it not clean the streets and free the rivers from pollution?" (6) "I believe a most serious problem for the American people to consider is the cultivation of better manners. It is the most noticeable, the most painful, defect in American civilisation."

Before he had been a day in the city invitations began to pour in; lunches, dinners, teas, receptions, dances, drives, theatre-parties, left him no hour that he could call his own; and since he was there to make money, and this was the performance of his choice, he had to be permanently "on view." At every function he was surrounded by women, who either adored him or thought they did, and who played up to him by appearing in the most extraordinary dresses which they believed to be aesthetic. He returned the compliment by clothing himself in the fashion he had made famous in London, by striking decorative attitudes, looking languid, talking of dress and colours and jewels, of poetry and prose and poetic prose, and by paying fanciful compliments. At one feminine party he was clearly on the brink of a mental breakdown, for he was heard to say "America reminds me of one of Edgar Allan Poe's exquisite poems, because it is full of belles"; whereat the belles screamed with delight and pelted him with flowers. He was so successful with women that several of their male friends determined to take a hand in the entertainment, hoping no doubt to show their superiority in more robust accomplishments. Two of them invited him to dinner at a chop-house on Broadway with the sole object of exposing him to the derision of their bibulous friends. Wilde ate everything that was placed before him and drank whisky, wine and whatever else came his way as a thirsty man drinks water. Eventually all but himself were drunk and he led them, staggering and drooping, to the street, where he helped them into hansom cabs and then walked back to his hotel. But he still had not completely vindicated his masculinity, and one evening at a club several youths suggested a round of brothels. Wilde was perfectly game, and proved that he could take his women, as he had taken his whisky, like a man.

The promoters of the lecture-tour felt aggrieved because he refused to parade the streets in his aesthetic attire. They wanted him to live up to *Patience*: he wanted to live it down. Though perfectly willing to lecture in knee-breeches, he declined to wear or carry a sunflower or a lily on the platform, and except for one brief reference to the opera "the original of Bunthorne" refused to be Bunthorne. The opening lecture was given to a full house on January 9th at Chickering Hall. His subject was The English Renaissance. The vast majority of the audience had no conception of what Wilde would talk about so that when he appeared in his odd garb they expected entertainment and waited happily for him to produce rabbits out of a hat. After he had been talking for some minutes it began to dawn on them that no conjuring tricks could be expected, that it was unlikely he would even stand on his head; but being a tough race, and well-trained in the exercise of listening to lectures, they saw it through without a murmur. They actually applauded his remark "To disagree with three-fourths of the British public on all points is one of the first elements of sanity, one of the deepest consolations in all moments of spiritual doubt," because it seemed patriotic to do so; and a slight titter ran through the hall when he summarised his credo: "Philosophy may teach us to bear with equanimity the misfortunes of our neighbours, and science resolve the moral sense into a secretion of sugar, but art is what makes the life of each citizen a sacrament."

All the same the more intellectual part of the audience was pleased and

impressed, and as the receipts had been exceptionally good it was decided
that he should visit all the leading cities. Most of the newspapers, taking
their tone from *Punch* and *Patience*, treated him by turns as a comedian
and a charlatan, and in a letter to a sympathiser, Joaquin Miller, he asked
"Who are these scribes who, passing with purposeless alacrity from the
Police News to the Parthenon, and from crime to criticism, sway with such
serene incapacity the office which they so lately swept?" Dion Boucicault,
the dramatist, was moved to anger by the way Wilde was treated in the
press and exhibited to the public, saying "He is too simple and gentle in his
nature to realise or even perceive his position ... There is no guile in him.
He is the easy victim of those who expose him to ridicule and to the censure
of the thoughtful. Those who have known him as I have, since he was a
child at my knee, know that beneath the fantastic envelope in which his
managers are circulating him there is a noble, earnest, kind and lovable
man." The people with whom he did not have to act a part liked him
very much, and during his stay in the country he enjoyed the society and
hospitality of, among others, Julia Ward Howe, Oliver Wendell Holmes,
Longfellow, Louisa Alcott, Kate Field, General Grant, Jefferson Davis,
Henry Ward Beecher, William Chase and Walt Whitman.

He met the last-named while staying at Philadelphia, where he dis-
coursed on Art and the Handicraftsman at the Horticultural Hall. A crowd
of people besieged the Aldine Hotel, but he was polishing up his lecture,
and his black servant stood outside his room informing callers that "Massa
Wilde is too busy to recept to-day." Americans, he told the audience, must
create their own art. "Let the Greek carve his lions and the Goth his
dragons: buffalo and wild deer are the animals for you." They ought to
produce masterpieces of the goldsmith's art. "The gold is ready for you in
unexhausted treasure, stored up in the mountain hollow or strewn on the
river sand, and was not given to you merely for barren speculation. There
should be some better record of it left in your history than the merchant's
panic and the ruined home." He referred briefly to the treatment he was
receiving from the press reporters. "You have heard me, I fear, through the
medium of your somewhat imaginative newspapers as ... a young man ...
whose greatest difficulty in life was the difficulty of living up to the level of
his blue china—a paradox from which England has not yet recovered." And
he went on to say that "at present the newspapers are trying hard to induce
the public to judge a sculptor, for instance, never by his statues but by the
way he treats his wife; a painter by the amount of his income; and a poet
by the colour of his necktie." Incidentally he asked one journalist how much

he had been paid for an article containing some nonsense about himself. Six dollars, was the reply. "Well," said Wilde, "the rate for lying is not very high in America. That's all I wished to ascertain. Good-day."

Wilde crossed the Delaware to call on Whitman at Camden. Whitman was 63, Wilde 27. They talked of Swinburne, Rossetti, Morris, Tennyson, Browning, on all of whom the young man was eloquent. A bottle of elderberry wine was produced by Walt's sister-in-law, and Oscar politely drank it as if it were nectar. Then they went up to the third floor and sat in the "den." "May I call you Oscar?" asked Whitman. "I like that so much," replied Wilde, settling himself on a stool at the other's feet. In the course of their conversation Wilde said "I can't listen to anyone unless he attracts me by a charming style or by beauty of theme." Whitman answered "Why, Oscar, it always seems to me that the fellow who makes a dead set at beauty by itself is in a bad way. My idea is that beauty is a result, not an abstraction." Wilde agreed: "Yes. I remember you have said 'All beauty comes from beautiful blood and a beautiful brain.' And, after all, I think so too." They had been talking for two hours when Whitman said "Oscar, you must be thirsty. I'll make you some punch." Wilde admitted that he could do with a drink, rapidly absorbed a large glass of milk punch, and took his leave. "Good-bye, Oscar: God bless you!" said Whitman, who described his visitor as a great big splendid boy: "We had a very happy time together. I think him genuine, honest and manly ... his youthful health, enthusiasm and buoyancy are refreshing."

It was at Philadelphia that Wilde found a publisher for his friend Rennell Rodd's poems. The publisher agreed to bring them out if Wilde would write a preface. He did so, and the appearance of the volume delighted its author, who wrote to the publisher that he had "seen no *édition de luxe* in England to compare with it." Unfortunately, for reasons that may be conjectured, Wilde had changed the title of the book and dedicated it to himself in these words:

TO
Oscar Wilde—
"Heart's Brother"—
These few Songs and many Songs to come.

Rodd was excessively annoyed. He did not like to think that he would have to write many more songs for Wilde; also he considered the dedication "too effusive" and asked the publisher to remove it "from all copies that go out for the future." Besides, he complained, "I am not over pleased at the way in which I find myself identified with much that I have no sympathy with" in the preface. The fact is that Rodd, who was by now ambitious for a career in politics or diplomacy, had at last been persuaded that continued friendship with a man who behaved as Wilde was reported in the English press to be behaving would do him no good. Scenting danger, he found a convenient excuse for breaking off their relationship in the title, dedication and preface which Wilde had supplied, and wrote sternly to the offender, warning him at the same time of the harm he was doing himself by his extravagant performances. Wilde, who had taken a great deal of trouble over the book, which would never have appeared in the States without the advantage of his introduction, was offended, and dismissed Rodd from his life with the remark "What he says is like a poor linnet's cry by the side of the road along which my immeasurable ambition is sweeping forward." This is the first time, as far as we know, that he took such a high tone towards a friend, and it shows, what his later behaviour will verify, that success went to his head as no drink ever could and deranged his judgment. It is what we should expect from a spoilt boy, not from an exceptionally intelligent man, and only explicable by the temporary ascendancy of his juvenile emotion.

From a financial point of view he was certainly a success; wherever he went people stared at him; and newspapers sent interviewers from near and far. At Washington, where he stayed at the Arlington Hotel, a card was brought to him bearing the name of a correspondent who represented eleven publications. "I was slightly flurried, as you may suppose," he related. "I said 'Now here is a man who moulds the thoughts of the West. I must be on my best behaviour.' In walked a boy of sixteen. 'Have you been to school much?' 'Oh, yes.' 'Have you learned French?' 'No.' 'If you wish to be a journalist you should study French.' Then I gave him a big orange and dismissed him. What he did with the orange I don't know; he seemed pleased to get it." Another reporter called to obtain details of his private life. "I told him I wished that I had one." He was taken through the parks and decided that "Washington has too many bronze generals." Afterwards he commented on public statues in a lecture: "To see the frock-coat of the drawing-room done in bronze, or the double waistcoat perpetuated in marble, adds a new horror to death." Whilst musing on the subject of America's national hero in the city named after him, it struck Wilde that George Washington had much to answer for. American lies were vulgar and unimaginative; their civilisation was equally so; and some years later, in a light-hearted mood, he explained how it came about: "The crude commercialism of America, its materialising spirit, its indifference to the poetical side of things, and its lack of imagination and of high unattainable ideals, are entirely due to that country having adopted for its national hero a man who, according to his own confession, was incapable of telling a lie; and it is not too much to say that the story of George Washington and the cherry-tree has done more harm, and in a shorter space of time, than any other moral tale in the whole of literature ... and the amusing part of the whole thing is that the story of the cherry-tree is an absolute myth."

Wilde's visit to Boston, where he lectured on January 31st in the Music Hall, was a diplomatic triumph. Sixty Harvard lads staged a rather mournful show which they thought would be funny. When the audience had assembled these sixty marched in pairs down the centre aisle to the empty seats in front that had been reserved for them. Each of them walked in the Bunthorne manner, wore the Bunthorne knee-breeches, etc., and carried, with affected admiration, sunflowers and lilies. Fortunately Wilde had got to hear in advance of this singularly feeble demonstration, and appeared on the platform in ordinary evening clothes, which completely stymied the sixty and made them look almost as foolish as they were. "As a college man, I greet you," were Wilde's opening words. His remark that he "seemed to see certain signs of an artistic movement in the lecture hall" was received with laughter; his epigram that "caricature is the tribute mediocrity pays to genius" was loudly applauded; and his statement, "I am impelled for the first time to breathe a fervent prayer 'Save me from my disciples,'" brought the house down. He completed their discomfort by saying that the statue of a Greek athlete would look well in their gymnasium: "I should like to present the students with such a statue myself if they would accept it." And he added that they ought to receive diplomas for painting beautiful pictures or modelling a fine piece of sculpture as well as for gaining a knowledge of "that dreadful record of crime known as history." He emphasised his view of education several times during the tour: "Give children beauty, not the record of bloody slaughters and barbarous brawls, as they call history, or of the latitude and longitude of places nobody cares to visit, as they call geography." And again: "You give the criminal calendar of Europe to your children under the name of history." It was generally agreed, even in the press, that he had scored off the silly sixty of Harvard, and when the students of Yale repeated the "joke" it fell completely flat.

His essential kindliness was displayed in a practical manner at Chicago. A young sculptor named John Donaghue wrote to say he was destitute and begged Wilde to help him. Wilde found him living, or rather starving, in a bare little room at the top of a building in a slum, liked his work, and praised it not only from the platform but wherever he went. As a result Donaghue was inundated with commissions, made enough money to improve his work by study in Europe, and became a rich and popular sculptor. But the things which the Chicagoans really admired and mistook for progress did not receive Wilde's unqualified approval. He could not agree that the possession of trains and telephones made people any more civilised than, say, the Athenians in the age of Socrates:

"Of what use is it to a man to travel sixty miles an hour? . . . Is he any the better for it? Why, a fool can buy a railway ticket and travel sixty miles an hour. Is he any the less a fool?"

"People should not mistake the means of civilisation for the end. The steam engine and the telephone depend entirely for their value on the use to which they are put."

"The value of the telephone is the value of what two people have to say."

He was even unimpressed by the miracles of Nature in the New World, being "disappointed in the outline" of Niagara Falls, which he described as "simply a vast unnecessary amount of water going the wrong way and then falling over unnecessary rocks." "But at least you'll admit they are wonderful waterfalls?" asked someone. "The wonder would be if the water did not fall," he replied. "Every American bride is taken there," he afterwards declared, "and the sight of the stupendous waterfall must be one of the earliest, if not the keenest, disappointments in American married life."

His early lectures drew so many people that he had to give additional ones in all the larger cities, and instructions were issued by his manager that he was to be provided with good rooms, including a private sitting-room for callers and meals, that the stage was to be fitted up as he required it, that returns were to be made after each lecture, and that he was to be allowed to draw money whenever he wished. He was advertised everywhere on the boardings in letters six feet high, "printed, it is true, in those primary colours against which I pass my life protesting"; he drove about in a carriage with a black servant to look after him; and was followed, watched and listened to by crowds of women, who clustered round him in shops and restaurants and waited patiently in public places for a glimpse of him. People told him that there had been "nothing like it since Dickens," he wrote to a friend; and on his return he informed Beerbohm Tree that when he landed in America he had two secretaries, one for autographs, the other for locks of hair: "Within six months the first had died of writer's cramp, the second was completely bald." The press reporters went on asking absurd questions, and to one batch he replied: "I am at a loss to catch your drift. I am in America to lecture on the decorative in art, not to cure rheumatism or restore hirsute appendages." Asked what he thought of two rival preachers, he said "It is monstrous to compare Thomas De Witt Talmage to the Rev. Henry Ward Beecher: it is like comparing Clown to Pantaloon." Pressed on the subject of his next lecture, he declared that he would begin at the doorknob and end with the attic: "Beyond that there remains only heaven, which subject I leave to the church." He described the conscience of an editor as "purely decorative," said that American newspapers were "comic without being amusing," but expressed his gratification at having "provided a permanent employment to many an ink-stained life."

Having filled his pockets by expounding his creed in the leading cities, he went on to places where they were not so willing to pay cash for his particular gospel. Indeed at Cincinnati he had to compete with a big religious revival, multitudes singing in the streets:

> Oh, wondrous bliss! oh, joy sublime!—
> I've Jesus with me all the time—

which clashed with his view of art and cut into his receipts. Under the circumstances he formed a jaundiced opinion of the place. On seeing a "No smoking" notice in the Academy of Design, he exclaimed "Great heaven! they speak of smoking as if it were a crime. I wonder they don't caution the students not to murder each other on the landings." The town distressed him. "I wonder your criminals don't plead the ugliness of your city as an excuse for their crimes," he said to a reporter. At Louisville he met the niece of Keats and spent a day with her reading the letters of the poet to her father, some of which were then unpublished. A few weeks later she sent him as a gift the original manuscripts of Keats's sonnet beginning "Blue! This the life of heaven . . . " At Indianapolis he annoyed the farmers by speaking of them as "peasants," no doubt because it sounded more poetical. Fifteen hundred people gave him a restless hearing at St. Louis, and again his attitude was slightly coloured by the treatment: "Several St. Louis citizens told me the city was not at its best. I should have thought so, even though the information was lacking." The Mississippi was in flood, yellow, raging, hissing, rushing, and he remarked that "no well-behaved river ought to act that way." He was unimpressed by the prairies, which reminded him of a piece of blotting-paper and possibly suggested his explanation of transatlantic humour:

"It is only fair to admit that he (the American) can exaggerate; but even his exaggeration has a rational basis. It is not founded on wit or fancy; it does not spring from any poetic imagination; it is simply an earnest attempt on the part of the language to keep pace with the enormous size of the country. It is evident that where it takes one twenty-four hours to go across a single parish, and seven days' steady railway travelling to keep a dinner engagement in another State, the ordinary resources of human speech are quite inadequate to the strain put on them, and new linguistic forms have to be invented, new methods of description resorted to. But this is nothing more than the fatal influence of geography upon adjectives; for naturally humorous the American man certainly is not."

When Wilde went further west he entered into a new business arrangement, whereby he received sixty per cent of the gross takings, a minimum guarantee of two hundred dollars a night to be paid in advance, and his travelling expenses. In the eastern cities he had dressed with elegance and had carried an actor's make-up box with him, rouging his face before going on the stage and sometimes having his hair dyed. But he journeyed towards San Francisco in plainer clothes, wearing a broad-brimmed white sombrero, Spanish-style, and he dropped some of his affectations, feeling perhaps that cowboys would not appreciate them. Before starting for the Rockies he had an adolescent mental picture of the west, which he believed to be exclusively populated by cowboys, redskins and outlaws, and he was surprised to find that many of his fellow-travellers were reading Mrs. Humphry Ward's best-seller in paper covers. "As each page is finished, it is torn out and flung through the window," he reported, "so that in the end the American prairie will get a top-dressing of Robert Elsmere."[1] He had no high opinion of American novels, which he called "American dry goods"; and though glad to see that copies of his *Poems* were selling on the train like hot cakes at ten cents a time, he was revolted by the get-up of the volume and annoyed by the knowledge that it was pirated. "Calling these boys on one side I told them that though poets like to be popular they desire to be paid, and selling editions of my poems without giving me a profit was dealing a blow at literature which must have a disastrous effect on poetical aspirants. The invariable reply they made was that they themselves made a profit out of the transaction and that was all they cared about." In spite of the long and tedious journey

[1] A later invention by Wilde, as *Robert Elsmere* was not published till 1888.

he was definitely impressed by the Rockies, and he had his greatest
success at San Francisco, where he stayed at the Palace Hotel and gave five
lectures at Platt's Hall.

Art, he found, flourished in Chinatown if nowhere else in the city:
"When I was in San Francisco I used to visit the China Quarter frequently. There I used to watch a great hulking Chinese workman at his
task of digging, and used to see him every day drink his tea from a little
cup as delicate in texture as the petal of a flower; whereas in all the grand
hotels of the land, where thousands of dollars have been lavished on great
gilt mirrors and gaudy columns, I have been given my coffee or my
chocolate in cups an inch and a quarter thick. I think I have deserved
something nicer." The attempts to make plates picturesque was also not to
his taste: "I do not see the wisdom of decorating dinner-plates with
sunsets and soup-plates with moonlight scenes . . . we do not want a
soup-plate whose bottom seems to vanish in the distance. One feels neither
safe nor comfortable under such conditions." Here, as elsewhere, he told
his listeners that pictures ought to be hung on the eye-line: "The habit
in America of hanging them up near the cornice struck me as irrational
at first. It was not until I saw how bad the pictures were that I realized
the advantage of the custom." But his was a voice crying in the wilderness:
"So infinitesimal did I find the knowledge of Art, west of the Rocky
Mountains, that an art patron—one who in his day had been a miner—
actually sued the railroad company for damages because the plaster cast
of Venus of Milo, which he had imported from Paris, had been delivered
minus the arms. And, what is more surprising still, he gained his case
and the damages." Another reminiscence: "In California I dined with a
gentleman who had fired eleven shots at a predatory poet and could not
be convinced that he had been guilty of want of respect for literature
in doing so."

All the arts were represented in the Bohemian Club, which made no
effort to entertain Wilde; but a group of the younger and livelier members,
who thought him a "Miss Nancy," decided to test him in the usual way.
They invited him to dinner with the single intention of making him
drunk; but Oscar took all the drinks as fast as they came and never stopped
talking. As the evening wore on his hosts were rolling about speechless
from drink and laughter. One by one they disappeared beneath the table,
and at length, finding himself alone, Oscar got up and sauntered off to the
Palace Hotel. The feat made him famous: it was noised abroad that "the
man who wears knee-pants and makes woman-talk is a three-bottled

man and then some." A committee from the Bohemian Club waited on him and asked if he would sit for a portrait. He agreed, and the picture was hung in the Club, whether on the eye-line or near the cornice is not recorded. Shortly afterwards, at the Cliff House, a famous roadhouse seven miles from the city, he was asked to prove himself a man in yet another direction by taking a hand at poker, which, he once said, "like most of the distinctly national products of America, seems to have been imported from abroad." Invited to the bar he was requested to play a game of "dollar ante." "What is 'dollar ante'?" he asked drearily. They explained. He sat down sadly, sighed deeply, and seemed to be wrapped in melancholy. When his turn came to deal, he distributed the cards mournfully, "like crumbs at communion." The rest must be told by an onlooker:

"Everybody went in. The captain took two cards; Fry took one and Oscar one. The captain bet five dollars, and Fry raised him five. Oscar murmured dubiously, but put up his portion. 'Ten harder,' said the captain. 'Ten more than you,' said Fry. Oscar knit his brow and said 'The o'ershadowing sky is murky, but I must stay. I will—how do you phrase it?—call. I will call on you.' The captain laid down his cards with a smile of triumph. 'Three aces,' said he. 'Full hand,' said Fry, reaching for the money. 'Too-too,' said the poet, and laid down four aces. He rose and drawled 'Now that I remember it, gentlemen, we used to indulge in this little recreation at Oxford. Come and take a snifter with me.'"

At the end of his stay we find him in more congenial surroundings. Two young artists met him at the Bohemian Club and invited him to their studio. Arrangements for his reception were undertaken by their wives, who made the place look as nice as possible and, for comic relief, dressed up the life-sized female dummy which they used for portraits, to save their subjects from the boredom of sitting when only their clothes were being painted. With the sky-light dimmed Miss Piffle (as they called the dummy) looked lifelike, her gloved hand holding a black feather fan. Oscar arrived and was enchanted. "This is where I belong!" he exclaimed: "This is my atmosphere! I didn't know such a place existed in the whole United States." He reproached them for not having invited him before. "I'm leaving to-morrow. I've been here three mortal weeks. If you'd only opened your door to me, I'd have come here every day." He behaved in a perfectly natural and sincere manner, and, as always when he did so, his company was delightfully exhilarating. He wandered round the studio admiring the costumes, the Indian relics, the paintings; and then he came to Miss Piffle. Isobel Field, who records the incident, must continue:

"I think he was a little near-sighted, for he almost tumbled against her. Bowing, he apologised to the quiet lady sitting there so demurely, and made some casual remark. It may have been our watchful attitude that gave him an inkling of the situation, for without changing his voice he began a conversation with Miss Piffle that was a marvel of impromptu humour. He told her his opinion of San Francisco, and incidentally of the United States and its inhabitants; he replied to imaginary remarks of hers with surprise or approval so cleverly that it sounded as though Miss Piffle were actually talking to him. It was a superb performance, a masterpiece of sparkling wit and gaiety. Never before, or since, have I heard anything that compared to it. When he left we all felt we had met a truly great man."

On his way back to the eastern States Wilde lectured at Salt Lake City, Denver and Leadville. At the first he spoke in the Opera House, which he said was a huge building about the size of Covent Garden, "and holds with ease fourteen families." He thought polygamy prosaic: "How much more poetic it is to marry one and love many!" The reporters wanted to know why he carried his fur coat about with him. "To hide the hideous sofas in all the hotel rooms," he replied. Next to the Tabernacle the most important building in Salt Lake City was the Amelia Palace, built in honour of one of Brigham Young's wives. According to Oscar, when Young died "the present President of the Mormons stood up in the Tabernacle and said that it had been revealed to him that he was to have the Amelia Palace, and that on this subject there were to be no more revelations of any kind." Someone who met Wilde at an entertainment given him in Denver thought that he looked rather vague and preoccupied, but he became interested when the subject of printing cropped up. "Printing is so dull," he said. "There is nothing exquisite about it at present. In my next publication I am hoping to give examples of something more satisfying in this way. The letters shall be of a rarer design; the commas will be sunflowers, and the semicolons pomegranates." While at Denver he received a message that if he went to Leadville, as he proposed to do, the tougher spirits would be sure to shoot him or his travelling manager. "I wrote and told them that nothing that they could do to my travelling manager would intimidate me." So up the Rocky Mountains he went on a gloomy wet day, one hundred and fifty miles of jolting, to arrive at a cheerless snow-covered station. That night a baby added to the fun, and when Wilde declared "There is no better way of loving nature than through art" it burst out crying. "I wish the juvenile enthusiast would restrain its raptures," said Wilde, whose own account of what took place, though it differed slightly at each recital, gives a pleasing picture of culture in the Rockies. His audience was composed of miners, whose red shirts, knotted handkerchiefs, loose corduroys and high boots reminded him of seventeenth century cavaliers:

"In all my journeys through the country," said he, "the only well-dressed men that I saw . . . were the Western miners. . . . As I looked at them I could not help thinking with regret of the time when these picturesque miners would have made their fortunes and would go East to assume again all the abominations of modern fashionable attire. Indeed, so concerned was I that I made some of them promise that when they again appeared in the more crowded scenes of Eastern civilisation they would still continue to wear their lovely costume. But I do not believe they will.

"I spoke to them of the early Florentines, and they slept as though no crime had ever stained the ravines of their mountain home. I described to them the pictures of Botticelli, and the name, which seemed to them like a new drink, roused them from their dreams. . . . I read them passages from the autobiography of Benvenuto Cellini, and they seemed much delighted. I was reproved by my hearers for not having brought him with me. I explained that he had been dead for some little time, which elicited the enquiry 'Who shot him?' . . . I had almost won them to reverence for what is beautiful in art when unluckily I described one of Jimmy Whistler's 'nocturnes in blue and gold.' Then they leapt to their feet and swore that such things should not be. Some of the younger ones pulled their revolvers out and left hurriedly to see if Jimmy were 'prowling about the saloons.' Had he been there, so bitter was their feeling that I fear he would have been killed. Their enthusiasm satisfied me, and I ended my lecture.

"They afterwards took me to a dancing saloon, where I saw the only rational method of art criticism I have ever come across. Over the piano was printed a notice: *Please do not shoot the pianist: he is doing his best.* The mortality among pianists in that place is marvellous. Then they asked me to supper, and having accepted I had to descend a mine in a rickety bucket in which it was impossible to be graceful. My dress was of India rubber. 'This cloak reminds me of the togas worn by Roman senators,' I said. 'The lining, however, should be of purple satin and there should be storks embroidered upon the flaps, with fern embroidery around the edges.' At the bottom of the mine we sat down to a banquet, the first course being whisky, the second whisky, and the third whisky. The amazement of the miners when they saw that art and appetite could go hand in hand knew no bounds; when I lit a long cigar they cheered till the silver fell in dust from the roof on our plates; and when I quaffed a cocktail without flinching, they unanimously pronounced me 'a bully boy with no glass eye' . . . I opened a new vein, or lode, with a silver drill, the lode being named 'The Oscar.' I had hoped that in their grand simple way they would have offered me shares in 'The Oscar,' but in their artless untutored fashion they did not."

Their failure to act handsomely may have been responsible for a remark in one of his last lectures: "When I was at Leadville, and reflected that all the shining silver that I saw coming from the mines would be made into ugly dollars, it made me sad." Otherwise his subterranean trip was a huge success. While the miners became dizzier and dizzier he remained cool and steady, chatting incessantly and showing no sign of fatigue when towards dawn he returned to the surface in a bucket. His fame as a drinker spread abroad in the land, and it is to be feared that he impressed America more as a Bacchanalian than as an aesthete, for long afterwards Frank Benson heard some cowboys say of him "That fellow is some art guy, but he can drink any of us under the table and afterwards carry us home two at a time." One trip to an outlandish spot was sufficient to go on with, and when at Kansas City he received a wire from Griggsville "Will you lecture us on aesthetics?" he replied "Begin by changing the name of your town."

Back on the Atlantic border Wilde lectured again at New York and Boston, and in the middle of May addressed large audiences at Montreal, where he stayed at the Windsor hotel, at Toronto, where he stayed at the Queen's and witnessed a game of lacrosse, and at Ottawa. Then he went south, where he was not so successful, though a crowded house at New Orleans pleased him so much that he spoke for an hour and a half, telling them that in America he had found picturesqueness of costume and habits only among the Indians and Negroes, "and I am surprised that painters and poets have paid so little attention to them, particularly to the Negro, as a subject of art." The painters and poets, to say nothing of the musicians, have since rectified this omission. He travelled through Texas and Georgia, lectured at Charleston, Richmond and other places, and noted the peculiarities of the inhabitants:

"It is a popular superstition that a visitor to the more distant parts of the United States is spoken to as 'Stranger.' But when I went to Texas I was called 'Captain'; when I got to the centre of the country I was addressed as 'Colonel'; and, on arriving at the borders of Mexico, as 'General.'"

"Among the more elderly inhabitants of the South I found a melancholy tendency to date every event of importance by the late war. 'How beautiful the moon is to-night,' I once remarked to a gentleman standing near me. 'Yes,' was his reply, 'but you should have seen it before the war.'"

He thought that the South produced the prettiest women, and described a certain Alabama lady as the most beautiful he had seen in the States. When a reporter who was not from Alabama asked him whether he had really put forward such an outrageous assertion, he said "That is a remark, my dear fellow, that I have made of some lady in every city in this country." To another interviewer, who wanted to know whether he thought European or American women the more beautiful, he replied that he would answer that question in mid-ocean, out of sight of both continents. After his return to England he said that American girls were "pretty and charming— little oases of pretty unreasonableness in a vast desert of practical common sense." He was not so complimentary about American men: "I can stand brute force, but brute reason is quite unbearable. There is something unfair about its use. It is hitting below the intellect." Also: "The Americans are certainly great hero-worshippers, and always take their heroes from the criminal classes." His final summary ran: "American women are charming, but American men—alas!"

He spent the summer of '82 in various holiday resorts, sometimes speaking, always gazed at, constantly chased by women "in silks and crêpes and laces, with diamonds in their ears," and occasionally writing blank verse for a play called *The Duchess of Padua*, which he hoped Mary Anderson would produce. His meetings were now smaller and more intimate: he talked to select circles of women, each of whom was busy embroidering and stitching an "Oscar Crazy Quilt," the season's rage, thus described by an expert: "On a piece of cambric half a yard square there is basted in the centre a sunflower made of either yellow broadcloth, silk, or velvet; or else a lily, daisy, or pansy. The squares are filled with bits of silk or velvet of all colours, the edges turned in, and the piece is sewed down firmly with a chain stitch of old gold colour, alternating with cardinal sewing-silk."

That seemed to exhaust the interest in Oscar; for though he toured a few minor towns in the autumn, he was content to accept as little as seventy-five dollars at one of them. Altogether he had delivered over eighty lectures, and had made enough money to repay what he had borrowed from his mother and to live for some months in comfort upon his return from the

States. The limelight which he had enjoyed was flashed on to Mrs. Langtry
from the moment she landed at New York in October. Of course he met
her on the boat and accompanied her all over the place. The reporters said
that he was love-smitten and one of them suggested that he had discovered
her. "I would rather have discovered Mrs. Langtry than have discovered
America," was his retort. He told her that he was going to Australia. She
asked why. "Well, do you know, when I look at the map and see what an
awfully ugly-looking country Australia is, I feel that I want to go there and
see if it cannot be changed into a more beautiful form." At which, in the
words of a journalist who was present, "he threw back his long locks and
laughed." Mrs. Langtry opened her season at Wallack's Theatre with *An
Unequal Match* by Tom Taylor, and Wilde was present on the first night
as guest-critic for the *New York Herald*; but as he could not praise her acting
he overpraised her beauty.

His lecture tour had come to an end, but he stayed on because Marie
Prescott seemed anxious to appear in *Vera*. She and her husband suggested
a few alterations, but Wilde was not helpful. "Who am I to tamper with
a masterpiece?" he objected. During these last months he lived in furnished
rooms in New York, first at the south-west corner of Irving Place and
17th Street, next to the house once occupied by Washington Irving, and
latterly in Greenwich Village at 48 West 11th Street. One day he was walking up Fifth Avenue when, close to 15th Street, a thin-faced youth stopped
him and introduced himself as the son of Anthony J. Drexel. Wilde had
visited the office of Morgan's partner, Drexel, and courteously invited the
lad to lunch, over which Drexel Junior said he had just won a lottery
prize and needed help to get the money: would Oscar go with him? Sus-
pecting nothing, the poet accompanied him to a luxurious house where
well-to-do men were shaking dice for heavy stakes. Wilde was induced to
take part, and soon lost so heavily that he had to pay by cheque. Leaving
the house in a thoughtful mood, it dawned on him that he had been
cheated; so, after calling at his bank to stop payment of the cheque, he
visited a police station, said "I've just made a *damned* fool of myself!"
and explained what had happened. Pictures of criminals were produced;
he recognised the young man at once, and was informed that "Drexel"
was "one of the cleverest bunco-steerers in New York." He was advised to
prosecute, but this he refused to do, and the police liked him so much that
they promised to keep the episode out of the papers until he was out of
the country.

He left New York on December 27th, '82, on board the *Bothnia*, and during the voyage revised his first impression of the ocean. "The Atlantic," he said, "has been greatly misunderstood." His teaching had some influence on American house decoration, furniture and ornaments, and, among other tributes, he received from a potter a pair of vases in gratitude for the effect of his lectures on the sale of underglazed pottery. The effect of America on Wilde was more pronounced. He never spoke in praise of the country or its inhabitants. For the American, he believed, "Art has no marvel, and Beauty no meaning, and the Past no message." When good Americans die they go to Paris, bad Americans to America, he used to say. And on hearing that Rossetti, in order to get rid of a poet who was always cadging, had given him enough money to go to the States, Wilde drawled "Of course, if one had the money to go to America, one would not go."

CHAPTER SEVEN

THE PLAGIARIST

HAVING entertained several dinner-parties with his reminiscences of America, and such comments as "The English have really everything in common with the Americans, except of course language," Oscar Wilde left for Paris in February '83 and remained there for three months, when his money ran out. He had decided to work hard on the blank verse play he was writing for Mary Anderson; but hard work did not come naturally to him, so in order to simplify his labours he cast himself for a fresh part. In common with many young men who set out in the world with vast, if unformulated, ambitions, he had an unqualified admiration, which he never outgrew, for Balzac, the mere size of whose concepts has an overwhelming effect on the impulsive emotions of youth. Wilde took a suite of second-floor rooms in the Hotel Voltaire, on the Quai Voltaire, and proceeded to model himself on Balzac, working in a white dressing-gown, which resembled the monkish garment worn by Balzac when writing, surrounding himself with books by and about the famous novelist, and even carrying in the street an ivory cane, the head set with turquoises, which was an exact copy of Balzac's walking-stick. "The Oscar of the first period is dead," he confided to a friend. "We are now concerned with the Oscar of the second period, who has nothing whatever in common with the gentleman who wore long hair and carried a sunflower down Piccadilly." He was much taken by the bust of Nero in the Louvre, asked a hairdresser, after studying it, to reproduce the effect on his own head; and then, dressing himself rather in the style of a Balzacian dandy, he went forth to mingle with the aristocracy of letters. On his arrival in Paris he had paved the way by sending notes, with copies of his *Poems*, to various writers and painters, who received him with the courtesy due to such attention.

Englishmen said that he spoke French haltingly with an atrocious pronunciation. Frenchmen said that he spoke it fluently with a perfect pronunciation. Since the natives of a country usually know more about their own language than the aliens, we must accept the French verdict. But strangely enough the countrymen of Rabelais have very little sense of humour. Their wit is polished, precise, direct and logical: they lack the sudden bursts of poetic imagery and self-criticism, of irresponsibility and frivolity, which are the essential ingredients of humour. Wilde was a master of wit and humour, but with him, as with his only rival in conversational English, Sydney Smith, humour transcended wit; and the French could not rise to his imaginative level. They thought him charming but odd. One of them, Alphonse Daudet, on hearing him say that he had spent hours in rapt admiration before the Venus of Milo, thought it excessive. Another, Edmond de Goncourt, gravely entered in his diary that, according to Wilde, the part of Lady Macbeth was played in Texas by a real murderess, whose name on the posters was followed by the statement "ten years penal servitude." A conversation with the actor Coquelin was recorded by Wilde himself:

"What is civilisation, M. Wilde?"

"Love of beauty."

"And what is beauty?"

"That which the bourgeois call ugly."

"And what do the bourgeois call beautiful?"

"It does not exist."

He told Coquelin that the play he was writing, *The Duchess of Padua*, consisted solely of style, and added: "Between them, Hugo and Shakespeare have exhausted every subject. Originality is no longer possible, even in sin. So there are no real emotions left—only extraordinary adjectives." Coquelin could make nothing of all this, and when they met again some years later Wilde dumbfounded him. Following a performance of *The Taming of the Shrew* William Rothenstein took Wilde to the actor's dressing-room, and after the usual compliments Coquelin asked his visitor to call at his house. Wilde said he would be delighted to do so and wanted to know when he would find Coquelin at home.

"I am always at home about nine o'clock."

"Good. Then I will come one of these evenings."

"But, Monsieur, I mean nine o'clock in the morning."

"My dear M. Coquelin," said Wilde, stepping back and regarding the actor with amazed admiration, "you are really a remarkable man. I am much more bourgeois than you. I am always in bed by four or five. I could never stay awake as late as that. Really you *are* a remarkable man!"

Hugo was alive, or half-alive, in '83 and Wilde went to one of his receptions, being given the place near the great man which was reserved for

visitors of distinction; but he had not been talking for long before Hugo's
eyes closed; at once it was whispered round the room "The master sleeps";
and Wilde had to be brilliant to the circle in bated breath. A more enervating
experience was a meeting with Paul Verlaine at the Café François Premier.
Though Wilde did his best to entertain the poet, it was uphill work, because Verlaine was far more interested in the quantity of absinthe he could
make the other pay for than in the quality of the conversation. Moreover
Verlaine was excessively ugly, and this to Wilde was as repellent as de-
formity; so his meeting with the man was an act of self-sacrifice which he
did not repeat. "I consider ugliness a kind of malady," he once said,
"and illness and suffering always inspire me with repulsion. A man with
the toothache ought, I know, to have my sympathy, for it is a terrible
pain, yet he fills me with nothing but aversion. He is tedious; he is a bore;
I cannot stand him; I cannot look at him; I must get away from him." A
later epigram was not merely meant to be funny: "It is better to be beautiful
than to be good, but it is better to be good than to be ugly." He thought
physical pain "a thousand times worse than any mental suffering," and he
attributed the heroism of martyrs to a kind of hysterical insanity. If he had
called it insane egotism he would not have been far wrong.

Among other notable Frenchmen of the time he met Mallarmé, Henri de
Régnier and Jean Richepin; he often dined with Paul Bourget, who admired
him greatly; he talked about painting with Degas, Pissarro, De Nittis and
Sargent, all of whom listened with interest to what he had to say; and he
went to see Zola, who did not feel quite at ease with him, a feeling that
got the better of the novelist when, a few years afterwards, he had to
propose the toast of "The Arts," coupling it with the name of Wilde, at
some dinner given in Paris. Zola concluded his speech with the words
"Malheureusement M. Wilde sera obligé de répondre dans sa langue barbare".
Wilde showed that he could be quite at ease with Zola by beginning his
reply in French: "Je suis Irlandais de naissance, Anglais de race, et comme
le dit M. Zola, condamné à parler la langue de Shakespeare." On a different occasion he remarked that Zola "is determined to show that, if he has
not got genius, he can at least be dull. And how well he succeeds!"

Wilde's clothes did not help to remove the misunderstanding created
by his sayings. He wore fur-lined coats, one of which was made of green
cloth and faced with black braid; and as the only Frenchmen who wore
fur were prosperous stockbrokers or bookmakers, his appearance antago-
nised the circles he moved in. His curled Neronic hair, the rings on his
fingers, which he constantly changed, his clothes, which were fashionable

a generation earlier, and the turquoise-headed stick, did not help to neutralise the effect of the bottle-green coat; while his carefully managed voice, which he had trained as other men train their lungs or their limbs, the pauses in his conversation, and the bizarre contrast between the slightly pontifical manner and the sometimes frivolous matter, gave Frenchmen the not wholly erroneous impression that he was playing a part. But when they deduced from this that he was utterly insincere, they displayed their own shallowness; for self-dramatisation was as necessary to his nature as preaching is to a parson's or platitudinising to a politician's or moralising to nearly everybody's. "What people call insincerity," he used to say, "is simply a method by which we can multiply our personalities."

Fortunately one French writer of that time, Jean Joseph-Renaud, heard Oscar play all his parts, one after the other, in a fashionable *salon*, and left a record of the occasion. Without listening to the names of the people who were being introduced to him, Wilde sat down, and with an air of exhaustion begged his hostess to have the shutters of the dining-room closed and the candles lit, as he could not endure the light of day, also the table decorations altered, as mauve flowers were unlucky. His conversation at first was pretentious and rather disconcerting. He asked questions and did not wait for the replies: "You have never seen a ghost? No! Ah! Now you, Madame, yes, you, Madame, your eyes seem to have looked upon ghosts . . . " and so on. Next he told some simple tales, almost whispering them as if imparting secrets of great consequence. Then, over coffee in the drawing-room, he passed on to French history and dealt wittily with men, deeds, treaties, bringing the past back to life and making it "glitter under the light of his words." Finally, on the subject of Lady Blessington, "he little by little raised himself to a lofty and intoxicating lyricism; his fine voice hymned, grew tender, rang out, like a viol in the midst of the emotional silence. This Englishman, who just before had appeared grotesque, reached, reached with simplicity, and surpassed, the expressive power of the most admirable odes to humanity. Many of us were moved to tears. One had never thought that the words of man could attain to such splendour. And this took place in a drawing-room, and the man who was speaking never spoke otherwise than one speaks in a drawing-room. We understood why a great lady had said of him 'When he is speaking I see round his head a luminous aureole!'"

It was during these three months in Paris that Oscar met one of his future biographers, Robert Harborough Sherard, who was in his early twenties at the time and had not yet "come through early poems, a three-volume novel, and other complaints common to his time of life," as Oscar was to write of him a few years later. Sherard was a born hero-worshipper, his loyalty to his heroes being so extreme that he could not or would not see them with the naked eye: at least one would suppose from his writings that he saw them through rose-coloured glasses, though he could sometimes be frank enough about them in private conversation. His egotism demanded that they should appear to the world as he wished them to appear, and Wilde frequently declared that he could not possibly live up to Sherard's conception of him. It was impossible not to feel flattered by Sherard's championship, but it was also impossible to feel quite comfortable with a man who insisted on such a high standard, and as the years went by their friendship wore thin. Their rather awkward companionship some seven years after their first meeting was shown when William Rothenstein and Stuart Merrill accompanied them on a round of low haunts in Paris, under the illusion, common enough in the nineties, that they were "seeing life." At one place, the Château Rouge, a refuge of criminals and other types who came under the heading of "life," Sherard asserted himself and kept shouting, to the acute discomfort of his party, that anyone who meddled with his friend Oscar Wilde would quickly regret it. "Robert, you are defending me at the risk of my life," said Wilde. But in the early months of their friendship Sherard had not appropriated Wilde, perhaps because Wilde had not yet become a property.

Their first meeting would have been their last if something in the younger man had not appealed to the older. Sherard was rather morose by nature, disinclined to like anyone whom he could not wholeheartedly admire, and what he had heard about Wilde did not dispose him to a favourable view He accepted the invitation to meet the poet with the firm intention of disliking him, and when he caught sight of the dandified figure he was "taken with a desire of hysterical and irrepressible laughter." Pulling himself together, he sat down to dinner with the rest of the company and listened to what Wilde had to say. "His conversation was as exhilarating as wine; his presence diffused a stimulating atmosphere; we felt ourselves exalted by his joyous enthusiasms." Even so Sherard would not surrender until he had fired a shot, until he had vented his annoyance at having to change from antagonism to admiration; and when Wilde expressed the sense of physical pleasure given him by the Venus of Milo in the Louvre, Sherard, who had been silent during the meal, burst out "I have never been to the Louvre. When that name is mentioned, I always think of the Grands Magasins du Louvre, where I can get the cheapest ties in Paris." Oscar's immediate comment was surprising: "I like that. That is very fine." Afterwards, when Sherard confessed that he had felt hostile merely because Wilde had made a reputation in a way that he had not the courage to copy, Oscar said with a laugh "That was very wrong of you," and told him that pleasure in the success of others made life rich and joyous. Oscar also explained why Sherard's irritable interruption had appealed to him: "From your appearance, your long hair and so forth, I fancied you were Herr Schultze on the violoncello. When you bluntly disclaimed all artistic interests, I discovered that you had scientifically thought out a pose that interested me.

Next day Sherard called at the Hotel Voltaire and remarked on the lovely view of the Louvre over the Seine. "Oh," returned Wilde, "that is altogether immaterial, except to the proprietor, who of course charges it in the bill. A gentleman never looks out of the window." They dined together at a restaurant. "If I were all alone, marooned on some desert island, and had my things with me, I should dress for dinner every evening," Wilde had said at Oxford, and in accordance with his wish Sherard had dressed for the occasion. Wilde seemed to find interest and beauty in everything. "It was always springtime once in my heart," he wrote in his last years: "My temperament was akin to joy." But Sherard was not in tune with this feeling, and rubbing his cigar-end into the coffee in his saucer he asked whether there was any beauty in the mess. "Oh, yes," said Wilde pleasantly; "it makes quite an effective brown." After dinner they strolled through the streets, and Wilde remarked as they passed the Tuileries "There is not there one little blackened stone which is not to me a chapter in the Bible of Democracy."

But although he used often to quote from Carlyle's *French Revolution,* many passages of which he knew by heart, he was not at that period much concerned with the Bible of Democracy. He was finishing his blank verse tragedy, *The Duchess of Padua,* and trying to find difficult rhymes for awkward words in his poem *The Sphinx.* Mary Anderson had already paid him a thousand dollars for *The Duchess;* another four thousand were due on acceptance; and it was for him a matter of vital importance to have it produced, the alternative being hard work at some uncongenial job. The tragedy was completed in March and sent off at once. Money was running short, and having allowed sufficient time for the arrival of the manuscript in America he cabled for the verdict. Sherard was with him when the answer came: the play was refused. He showed no sign of disappointment, but tore a small piece off the blue form, rolled it into a pellet, popped it into his mouth—a curious habit of his when handling a book or a paper

—passed the cable over to Sherard with the words "This is rather tedious, Robert," made no further reference to it, and a minute later was chatting away about something else. In those days his favourite word to express pleasure was "amazing," to express displeasure "tedious." Sherard heard nothing more of the subject, though when they went out to dinner that evening Wilde said "We shan't be able to dine with the Duchess to-night," their previous meals having been enjoyed at more luxurious restaurants in anticipation of the £800 advance on royalties.

Mary Anderson's verdict was justified, though it would not have hurt her to send the cash and shelve the play. At the end of his life Wilde admitted that "*The Duchess* is unfit for publication—the only one of my works that comes under that category." In many places the blank verse faintly echoes Shakespeare's, while the comic passages are depressing enough to recall the heavy humour of Shakespeare's clowns at their feeblest. A line from one of Wilde's sonnets, "Murder with his silent bloody feet," reappears in one of the scenes, and Mary Anderson could not have felt complimented when the character specially created for her was described in words that had already done service in a sonnet to Ellen Terry:

> O hair of gold, O crimson lips, O face
> Made for the luring and the love of man!

There is little to be said in favour of the piece, except that already Wilde shows he can bring down a curtain effectively and that the born dramatist in him puts up a good fight against the uninspired quality of the verse. *The Duchess* was a failure in Germany and only ran for three weeks in 1891 when, under the title *Guido Ferranti*, it was produced without the author's name at the Broadway Theatre, New York.

As a key to Wilde's character, his poem *The Sphinx* is far more important. He had an actor's love of high-sounding phrases; coloured words attracted him as coloured marbles attract some boys; and it gave him a double delight when his youthful love of shocking respectable people could find expression in ornate language. Although *Dorian Gray* and *Salomé* were to be more complete illustrations of his boylike enjoyment of scandalising the bourgeoisie by a ritualistic indulgence in bizarrerie and devilry, *The Sphinx* is the first of his works to hint at hidden vices. He began to write it at Oxford, more or less completed it at Paris in '83, but tinkered with it off and on for another ten years. It eventually appeared in 1894, and he said that he had hesitated to publish it "as it would destroy domesticity in England." But a careful study of it would be more likely to establish domesticity in England

and place monogamy on an enduring basis. Wilde, like the Fat Boy in *Pickwick*, wanted to make people's flesh creep; but he was too childlike by nature to succeed in his plan, and the adult reader is more inclined to shake with laughter than to shudder with horror. No doubt *The Sphinx* could pass as poetry in an age that had forgotten how to write it and mistook word-patterns for the real thing. Take two verses:

> But you can read the Hieroglyphs on the great sandstone obelisks,
> And you have talked with Basilisks, and you have looked on Hippogriffs.

> White Ammon was your bedfellow! Your chamber was the steaming Nile!
> And with your curved archaic smile you watched his passion come and go.

This kind of thing has about it the interest of the cross-word puzzle, for those who find cross-word puzzles interesting, and the reader is kept wondering what quaint word the author will come across when next he dips into the dictionary. Its general effect is comical, although one is never quite sure that Wilde himself did not enjoy the joke, and sometimes we seem to catch his "curved archaic smile." When an acquaintance said to him that the metre was that of Tennyson's *In Memoriam*, he gravely replied "No, it is printed quite differently." Possibly he chose the metre of the most famous poem by the most moral of poets in order to heighten the contrast between his theme and the Laureate's and add to the reader's embarrassment, though he knew that his effort would not have as wide an appeal as Tennyson's and explained to a friend why so small an edition had been printed: "My first idea was to print only three copies: one for myself, one for the British Museum, and one for Heaven. I had some doubt about the British Museum."

Spontaneity in a work of this order being out of the question, we are not surprised to learn that Wilde equipped himself with a rhyming dictionary and went about asking his friends for words of three syllables to rhyme with "nenuphar," "catafalque" and so on. "Why have you brought me no rhyme from Passy?" he used to ask Sherard, who was living out there at the time and once induced his new friend to lunch at his house. Wilde declined to repeat the visit, excusing himself on the ground that Passy was a dreadful place to get to: "It is so far off that one's coachman keeps getting off his box to ask for something on account of his *pourboire*." So in future they lunched or dined in Paris at Wilde's expense, sometimes at the Café de Paris, Oscar excusing the luxury with "It's a duty we owe to

the dignity of letters." But they had to confine themselves to cheaper
restaurants after *The Duchess* was turned down.

Apart from the writing of one more poem, *The Harlot's House*, which
caused some stir at the time because it was not the custom of Victorian
poets to write on brothels, Wilde lazed away his three months in Paris in
the manner most agreeable to himself: in studio, in *salon* and in café he
mixed with the three classes of people whose company he really enjoyed:
artists, aristocrats and outcasts. He could get on with anyone who was not
conventional, respectable, prudent, middle class, and to Sherard's amazement he would sit for hours in a boulevard café talking with such notorious
characters as André Salis, known as Bibi-la-Purée, known also as a thief, a
beggar, a pariah, a poet and a police spy. The sight of the elegant Oscar
sitting in animated conversation with this disreputable figure was too much
for Sherard, whose discomfort was increased when Oscar invited the drug-
demented poet Maurice Rollinat to dinner at the Hotel Voltaire and begged
him to recite his morbid verses, which he did with such frightening effect
that Oscar bubbled over with enthusiasm and Sherard passed a sleepless
night. It was therefore with simple sincerity that Wilde said from the witness-
box "I would talk to a street arab with pleasure." Carson, who was cross-
examining him, affected to be shocked: "You would talk to a street arab!?"
"If he would talk with me. Yes, with pleasure."

Though he deprecated such curious tastes, Sherard was completely captivated by Wilde. "It was for me a new and joyous life, an unending feast
of the soul, and each day my admiration for my new friend grew more
enthusiastic." Temperamentally disposed to melancholy, with a strain of
puritanism in him, Sherard's whole nature seemed to change in Oscar's
company: "This joyous Celt showed me the gladness of things, suggested
the possibility of great and buoyant happiness in the world, and with his
exuberant vitality scattered the black butterflies that enc0loud my spiritual
vision." Sherard was passing through a suicidal phase from which Wilde
rescued him: "If he had taught me nothing but the great value and happiness of life, I should still owe him an unpayable debt." Oscar described
suicide as "the greatest compliment that one can pay to society," and when
Sherard asked him "If you saw a man throw himself into the river here,
would you go after him?" he promptly replied "I should consider it an act
of gross impertinence to do so. His suicide would be a perfectly thought-
out act, the definite result of a scientific process, with which I should
have no right whatever to interfere." He might have added that the prospect of a wetting for himself, with its attendant discomfort, would have

contributed to his inaction, for in his philosophy there was no cant about self-sacrifice or one's duty to others. What he did for others he enjoyed doing and never pretended there was any duty or self-denial about it. He was naturally kind-hearted, which meant that he was also kind-hearted to himself. He loved the luxurious things of life, took immense pleasure in good food, comfortable clothes, delightful surroundings, and it added to his own pleasure when he could help others to the same things, or to the things in which they took pleasure. Thus he was boundlessly generous: his money belonged to his friends, and such was his joy in making others happy that he would do things for them which he was far too lazy to do for himself. "Friends always share," he used to say; but the record of his life proves that his friends shared more in his good fortune than he in theirs. Amongst many instances of his generosity in these early days at Paris, Sherard tells us that a dancer known as "Le Petit Louis" wanted to quit his sordid life and join the navy, and that Wilde provided him with the money. Sherard, too, had cause to be grateful, for Wilde, though very hard-up at the time, gave him the sum he needed to leave Paris and settle in England. Wilde was so friendly by nature that he found it difficult to remain on formal terms with anyone he really liked, and soon after their first meeting he said to Sherard: "I don't want you to call me Wilde, and I certainly don't intend to call you Sherard. We are going to be friends: I think we are friends already. Now if we are friends we ought to call each other by our christian names. If we are not, then I am Mr. Wilde and you are Mr. Sherard." Sherard's less expansive nature could not immediately reciprocate; and needless to say Wilde himself did not always make a practice of his precept.

It was not only the pleasures of the senses which Wilde quickened in his friends; he stimulated their minds and broadened their interests. Sherard describes how, during a moonlit walk through Paris, Wilde told him the story of *Eugénie Grandet*, and how, when he read Balzac's novel, the original seemed far inferior to the version he had heard that evening. Wilde's love of Baudelaire, which he carried to the length of drinking the poet's favourite tipple absinthe, was also communicated to Sherard; and one night they went on a pilgrimage in the footsteps of Gerard de Nerval, whose personality Wilde made vivid to his friend. Twice they called on Sarah Bernhardt together, the first time at the Vaudeville Theatre, where she was appearing in a play by Sardou; and the joy with which she received Wilde seemed to irritate Jean Richepin and the other men who were in the *salon* adjoining her dressing-room. The second time they went to her house in the Avenue de Villiers, and she was delighted with an armful of wallflowers which Oscar had brought for her. He was seen so often in the company of another well-known actress that the newspapers referred to it, and people wondered whether anything would come of it. Nothing did.

In May '83 Wilde returned to London, with so little money in his pocket that one of the first things he did was to pawn his Berkeley Gold Medal. Yet he must have raised some cash elsewhere, possibly a final instalment from the parental acres, because we find him enjoying "the splendid whirl and swirl of life in London" and displaying his "Neronian coiffure" in society with the childlike pleasure of an actor who admires his own make-up. "I am hard at work being idle," he wrote to Sherard, and for a while he was; but the need for money once more drove him to the lecture-platform, and on June 30th he addressed the students of the Royal Academy at their club in Golden Square on The House Beautiful, among other matters referring to the hideous London thoroughfares where "wearied of the houses you turn to contemplate the street itself, you have nothing to look at but chimney-pot hats, men with sandwich boards, vermilion letter-boxes, and do that even at the risk of being run over by an emerald-green omnibus." Nine days later he gave his Personal Impressions of America in a lecture at Princes' Hall, Piccadilly, and this settled his immediate future; a firm of lecture-agents booking him for a provincial tour in the autumn and winter. But before that started he had to keep an appointment in America. Marie Prescott was going to produce Vera, and he wanted to be present at the final rehearsals. On July 30 he lectured at Southport, and on August 2nd, after welcoming Mrs. Langtry at Liverpool on her return from the States, he left for New York. The play, which was produced on August 20th at the Union Square Theatre in that city, started well, and Wilde received an ovation when he appeared in response to loud calls after the second act; but it seems that a later appearance of the heroine in a flaming vermilion gown, for which the author had obtained the material, was too much for the audience; and as her emotions were of a kind to match the gown, the earlier cheers had developed into cat-calls by the end of the evening. The piece ran for a week; but Marie Prescott had an inspiration. She liked her part and intended to take the play on tour. If only Oscar would play Prince Paul, their success was assured. There is no doubt that he would have been extremely good as Prince Paul, since that character displayed an aspect of himself, but the play he wished to appear in contained only one part, and he returned home to perform it, being greeted by Punch on his arrival in England with the statement that *Vera* was "vera bad."

At this period he had rooms in Charles Street (afterwards Carlos Street), Grosvenor Square, in an old house which then stood opposite the mews of the Coburg Hotel. It was kept by a retired butler, whose wife was a very good cook, a fact that appealed to Wilde, who once remarked that "The British cook is a foolish woman who should be turned for her iniquities into a pillar of salt which she never knows how to use." With his usual generosity he asked Sherard, who was almost penniless, to stay with him, and whenever he returned from lecturing in the provinces he produced the sum he had earned and told Sherard to help himself. "It's as much yours as mine," he said. "You know I have no sense of property." On such occasions they gave breakfasts to their friends which lasted well into the afternoons, or lunched at the Café Royal, often in the company of Whistler. Incidentally Wilde began to study German, and went lecturing with a volume of Heine and a small German dictionary in his pocket. Sherard relates a quaint incident of the Charles Street days. When at New College, Oxford, he had made the acquaintance of a Scot named John Barlas, whom he now invited to meet Wilde. At this time Barlas was writing poetry and living with a girl in a Lambeth slum. They were both red-hot anarchists, and the girl, whom he brought along with him to Charles Street, wore flannel underclothing of a blood-red hue to denote the colour of her convictions. Neither her clothes nor her manners were up to Mayfair standard, but Wilde showed no surprise and treated her as if she were a duchess. The contrast between the girl and her surroundings, however, upset Barlas, who decided that she had not received the attention due to a queen, and when they all left the house together he was excessively put out because Wilde did not offer an arm to the lady across Grosvenor Square. He therefore hailed a hansom, shoved the girl into it, and after expressing his sense of grievance in forcible terms gave the Lambeth slum address to the cabby, who seemed unwilling to drive to such a place. Instantly Wilde, who had just been the public victim of Barlas's unjustifiable wrath, stepped forward and assured the man that all was well. The cabby touched his cap, called Wilde "my lord," and whipped up his horse. Barlas, who had an excitable and quarrelsome disposition, brooded intensely on the condition of the world, the greed and wickedness of man, and eight years after he had anathematised Wilde his indignation got the better of him: he rushed from his slum to the House of Commons and fired a revolver at it. This relieved him but did not relieve the oppressed peoples on whose behalf the gesture was made. He was arrested, and Wilde, without thinking twice about it, went bail for him, becoming one of his sureties for good behaviour. Barlas, being a kind-hearted fellow, bore Wilde no malice for his timely help, and in a letter some five years after Wilde's death said that he "was and remains my ideal of a man of genius in this generation."

Lecturing was a dreary business now, and Wilde was bored before he began. He was billed everywhere as "The Great Aesthete," and people came to gape at him as at something in a zoo, being much disappointed when they saw an ordinary man in dress clothes, many of them leaving long before the lecture was over, some of them demanding their money back. He did not care one way or the other; he just "walked through" a part of which he was thoroughly tired, and hurried off at the conclusion of the performance as if he had a train to catch. From the opening of the tour, on September 24th at Wandsworth Town Hall, to the close, on March 5th at the Crystal Palace, he dealt with The House Beautiful and The Value of Art in Modern Life, but his most popular lecture described his Personal Impressions of America. We have a snapshot of him from a youth named Richard Le Gallienne, who was taken by his father to hear Wilde talk on America at Birkenhead. It was an afternoon lecture, and Wilde was dressed in his Balzacian costume, suggestive of the Regency period, with tight pantaloon trousers and a huge stock. The curled amber-dyed hair looked like a wig. Though handsome in a way, there was something excessive about his appearance which reminded Le Gallienne of an enormous doll; but this impression was contradicted by his wonderful voice, his humourous haughty eyes and his superb insolent aplomb. Recovering from the state of bewilderment into which his appearance usually threw an audience, everyone was soon laughing heartily at his description of life in the United States, and Le Gallienne's father, a shrewd business man, said "Don't make any mistake; that man is no fool." The son agreed, for Wilde seemed to be expressing exactly what Richard was feeling. At Edinburgh Wilde met an old college friend, David Hunter Blair, now a priest in the Roman Church. After the lecture Blair went round to see him and took him to task for a passage in Ravenna. "You know that all your sympathies were with the dethroned Pope, not with the invading and usurping King—you know they were!" complained Blair. "Don't be angry, Dunsky," appealed Oscar. "You must know that I should never, never have won the Newdigate if I had taken the Pope's side against the King's." As Blair rose to go, Oscar suddenly knelt and kissed his hand. "Pray for me, dear old Dunsky," he said, and the priest thought there were tears in his eyes.

Provincial lionising was not much to his taste, but he played the lion when called upon to do so, and noticed that the women had misunderstood his message. "Some women try to follow what they think my ideas, but only succeed in looking dowdy and untidy," he told a friend. The repulsive northern towns depressed him. He thought that all factory chimneys, workshops, etc., should be removed to some out-of-the-way island, and that to make England beautiful again Manchester should be given back to the shepherds and Leeds to the stock-farmers. While staying at the Station Hotel, Newcastle-on-Tyne, and meditating on the prevailing ugliness, he came to the conclusion that if he were to be born again he would like to come to life as a flower, even though, for his sins, he might be made a red geranium. He recalled the grey misty quadrangles of Oxford and his joyous life there and what he loved best in the world, "poetry and paradox dancing together," and he contrasted it all with the hideous manufacturing centres he was doomed to visit and the sort of life he was now living. Gone were the days when he could write:

> In that wild throb when all existences
> Seemed narrowed to one single ecstasy,

and from the Central Station Hotel, Glasgow, he announced to a young Oxford friend that there was no such thing as a romantic experience: "There are romantic memories, and there is the desire of romance—that is all. Our most fiery moments of ecstasy are merely shadows of what somewhere else we have felt, or of what we long some day to feel." Also there was no such thing as a new experience of any kind: there were only moods, the mystery of which fascinated him. "There is an unknown land full of strange flowers and subtle perfumes, a land of which it is joy of all joys to dream, a land where all things are perfect and poisonous. I have been reading Walter Scott for the last week—you too should read him, for there is nothing of all this in him."

On his visits to London between his lecturing dates he saw a great deal of Whistler, whom he both liked and admired. But he had not yet discovered the real character which lay beneath the surface charm, the debonair exterior, the arresting manner of the man. Whistler was twenty-two years older than Wilde, having been born on July 10th, 1834: he was therefore about fifty when the two saw so much of each other and would shortly reach that stage in the development of an out-and-out egotist when the slightest breath of criticism could ruffle him, when he would be right and everyone who disagreed with him wrong about everything, and when the whole world would seem to be in a conspiracy against him. All human beings are egotists more or less, but they are roughly divisible into two classes: the civilised ones who recognise that they are only important to themselves and are capable of taking an interest in others, and the uncivilised ones who are wretched unless their importance is generally recognised and who demand an interest in themselves which they cannot give to others. Whistler belonged to the second class. He was interested in no one but Whistler, and expected the rest of the world to take him at his own valuation. When they did not, he either insulted them or assaulted them. In his case the natural egotism of the artist was inflamed by the frustrated egotism of the man of action. His father had been a soldier, and he was brought up to be one too, but he was too lazy and indifferent to go through with it, and another ambition was alive within him. Yet such was his egotism that he was not content with the joy which his art gave him; he wanted to be a man of the world, a personality of mark, and a dozen other things, though chiefly a warrior. This desire became acute after he had failed to take part in the American Civil War, when his ambition to fight was defeated by his instinct to paint, and in a sort of baffled fury he joined an expedition to help Chili and Peru against Spain; but when the Spanish gunboats began to shell Valparaiso, he made haste out of it on horseback. That was the last straw. Had he fought with Robert E. Lee in the Civil War, he might not have fought against Ruskin in the Law Courts. Had he been wounded by the enemy in Chili, he might not have wounded so many non-combatants in England. But his failure to do something in South America, following his failure to do anything at all in North America, rankled, and the story of his career is a story of quarrels, the number of folk who "never spoke to Whistler again" being considerable. Physically, he was small, but he had long arms and powerful shoulders, and he learnt how to box from a professional, trading on the fact that others had not learnt. He pushed his brother-in-law Seymour Haden through a plate-glass window, attacked a negro on a boat, fought an unknown man on the platform of Waterloo Station, went for a workman in the Quartier Latin who had accidentally dropped some plaster on his clothes, picked a quarrel with Legros, whom he struck violently on the face, and challenged friends to duels for reasons which seemed to them inadequate.

As he did not live in an age when physical combat was regarded as the normal pursuit of gentlemen, he was bellicose on paper, giving his one-time friends and patrons such names as "Judas Iscariot," and entitling his pen-pricks when published *The Gentle Art of Making Enemies*; but in the days when he and Wilde lunched at the Café Royal he had not gone out of his way to make enemies, and the hostility he had aroused had been due more to his genius than his bluster. He could be extremely charming, and in their early acquaintanceship he and Wilde cooed at each other in a manner that must have been rather trying.

They had some traits in common. Both were usually unpunctual. "Punctuality," Wilde declared, "is the thief of time"; though he also said "I am not punctual myself, but I do like punctuality in others." Whistler did not explain his behavior with aphorisms. Each drew attention to himself by oddities of dress, but Wilde's Polish cap and green overcoat, befrogged and befurred, were too much for Whistler, who admonished him: "Oscar—How dare you! What means this disguise? Restore those things to Nathan's, and never again let me find you masquerading the streets of my Chelsea in the combined costumes of Kossuth and Mr. Mantalini!" Both of them were extreme individualists, eschewing conformity, indulging eccentricity. Neither let his mind escape into the fantastic world of politics or theology or science, but nourished it in the real world of art. Where they disagreed was over the relative importance of the arts. There was only one art for Whistler, the art of painting, and only one painter worth talking about, himself. Wilde placed literature before all the other arts, though he loved painting and was himself no mean draughtsman. In England, for some mysterious reason, the word "art" is generally taken to mean painting. This may be because pictures make a more immediate appeal and are more easily understood by the average man than music and literature; or it may be because pictures are material things: one can possess them and handle them and exhibit them and take a pride in them: they have a commercial value. Whatever the reason, the State pays for picture galleries and museums, but ignores music and literature; while the English people call painters "artists" and all the other artists after the art they practise. Wilde was the first person to correct this error: he habitually spoke of good writers, good musicians, good architects, good sculptors, as artists, and when he made it clear that all the arts were closely related but that the greatest was poetry (by which he meant great literature, not necessarily in verse), Whistler became fretful.

Their views on the popular painters and pictures of the day were much the same. If he had made them himself, Whistler would have barked with pleasure over such remarks as these by Wilde:

"That curious mixture of bad painting and good intentions that always entitles a man to be called a representative British artist."

"On the staircase stood several Royal Academicians, disguised as artists."

"That poetic school of artists who imagine that the true way of idealising a sitter is to paint someone else."

"Varnishing is the only artistic process with which the Royal Academicians are thoroughly familiar."

"Is it really *all* done by hand?" he reverently asked on seeing Frith's Derby Day which was bought for the nation.

"Nature is always behind the age. It takes a great artist to be thoroughly modern."

"There is hardly a single person in the House of Commons worth painting, though many of them would be the better for a little whitewashing."

"Nature is elbowing her way into the charmed circle of art."

It is more than probable that Whistler did not see Wilde's first reference to his work in print, because he had a tenacious memory, and one passage in Wilde's review of the Grosvenor Gallery Exhibition, 1877, would have made a friendship impracticable. Of Whistler's two "Nocturnes," which showed rockets bursting, Wilde wrote "These pictures are certainly worth looking at for about as long as one looks at a real rocket, that is, for somewhat less than a quarter of a minute." Though there is praise for Whistler's Carlyle in the same article, the painter would have remembered the rocket and sooner or later produced a squib. Their early interchanges in public were harmless enough. Following an imaginary conversation between the two on art and life which *Punch* printed in the autumn of '83, Wilde sent a message to Whistler from Exeter: "*Punch* too ridiculous. When you and I are together we never talk about anything except ourselves." Whistler forwarded this to *The World*, which gave it with his reply: "No, no, Oscar, you forget. When you and I are together we never talk about anything except me." Oscar's riposte did not appear in Whistler's *Gentle Art*: "It is true, Jimmy, we were talking about you, but I was thinking of myself." Whistler was invited to Wilde's wedding, but just as the service was about to begin a wire arrived from him: "Am detained. Don't wait."

This spirit of pleasantry was soon to evaporate. The difference between the two men is shown in a brief incident. Seeing Wilde and George Du Maurier talking together one day, Whistler cried out in his disagreeable nasal voice "Which of you two discovered the other?" Wilde replied "We have both discovered you." Soft answers did not turn away Whistler's wrath, the reason in this case being that Wilde was gradually ousting the older man from his previously-held position as king of any social crush at which he happened to be present. At first Wilde played second fiddle gracefully enough and stood in the group that always gathered around "the master." But Oscar's amazing powers as a raconteur soon drew the attention of all who wished to be amused, and a group quickly formed round him the moment he appeared on the scene. Worse still, while his group waxed, Whistler's waned, and the latter's growing hostility was simply due to jealousy. He had no difficulty in finding an opening for his attack. Wilde's habit of absorbing whatever appealed to him in another man's style or philosophy, as though he were studying a part, and then presenting it in a slightly different guise as his own, has already been remarked. It did not occur to him that anyone could object to such conduct. Shakespeare had done it, Molière had done it, every creative artist did it. Why not? "I appropriate what is already mine," he proclaimed, "for once a thing is published it becomes public property." And although he also said "There are many things that we would throw away if we were not afraid that others might pick them up," he did not act on this principle, but scattered so many good things in all directions as he strolled through life that countless stories of his invention have been published under other men's names and hundreds of his sayings have brightened other men's books. Ideas, witticisms, tales, poured from him, and out of his abundance many were enriched. He did not mind, for he seemed to have an inexhaustible store. But Whistler, a man with relatively few ideas, snapped at anyone who borrowed from his hoard; and although the following story has been printed and retailed with sickening frequency, it must be told again here, let us hope for the last time, not, as is usual, to mark the superiority of the painter's wit, but as an example of Wilde's generosity and his opponent's pettiness.

Humphry Ward, art critic of *The Times*, was at an exhibition of Whistler's paintings, expressing his opinion that one work was good, another bad, and so on.

"My dear fellow," said Whistler, "you must never say this painting is good or that bad. Good and bad are not terms to be used by you. But you may say 'I like this' or 'I don't like that,' and you will be within your rights. Now come and have a whisky: you're sure to like that."

"I wish I had said that!" exclaimed Wilde delightedly.

"You will, Oscar, you will," retorted Whistler with his loud "Ha-ha!"

And there is not the least doubt that Wilde laughed louder than anyone else at this sally, as he usually did when the joke was a good one against himself. He could bring off the same sort of thing as easily as Whistler, but he was too soft-hearted to indulge in it unless provoked. It has been related that Lewis Morris, a popular poet of the eighties who expected to be made Laureate when Tennyson died, once complained to Oscar that there was a conspiracy of the press against him, a conspiracy of silence, and asked what he ought to do, receiving the advice "Join it." But this is not what happened. The complaint was made by Morris to Augustine Birrell, who did not know what to say and afterwards mentioned his quandary to Wilde. "You did not know what to say?" echoed Wilde. "No." "You should have said 'A conspiracy of silence? My dear fellow, join it at once!'" But Wilde would not have said that to Morris: he would have thought it, and then probably told someone that he had said it.

In the innocence of his heart Wilde had asked Whistler for a few tips for his lecture to the students of the Royal Academy. He was never to hear the end of it, for Whistler broadcast the fact that the poet had stolen the painter's thunder and passed it off as his own lightning. The situation was not eased by the humorous tang which accompanied Wilde's public praise of Whistler. Here, for instance, are some passages from his review of the other's famous "Ten O'Clock" lecture in February 1885:

"The scene was in every way delightful; he stood there, a miniature Mephistopheles, mocking the majority! He was like a brilliant surgeon lecturing to a class composed of subjects destined ultimately for dissection, and solemnly assuring them how valuable to science their maladies were and how absolutely uninteresting the slightest symptoms of health on their part would be. . . .

"Nothing could have exceeded their enthusiasm when they were told by Mr. Whistler that no matter how vulgar their dresses were, or how hideous their surroundings at home, still it was possible that a great painter, if there was such a thing, could, by contemplating them in the twilight, and half closing his eyes, see them under really picturesque conditions which they were not to attempt to understand, much less dare to enjoy. . . .

"But I strongly deny that charming people should be condemned to live with magenta ottomans and Albert-blue curtains in their rooms in order that some painter may observe the side-lights on the one, and the values of the other . . ."

After saying that the poet was the supreme artist, "and lord over all life and all arts," that the lecture was a masterpiece, and that Whistler was a master of painting and persiflage, Wilde concluded: "For that he is indeed one of the greatest masters of painting is my opinion. And I may add that in this opinion Mr. Whistler himself entirely concurs."

No one could have asked for a more generous and enthusiastic review; yet Whistler was annoyed because the whole tone of it was that of a rival, not a disciple, and the unforgivable thing was that the man who had once unblushingly borrowed from him should now dare to disagree with him. Worse was to come. In April '87 Oscar reviewed an account of Whistler's life and work in the Art Journal by Walter Dowdeswell. Clearly the article had been inspired by the subject, and the reviewer did not fail to notice the fact: "Mr. Dowdeswell displays a really remarkable power, not merely of writing, but of writing from dictation, especially in his very generous and appreciative estimate of Mr. Whistler's genius." Wilde's compliments, too, had an odd twist in them, as when he wrote that Whistler had "opened the eyes of the blind, and given great encouragement to the short-sighted." Taken in conjunction with his growing fame as a wit and talker, his increasing popularity at parties, his extraordinary social success, such genial remarks as we have quoted excited Whistler's envy and sharpened his malice. He could no longer feel satisfied with private gibes at Oscar's expense, and in November '88 he exploded in public, writing to the Committee of the National Art Exhibition about one of their members in these terms: "What has Oscar in common with art? except that he dines at our tables and picks from our platters the plums for the pudding he peddles in the provinces. Oscar—the amiable, irresponsible, esurient Oscar—with no more sense of a picture than of the fit of a coat, has the courage of the opinions ... of others!" Whistler got this published in *The World*, and Oscar's reply appeared in the next number: "Atlas, this is very sad! With our James vulgarity begins at home, and should be allowed to stay there." To which Whistler countered "'A poor thing,' Oscar! 'but,' for once, I suppose, 'your own.'" It will be noted that five years have elapsed since Oscar peddled Whistler's plum in the provinces, and that even in the full flow of his malice the writer could not help describing his victim as amiable. It was Oscar's natural amiability that prevented him from ever understanding the other's spitefulness: he felt Whistler's hostility keenly, and his gentle nature recoiled from it, but it remained a mystery to him. Perhaps he came nearest to comprehension when he described a certain type as one who "fancied that he could gain a reputation for wealth by crying out that he had been robbed." But it never struck him that printed references to Whistler would irritate that artist whenever they were not wholly flattering, and in '89 he made the mistake of saying in the course of a review that "Mr. Whistler always spelt art, and we believe still spells it, with a capital 'I,'" and further that Whistler "with all his faults was never guilty of writing a line of poetry, and is, indeed, quite incapable of doing anything of the kind." Also, in January '89, Oscar's genius as a talker was first manifested to the reading public by an essay entitled "The Decay of Lying" which appeared in *The Nineteenth Century*. Apart from the brilliance of its dialogue, there were several things in the essay that must have annoyed Whistler, above all Oscar's humorous handling of an aspect of nature which Whistler had made his own as a painter and which had been the theme of the most eloquent passage in his "Ten O'Clock" lecture. This was how Whistler had dealt with it:

"And when the evening mist clothes the riverside with poetry, as with a veil, and the poor buildings lose themselves in the dim sky, and the tall chimneys become campanile, and the whole city hangs in the heavens, and fairy-land is before us—then the wayfarer hastens home; the working man and the cultured one, the wise man and the one of pleasure, cease to understand, as they have ceased to see, and Nature, who, for once, has sung in tune, sings her exquisite song to the artist alone, her son and her master—her son in that he loves her, her master in that he knows her."

Wilde's variation ran as follows:

"There may have been fogs for centuries in London. I dare say there were. But no one saw them, and so we do not know anything about them. They did not exist till Art had invented them. Now, it must be admitted, fogs are carried to excess. They have become the mere mannerism of a clique, and the exaggerated realism of their method gives dull people bronchitis. Where the cultured catch an effect, the uncultured catch cold."

For a year Whistler smouldered in silence, and then erupted with violence. The final engagement took place in *Truth* in January 1890. Whistler wrote to that periodical applauding its attack on plagiarists and asking "How was it that, in your list of culprits, you omitted that fattest of offenders—our own Oscar?" He then dragged up the old old story: that he had crammed Wilde for a lecture to the Royal Academy students, but that the culprit had never acknowledged the fact; he went on to complain that his remark about Oscar having the courage of the opinions of others had been calmly appropriated without acknowledgment by the very man of whom it was written in "The Decay of Lying"; and he finished up by quoting a letter he had written to Oscar in which he had stated that the least any plagiarist could do was to say "Je prends mon bien là où je le trouve," but that "You, Oscar, can go further, and with fresh effrontery, that will bring you the envy of all criminal confrères, unblushingly boast 'Moi, je prends *son* bien là où je le trouve'!" Wilde was exasperated by this quite gratuitous attack, and decided to stand on his dignity, in which attitude he was never at his best:

"As Mr. James Whistler has had the impertinence to attack me with both venom and vulgarity in your columns, I hope you will allow me to state that the assertions contained in his letters are as deliberately untrue as they are deliberately offensive.

"The definition of a disciple as one who has the courage of the opinions of his master is really too old even for Mr. Whistler to be allowed to claim it, and as for borrowing Mr. Whistler's ideas about art, the only thoroughly original ideas I have ever heard him express have had reference to his own superiority as a painter over painters greater than himself.

"It is a trouble for any gentleman to have to notice the lucubrations of so ill-bred and ignorant a person as Mr. Whistler, but your publication of his insolent letter left me no option in the matter."

He had laid himself open, and Whistler was not the man to neglect the advantage:

"O Truth! Cowed and humiliated, I acknowledge that our Oscar is at last original. At bay, and sublime in his agony, he certainly has, for once, borrowed from no living author, and comes out in his own true colours—as his own 'gentleman.' "

Wilde never spoke resentfully of the treatment he had received at Whistler's hands. He remained amiable to the end.

CHAPTER EIGHT

THE FAMILY

ALTHOUGH Wilde felt that all the arts were related, and that he who could understand one could understand all, there is no evidence that music meant much to him. In fact it is fairly certain that he could hardly distinguish one tune from another, and his references to the subject convince us that he thought more of phrase-making than of the sounds which inspired it. The name of Dvořák appealed to him, and the composer would have been startled to hear him speak of "some mad scarlet thing by Dvořák," who was also credited with producing "passionate, curiously-coloured things." But Wilde made no claim to be an authority. At some "musical soirée" a woman, seeing him arrive and anxious that he should be impressed by her niece who was just then performing a Scottish reel on the piano, asked eagerly "Do you like music, Mr. Wilde?" "No, but I like that," he answered reassuringly. His general feeling was broadly defined in two remarks:

"I like Wagner's music better than anybody's. It is so loud that one can talk the whole time without other people hearing what one says."

"Musical people are so absurdly unreasonable. They always want one to be perfectly dumb at the very moment when one is longing to be absolutely deaf."

His interest in the other arts was enthusiastic if not acute. The theatre made a special appeal to him, and scarcely a week passed without a visit to it. Occasionally he wrote criticisms of what he had seen for The Dramatic Review, but his abandonment to the whole process of theatrical illusion was rather like a child's at a pantomime, and his brain seldom functioned. Now and then a gleam of the humorous Oscar appeared, as when he wrote of a performance of Helena in Troas that certain lines in the English translation owed "their blank verse character more to the courtesy of the printer than to the genius of the poet"; and again when he said that the behaviour of the characters and the rush and tumble of the situations in a farcical comedy "distribute a gentle air of lunacy over life. What our descendants will think of such a work of art is an open question. However, posterity has as yet done nothing for us!" The Lyceum remained his favourite playhouse, and he would not even admit that Irving's scenery could be at fault, writing of the production of *Olivia*: "A critic who posed as an authority on field sports assured me that no one ever went out hunting when roses were in full bloom. Personally, that is exactly the season I would select for the chase, but then I know more about flowers than I do about foxes, and like them much better." Which recalls his epigram: "One knows so well the popular idea of health. The English country gentleman galloping after a fox—the unspeakable in full pursuit of the uneatable." In private conversation he was a little less restrained, and those who know Sargent's portrait of Ellen Terry as Lady Macbeth will appreciate Oscar's comment on the Lyceum production: "Judging from the banquet, Lady Macbeth seems an economical housekeeper, and evidently patronises local industries for her husband's clothes and the servants' liveries; but she takes care to do all her own shopping in Byzantium." He went to a performance of *The Three Musketeers*, in which two of the leading parts had been miscast, and afterwards told a friend that the production ought to be called "Athos, Pathos and Bathos." But he usually enjoyed himself thoroughly in the theatre, and on one occasion even seemed pleased with the various "turns" at a Music Hall, though, after describing a mimic as "perfectly splendid," he felt compelled to add "And I do think it so kind of him to tell us who he is imitating. It avoids discussion, doesn't it?"

What with theatres, picture exhibitions and social engagements, Oscar was kept fairly busy when in London, but however urgent the calls upon his time he hardly passed a day without seeing his mother, whom he both loved and admired, taking a somewhat romantic view of her intelligence and social position. She had left Dublin shortly after her younger son left Oxford. Willie Wilde, finding life at the Irish bar rather irksome, decided to become a journalist instead and accompanied her to London. At first they lived at No. 1 Ovington Square, where Oscar joined them for a time and where their domestic staff consisted of one charwoman. Then Willie got work as a free-lance on *The World*, in which he never lost an opportunity of mentioning his brother, and afterwards on the staff of *The Daily Telegraph*, which enabled him to take a small house in Park Street, Grosvenor Square, next door to a large corner public house, the proximity of which probably influenced his choice of residence. He and his mother were living there when Oscar was in Charles Street nearby.

Many people have left descriptions of Lady Wilde's receptions. One went from the bright street into a small dark stuffy room, which was lit by candles or pink-shaded lamps, the curtains being drawn. The hostess was large, ungainly and grotesque; but she had a certain dignity and was very kind. Everyone was welcomed and introduced to as many people as possible, and no one was allowed to feel out of it. As in her Merrion Square days, her clothes were remarkable. Sometimes she would dress in white, her grey hair hanging down her back, like a Druid priestess. Other times she would be seen in purple brocade, with a towering headdress of velvet decorated with white streamers, or a crown of gilt laurels on her hair, enormous brooches fastening the lace across her breast. She wore long gold ear-rings, huge gold bracelets, and rings on every finger. She moved to a clatter of ornaments. All her dresses were striking, in and out of doors. In February '86 Marie Corelli went to a "grand crush" in Upper Phillimore Place, and described Lady Wilde as being "in a train-dress of silver grey satin, with a hat as large as a small parasol and long streamers of silver grey tulle all floating about her! She did look eccentric." Her voice was deep and she used it dramatically. She meant well, but some of her remarks made her visitors feel uncomfortable. "A highly intellectual countenance," she said to one girl: "I shall hear of you in the literary world." Upon which Oscar, who was standing by, laughed aloud: "Oh, come now, mother! That's too bad." Another female heard herself complimented from the other side of the room in a reverberating whisper: "Such a beautiful long neck! Do you see the glint on her hair as she turns? I wish Oscar were here to see it." A pretty chatterbox was reproved: "My dear Miss Potter, you must not talk so much. Not with that face. You should be still—still and grave." And when in oracular mood she would speak at large: "I have come to the conclusion that nothing in the world is worth living for except . . ." a pause before the last word was hissed out . . . "sin!"

Oscar's arrival at these receptions was an event. After bowing over his mother's hand, he took the centre of the stage, either seating himself on an ottoman or lounging gracefully with his arm on the mantelpiece. Lady Wilde would then do the honours: "This is Miss Hannah Lynch, Oscar: a young Irish genius." It was a habit of hers to give brief biographies of the people she introduced to one another, so that they could know to whom they were talking and have subjects for immediate discussion. In *Dorian Gray* Oscar satirised this aspect of his mother, and the fact that he omitted the greater part of the following passage when the novel appeared in book form suggests that he suffered a qualm of filial conscience:

"I know she goes in for giving a rapid *précis* of all her guests. I remember her bringing me up to a most truculent and red-faced old gentleman covered all over with orders and ribbons, and hissing into my ear, in a tragic whisper which must have been perfectly audible to everybody in the room, something like 'Sir Humpty Dumpty—you know—Afghan frontier—Russian intrigues: very successful man—wife killed by an elephant—quite unconsolable —wants to marry a beautiful American widow—everybody does nowadays— hates Mr. Gladstone—but very much interested in beetles: ask him what he thinks of Schouvaloff.' I simply fled. I like to find out people for myself. But poor Lady Brandon treats her guests exactly as an auctioneer treats his goods. She either explains them entirely away, or tells one everything about them except what one wants to know."

Most of the poets, painters and journalists who called at the little house in Park Street were Irish, though occasionally some temporary celebrity put in an appearance. The beauty of the hour, Miss Craigie Halkett, was one of the exhibits, another being the actress, Miss Fortescue, fresh from her breach of promise case against Lord Garmoyle, and very much the fashion of the moment. But when in 1886 Lady Wilde and Willie moved to 146 (now 87) Oakley Street, Chelsea, her Saturday receptions became so popular and fashionable that she had to give Wednesday ones as well. People were coming and going all the time, elbowing their way up the narrow staircase, or crushing against one another in the fuggy rooms, pushing, jostling, chattering; and the street outside was full of hansoms and broughams. Oscar's increasing fame was the real cause of all this. He contributed to his mother's support, and on his visits always looked to see if there were any bills in the rack at the side of the fireplace, leaving the money for them whenever he had any money to leave. All sorts of celebrities now turned up, political as well as artistic. Oliver Wendell Holmes, Ouida and Browning called, and came again. Oscar was not greatly impressed by Browning, of whom he was obviously thinking when he said "Good artists exist simply in what they make, and consequently are perfectly uninteresting in what they are. A great poet, a really great poet, is the most unpoetical of creatures. But inferior poets are absolutely fascinating. The worse their rhymes are, the more picturesque they look. The mere fact of having published a book of second-rate sonnets makes a man quite irresistible. He lives the poetry that he cannot write. The others write the poetry that they dare not realise." He reverted to this theme on more than one occasion: "The greatest artists are stupid and tiresome men as a rule. Flaubert was certainly a stupid man. But bad poets and novelists are romantic and delightful." Though not aware of Wilde's opinion, it is to Edmund Gosse's credit that he should have recorded their first meeting, at which Wilde expressed his pleasure. "I was afraid you would be disappointed," said Gosse, and got this reply: "I am never disappointed in literary men. I think they are perfectly charming. It is their works I find so disappointing."

When Oscar's fame was at its zenith in the nineties, and he could no longer find time to attend his mother's functions, the celebrities disappeared from Oakley Street and the crowd began to dwindle. But with the passing years Lady Wilde seemed to achieve greater dignity. She ceased to paint her face, and in default of visitors she let in the daylight. Her manner became aloof and detached. One afternoon a caller who had a train to catch asked her the time. "Does anyone here know what time it is?" she demanded. "We never know in this house about Time." She spoke with pride of her famous son: "He is always working and the world will not let him alone. No one in London is so sought after as Oscar." And occasionally she even indulged in a little joke at her own expense: "I want to live on some high place, Primrose Hill or Highgate, because I was an eagle in my youth."

She was, perhaps, fonder of Willie than of Oscar, and Willie remained with her until his marriage and returned to her after his divorce. He was a tall, bulky, bearded, vivacious, entertaining, easygoing, lazy bohemian, whose laughing eyes, jovial face and soft Irish voice made him popular with men and still more popular with women. In conversation he rambled amusingly from one topic to another, telling stories well and treating everything facetiously. It was said that a wealthy old lady paid him an annual salary of £300 for visiting her every afternoon and keeping her amused for two or three hours. His style of humour is best exemplified in the following anecdote. One night Augustus Moore, brother of George Moore, arrived at the Café Royal in a very brightly coloured necktie and asked Willie Wilde what he thought of it. "Well, my dear Gus, since you ask me, I should have thought that only a deaf man could have worn it with safety." Willie spoke in a rather flowery Micawberish manner, not unfamiliar to those who remember an older generation of journalists. Asked by Jimmy Glover to attend the wedding of a man with whom he had quarrelled on account of something the fellow had written about his mother, Willie replied: "My dear James, much as I sincerely appreciate your ambassadorial kindness of heart, there are certain circumstances which will ever prevent diplomatic relations being reopened with your unpleasant friend and my equally unpleasant enemy. The orange blosoms, the unnecessary shower of beautiful white rice, the not very elegant slipper, may all follow yonder person to the happiness which he little deserves, but I shall not be a contributory unless certain published apologies re forthcoming which I know would be impossible."

After he joined the staff of the *Daily Telegraph* he became known as one of the best leader-writers of the day, and his society gossip paragraphs in *The World* pleased the people who enjoyed that kind of thing, the editor, Edmund Yates, being one of them. Yates often asked him for stories, and he would stroll along to Charles Street, where Willie, sometimes in bed, would invent half a dozen in half an hour and send him happy away. Willie was a godsend to many snappers-up of unconsidered trifles, and one evening at the Café Royal he remarked to Cottsford Dick, who had used or paraphrased several of his pleasantries in *The World*, "You and I ought to call ourselves the agriculturists." "Why?" "Because while I *mot*, you reap." Willie's great triumph came when he reported the judicial proceedings of the Parnell Commission, his accounts being easily the best in the English press; and Oscar was delighted with his success.

But Willie's achievement and his charm were the cause of his undoing. A wealthy American widow, Mrs. Frank Leslie, who on the death of her first husband had become the proprietor of a well-known periodical, was much impressed by the combination in Willie of accomplishment and agreeability. She decided to marry him, and he raised no objection; but in the rush and excitement of the moment it did not occur to either of them to question the other's intentions, and it became clear, very soon after their arrival on the other side of the Atlantic, that they held different views on the obligations of the married state. She wanted him to be, not only attentive and faithful to herself, but a valuable accession to the periodical she had inherited. He, on the other hand, preferred jolly evenings at the Century Club and occasional outings with girls to a quiet domestic life, and considered that as his wife was rich it was absurd that he should have to work. The question was debated at length between them, she urging the necessity of hard work and early hours, he retaliating that already far too many people were working and much too much work was done in America, where one sadly felt the need of a leisured class, which he proposed to supply. They could not agree, and she divorced him, telling the reporters that "he was of no use to me either by day or by night." As she ran through several husbands without finding satisfaction, it is reasonable to suppose that she demanded more in the sex department than Willie was prepared or able to provide.

This episode in his life which lasted for two or three years, demoralised Willie, who returned to England a spent force. He went to America a clever if sluggish journalist; he came back a nervous wreck. He had always been fond of the bottle; he was now a confirmed toper. He never recovered his position, and though his second marriage was a happy one his ability as a

journalist had deserted him. His appearance deteriorated; he borrowed right
and left; and he was only sober when penniless. This was in the nineties
when brother Oscar was at the height of his fame and the most talked-of
writer in England. Before the American adventure Oscar had dealt indul-
gently with Willie's weakness: "Oh, he occasionally takes an alcoholiday."
But when his life became one long alcoholiday his younger brother, who
hated to see people dirty, drunken and disreputable, ceased to be indulgent.
"He sponges on everyone but himself," was Oscar's caustic summary.

It was during his lecture tour, in November 1883, that Oscar became engaged to his future wife, Constance Lloyd. They had first met at a young
people's party in '81, were instantaneously attracted to one another, and
wandered off together into a garden, where they exchanged confidences. He
promised to see her again soon, but America and Paris intervened before
their next meeting. She was the only child of a well-known Irish barrister,
who had died at an early age. Her mother had married again, and she was
not happy at home; so she lived in Ely Place, Dublin, with her grandfather,
whose fortune of about £1000 a year she would inherit at his death. Constance had three offers of marriage after her first meeting with Oscar, but
turned them down without hesitation; and imediately after they met again
in '83 he wrote asking her to be his wife. She agreed by return of post. It
has been said that Oscar married for money. If so, he had a poor financial
sense, because Constance could only hope for a moderate income until she
came into her grandfather's estate, while many wealthy women would have
snatched at the chance of marrying Oscar Wilde. In one of her letters to him
Constance described herself as the most fortunate of women because he had
chosen her from the crowds of his female adorers. Wilde himself was probably responsible for the rumour that he had married for money, because he
used to tell how his wife's grandfather "lying on what threatened to be his
deathbed, had no sooner joined our hands and given us his blessing than
for very joy of the occasion, he suddenly blossomed out into new health
and vigour." But the truth is that Oscar was very much in love with Constance, who was passionately in love with him. She was a shy, sensitive,
simple, serious, gentle soul, with glorious violet-coloured eyes and light
chestnut hair. She was slight in build, very pretty, with a lovely complexion
and though she had not much to say for herself she said it in a low attractive voice, and could, according to Oscar, "draw music from the piano so
sweet that the birds stop singing to listen to her."

After their marriage he was asked by a female acquaintance how he cam to fall in love with Constance. "She never speaks," was his reply, "and I am always wondering what her thoughts are like." Certainly he did most of the talking, but she was candid enough when her mind was made up. "I am afraid you and I disagree in our opinion on art," she wrote in the early days of their engagement, "for I hold that there is no perfect art without perfect morality, whilst you say they are distinct and separable things." She read *Vera*, but love could not blind her to its defects. In fact her opinions, though few, were definite. But all that mattered in her eyes was their love for each other, and he thought of little else. "We telegraph to each other twice a day," he confided to a friend, "and I rush back suddenly from the uttermost parts of the earth to see her for an hour, and do all the foolish things that wise lovers do." Her letters to him began "My darling Love," "My own darling Oscar," and she declared that she worshipped him more every time she saw him. On his own principle that "no man should have a secret from his wife —she invariably finds it out," he confessed to past misdemeanours, but she was "content to let the past be buried; it does not belong to me." She said that he deprived her of strength: "I have no power to do anything but just love you . . . my whole life is yours to do as you will with it . . . Do believe that I love you most passionately with all the strength of my heart and mind." She would do anything he asked her to do, and "When I have you for my husband, I will hold you fast with chains of love and devotion so that you shall never leave me, or love anyone as long as I can love and comfort." Sometimes, between lectures, he would cross the sea to Dublin for two or three hours, and sacrifice his meals in order to spend every minute in her company. She treasured the flowers he sent, keeping them alive as long as possible. She lay awake at nights thinking of him. "I wish you would not take all my sleep away with you," she wrote. His letters were read and read again until she knew them by heart. They made her "mad for joy," she told him, "and yet more mad to see you and feel once again that you are mine, and that it is not a dream but a living reality that you love me."

Better proof that he loved her than any of his protestations can be found in the verses he wrote in a copy of his *Poems* which he gave her. Except for certain stanzas in *The Ballad of Reading Gaol*, they are the best lines he ever produced, and like those quoted in chapter 5, they contain a hint of pre-destined tragedy. During his own lifetime the most popular poem in the 1881 volume, which appeared in several anthologies, was *Requiescat*, written at Avignon in memory of his little sister; but these lines to his wife are more sincere and less derivative:

I can write no stately proem
As a prelude to my lay;
From a poet to a poem
I would dare to say.

For if of these fallen petals
One to you seem fair,
Love will waft it till it settles
On your hair.

And when wind and winter harden
All the loveless land,
It will whisper of the garden,
You will understand.

A packed house witnessed their marriage on May 29th, 1884, at St. James's Church, Paddington. The crowd had collected, not to assist at a solemn celebration, but to stare at a spectacular show, and it was well rewarded. The dresses of bride and bridesmaids were of a kind to receive considerable attention in the papers that dealt with such matters, and doubtless afforded a topic of conversation to many ladies until the next dress-parade took their fancy. Enough to say that the predominant colour was yellow, or shades thereof, and that Lady Wilde provided a startling note of red.[1] Two points of interest may be noted in the church register: Oscar Wilde is described as

[1] Possibly not enough. For those who like this sort of thing, this is the sort of thing they like: "The bride's rich creamy satin dress was of a delicate cowslip tint; the bodice, cut square and somewhat low in front, was finished with a high Medici collar; the ample sleeves were puffed; the skirt, made plain, was gathered by a silver girdle of beautiful workmanship, the gift of Mr. Oscar Wilde; the veil of saffron-coloured Indian silk gauze was embroidered with pearls and worn in Marie Stuart fashion; a thick wreath of myrtle leaves, through which gleamed a few white blossoms, crowned her fair frizzed hair, the dress was ornamented with clusters of myrtle leaves; the large bouquet had as much green in it as white. The six bridesmaids were cousins of the bride. Two dainty little figures, that seemed to have stepped out of a picture by Sir Joshua Reynolds, led the way. They were dressed in quaintly-made gowns of Surah silk, the colour of a ripe gooseberry; large pale yellow sashes round their waist; the skirts falling in straight folds to the ankles displayed small bronze, high-heeled shoes. Large red silk Gainsborough hats decked with red and yellow feathers shaded the damsels' golden hair; amber necklaces, long yellow gloves, a cluster of yellow roses at their throats, a bouquet of white lilies in their hands, completed the attire of the tiny bridesmaids. The four elder bridesmaids wore skirts of the same red Surah silk, with over-dresses of pale blue *mousseline de laine*, the bodices made long and pointed; high crowned hats with cream-coloured feathers and red knots of ribbon, lilies in their hands, amber necklaces and yellow roses at their throats made up a sufficiently picturesque *ensemble*. One of the ladies present wore what was described as a 'very aesthetic costume.' It was composed of an underdress of rich red silk with a sleeveless smock of red plush, a hat of white lace trimmed with clusters of red roses under the brim and round the crown."

"gentleman," which he preferred to "writer," and his age is given as twenty-eight, which he preferred to twenty-nine. After the ceremony there was a small family gathering at 100 Lancaster Gate, and then Oscar and Constance left from Charing Cross for Paris, where they stayed at the Hôtel Wagram in the Rue de Rivoli. The morning following their arrival Sherard called, and was enchanted with their rooms, which were on one of the upper storeys. "The lovely young wife seemed supremely happy. There was bright sunlight, as one only sees it in Paris, on the Tuileries without, yet the room where I first met her was just as gladsome. It was full of flowers and youth and laughter." The two friends went for a walk and on their way through the Marché St. Honoré Oscar "stopped and rifled a flower-stall of its loveliest blossoms, and sent them, with a word of love on his card, to the bride whom he had quitted but a moment before." Oscar's first topic of conversation was curious, though Sherard's sense of personal loyalty prevented him from recording its nature. The present biographer, having learnt it from Sherard, has no such compunction. Just as a boy is bursting to tell a companion all about some wonderful new experience, so was Oscar bursting to tell Sherard all about the marvellous night he had just spent with his wife. It came forth in a stream of superlatives, and Sherard felt rather awkward; but when Oscar began to elaborate the physical details, Sherard felt acutely embarrassed, and checked the enthusiastic hierophant.

The Wildes returned to Oscar's old rooms at No. 9 Charles Street while their home in Tite Street, Chelsea, was being prepared. They were together nearly all the time, wrapped up in each other. He even accompanied her when she went out shopping, openly delighting in all the window-gazing and pattern-fingering that drives most men to drink. While waiting for her one day outside Swan and Edgar's shop, a hard-eyed sinister young woman passed by, gazed at him, and went on with a mocking laugh: at least that is how he described the incident, adding "I felt as if an icy hand had clutched my heart." But Constance emerged and the sun shone again. Childlike he could not help dramatising occurrences which other people would dismiss as trivial: it was all part of the great Oscar melodrama or comedy, according to the mood of the moment. Vincent O'Sullivan tells us that at the Café Royal, one day in the nineties, Oscar said to him "There is a dreadful youth waiting for me in Regent Street. He is pacing up and down before the door like a wonderful black panther. I think he must be there yet. Do go and see. If he is, I shall go out by the side door." O'Sullivan did as he was asked, and noticed a fellow hanging about who reminded him of anything but a wonderful black panther. He gives us another instance which he heard from Marcel Schwob, the French writer. Calling on Wilde in Paris, Schwob found him on the point of going out and searching for his stick. "My gold-headed cane has disappeared," he said. "Last night I was with the most terrible creatures—bandits, murderers, thieves—such company as Villon kept. They stole my gold-headed cane. There was a youth with beautiful sad eyes who had slain his mistress that morning because she was unfaithful. I feel sure it was he who stole my gold-headed cane." While Schwob was glancing round the room, Oscar continued the performance: "My gold-headed cane is now between the hands that slew the frail girl who had the grace of a spent rose-bush in the rain." Schwob spotted the stick in a corner and drew Wilde's attention to it. "Ah, yes," said Wilde, grieved that the play was over, "so it is. There is my gold-headed cane. How clever of you to find it!"

In a few weeks No. 16 (now 34) Tite Street was ready for them and they moved in. Constance's dowry had enabled them to take the lease and to convert the interior of a very commonplace Victorian house into something quite unlike the interior of any other Victorian house. One day Oscar found a reason for having chosen that particular locality. Sargent painted his famous portrait of Ellen Terry as Lady Macbeth in a studio nearby, and Oscar watched its progress: "The street that on a wet and dreary morning has vouchsafed the vision of Lady Macbeth in full regalia magnificently seated in a four-wheeler can never again be as other streets: it must always be full of wonderful possibilities." Some of its possibilities were realised at Number 16, which was decorated by E. W. Godwin, with help from Whistler. The walls of the dining-room on the ground-floor were white, blended with delicate tints of blue and yellow. The mantelpiece, carpet and chairs were also white. Oscar's study at the top of the first flight of stairs facing the drawing-room had an eastern flavour: oriental divans, Japanese prints, Moorish casements, etc., and the shelves contained his valuable books, *éditions de luxe,* and so forth. But he only used the place as a smoking lounge, doing his writing in a small room downstairs facing the street, on a table which had once been Carlyle's and which he hoped would be an incentive to work. Here the walls were buttercup-yellow, the woodwork lacquered red; a cast of the Hermes of Praxiteles stood in a corner on a red stand; and the pictures were a Monticelli, a drawing by Simeon Solomon, and a Japanese painting of children at play. Constance was responsible for her drawing-room on the first floor. The decorative scheme was one of faded brocades against a background of white and cream paint. Along two sides of the room engravings and etchings, including some of Whistler's Venetian studies presented by the artist, formed a deep frieze against a background of dull gold. Above a carved white mantelpiece was a large gilt copper bas-relief by Donaghue, the subject suggested by Wilde's poem *Requiescat*. An oil-painting of Oscar by an American, Harper Pennington, hung on the opposite wall. The ceiling, let into which were two many-hued Japanese feathers, was designed by Whistler.

Constance had to live up to her background, and we hear of her appearance in all sorts of dresses. Her husband was attracted to the styles of certain historical periods, and she was so fond of him that his whims were laws. Noticing her rather sad expression, with its innocent appeal, people wondered whether she enjoyed her receptions, at which she was shown off in gowns that may have enhanced her prettiness but which certainly depressed her spirits. She was presented at Court shortly after her marriage, and in compliment to the Queen her dress was an exact copy of something that would have been exactly right when Victoria ascended the throne nearly fifty years before. Fashionable and artistic society thronged to her At Homes, and she was uncomfortably aware that her clothes had to be as unconventional as her husband's conversation. For his sake she posed in Grecian, early Venetian, Mediaeval, Caroline, Dutch and *Directoire* attires, and she did not like it a bit. He encouraged her always, and was once overheard to murmur in her ear "You are looking lovely, Constance—not a bit too tired with all these people." She smiled bravely; but, if she looked lovely, she felt miserable, and was only too happy when he took the centre of the stage and she could listen with the rest. Fortunately he could appreciate the fun of the show, for he related how once, when he and his wife were walking along Kings Road, Chelsea, in rather striking clothes, an urchin stared at them and shouted derisively "'Amlet and Ophelia out for a walk, I s'pose!" To which he returned "My little fellow, you are quite right. We are." In her eyes he could do no wrong, and his remark, "There's nothing in the world like the devotion of a married woman—it's a thing no married man knows anything about" was coined from observation, not his experience with Constance. Indeed, as time went on, his wife's devotion became rather overpowering, and his epigrams on the subject of marriage harmonised less and less with the Dickensian ideal of nuptial bliss. For instance:

"The proper basis for marriage is a mutual misunderstanding."

"The worst of having a romance is that it leaves one so unromantic."

"The only difference between a caprice and a lifelong passion is that the caprice lasts a little longer."

"Faithfulness is to the emotional life what consistency is to the life of the intellect—simply a confession of failure."

"Women never know when the curtain has fallen. They always want a sixth act, and as soon as the interest of the play is entirely over they propose to continue it."

"In married life three is company and two is none."

"One should always be in love. That is the reason one should never marry."

"A man can be happy with any woman, as long as he does not love her."

"When one is in love, one always begins by deceiving oneself, and one always ends by deceiving others. That is what the world calls a romance."

"The happiness of a married man depends on the people he has not married."

"When a man has once loved a woman, he will do anything for her, except continue to love her."

Thus it is scarcely surprising to learn that at some social crush in the late eighties he joined with others in admiring his wife, but was heard to mutter "If only I could be jealous of her!" Her motherhood did not improve her as a mannequin. Their first child, Cyril, was born in 1885; a second son, Vyvyan, followed in '86; and as she became involved in household and parental duties Oscar began to accept invitations without her. He was not by inclination a domestic man, and though he would refuse engagements which clashed with his wife's parties, saying *"C'est le jour de ma femme,"* and would exert himself to entertain her friends and relations, he did not enjoy himself at her homely functions, and only attended them to please her. The two women who wrote under the name of "Michael Field" called at Tite Street one afternoon and were received by Constance, who was dressed in turquoise blue, white frills and amber stockings. "The afternoon goes on in a dull fashion till Oscar enters," they noted in their diary, after which they enjoyed "A gay charming time!"

We have three glimpses of the Wildes together at home, none of which suggests that they were quite at home together. One evening some friends were dining with them. Oscar at the time was supposed to be in love with a beautiful actress then touring the provinces. "Where have you been this week?" he was asked. He launched into a poetic description of his visit to a marvellous Elizabethan mansion, with velvet emerald lawns, great yew hedges, lovely lily-ponds, glorious rose-gardens, stately oaks and strutting peacocks. The guests were enthralled by his eloquence. When he had finished, Constance said "And did she act well, Oscar?"

The second incident was given me by Robert Ross: "Oscar was always the essence of charm and good nature, and would never do anything to disappoint his wife. One day, when I was with them in Tite Street, she asked him if he would come in for lunch the following day, as some old Dublin friends (a clergyman among them) were coming to see her and very much wanted to meet him. Oscar, to whom this sort of thing was the reverse to attractive, said 'All right, my dear, if Bobbie can come as well.' Of course she asked me, though I knew she didn't want to, and it was then and there arranged. We found his wife's friends the typical provincial sort, full of their own local news and nothing much else. Oscar talked during lunch as I never heard him talk before—divinely. Had the company included the Queen and all the Royal Family, he couldn't have surpassed himself. Humour, tale, epigram, flowed from his lips, and his listeners sat spellbound under the influence. Suddenly in the midst of one of his most entrancing stories—his audience with wide eyes and parted mouths, their food untasted—his wife broke in: 'Oh, Oscar, *did* you remember to call for Cyril's boots?'" In fairness to Constance it may be said that, though her husband spoke with the tongue of an angel, his lunchtime conversation might pall if she had also had a dose over the toast and marmalade that morning, and that Ross's presence no doubt irritated her.

Richard Le Gallienne is our authority for a third peep into the Tite Street dining-room. He tells us that Constance was evangelically religious, that her bosom friend was Lady Sandhurst, a zealous worker for the Church, and that she took a great interest in missionaries. The subject cropping up once at dinner, Oscar spoke in the accents of Sydney Smith: "Missionaries, my dear! Don't you realise that missionaries are the divinely provided food for destitute and underfed cannibals? Whenever they are on the brink of starvation, Heaven, in its infinite mercy, sends them a nice plump missionary." Constance was not equal to this: "Oh, Oscar, you cannot surely be in earnest! You can only be joking!"

Towards the close of their married life Constance was drawn to theosophy. She was deeply impressed by Madame Blavatsky and believed all the legends that had grown up around that lady. But long before this happened Oscar had found it necessary to explain his longer absences from home in the oddest possible manner. "The one charm of marriage," he said, "is that it makes a life of deception absolutely necessary for both parties." A letter that Constance wrote to Clyde Fitch's mother illustrates her simplicity as nothing else could, for it shows that she swallowed a story that would have deceived no one else. Oscar, she reported, "has become mad about golf, and spends two or three hours on the links every day, and this is so good for him." His description of the game would have amazed a golfer; but one wonders whether he did the thing properly and carried a bag of clubs to the Café Royal every morning.

Meanwhile, the dinners in Tite Street and the lunches at the Café Royal, to say nothing of the rates and taxes, had to be paid for; and within a few months of his marriage it became evident that Oscar would have to work. His wife's income might have enabled them with strict economy to live a quiet life in the suburbs; but no one was ever less suited to a quiet life in the suburbs than he, and the alternative was uncongenial labour. At first, loathing the job, he accepted a few more lecture-engagements, explaining to audiences in Edinburgh, Dublin and elsewhere that large mirrors in rooms were one of the unpunished crimes of the 19th century, that the endless array of antimacassars in most homes reduced life to the level of an eternal washing-day, that fashions in colours were just as silly as it would be to have fashions in musical notes ("How we should smile if it were to be announced that B Flat would for some months be the fashionable note!"); and that education should be primarily aesthetic: "A school should be the most beautiful place in every town and village—so beautiful that the punishment for undutiful children should be that they should be debarred from going to school the following day." From a letter which he wrote to his wife while staying at the Balmoral Hotel, Edinburgh, in December '84, we can guess that he was not having the time of his life. "I feel incomplete without you," he told her. It soon transpired that lectures would not keep the tax-gatherer from the door, and one day he was accosted on his doorstep in Tite Street.

"I have called about the taxes," said a humble little man.

"Taxes! Why should I pay taxes?" said Wilde majestically.

"But, sir, you are the householder here, are you not? You live here, you sleep here."

"Ah, yes; but then, you see, I sleep so badly."

At one period in the early years of their married life money was so scarce that Constance had to borrow small sums from a neighbour, and Oscar even applied for an Inspectorship of schools, soliciting Professor Mahaffy's influence to that end. In the spring of '85 he managed to get a job as book-reviewer for *The Pall Mall Gazette*. This helped, but Constance's income was still their chief means of support. Then, in June '87, he was appointed by Cassell & Co. editor of *The Lady's World*, a shilling monthly, the first number of which had appeared in November '86. Wilde contributed nothing to it, but after the twelfth number it was enlarged and came out as *The*

Woman's World with his name as editor on the wrapper. Thenceforward he wrote Literary Notes for it, and continued to do so until June '89, relinquishing his editorship after the October number of that year. The magazine survived him for twelve months.

He commenced duty with the high spirits which novelty always excited in him, and for a while he allowed himself to feel his editorial importance. He persuaded all sorts of notabilities to write for him: Princess Christian, the Queen of Roumania, the Countess of Portsmouth, Marie Corelli, Olive Schreiner, Ouida, E. Nesbit, Oscar Browning, Blanche Roosevelt, and many others whose names meant more to their contemporaries than they do to their descendants. His delight over the new toy was such that he would have been quite willing to write the whole magazine himself if only he could have induced a number of well-known women to sign the various essays from his pen. He asked Sarah Bernhardt for an article on "The History of My Tea-Gown," and for another about her American tour. His readers would not tolerate any glorification of the Americans, he informed her, "so they should not be treated as civilised altogether," and he advised her to begin the article with the statement that the Americans, according to their own explanation, visited France in order to complete their education, and that the French had to "tolerate people who are so fascinatingly unreasonable as to attempt to finish in a foreign land what they never had the courage to begin in their own!" He suggested that he should write the article for her, and then print it under her name. As Sarah fully intended to revisit America, she declined the offer. He overflowed with ideas, thinking out the titles and subjects of many contributions, from cookery to corsets, from shorthand to servants.

Naturally he cooled off fairly soon. He found punctuality excessively annoying, the editorial drudgery inconceivably boring, and the prohibition of smoking unimaginably irritating. But he put up with these things in the early enthusiastic days, and when asked how he managed to exist without smoking he replied "One makes up one's mind that one cannot, and one does not." Dressed with an elegance never before or since seen in an editor, he travelled by the Underground Railway from Sloane Square, alighted at Charing Cross, and walked down the Strand and Fleet Street, arriving at the office in La Belle Sauvage Yard, Ludgate Hill, at an hour that he could never regard as healthy. An official in the firm of Cassell's described him as "so indolent but such a genius"; while his assistant editor, Arthur Fish, has left an account of his comings and goings which implies that the magazine's readers owed several numbers more to the exertion of the assistant than to

the energy of the editor: "At first the work was taken quite seriously and
11 o'clock on his appointed morning saw the poet entering the dingy
portals of 'the Yard,' but after a few months his arrival became later and
his departure earlier, until at times his visit was little more than a call.
After a very short time in my association with him I could tell by the sound
of his approach along the resounding corridor whether the necessary work
to be done would be met cheerfully or postponed to a more congenial period.
In the latter case he would sink with a sigh into his chair, carelessly glance
at his letters, give a perfunctory look at proofs or make-up, ask 'Is it necessary to settle anything to-day?,' put on his hat, and, with a sad 'Good-
morning,' depart again. On his cheerful days, however, everything was
different. These were fairly constant in the spring days of the year: there
would be a smiling entrance, letters would be answered with epigrammatic
brightness, there would be a cheery interval of talk when the work was
accomplished, and the dull room would brighten under the influence of
his great personality."

W. E. Henley, who had edited a magazine published by the same firm,
met Wilde during the last year of his servitude, and asked: "How often
do you go to the office?"

"I used to go three times a week for an hour a day, but I have since
struck off one of the days."

"My God!" exclaimed Henley: "I went five times a week for five hours a
day, and when I wanted to strike off a day they had a special committee
meeting."

"Furthermore," continued Wilde, "I never answered their letters. I have
known men come to London full of bright prospects and seen them complete wrecks in a few months through a habit of answering letters."

CHAPTER NINE

THE CRITIC

"I HAVE never been able to see how the duties of a critic, which consist largely in making painful remarks in public about the most sensitive of his fellow-creatures, can be reconciled with the manners of a gentleman."

This saying of Bernard Shaw's will explain why Oscar Wilde's journalistic criticism was on the whole so flat. He was too gentle a man to hurt people's feelings, too good-natured to make a good critic. Such "painful remarks" as he did utter in public were usually called forth by hostility to himself. From the first of his reviews in *The Pall Mall Gazette* (March 7, 1885) to the last (May 24, 1890) he was, except on rare occasions, more kind to the authors than critical of their works; and though his anonymous contributions to *The Pall Mall Gazette* are more readable because a trifle less polite than his editorial contributions to *The Woman's World*, it cannot be said that any of them would be worth reprinting to-day on their own merits.

Nevertheless his levity sometimes got the better of his kindliness and expressed itself in his distinctive form of humour and perception, the best examples of which must be rescued from their innocuous contexts and set forth here.

As a reviewer he suffered from novels more than from any other class of literature, though perhaps his pain was never excessive. "The nineteenth century may be a prosaic age, but we fear that, if we are to judge by the general run of novels, it is not an age of prose." That was his chief ground of complaint, but he decided that "one should not be too severe on English novels: they are the only relaxation of the intellectually unemployed." He made a further point: "The difficulty under which the novelists of our day labour seems to me to be this: if they do not go into society, their books are unreadable; and if they do go into society, they have no time left for writing." A strong moral purpose was a poor substitute for a feeble book, and one author was told that he had "every form of sincerity except the sincerity of the artist, a defect that he shares with most of our popular writers." This needed rubbing in: "It is a curious fact that the worst work is always done with the best intentions, and that people are never so trivial as when they take themselves very seriously." And again: "The aim of most of our modern novelists seems to be, not to write good novels, but to write novels that will do good." It was therefore "pleasant to come across a heroine (in Bret Harte's *Cressy*) who is not identified with any great cause, and represents no important principle."

Once a note almost of irritation escaped our critic: "We sincerely hope that a few more novels like these will be published, as the public will then find out that a bad book is very dear at a shilling." And an early "thriller," by G. Manville Fenn, drew this from him: "Shilling literature is always making demands on our credulity without ever appealing to our imagination," which can be said of most modern "crime" fiction. Demands on the reader's credulity were not however confined to "thrillers," and his review of *Jenny Jennet: A Tale Without a Murder* began thus: "Mr. Gallenga has written, as he says, 'A tale without a murder,' but having put a pistol-ball through his hero's chest and left him alive and hearty notwithstanding, he cannot be said to have produced a tale without a miracle."

Although Wilde admitted that "to be put into fiction is always a tribute to one's reality," he deprecated the fashion: "The only form of fiction in which real characters do not seem out of place is history. In novels they are detestable." Besides, great fictional creations made even real people seem colourless: "A steady course of Balzac reduces our living friends to shadows, and our acquaintances to the shadows of shades. Who would care to go out to an evening party to meet Tomkins, the friend of one's boyhood, when one can sit at home with Lucien de Rubempré? It is pleasanter to have the entrée to Balzac's society than to receive cards from all the duchesses in Mayfair." As he received cards from a good sprinkling of Mayfair duchesses, he was in a position to know.

A typical specimen of romance was dismissed with the remark that it could "be read without any trouble and was probably written without any trouble also," though a tale called *Astray* by Charlotte M. Yonge and three other writers had the opposite effect: "It has taken four people to write it, and even to read it requires assistance"; all the same "it is a book that one can with perfect safety recommend to other people."

Following the example of Disraeli novelists were busily sketching the contemporary political scene, and one of them received Wilde's attention: "As a concession to humanity, each of the politicians is made to fall in love, and the charm of their various romances fully atones for the soundness of the author's theory of rent." Other novelists felt they were on safer ground with the aristocracy, and he noticed a book by Ouida in a way that possibly accounted for her statement some years later that she did not think much of him as a writer: "The book may be described as a study of the peerage from a poetical point of view . . . What is the story? Well, we must admit that we have a faint suspicion that Ouida has told it to us before . . . The noblest character in the book is Lord Aubrey. As he is not a genius he, naturally, behaves admirably on every occasion."

After reviewing many works of fiction Wilde came to the conclusion that "there is a great deal to be said in favour of reading a novel backwards. The last page is, as a rule, the most interesting, and when one begins with the catastrophe or the *dénouement* one feels on pleasant terms of equality with the author. It is like going behind the scenes of a theatre. One is no longer taken in, and the hairbreadth escapes of the hero and the wild agonies of the heroine leave one absolutely unmoved." In the case of the novel which produced this reflection, he admitted that if he had not known what was in store for one of the characters he would hardly have got through the book.

On the whole it was a relief to turn to the poets, though he sometimes expressed it in a form known as comic relief. He took one poet to task for making a trisyllable of "tuberose." The poet retorted that it was a trisyllable if properly derived from the Latin *tuberosus*, the lumpy flower. Wilde replied that there must in future be two derivations for every word, one for the poet and one for the scientist: "and in the present case the poet will dwell on the tiny trumpets of ivory into which the white flower breaks, and leave to the man of science horrid allusions to its supposed lumpiness and indiscreet revelations of its private life below ground. In fact 'tuber' as a derivation is disgraceful. On the roots of verbs Philology may be allowed to speak, but on the roots of flowers she must keep silence. We cannot allow her to dig up Parnassus." Of another poet who dealt with a great variety of subjects, from popular watering-places and universal providers to the immortality of the soul, he wrote: "We fear that he will never produce any real good work till he has made up his mind whether destiny intends him for a poet or for an advertising agent."

Although, as he said, "a poet can survive everything but a misprint," it appears from such pious verse as came his way that poetry could not survive religion. "I must confess," he wrote, "that most modern mysticism seems to me to be simply a method of imparting useless knowledge in a form that no one can understand." And he described the mystics as possessing "that quality of absolute unintelligibility that is the peculiar privilege of the

verbally inspired." Those who adhered to the orthodox beliefs were no
more to his taste. "There seems to be some curious connection between
piety and poor rhymes," he complained. But he perceived the true reason:
"Ordinary theology has long since converted its gold into lead, and words
and phrases that once touched the heart of the world have become wearisome
and meaningless through repetition. If Theology desires to move us, she
must re-write her formulas." Yet poets were still assuming that humanity
had remained stationary since the fourteenth century. For instance: "*Andia-
toroctè* is the title of a volume of poems by the Rev. Clarence Walworth,
of Albany, N. Y. It is a word borrowed from the Indians, and should, we
think, be returned to them as soon as possible. . . . Poems of this kind were
popular in the Middle Ages when the cathedrals of every Christian country
served as its theatres. They are anachronisms now, and it is odd that they
should come to us from the United States. In matters of this kind we
should have some protection."

Poetry about the saints was no better than poetry by a saint:

"K. E. V.'s little volume is a series of poems on the Saints. Each poem is
preceded by a brief biography of the Saint it celebrates—which is a very
necessary precaution, as few of them ever existed. It does not display much
poetic power and such lines as these on St. Stephen . . . may be said to add
another horror to martyrdom. Still it is a thoroughly well-intentioned book
and eminently suitable for invalids."

"As truly religious people are resigned to everything, even to mediocre
poetry, there is no reason at all why Madame Guyon's verses should not be
popular with a large section of the community. Their editor, Mr. Dyer, has
reprinted the translations Cowper made for Mr. Bull, added some versions
of his own, and written a pleasing preface about this gentle seventeenth
century saint whose life was her best, indeed her only true poem."

Nor was Wilde greatly impressed by the verses of those more modern
religious crusaders, the socialists. Having quoted one of E. Nesbit's vigorous
revolutionary poems, he said: "The only consolation that we can offer to the
timid and the Tories is that as long as so much strength is employed in blowing the trumpet, the sword, so far as Miss Nesbit is concerned, will probably
remain sheathed." But at least the socialists had variety. In 1889 Edward
Carpenter brought out an anthology called *Chants of Labour: A Song-Book of
the People*, from which collection Wilde drew the optimistic conclusion that
"Socialism is not going to allow herself to be trammelled by any hard
and fast creed or to be stereotyped into an iron formula. She welcomes many
and multiform natures. She rejects none and has room for all. She has the

attraction of a wonderful personality and touches the heart of one and the brain of another, and draws this man by his hatred of injustice, and his neighbour by his faith in the future, and a third, it may be, by his love of art or by his wild worship of a lost and buried past. And all of this is well. For, to make men Socialists is nothing, but to make Socialism human is a great thing."

Jeremiads were as common then as now, but Wilde refused to be stampeded:

"Mr. Gladstone Turner believes that we are on the verge of a great social cataclysm, and warns us that our *cradles* are even now being rocked by *slumbering volcanoes*! We hope that there is no truth in this statement, and that it is merely a startling metaphor introduced for the sake of effect, for elsewhere in the volume there is a great deal of beauty which we should be sorry to think was doomed to immediate extinction."

The subject of temperance has inspired few notable contributions to literature, and in reviewing a volume devoted to that theme Wilde hinted at the reason: "Compared to real poetry these verses are as 'water unto wine,' but no doubt this was the effect intended." Unlike so many of his contemporaries, Wilde seldom depended upon puns for his humour, but whenever he did so the result fully justified the method, as in this case: "*The Chronicle of Mites* is a mock-heroic poem about the inhabitants of a decaying cheese who speculate about the origin of their species and hold learned discussions upon the meaning of evolution and the Gospel according to Darwin. This cheese-epic is a rather unsavoury production and the style is at times so monstrous and so realistic that the author should be called the Gorgon-Zola of literature."

It is pleasant to record that Wilde did not go out of his way to praise the famous men of his time. The following passages will show that he had almost as little reverence for his well-known contemporaries as was displayed by his fellow-Celt Bernard Shaw:

"Judges, like the criminal classes, have their lighter moments, and it was probably in one of his happiest and, certainly, in one of his most careless moods that Mr. Justice Denman conceived the idea of putting the early history of Rome into doggerel verse for the benefit of a little boy of the name of Jack." After quoting some, he concludes: "If Jack goes to the bad, Mr. Justice Denman will have much to answer for."

"Homer has always been a great favourite with our statesmen," he remarked in reviewing the Earl of Carnarvon's translation of the *Odyssey*, "and indeed may be said to be almost a factor in our political life . . . Many of our leaders have sulked in their tents with Achilles after some violent political crisis and, enraged at the fickleness of fortune, more than one has given up to poetry what was obviously meant for party."

"Writers of poetical prose are rarely good poets," he said, in criticising *With Sa'di in the Garden* by Sir Edwin Arnold: "He knows India better than any living Englishman knows it, and Hindoostanee better than any English writer ought to know it." After quoting some of Arnold's verse, which was liberally sprinkled with Indian words, he finished up: "Sir Edwin Arnold has translated Sa'di and someone must translate Sir Edwin Arnold."

(On a book glorifying the poetry of Longfellow): "To a land out of breath in its greed for gain he showed the example of a life devoted entirely to the study of literature . . . But his poems are not of the kind that call for intellectual analysis or for elaborate description or, indeed, for any serious discussion at all."

While praising the poetical work of a friend, who had been imprisoned for political agitation in Ireland, Wilde said what he thought of the philosophical work of an acquaintance, who was then a power in the land.

"Prison has had an admirable effect on Mr. Wilfred Blunt as a poet . . . Literature is not much indebted to Mr. Balfour for his sophistical *Defence of Philosophic Doubt* which is one of the dullest books we know, but it must be admitted that by sending Mr. Blunt to gaol he has converted a clever rhymer into an earnest and deep-thinking poet."

At a time when Swinburne was the god of youth's idolatry, Wilde asserted what everyone would now agree with:

"It has been said of him, and with truth, that he is a master of language, but with still greater truth it may be said that language is his master. Words seem to dominate him. Alliteration tyrannises over him. Mere sound often becomes his lord. He is so eloquent that whatever he touches becomes unreal."

An eminent versifier of those days, as prolific as he was not poetic, did not laugh very heartily when he came across this:

"Most modern calendars mar the sweet simplicity of our lives by reminding us that each day that passes is the anniversary of some perfectly uninteresting event." Wilde therefore hailed the arrival of a calendar "in which every day in the year is made beautiful for us by an elegant extract from the poems of Mr. Alfred Austin." Indeed he did not even quarrel with the compiler for constantly repeating the same quotation twice over, because "it was difficult to find in Mr. Austin's work three hundred and sixty-five different passages really worthy of insertion in an almanac; and, besides, our climate has so degenerated of late that there is no reason at all why a motto perfectly suitable for February should not be equally appropriate when August has set in with its usual severity."

Occasionally Wilde dealt with a biography, but such specimens as came his way were not of the highest class and one is not surprised by his remark: "Every great man nowadays has his disciples, and it is usually Judas who writes his biography." A "Great Writers" series had recently been launched, and a well-known journalist named Joseph Knight had been chosen to contribute a Life of Dante Gabriel Rossetti. Wilde described it as "just the sort of biography Guildenstern might have written of Hamlet." After expressing his sorrow that an English dramatic critic should misquote Shakespeare, "as we had always been of opinion that this was a privilege reserved specially for our English actors," he closed: "We sincerely hope that there will soon be an end to all biographies of this kind. They rob life of much of its dignity and its wonder, add to death itself a new terror, and make one wish that all art were anonymous." After which it is scarcely surprising that Joseph Knight did not give Wilde's comedies a friendly welcome in *The Athenaeum* and other papers.

Wilde had long outgrown his early admiration for professors, and in advising the removal of certain statements in a book on Italian literature he explained "They show a want of knowledge that must be the result of years of study." Even his old friend and mentor J. P. Mahaffy did not escape. Of the professor's *Greek Life and Thought* he wrote: "There is always something peculiarly impotent about the violence of a literary man. It seems to bear no reference to facts, for it is never kept in check by action. It is simply a question of adjectives and rhetoric, of exaggeration and over-emphasis." Mahaffy had become a strong Tory in politics for purely snobbish reasons, and Wilde dressed him down for fawning on the English governing oligarchy, as shown by his attacks on Greek nationalism and patriotism. Wilde revealed his own attitude to such matters when noticing an Irish romance by J. A. Froude: "If in the last century she [England] tried to govern Ireland with an insolence that was intensified by race hatred and religious prejudice, she has sought to rule her in this century with a stupidity that is aggravated by good intentions." And Froude was also told that "Like most penmen he overrates the power of the sword."

The Irish professor received another jolt from his old pupil when his book on the art of conversation was published: "If Mr. Mahaffy would only write as he talks, his book would be much pleasanter reading." Mahaffy had suggested in his book that intelligent questions addressed to a pure mathematician would elicit many curious facts that would pleasantly beguile the time.

Wilde drew the line at this: "Here, in the interest of Society, we feel bound to enter a formal protest. Nobody, even in the provinces, should ever be allowed to ask an intelligent question about pure mathematics across a dinner table."

Writers in the latter half of last century were beginning to import wisdom from the East, and Wilde wrote a delightful essay for *The Speaker* on a book about a Chinese sage and mystic, whose philosophy had a great deal in common with his own, for he had preached the creed of Inaction, showed the stupidity of everything the vast majority of men think noble and right, and asserted the inutility of everything they think useful: "Chuang Tzŭ, whose name must carefully be pronounced as it is not written . . . is a very dangerous writer, and the publication of his book in English, two thousand years after his death, is obviously premature, and may cause a great deal of pain to many thoroughly respectable and industrious persons. It may be true that the ideal of self-culture and self-development, which is the aim of his scheme of life, and the basis of his scheme of philosophy, is an ideal somewhat needed by an age like ours, in which most people are so anxious to educate their neighbours that they have actually no time left in which to educate themselves. But would it be wise to say so? It seems to me that if we once admitted the force of any one of Chuang Tzŭ's destructive criticisms we should have to put some check on our national habit of self-glorification; and the only thing that ever consoles man for the stupid things he does is the praise he always gives himself for doing them."

On several occasions as a reviewer Wilde rightly distinguished between the imaginative and inventive faculties. He spoke of "the fatal originality of inexperience," said of one poet that he "makes a distinct attempt to be original and the result is extremely depressing," claimed the "true originality is to be found rather in the use of a model than in the rejection of all models and masters," and pronounced: "The originality which we ask from the artist is originality of treatment, not of subject. It is only the unimaginative who ever invent. The true artist is known by the use he makes of what he annexes, and he annexes everything."

In his final journalistic criticism Wilde gave a courteous reception to *Primavera*, a volume of poems by four young Oxford friends, two of whom, Laurence Binyon and Stephen Phillips, were later to be well-known as dramatists. This last review ends characteristically:

"On the whole *Primavera* is a pleasant little book, and we are glad to welcome it. It is charmingly 'got up,' and undergraduates might read it with advantage during lecture hours."

CHAPTER TEN

THE ARTIST

"ONLY mediocrities progress," Wilde informed the readers of a newspaper in September '94. "An artist revolves in a cycle of masterpieces, the first of which is no less perfect than the last." No one had the gumption to ask him whether he thought *Vera* or *The Duchess of Padua* as perfect as *Salomé* or *Lady Windermere's Fan*; but as neither *Vera* nor *The Duchess of Padua* had been published he must have felt, if he remembered them at all, that he ran no risk in making the astonishing assertion just quoted. Besides, he might have got out of the difficulty by saying that when he wrote those two early plays he was not an artist.

While editing *The Woman's World* and reviewing for *The Pall Mall Gazette* and other papers, he was also producing short stories, fairy tales, essays and a novel, some of which were serialised before publication in book form. His first appearance before the public as an artist of any individuality was in *The Court and Society Review*, which printed his short story *The Canterville Ghost* in February, 1887. It is an unequal story, which begins as a social satire, continues as a pure burlesque, and closes in an atmosphere of romantic sentiment. Thus the main aspects of Wilde's nature—his quick intelligence, his sense of fun, and his emotional unreality—are manifested, briefly and together, in his earliest attempt at fiction. He wrote three more short tales with a modern flavour, all of which appeared in magazines during the first half of '87, the collection coming out in '91 under the title of *Lord Arthur Savile's Crime and other Stories*. They were the class of thing he could have gone on writing for ever; dozens of such yarns occurred to him in the course of conversation, and he told them at lunch-parties, over a drink, during the intervals of a play, while smoking in bed or watching a painter at work, in fact at any odd moment of the day or night: and most of them made their appearance under the names of other authors. The exertion required to write them down irked him; the excitement of talk, the presence of an audience, even of one, called them forth; their spontaneity was the effect of company; and their freshness seemed to fade when he sat down alone to recreate them with pen and ink. He once said that Mrs. Chapone's *Ode to Solitude* always filled him with the wildest passion for society; but no poem was needed to do that. Social life was the very breath of his being, and his written work was his talk gone rather flat: solitude took much of the sparkle out of it. None the less he thought well of the longest story in this book, *Lord Arthur Savile's Crime*, which is a résumé of his personality. Typical epigrams, some to be improved and transferred to his plays, were seen for the first time:

"Nothing looks so like innocence as an indiscretion."

"Surely Providence can resist temptation by this time."

"No one cares about distant relations nowadays. They went out of fashion years ago."

"The world is a stage, but the play is badly cast."

"Not being a genius, he had no enemies."

His picture of low life in London has the unreal melodramatic quality one might expect from a youth who is making the most of his first contact with things beyond his normal experience: "Then he wandered across Oxford Street into narrow, shameful alleys. Two women with painted faces mocked at him as he went by. From a dark courtyard came a sound of oaths and blows, followed by shrill screams, and, huddled upon a damp doorstep, he saw the crook-backed forms of poverty and eld." Also there is the note of personal doom which appears so often in Wilde's work, signifying his love of self-dramatisation: "Perhaps, some day, his own name might be placarded on the walls of London. Some day, perhaps, a price would be set on his head also." And again: "He thought of all the days that break in beauty, and set in storm."

Just as his epigrams were polished and perfected by repetition, so were his stories elaborated and even completely altered in the re-telling. In their first form they consisted of little more than brief anecdotes, and some of them would have been better left as such; but if his audience seemed to be in a receptive mood he would build up an episode until it became a lengthy narrative with a number of side-issues and digressions and new points of view: so much would depend on the need or the inspiration of the moment. In the case of *Lord Arthur Savile's Crime* he spun it out on one occasion because he required a rest. Graham Robertson relates that he went for a short stroll in the country with Wilde, who, hating exercise, was toiling behind in silence. Returning through a wood he suddenly said "Let's sit down."

"What for?"

"Well, what do people usually sit down for?"

"You can't be tired. We have been no distance, and we can't sit down now. We shall never get home if we do."

"I shall never get home if we don't," said he, and down he went. "Do sit down. Look here, if you sit down I'll tell you a story. Did I ever tell you about George Ellison and the palmist?"

"No, and I don't know George Whathisname."

"If you don't know him you certainly must——" and he lingered over the story of Lord Arthur Savile's crime.

On the other hand, at a lunch when Wilde told so many yarns that each had to be presented in skeleton form, H. B. Irving heard Lord Arthur's adventure described in five minutes; and at a time when H. B. was full of the subject, having just obtained a dramatic version of the story which he wished to produce, he gave a few of us the anecdote as he had received it from Wilde:

"It was at Lady Thirlmere's great reception that Lord Arthur Savile met Mr. Ransom the palmist. He had always wanted to know what the future held in store for him, and he watched the palmist inspect his hand with an interest he could hardly conceal. Mr. Ransom frowned and looked uncomfortable; then he trembled, his complexion turned white, and his voice shook. 'You are fated to kill someone,' he whispered, 'and you cannot escape your fate.' By the time Lord Arthur had recovered from the shock Mr. Ransom had disappeared. It was indeed an unpleasant predicament to find oneself in, but Lord Arthur reflected that it would be still more unpleasant for the person he had to kill, and this consoled him. His real difficulty as a gentle good-natured man was to provide his victim with a quick and painless death. Surely nothing could be simpler, he thought. But he was to find that it was not so simple as he thought. The clergyman whom he tried to push under the wheels of an omnibus stepped back suddenly, trod on his feet, and went away without apologising. The next attempt ended even more dismally. He sent some poison by post to an uncle who had been ill for a long time, whose murder would be an act of humanity, and from whose will he expected to benefit. But what is one person's poison is another's cure, and a fortnight later his uncle gave a dinner-party to celebrate his return to health. Driving his dogcart in Hyde Park one morning, Lord Arthur saw a man leave the path and start to walk slowly across the road. As he seemed to be an invalid Lord Arthur felt not only hopeful but happy to serve the cause of humanity; he whipped up his horse and drove straight at the man, who, however, thinking that it was a runaway carriage, jumped lightly to one side, seized the bridle, and brought the horse to a standstill. Lord Arthur had to tip him a sovereign. Again and again his attempts to murder were frustrated; the explosive he sent to an aunt did not explode; the lady he tripped into a canal was saved by a passer-by, and both of them had to be recompensed; the child he overturned in a pram was highly entertained, laughed heartily, and asked him to do it again. It really seemed that Fate was against him.

"One night he was walking along the Thames Embankment in despair, and wondering whether suicide would count as murder, when he saw someone leaning over the parapet. No one was in sight, and the river was in flood. It was a heaven-sent opportunity, the answer to his prayer. Leaning down quickly, he seized the unknown's legs; there was a splash in the dark swirling waters, and peace descended upon Lord Arthur. His duty done, he slept well, and did not rise till the following afternoon. One of the first things to catch his eye as he opened the paper was a paragraph headed: Well-known Palmist drowned—Suicide of Mr. Ransom. Inscribed on the wreath which Lord Arthur sent for the funeral were the words 'In Gratitude.'"

Most people who had heard Wilde tell the story at length were disappointed when they read the published version; amongst others Sir Bernard Partridge, who writes to me: "I remember once his calling on me at my studio in Devonshire Street, and telling me, with exquisite humour and fancy, his story *Lord Arthur Savile's Crime*. The recital took nearly an hour, and when at the end of it I said 'Of course you'll publish that story, Oscar,' he replied wearily 'I don't think so, my dear fellow: it's such a bore writing these things out.' But of course that was all *blague*: he meant to publish it all right. But when I afterwards read the story in print the effect was as nothing compared with that produced by his extempore recital that afternoon in Devonshire Street."

In May 1888 *The Happy Prince and Other Tales* was published, and Oscar Wilde was seen in a fresh character: as a writer of fairy stories. He revelled in it, and in November '91 gave a more ornate representation in *A House of Pomegranates*. Although he frequently declared that technically speaking all his works were equally perfect, until his imprisonment he expressed a preference for the story of *The Young King* in his second volume of fairy tales. After his release he thoroughly disliked all his works, saying that they were inadequate expressions of his genius. *The Happy Prince* and *The Young King* are sermons in practical Christianity, and are, on the whole, the two most effective stories in the collection. But to the biographer there are four interesting points about these tales which bear on the nature of their author. The first is that Wilde was becoming extremely interested in the personality of Jesus Christ, an interest that increased every year until at length he almost identified himself with Christ and often spoke in parables. The second point to notice is Wilde's sympathy with the poor and the down-trodden, which eventually found direct expression in *The Soul of Man Under Socialism*, an essay that aroused the secret enmity of the rich and powerful classes at whose house-parties he was an invaluable entertainer. Next we observe his growing addiction to the use of words merely for the sake of their sounds. Two stories, *The Birthday of the Infanta* and *The Fisherman and His Soul* are full of descriptions of jewels, flowers, clothes, furniture, fruits, embroideries, and so on. He took a sensuous pleasure in all this; but the queer thing is that he seemed to think he was producing literature, pos-sibly because Pater and Flaubert had done something of the sort; and at his worst and weakest he resembled them. In style he thought *The Birthday of the Infanta* his best story, and he gravely told some friends that he had conceived it "in black and silver," but that, when translated into French, it had come out "pink and blue," which had taught him that there were certain colour-forces in English, a power of rendering gloom, which were not in French. In the nineties another school of writers laboured under the same misapprehension that it was producing literature by cataloguing machine parts; and the best that we can say for Wilde is that his tapestries and jewels are at least more picturesque and therefore nearer to literature than Kipling's nuts and bolts. There was also no scientific humbug about Wilde, who said that it was "better to take pleasure in a rose than to put its root under a microscope." The last personal point to note in connection with Wilde's fairy tales is the fact that he should have written fairy tales at all. The ex-planation has been given in an earlier chapter. Like all who have expressed themselves in stories or plays for children, from Hans Andersen to James Barrie, he was emotionally undeveloped. Even Dean Swift, who must have been revolving in his grave ever since Gulliver became a favourite in the nursery, was strangely immature in that respect and has delighted children for two centuries in spite of himself. Wilde answered a critic of his second book of fairy tales with the words "I had about as much intention of pleasing the British child as I had of pleasing the British public." True; but he had thoroughly pleased an Irish child: himself.

Loving books that were beautifully printed and handsomely bound, he got Charles Ricketts and C. H. Shannon to design and decorate *A House of Pomegranates*, and told Katherine Bradley and Edith Cooper ("Michael Field"), after praising their *Tragic Mary* as, in appearance, one of the two most beautiful books of the century, that he was going to surpass them and would send them an early copy of his tales which would make them "very unhappy." The illustrations, he informed them, were not taken from anything in the book, only suggested by it, for in his opinion literature, being more graphic than painting, should never be illustrated in itself, but solely by what it evoked. His delight in luxuriously produced books was even keener than his pleasure in rare gems, rich materials, and so forth, and when he was asked to send a copy of a new edition of his poems to a newspaper for review he replied that the edition was limited to 200 copies, which were for lovers of poetry, not reviewers: "Its raiment, gold smeared on tired purple, might attract attention in the Strand, and that would annoy it, books being very delicate and most sensitive things." When he reached heaven, he once said, he would like to find a number of volumes in vellum and to be told that they were his.

Considering his natural indolence and love of society, Oscar Wilde was pretty active during the four years, 1887 to 1890. He reviewed books all the time, edited a magazine for two of the years, wrote a volume of short stories, two volumes of fairy tales, a novel, and six long essays, all of which appeared in monthly reviews and four of which, with an earlier one, were collected and published under the title of *Intentions* (1891). The peace of the countryside was not to him a necessary condition for creative effort, and all his writing was done in Tite Street. "Town life nourishes and perfects all the more civilised elements in man," he said. "Shakespeare wrote nothing but doggerel lampoon before he came to London and never penned a line after he left."

His interest in the theatre and in clothes prompted his first considerable essay, which appeared in *The Nineteenth Century* in May 1885 under the heading *Shakespeare and Stage Costume*, but re-entitled *The Truth of Masks* when published in *Intentions*. Nothing in it need detain us except the characteristic close: "Not that I agree with everything that I have said in this essay. There is much with which I entirely disagree. The essay simply represents an artistic standpoint, and in aesthetic criticism attitude is everything." That was not the way to satisfy or conciliate an age which mistook seriousness for profundity and sincerity for truth; and his next essay, *The Decay of Lying*, which came out in *The Nineteenth Century* for January '89, strengthened the impression that he was trifling with his readers. Here we get Wilde as a talker for the first time in his writings. Adela Schuster, who knew him well, told me that if one took the duologues in *Intentions* with *The Importance of Being Earnest* and stirred them up together one would have a faint idea of what his conversation was like. It would be necessary, I fancy, to add *Poems in Prose* to the mixture. Anyhow, *The Decay of Lying* is Wilde in one of his veins, and a delightful one.

The thesis is that the Victorian age had become hideously prosaic in its insistence on facts, whilst imaginative lying, the basis of romantic literature, had practically died out: "Many a young man starts in life with a natural gift for exaggeration which, if nurtured in congenial and sympathetic surroundings, or by the imitation of the best models, might grow into something really great and wonderful. But as a rule, he comes to nothing. He either falls into careless habits of accuracy, or takes to frequenting the society of the aged and well-informed ... and in a short time he develops a morbid and unhealthy faculty of truth-telling, begins to verify all statements made in his presence, has no hesitation in contradicting people who are much younger than himself, and often ends by writing novels which are so life-like that no one can possibly believe in their probability." Even newspapers had degenerated: "They may now be absolutely relied upon." Modern writers of romance had gone irretrievably astray and were even base enough to buttress their fancies with facts: "If a man is sufficiently unimaginative to produce evidence in support of a lie, he might just as well speak the truth at once." Recent poets, however, "with the unfortunate exception of Mr. Wordsworth, have been really faithful to their high mission, and are universally recognised as being absolutely unreliable." Barristers, too, are given a word of encouragement: "Their feigned ardours and unreal rhetoric are delightful. They ... have been known to wrest from reluctant juries triumphant verdicts of acquittal for their clients, even when those clients, as often happens, were clearly and unmistakeably innocent." The discussion ranges over several topics: the superiority of art to nature, the way in which nature imitates art, and the cleavage between art and life, each viewpoint clarifying our recognition of the essential cleavage between Wilde's intellect and his emotions.

That same month, January '89, *The Fortnightly Review* printed his brief biography of Thomas Griffiths Wainwright, called *Pen, Pencil and Poison.* Wilde had a distaste for the sort of biography that was written in his day and once remarked, concerning two "Lives" of Rossetti which had appeared almost before he was cold in his grave, "Whenever a great man dies, Hall Caine and William Sharp go in with the undertakers." He therefore showed how the thing ought to be done by adopting an urbane and scholarly attitude to a man whose forgeries and murders would have received moral castigation from most Victorian biographers, but whose real crime in Wilde's view was his misuse of the English language. Of Wainwright's description of a picture by Giulio Romano, Wilde says "Were this description carefully re-written it would be quite admirable"; while on the subject of the forger's sentence to transportation for life, he states "This heavy punishment was inflicted on him for what, if we remember his fatal influence on the prose of modern journalism, was certainly not the worst of all his sins." Wilde's attraction to the man was the attraction of a juvenile temperament to crime, to the thrilling mystery of something abnormal. "One can fancy an intense personality being created out of sin," he says, putting himself in the other fellow's place with his usual flair for personal drama, and, building up the effect, "The fact of a man being a poisoner is nothing against his prose. The domestic virtues are not the true basis of art."

In July and September 1890, *The Nineteenth Century* published Wilde's next two essays, which consisted of duologues on *The Critic as Artist*. The main idea, set forth with much wit and more rhetoric, is that criticism need not concern itself with the thing criticised, that it should record the emotions aroused in the critic by his subject, that it is a form of spiritual autobiography, and that it can be just as independent and creative as a novel, a play, or a picture, if not more so. "This was sometimes a paradox," as Hamlet says, "but now the time gives it proof." No one could have outlined the new creed so persuasively as Wilde, because it fitted his outlook, or rather inlook, so exactly. "We watch ourselves, and the mere wonder of the spectacle enthralls us," said he, and "I am the only person in the world I should like to know thoroughly, but I don't see any chance of it just at present." One thing at least he knew about himself: that he was not what is commonly called a man of action. Perhaps the most absurd statement ever made about him was that by W. B. Yeats: "I considered him essentially a man of action, that he was a writer by perversity and accident, and would have been more important as soldier or politician." Nothing could be further from the truth, except in the sense meant by Wilde when he said "We have been deluded by the name of action: to think is to act." But the whole bent of his mind, to say nothing of the inclination of his body, was hostile to action in any shape or form, except the action of the tongue in conversation. He knew, none better, that "those who try to lead the people can only do so by following the mob," and that the chief justification for men of action is that they furnish subjects for discussion and recreation to men of reflection. Hear him on the subject:

"When man acts he is a puppet. When he describes he is a poet."

"Action! What is action? It dies at the moment of its energy. It is a base concession to fact. The world is made by the singer for the dreamer."

"Action is limited and relative. Unlimited and absolute is the vision of him who sits at ease and watches, who walks in loneliness and dreams."

"To do nothing at all is the most difficult thing in the world, the most difficult and most intellectual."

"Anybody can make history. Only a great man can write it. There is no mode of action, no form of emotion, that we do not share with the lower animals. It is only by language that we rise above them—by language, which is the parent, and not the child, of thought."

"While, in the opinion of society, contemplation is the gravest thing of which any citizen can be guilty, in the opinion of the highest culture it is the proper occupation of man."

"Don't talk about action. It is a blind thing dependent on external influences, and moved by an impulse of whose nature it is unconscious. It is a thing incomplete in its essence, because limited by accident, and ignorant of its direction, because always at variance with its aim. Its basis is the lack of imagination. It is the last resource of those who know not how to dream."

The three duologues in *Intentions* are peppered with such aperçus as were constantly cropping up in his talk, when he would say in a phrase what other men would have expanded into an essay. To give a few examples:

"Wordsworth went to the lakes, but he was never a lake poet. He found in stones the sermons he had already hidden there."

"Man can believe the impossible, but man can never believe the improbable."

"The public is wonderfully tolerant. It forgives everything except genius."

"Meredith is a prose Browning, and so is Browning."

"We are born in an age when only the dull are taken seriously, and I live in terror of not being misunderstood."

"Anybody can write a three-volumed novel. It merely requires a complete ignorance of both life and literature."

"For he to whom the present is the only thing that is present, knows nothing of the age in which he lives."

"It is enough that our fathers have believed. They have exhausted the faith-faculty of the species. Their legacy to us is the scepticism of which they were afraid."

"One is tempted to define man as a rational animal who always loses his temper when he is called upon to act in accordance with the dictates of reason."

"That the desire to do good to others produces a plentiful supply of prigs is the least of the evils of which it is the cause."

"It is only an auctioneer who can equally and impartially admire all schools of art."

"As long as war is regarded as wicked, it will always have its fascination. When it is looked upon as vulgar, it will cease to be popular."

"It is always with the best intentions that the worst work is done."

"We are never more true to ourselves than when we are inconsistent."

Wilde put a good deal of himself into *Intentions*, and four years after he had finished it he wrote to a friend "I simply love that book." It was published by a new firm, Osgood, McIlvaine & Co., which brought out his *Lord Arthur Savile's Crime* and *A House of Pomegranates* in the same year, 1891, and which made a point of announcing in every advertisement that their books appeared simultaneously in London and New York. Walking along Piccadilly one morning, Richard Le Gallienne met Wilde, who, after the usual greetings, assumed an air of deep grief and said "Did you see in the papers this morning that Osgood is dead?" Le Gallienne looked sympathetic. "Poor Osgood!" Wilde went on: "He is a great loss to us all. However," he added, suddenly brightening up, "I suppose they will bury him simultaneously in London and New York."

In June '89 an essay by Wilde entitled *The Portrait of Mr. W. H.* appeared in *Blackwood's Magazine*. It dealt with Shakespeare's *Sonnets*, which he loved "as one should love all things, not wisely but too well." After writing it he found that he had more to say on the subject and wished to make a short book of it: otherwise it might have gone into *Intentions*. In addition to the main theme it expounded a favourite notion of his: that when you convert someone to an idea, you lose your own belief in it. "Whenever people agree with me, I always feel I must be wrong," he used to say. Whether he really believed the theory with regard to the *Sonnets* which he advanced in the essay is immaterial, for on this point too he had something interesting to say: "If one puts forward an idea to a true Englishman—always a rash thing to do—he never dreams of considering whether the idea is right or wrong. The only thing he considers of any importance is whether one believes it oneself. Now, the value of an idea has nothing whatsoever to do with the sincerity of the man who expresses it. Indeed, the probabilities are that the more insincere the man is, the more purely intellectual will the idea be, as in that case it will not be coloured by either his wants, his desires, or his prejudices." Wilde, who could live a part as well as any great player, was so convincing when he discussed his theory that he won over a politician, A. J. Balfour, to the view that "Mr. W. H." in Shakespeare's *Sonnets* was a young actor named Willie Hughes, who had inspired the poet to create some of his finest female characters, and was "the onlie Begetter" of the *Sonnets*. In Wilde's opinion Plato dominated the renaissance, and Shakespeare's sonnets expressed Platonic thought in modern form. "Had Mr. W. H. not made Shakespeare suffer," he said to Charles Ricketts, "we should not possess the *Sonnets*, and England would be glad." In his usual manner he turned an idea into an anecdote, the anecdote into a story, embroidering as he went along, and the freer play he gave to his imagination the deeper conviction he imparted to others and the more inclined was he to believe the story himself. "You *must* believe in Willie Hughes," he said after one recital, which had so much impressed his listeners that he added sceptically "I almost do myself." He predicted that "Our English homes will totter to their base when my book appears"; but it did not appear in his lifetime, because the expanded manuscript was stolen from his home after his arrest; and the essay in *Blackwood's*, though it caused some annoyance to people who thought the writer serious, and more annoyance to people who thought him not serious, failed to frighten the Victorians out of their apathy to Shakespeare.

A year later, however, he managed to create considerable unrest amongst the critics and not a little discomfort in literary quarters. A curious conjunction in the history of English letters is recorded by Conan Doyle, then an unsuccessful doctor and almost unknown author, who had travelled from Southsea to London in order to dine with a representative of Lippincott, the American publisher. His fellow-guests were an Irish M.P. named Gill and Oscar Wilde, who immediately put Doyle at his ease by praising *Micah Clarke*. Wilde's conversation left an indelible impression on the mind of Doyle: "He towered above us all, and yet had the art of seeming to be interested in all that we could say. He had delicacy of feeling and tact, for the monologue man, however clever, can never be a gentleman at heart. He took as well as gave, but what he gave was unique." Though his gestures were slight and his speech precise, he was able without effort to make an episode equally vivid and amusing, as when, in discussing the wars of the future, he said "A chemist on each side will approach the frontier with a bottle," his serio-comic expression and manner sending his hearers into fits of laughter. Doyle gives us one of Wilde's brief impromptus. They were discussing the commonly-held view that the good fortune of one's friends makes one discontented. Said Wilde: "The devil was once crossing the Libyan desert, and he came upon a spot where a number of small fiends were tormenting a holy hermit. The sainted man easily shook off their evil suggestions. The devil watched their failure, and then he stepped forward to give them a lesson. 'What you do is too crude,' he said. 'Permit me for one moment.' With that he whispered to the holy man. 'Your brother has just been made Bishop of Alexandria.' A scowl of malignant jealousy at once clouded the serene face of the hermit. 'That,' said the devil to his imps, 'is the sort of thing which I should recommend.'" As a result of the meeting, Doyle wrote *The Sign of Four* for Lippincott, and Wilde *The Picture of Dorian Gray*.

Wilde was unable to understand how a man could sit down day after day and work on the same book for years. "Now when I start a thing," he confided to Vincent O'Sullivan, "I must write desperately day and night till it is finished. Otherwise I should lose interest in it, and the first bus passing in the street would distract me from it." *Dorian Gray* was probably the only thing he ever wrote that took him more than a few weeks, though he sometimes went on touching up a story or a poem over a longish period. Originally it was, as we might guess, a short story on the lines of Balzac's *Peau de Chagrin* and Poe's *William Wilson*; then another short story was added, of an actress who loses her genius by falling in love; then a third, based on the discovery of Christ's body in a tomb near Jerusalem, though how this was worked into the scheme of the book it is difficult to say; but the main idea came from an actual episode. In the year 1884 Wilde used often to drop in at the studio of a painter, Basil Ward, one of whose sitters was a young man of exceptional beauty. Incidentally, Wilde must have been a godsend to many painters of the time, as his conversation kept their sitters perpetually entertained. When the portrait was done and the youth had gone, Wilde happened to say "What a pity that such a glorious creature should ever grow old!" The artist agreed, adding "How delightful it would be if he could remain exactly as he is, while the portrait aged and withered in his stead!" Wilde expressed his obligation by naming the painter in his story "Basil Hallward."

The book is a strange concoction. It is, one may say, the most lifelike thing he ever produced, but it is utterly unlike life; in other words, it contains a full-length portrait of himself as a talker in the character of Lord Henry Wotton, with many of his most searching comments on life, side by side with a complete revelation of his emotional unreality in portraying human nature and the morbid strain in him which eventually wrecked his life. Wilde is one of our most autobiographical writers; his personality is paramount in all his works, nearly every phrase in which is stamped with his individuality: his profundity as a critic, his superficiality as a creator Until he went to prison he only touched reality through his intelligence never through his emotions; of which limitation he was perfectly conscious. Speaking of reality in fiction to a female friend, he once said:

"I could never have dealings with Truth. If Truth were to come unto me, to my room, he would say to me 'You are too wilful.' And I would say to him 'You are too obvious.' And I should throw him out of the window."

"You would say to *him*. Is not Truth a woman?"

"Then I could not throw her out of the window; I should bow her to the door."

And with regard to *Dorian Gray* he admitted to Conan Doyle "Between me and life there is a mist of words always. I throw probability out of the window for the sake of a phrase, and the chance of an epigram makes me desert truth. Still I do aim at making a work of art . . ." The mist of words was an opaque fog in chapter XI of his novel, where he suffers from a severe attack of logomania, giving us lists of perfumes, musical instruments, jewels, embroideries, ecclesiastical vestments, and much else. As in *Lord Arthur Savile's Crime* we are treated to sketches of working-class life seen histrionically: "Women with hoarse voices and harsh laughter had called after him. Drunkards had reeled by cursing, and chattering to themselves like monstrous apes. He had seen grotesque children huddled upon door-steps, and heard shrieks and oaths from gloomy courts." "From some of the bars came the sound of horrible laughter. In others, drunkards brawled and screamed." Each facet of Wilde's nature is discernible in the book: his theatricality, his acute perception, his false emotion, his conversational charm, his laziness (he copied out the description of embroideries from his review of a book on that subject), his snobbery, his love of paradox, his showmanship, his attraction to the Roman ritual, his taste for "purple patches" of prose (the phrase is his own invention), his passion for luxury, his adoration of beauty, and his delight in scandalising the bourgeois.

The novel came out on June 20th, 1890, in the July number of *Lippincott's Monthly Magazine*, being published as a book in April '91 with a preface, and six additional chapters to meet the needs of the fiction market. Apart from those new chapters, Numbers 3, 5, 15, 16, 17 and 18, many passages appeared in the book which were not in the magazine version, while a number of passages appeared in the magazine which were omitted from the book or altered in it. One of the readers for Ward Lock & Co., the firm which published the novel in England, was Coulson Kernahan, who had been asked by Wilde to correct if necessary the "wills" and "shalls" and "woulds" and "shoulds," about which he never felt certain, and pass the proofs for press. Wilde then left for Paris. Just after passing the proofs

Kernahan received a wire from the author: "Terrible blunder in book. Coming back specially. Stop all proofs." Wilde arrived in a hansom with a look of strained anxiety on his face.

"It is not too late? For heaven's sake tell me it is not too late," he gasped.

"Make yourself easy. It was not too late. I stopped the proofs," said Kernahan.

"Thank God!" With a great sigh of relief, Wilde sank into a chair and mopped his forehead with a handkerchief. "I should never, never have forgiven myself, or you, had my book gone out disfigured by such a blunder—by such a crime, as I count it, against art." Pausing to obtain control of himself, he then half-whispered "There's a picture-framer—a mere tradesman—in my story, isn't there?"

"Yes."

"What have I called him?"

"Ashton, I think. Yes, Ashton."

"Don't repeat it! Don't repeat it!" He shuddered. "It is more than my shattered nerves can stand . . . Ashton . . . " his voice broke . . . "Ashton is a gentleman's name, and—God forgive me!—I've given it to a tradesman. It must be changed to Hubbard. Yes, Hubbard positively smells of the tradesman."

Kernahan tells us that, after Wilde had successfully brought that off and enjoyed a good laugh, he became natural.

"Praise makes me humble, but when I am abused I know I have touched the stars." If this statement of Wilde's was honest, he must have felt that he had touched a constellation after the critics had relieved themselves on the subject of *Dorian Gray*. Here are some of their less restrained comments on the book:

"Esoteric prurience"—"stupid and vulgar"—"dull and nasty"—"disgusting"—"malodorous putrefaction"—"delights in dirtiness"—"ought to be chucked into the fire"—"garish vulgarity"—"coarse and crude"—"will taint every young mind that comes in contact with it"—"grubbing in muckheaps" —"the book is unmanly, sickening, vicious . . . and tedious."

"Whether the Treasury or the Vigilance Society will think it worth while to prosecute Mr. Oscar Wilde or Messrs. Ward Lock & Co. we do not know." (*St. James's Gazette.*)

"It is a tale spawned from the leprous literature of the French *Décadents* —a poisonous book, the atmosphere of which is heavy with the mephitic odours of moral and spiritual putrefaction." (*Daily Chronicle.*)

"It is false to morality—for it is not made sufficiently clear that the writer does not prefer a course of unnatural iniquity to a life of cleanliness, health and sanity. The story—which deals with matters only fitted for the Criminal Investigation Department or a hearing in camera—is discreditable alike to author and editor (of *Lippincott's Monthly Magazine*). Mr. Wilde has brains, and art, and style; but if he can write for none but outlawed noblemen and perverted telegraph boys, the sooner he takes to tailoring (or some other decent trade) the better for his own reputation and the public morals." (*Scots Observer*.)

Such press notices nowadays would send a book through half a dozen editions in as many days, but Wilde lived at a time when a high moral tone was good for sales, even among regular readers, and none of the reviewers hinted that *Dorian Gray* had been written by a churchman. Walter Pater dealt with it in *The Bookman*, but his polite and non-committal remarks were not of a kind to stimulate interest in the work. A few phrases from Wilde's replies to his critics may be quoted:

"My story is an essay on decorative art. It reacts against the crude brutality of plain realism. It is poisonous if you like, but you cannot deny that it is also perfect, and perfection is what we artists aim at."

"The sphere of art and the sphere of ethics are absolutely distinct and separate."

"Yes, there is a terrible moral in *Dorian Gray*—a moral which the prurient will not be able to find in it, but it will be revealed to all whose minds are healthy. Is this an artistic error? I fear it is. It is the only error in the book."

"I write because it gives me the greatest possible artistic pleasure to write. If my work pleases the few I am gratified. If it does not, it causes me no pain. As for the mob, I have no desire to be a popular novelist. It is far too easy."

He replied more compactly in *A Preface to Dorian Gray*, which was printed first of all in *The Fortnightly Review* for March '91, and then took its place in the published novel. His critics read without enjoyment the following sentences in the preface, which they guessed, and rightly guessed, referred to themselves:

"Those who find ugly meanings in beautiful things are corrupt without being charming. This is a fault."

.   .   .   .   .

"The nineteenth-century dislike of Realism is the rage of Caliban seeing his own face in a glass.

"The nineteenth-century dislike of Romanticism is the rage of Caliban not seeing his own face in a glass."

.   .   .   .   .

"It is the spectator, and not life, that art really mirrors."

.   .   .   .

"When critics disagree the artist is in accord with himself."

In the book this preface was printed in italics, and as Frank Harris is not our only authority we may accept as true an episode in his Life of Wilde. In the early summer of '91, just after the publication of the novel, there was a house-party at Taplow Court, the home of the Willy Grenfells, and among the guests were the Asquiths, the Beerbohm Trees and Oscar Wilde. In 1919 Lady Desborough, formerly Mrs. Grenfell, recalled a day in that summer of 28 years before when Wilde had stepped in mid-river from her punt to another in which Mrs. Tree had greeted him with the words "Welcome, little stranger." In view of his weight, and the narrow escape from submersion of both parties, this had caused some merriment. Lady Desborough also remembered that they had played a good game in the evening: composing "an imaginary letter from a woman thanking a man for flowers when she wasn't *quite* certain whether he'd sent them or not!" It was during dinner that Asquith made fun of Wilde's italics, saying that they reminded him of the man who raised his voice in conversation, talking loudly so that everyone should hear what he said.

"How delightful of you, Mr. Asquith, to have noticed that!" Wilde rejoined. "The brilliant phrase, like good wine, needs no bush. But just as the orator marks his good things by a dramatic pause, or by raising or lowering his voice, or by gesture, so the writer marks his epigrams with italics, setting the gems, as it were, like a jeweller—an excusable love of one's art, not all mere vanity, I like to think."

The editor of *The Scots Observer*, which had made one of the most violent attacks on *Dorian Gray*, was W. E. Henley, an embittered and envious being who had surrounded himself with a group of fanatical young admirers, all of whom thought him the most wonderful personality of the age. Undoubtedly he was a first-class journalist and one of the two outstanding editors of the nineties, the other being Frank Harris. Both men could write powerful articles, the main difference between them being that Henley had nothing much to say but said it very well, while Harris had a lot to say which others had said before him but said it better than they. Of Harris we shall hear more in the next chapter. Of Henley all we need to know here is that, being a cripple, he had an exaggerated admiration for physical strength, toughness and endurance, that he exalted Imperialism, went into raptures over Kipling, and was hostile to anyone who thought more highly of art than of conflict. It is hardly necessary to add that Wilde's works were not amongst his bedside books, and that for Wilde himself, as aesthete and revolutionary wit, he entertained feelings which were vocal but unprintable. When at last they met Henley was compelled to change his opinion. There were at least twenty other men present, says Lewis Hind, "all voluble talkers, all ready to shout each other down, all straining at the leash of utterance. But all were content to stand back and let two hold the stage, a duel, a combat of giants—broadsword and rapier. These two were Henley and Oscar Wilde." Though another witness states that it was Wilde who said all the brilliant things at that contest, we are not surprised to learn from W. B. Yeats that Wilde gave Henley more than his due: "I had to strain every nerve to equal that man at all." And we can infer that Henley's broadsword was often used as a bludgeon from Wilde's further statement: "To converse with him is a physical no less than an intellectual recreation." Henley of course would not allow that Wilde had put up a real fight, because that might have implied that Henley had found his match, but he handsomely admitted to Yeats: "No, he is not an aesthete; one soon finds that he is a scholar and a gentleman."

Wilde's novel did him a great deal of harm. Hating the book, especially when they had not read it, people hated the author, and the journalists almost to a man were thenceforward among his bitterest enemies. In the Queensberry case it was used in evidence against him, and there are no more instructive passages in forensic records than his cross-examination on the subject by Edward Carson, a contemporary of his at Trinity College, Dublin:

Carson: You are of opinion, I believe, that there is no such thing as an immoral book?

Wilde: Yes.

Carson: Am I right in saying that you do not consider the effect in creating morality or immorality?

Wilde: Certainly I do not.

Carson: So far as your works are concerned, you pose as not being concerned about morality or immorality?

Wilde: I do not know whether you use the word "pose" in any particular sense.

Carson: It is a favourite word of your own.

Wilde: Is it? I have no pose in this matter. In writing a play or a book I am concerned entirely with literature: that is, with art. I aim not at doing good or evil, but in trying to make a thing that will have some quality or form of beauty or wit.

Carson: After the criticisms that were passed on *Dorian Gray,* was it modified a good deal?

Wilde: No. Additions were made. In one case it was pointed out to me—not in a newspaper or anything of that sort, but by the only critic of the century whose opinion I set high, Mr. Walter Pater—that a certain passage was liable to misconstruction, and I made one addition.

(Wilde admitted the following day, on re-examination by Sir Edward Clarke, that Walter Pater had written several letters to him about *Dorian Gray,* "and in consequence of what he said I modified one passage.")

Carson: This is in your introduction to *Dorian Gray:* "There is no such thing as a moral or an immoral book. Books are well written or badly written. That is all." That expresses your view?

Wilde: My view on art, yes.

Carson: Then I take it that no matter how immoral a book may be, if it is well written it is, in your opinion, a good book?

Wilde: Yes; if it were well written so as to produce a sense of beauty, which is the highest sense of which a human being can be capable. If it were badly written it would produce a sense of disgust.

Carson: Then a well-written book putting forward perverted moral views may be a good book?

Wilde: No work of art ever puts forward views. Views belong to people who are not artists.

Carson: A perverted novel might be a good book?

Wilde: I do not know what you mean by a perverted novel.

Carson: Then I will suggest *Dorian Gray* as open to the interpretation of being such a novel.

Wilde: That could only be to brutes and illiterates. The views of Philistines on art are incalculably stupid.

Carson: An illiterate person reading *Dorian Gray* might consider it such a novel?

Wilde: The views of illiterates on art are unaccountable. I am concerned only with my view of art. I don't care twopence what other people think of it.

Carson: The majority of persons would come under your definition of Philistines and illiterates?

Wilde: I have found wonderful exceptions.

Carson: Do you think the majority of people live up to the position you are giving us?

Wilde: I am afraid they are not cultivated enough.

Carson: Not cultivated enough to draw the distinction between a good book and a bad book?

Wilde: Certainly not.

Carson: The affection and love of the artist for Dorian Gray might lead an ordinary individual to believe that it might have a certain tendency?

Wilde: I have no knowledge of the views of ordinary individuals.

Carson: You did not prevent the ordinary individual from buying your book?

Wilde: I have never discouraged him.

(Counsel then read a long extract from *Dorian Gray* using the Lippincott version, which describes the meeting between Dorian and the artist, Basil Hallward.)

Carson: Now I ask you, Mr. Wilde, do you consider that description of the feeling of one man towards another, a youth just grown up, was a proper or an improper feeling?

Wilde: I think it is the most perfect description of what an artist would feel on meeting a beautiful personality that was in some way necessary to his art and his life.

Carson: You think that is a feeling a young man should have towards another?

Wilde: Yes, as an artist.

(Counsel read another extract. Wilde asked for a copy, and was given one of the complete edition in book form. Carson, in calling his attention to the place, remarked "I believe it was left out in the purged edition.")

Wilde: I do not call it purged.

Carson: Yes, I know that; but we will see. (Counsel read a further extract.) Do you mean to say that that passage describes the natural feeling of one man towards another?

Wilde: It would be the influence produced on an artist by a beautiful personality.

Carson: A beautiful person?

Wilde: I said "a beautiful personality." You can describe it as you like. Dorian Gray was a most remarkable personality.

Carson: May I take it that you, as an artist, have never known the feeling described here?

Wilde: I have never allowed any personality to dominate my art.

Carson: Then you have never known the feeling you describe?

Wilde: No; it is a work of fiction.

Carson: So far as you are concerned you have no experience as to its being a natural feeling?

Wilde: I think it is perfectly natural for any artist to admire intensely and love a young man. It is an incident in the life of almost every artist.

Carson: But let us go over it phrase by phrase. "I quite admit that I adored you madly." What do you say to that? Have you ever adored a young man madly?

Wilde: No; not madly. I prefer love; that is a higher form.

Carson: Never mind about that. Let us keep down to the level we are at now.

Wilde: I have never given adoration to anybody except myself.

Carson: I suppose you think that a very smart thing?

Wilde: Not at all.

Carson: Then you never had that feeling?

Wilde: No; the whole idea was borrowed from Shakespeare, I regret to say; yes, from Shakespeare's sonnets.

Carson: I believe you have written an article to show that Shakespeare's sonnets were suggestive of unnatural vice?

Wilde: On the contrary, I have written an article to show that they are not. I objected to such a perversion being put upon Shakespeare.

Carson (continuing to read): "I adored you extravagantly—"

Wilde: Do you mean financially?

Carson: Oh, yes, financially. Do you think we are talking about finance?

Wilde: I do not think you know what you are talking about.

Carson: Don't you? Well, I hope I shall make myself very plain before I have done. "I was jealous of everyone to whom you spoke." Have you ever been jealous of a young man?

Wilde: Never in my life.

Carson: "I wanted to have you all to myself." Did you ever have that feeling?

Wilde: No; I should consider it an intense nuisance, an intense bore.

Carson: "I grew afraid that the world would know of my idolatry." Why should you grow afraid that the world should know of it?

Wilde: Because there are people in the world who cannot understand the intense devotion, affection and admiration that an artist can feel for a wonderful and beautiful personality. These are the conditions under which we live. I regret them.

Carson: These unfortunate people, that have not the high understanding that you have, might put it down to something wrong?

Wilde: Undoubtedly; to any point they chose. I am not concerned with the ignorance of others. I have a great passion to civilise the community.

Carson: In another passage Dorian Gray received a book. Was the book to which you refer a moral book?

Wilde: Not well written; but it gave me an idea.

(Pressed as to whether the book concerned had a certain tendency, Wilde declined with some warmth to be cross-examined upon the work of another artist. It was, he said "an impertinence and a vulgarity." He admitted that he had had in mind *A Rebours* by Huysmans. Counsel wanted to elicit Wilde's view as to the morality of that book, but Sir Edward Clarke succeeded, on appeal to the judge, in stopping further reference to it. Counsel then quoted yet another extract from the Lippincott version of *Dorian Gray*, in which the artist tells Dorian of the scandals about him and asks him "Why is your friendship so fateful to young men?" In reply to the question as to whether the passage in its ordinary meaning did not suggest a certain charge, Wilde said that it described Dorian Gray as a man of very corrupt influence, though there was no statement as to the nature of his influence. "But as a matter of fact," he added, "I do not think that one person influences another, nor do I think there is any bad influence in the world.")

Carson: A man never corrupts a youth?

Wilde: I think not.

Carson: Nothing he could do would corrupt him?

Wilde: If you are talking of separate ages——

Carson: No, sir, I am talking common sense.

Wilde: I do not think one person influences another.

Carson: You do not think that flattering a young man, making love to him in fact, would be likely to corrupt him?

Wilde: No.

Wilde once confessed that he liked to amuse the mob, to infuriate the respectable middle classes, and to fascinate the aristocrats. Up to the beginning of 1891 his efforts had been crowned with success, but in February of that year his essay *The Soul of Man Under Socialism* came out in *The Fortnightly Review*, and the aristocrats were no longer fascinated, though he was much too valuable an acquisition at house-parties and dinner-parties to be struck off the lists of eligible guests at Mayfair mansions and country castles.

The origin of that remarkable essay was an address on socialism by Bernard Shaw in Westminster. Wilde went to the meeting and spoke; after which he decided to put his faith on paper. The personal relationship between these two men, who are now more widely known and appreciated on the continent of Europe than any writer of the English language except Shakespeare, has an interest which could only be surpassed by the discovery of evidence concerning Shakespeare's relationship with an equally famous contemporary, if there were such a person. The extraordinary fact of two Irishmen, born within two years of one another, coming to London and winning an unexampled notoriety with the aid of their wit, humour and personal oddity, is sufficiently curious; but when it is added that they were two of the greatest personalities in literary history, and further that they were utterly dissimilar by nature in nearly every respect, the story of their impact on one another has an unique fascination. Shaw himself would have been our sole witness if I had not by a stroke of luck discovered one other.

Although, according to themselves, their motives were different, each of them went through a fancy-dress phase in public, Wilde claiming beauty as his object when he appeared as an aesthete, Shaw claiming hygiene as his object when he appeared in a suit of brown knitted wool, combining jacket, waistcoat and trousers all in one piece, the creation of a German doctor named Jaeger. "Oh, Shaw!—that's the man who smokes the Jaeger cigarettes," someone reported Wilde as saying. They first met at one of Lady Wilde's at-homes, when Wilde "came and spoke to me with an evident intention of being specially kind to me," Shaw relates. "We put each other out frightfully; and this odd difficulty persisted between us to the very last . . ." They met again in '86 at Arthur Macmurdo's house in Fitzroy Street, where, Ernest Rhys tells us, they "had a characteristic passage of arms, both gay and bitter," but Rhys could remember nothing more when I applied for details. Another meeting was near the stage door of the Haymarket Theatre, "at which our queer shyness of one another made our resolutely cordial and appreciative conversation so difficult that our final laugh and shake-hands was almost a reciprocal confession." Shaw amplified this in conversation with me: "The press treated both of us as jokes; he was Oscar the comic, I was G.B.S. the clown. The result was that we treated one another with elaborate courtesy, 'mistering' each other with such formality and regularity that we never got on familiar terms, and our relationship was really unendurable for both of us."

Fortunately they did spend one "really pleasant afternoon" together, when their meeting was a complete success and Shaw was able to understand why William Morris, "when he was dying slowly, enjoyed a visit from Wilde more than from anybody else." They ran into each other at a naval exhibition in Chelsea. Wilde was in a tweed suit and low hat, and admitted that he was going to spend a restful afternoon at Rosherville Gardens away from social engagements. As Shaw was off on a similar errand to escape from work, they were both in holiday mood. "It was my sole experience of Oscar's wonderful gift as a raconteur . . . Wilde and I got on extraordinarily well on this occasion. I had not to talk myself, but to listen to a man telling me stories better than I could have told them . . . And he had an audience on whom not one of his subtlest effects was lost." One story in particular remained in Shaw's memory. The version he gave me varies slightly from the one he gave to Frank Harris:

"Oscar's story was of a young man who invented a theatre stall which economised space by ingenious contrivances which were all described. A friend of his invited twenty millionaires to meet him at dinner so that he might interest them in the invention. The young man demonstrated that by his invention a theatre holding six hundred people could be made to accommodate a thousand; at which point the millionaires were eager and ready to make his fortune. Unfortunately he went on to calculate the annual gain in all the theatres and concert halls in the world; then in all the church offertories, and so on, piling up the pecuniary, moral and religious effects of the invention, until at the end of an hour he had estimated a profit of several thousand millions, plus the millennium: the climax of course being that the millionaires folded their tents and silently stole away, leaving the ruined inventor a marked man for life."

The contrast between Wilde and Shaw as companions is illustrated by something I heard from Robert Ross:

"I once met Shaw in Chartres Cathedral. He asked me to take him round and tell him everything I knew about the stained-glass windows. By dint of relentless examination he pumped me dry of every scrap of information I possessed, and at the end of an hour I was fit only for a Turkish bath and alcoholic stimulants. Now Oscar would have told me wonderful stories about those windows—all made up on the spur of the moment of course—and at the end of an hour I should still have been begging for more."

Apart from their usual diffidence in one another's company, Shaw was hostile to what he considered Wilde's snobbery, and, being Irish himself, impervious to his charm. But he greatly admired and benefited from Wilde's method of shattering conventional morality with a phrase; and when he tried to get several literary men, "all heroic rebels and sceptics on paper," to sign a memorial asking for the reprieve of the Chicago anarchists, the only signature he got was Wilde's: "It was a completely disinterested act on his part; and it secured my distinguished consideration for him for the rest of his life." Equally, Wilde always made a point of recognising Shaw as a person of consequence at a time when it was customary to treat him as a jester; and I have failed to discover who first attributed to Wilde the statement that Shaw "has not an enemy in the world, and none of his friends like him." I am not at all sure that G.B.S. did not spot the following in *Dorian Gray* and in an impish moment make the necessary adaptation: "Ernest Harrowden, one of those middle-aged mediocrities so common in London clubs, who have no enemies, but are thoroughly disliked by their friends." Wilde was much too shrewd a judge to make such a singularly inappropriate summary of Shaw, whose printed criticisms made him thousands of enemies and who was only disliked by people who did not know him. What has not been made public before is that Wilde admired Shaw's early works. He described *The Quintessence of Ibsenism* as "such a delight to me that I constantly take it up, and always find it stimulating and refreshing." England, he said, was a land of intellectual fogs, and Shaw had done much to clear the air. He even admired "the horrible flesh and blood" of Shaw's "creatures" in *Widowers' Houses*, the preface to which he considered "a real masterpiece of trenchant writing and caustic wit and dramatic instinct." So, however awkward their personal relationship, each of them had a proper appreciation of the other's genius.

The sole record by an onlooker of a meeting between the two was sent me by Sir Bernard Partridge:

"I was present at their meeting in the rooms of the late Fitzgerald Molloy in Red Lion Square. There were only the four of us. Shaw was on the threshold of his career; Oscar had already 'arrived.' But for once he was content to listen, and Shaw, delighted to meet such a listener, let himself go. His subject was a magazine, the founding of which he had in mind, and he held forth at great length on its scope and outlook. When he came to a halt, Oscar said 'That has all been most interesting, Mr. Shaw; but there's one point you haven't mentioned, and an all-important one—you haven't told us the *title* of your magazine.' 'Oh, as for that,' said Shaw, 'what I'd want to do would be to impress my own personality on the public—I'd call it *Shaw's Magazine*: Shaw—Shaw—Shaw!': and he banged his fist on the table. 'Yes,' said Oscar, *'and how would you spell it?'* Shaw joined heartily in our laughter against him."

Wilde's essay on *The Soul of Man Under Socialism* may have been prompted by a Shavian lecture, but his whole trend of thought was antagonistic to the Webbshavian deification of the state; and as our age has suffered terribly from state-worship, Wilde's attitude now appears more intelligent, more humane, more vital, and more imaginative than the Marx-Fabian creed. For once in a way, too, Wilde was solely concerned with what he was saying, not with how he was saying it, so he ceased to be "literary" and wrote literature. He had the instinct of genius for stating truths without having to consult text-books; and no one has ever de-canted so much humbug in so few and such witty phrases. In this essay more than anywhere else in his work he symbolised the spirit of youth's revolt against age, of frivolity against decorum, of irreverence against acceptance, of anarchy against institutionalism, of the individual against society, of beauty against ugliness, of art against commerce, of freedom against convention. In speaking for the rebellious spirits of his own age, he spoke for those of all ages, which explains his appeal to the intelligent youth of every generation. This is largely because he maintained the outlook of a boy, though mentally a most precocious one, throughout his life, and could find effortless expression for the feelings and thoughts of the young. Even his appearance was that of an oversized boy: physically and mentally he never reached the crusty disillusioned age. Listen to him on the socialistic dream of all busy-bodies and bureaucrats:

"If the Socialism is Authoritarian; if there are Governments armed with economic power as they are now with political power; if, in a word, we are to have Industrial Tyrannies, then the last state of man will be worse than the first."

"It is to be regretted that a portion of our community should be practically in slavery, but to propose to solve the problem by enslaving the entire community is childish."

"While to the claims of charity a man may yield and yet be free, to the claims of conformity no man may yield and remain free at all."

"Wherever there is a man who exercises authority, there is a man who resists authority."

"All authority is quite degrading. It degrades those who exercise it, and it degrades those over whom it is exercised."

"Whenever a community . . . or a government of any kind, attempts to dictate to the artist what he is to do, Art either entirely vanishes, or becomes stereotyped, or degenerates into a low and ignoble form of craft."

"The form of government that is most suitable to the artist is no government at all."

A good deal of the essay, which by the way should have been called *The Soul of Man Above Socialism*, deals with questions concerning art and the artist, because Wilde recognised, what very few people have yet discovered, that the arts are the only civilising influences in the world, and that without them people are barbarians. He knew, as no one else in his age knew except perhaps Ruskin, that an aesthetic education, which humanises people, is far more important even for politicians than an economic education, which does the opposite; and since institutions are made for man, not man for institutions, he advocated socialism solely because he believed that it would lead to individualism, an intensification of which was also the effect of art. Property, he said, should be abolished because possessions cramped individuality: "The true perfection of man lies, not in what man has, but in what man is." Therefore "in the interest of the rich we must get rid of property." Poverty too should be abolished because it debased people and retarded their individual development: "There is only one class in the community that thinks more about money than the rich, and that is the poor." The best among the poor were never grateful for charity: "They are ungrateful, discontented, disobedient and rebellious. They are quite right to be so." "A man who would not be discontented with such surroundings and such a low mode of life would be a perfect brute." "Starvation, and not sin, is the parent of modern crime." "It is through disobedience that progress has been made, through disobedience and through rebellion." "To recommend thrift to the poor is both grotesque and insulting. It is like advising a man who is starving to eat less . . . Man should not be ready to show that he can live like a badly fed animal. He should . . . either steal or go on the rates . . . It is safer to beg than to take, but it is finer to take than to beg." "As for the virtuous poor, one can pity them, of course, but one cannot possibly admire them." Their existence, however, called forth a class of people whom many regarded as the pests of society: "Agitators are a set of interfering, meddling people, who come down to some perfectly contented class of the community and sow the seeds of discontent amongst them. That is the reason why agitators are so absolutely necessary." The need for agitation had hindered the growth of the best natures: "Most personalities have been obliged to be rebels. Half their strength has been wasted in friction."

He dismisses in a sentence the nonsense talked about the dignity of manual labour: "Man is made for something better than disturbing dirt." In his view machinery must do all the dull and dirty work, the state's job being the manufacture and distribution of the various commodities. Machines must be the slaves, not as at present the competitors, of human beings; and the state should be the servant, not the master, of mankind. "Cultivated leisure is the aim of man." There is no doubt whatever that machines can produce enough and to spare for everybody, and that the state can make an equitable distribution of their products; but the drawback to all perfectibility plans for the universe lies in the imperfectibility of man, and the undeniable fact that the worst types of men, who can always be depended upon to abuse whatever system is in operation, are the very types which inevitably gravitate towards power and politics. It is difficult to conceive a state of society in which a sufficient number of disinterested and civilised and imaginative people would, even if given the chance, voluntarily undertake what would be to them the suffocating boredom of government. Wilde, more intelligent than other socialists, seems to feel that there is a snag somewhere, but he brushes it aside and forges gaily ahead: "It will, of course, be said that such a scheme as is set forth here is quite unpractical, and goes against human nature. This is perfectly true. It is unpractical, and it goes against human nature. This is why it is worth carrying out, and that is why one proposes it." In any case there was no harm in trying, for "all the results of the mistakes of governments are quite admirable," and "A map of the world that does not include Utopia is not worth even glancing at, for it leaves out the one country at which Humanity is always landing. And when Humanity lands there, it looks out, and, seeing a better country, sets sail. Progress is the realisation of Utopias."

The people at whose tables he dined were entirely satisfied with things as they were, and had no wish to set sail for any utopia. The essay did him a greater disservice with the governing classes than anything else he could have said or done, and at a time when they might have lent him a helping hand they turned a cold shoulder.

CHAPTER ELEVEN

THE MAN ·

PICTURE a tall, broad, thick-set, slow-moving man, inclined to corpulence; with a large bloodless coarse-skinned face, clean-shaven at a time when moustaches were in vogue, a powerful well-shaped nose, thick purple-tinged sensual lips, long crowded uneven discoloured teeth, fleshy cheeks, heavy jaw, firm mouth, fine brow, long dark carefully-waved hair, and expressive heavy-lidded eyes. It was a proconsular face, masklike at moments of introspection, lit up in conversation by a smile which radiated good-will. The dominant expression was one of humour, and sometimes he appeared to be smiling ironically at himself, the critic in him being entertained by the actor. His hands were fat and flabby; his handshake lacked grip, and at a first encounter one recoiled from its plushy limpness, but this aversion was soon overcome when he began to talk, for his genuine kindliness and desire to please made one forget what was unpleasant in his physical appearance and contact, gave charm to his manners, and grace to his precision of speech. The first sight of him affected people in various ways. Some could hardly restrain their laughter, others felt hostile, a few were afflicted with "the creeps," many were conscious of being uneasy; but except for a small minority who could never recover from the first sensation of distaste and so kept out of his way, both sexes found him irresistible, and to the young men of his time, says W. B. Yeats, he was like a triumphant and audacious figure from another age. There was nothing extraordinary about his mannerisms and clothes during the period at which we are picturing him. It was noticed that when talking he frequently put a bent forefinger over his mouth, which showed that he was conscious of his unattractive teeth. Gestures, usually slight, always effective, gave significance to his speech. He wore the conventional garb of the day, with flowers, preferably violets, in the buttonhole of his tightly-fitting frockcoat. A scarab ring adorned one finger, and he carried an old-world stick, but, unlike Whistler, he aimed at no eccentricities of dress, his clothes being those of a man of fashion, though in his case, largely because of his massive build and un-

English face, the fashion seemed a little over-emphasised. Such was the external Oscar Wilde from, roughly, the early part of 1885 to the beginning of 1892. Let us now explore beneath that smiling, self-confident, somewhat exotic, at first repellent surface.

It must have been mainly due to his perennial boyishness that Wilde never experienced a day's unhappiness until he was forty years old; and although he was to know what it felt like to be wretched from his forty-first year onwards, his resilience was such that he could not remain in the depths for many hours at a time. Throughout life the chief strand in his nature, which explains his social success and his effect on others, was an invincible happiness. The mark of a happy man is that he is more interested in other people or other things than in himself; and so we find the happiest natures amongst painters, scientists, sculptors, architects, and those writers and composers whose absorption in their themes transcends self-absorption. Contrary to the usual belief the unhappiest among mankind are those whose religion encourages them to be concerned with their souls' salvation, a condition which inflames their egotism and dehumanises them. Wilde was a life-lover, and his interest in himself, which was considerable, was dependent on his interest in the world about him, which was immeasurable. With that curious sixth sense which foretold his ruin, he once wrote:

> But strange that I was not told
>   That the brain can hold
> In a tiny ivory cell
>   God's heaven and hell.

Yet this was merely the destiny he liked to dramatise, and hell was a state of mind unrealised by him until he appealed to the law to protect him from a man whose spiritual home was in hell. Wilde's natural feeling was expressed in a casual remark: "Give me *The Winter's Tale*—'Daffodils that come before the swallow dares'—but not *King Lear*. What is *King Lear* but poor life staggering in the fog?" Happiness, he felt, was synonymous with virtue: "When we are happy we are always good, but when we are good we are not always happy . . . To be good is to be in harmony with oneself. Discord is to be forced to be in harmony with others."

Because of his innate happiness he never lost his sense of the miraculous in everyday life. One day was not a mere repetition of another: he awoke each morning "into something rich and strange"; the novelty of existence did not wear off. "The season with its red roses of pleasure has absorbed me quite," he told a friend, "and I have almost forgotten how to write a letter." This was a bare statement of fact; he enjoyed every minute of his life, because he mentally created a fresh universe with every minute. "The only horrible thing in the world is *ennui*. That is the one sin for which there is no forgiveness." He rejoiced with those who rejoiced, but he did not weep with those who wept: he tried to laugh them out of their tears. "All sympathy is fine," he would say, "but sympathy with suffering is the least fine mode. There is in it a certain element of terror for our own safety." "One should sympathise with the colour, the beauty, the joy of life. The less said about life's sores the better." He lived up to this principle, and no one ever heard him complain of his state of health, or even refer to his physical condition, until near the end of his life. Beauty was his religion, and so responsive to it was he that, while pathos left him unmoved, beauty brought tears to his eyes. "To me beauty is the wonder of wonders," he said. "It is only shallow people who do not judge by appearances. The true mystery of the world is the visible, not the invisible." As we have seen, he derived an exquisite pleasure even from the sounds of syllables, and in conversation would dwell on such words as "vermilion," "narcissus," "amber," "crimson," pronouncing them as if tasting them. Vincent O'Sullivan once suggested to him that his real reason for writing plays was a desire for the immediate applause. "Yes, the immediate applause," he replied. "What a charming phrase of yours!". . . he savoured it again . . . "the immediate applause." He loved to roll on his tongue such titles as "The Marquess of Dimmesdale," but took no pleasure in saying "The Duke of York"; and certain words, those ending with "ette" for example, gave him physical discomfort. Equally he could not endure ugly surroundings. Once he called to see Sherard, who was then living in rooms off the Strand, and was asked to wait downstairs in the drawing-room. Three minutes of its furniture, pictures and ornaments saw the limit of his staying-power, and Sherard heard him calling plaintively from the landing "Do let me come up, Robert, or I shall have to sit on the steps. If I stay a moment longer in that drawing-room, I shall become very ill." He exercised a considerable influence on furniture, ornaments, wall-paper, window-curtains, women's clothes, and the rest of it; and by the nineties the restrained decorative schemes of William Morris, Ford Madox Brown and the pre-Raphaelites had given place to the rich brocades, rose-coloured tinted ceilings, yellow satins, luminous jewels and lavish flowers admired by Wilde. People now question the merits of his innovations, which have had strange developments. Their disagreement would merely have confirmed him in the impeccability of his taste; but as, in his view, time transforms the individuality of human beings so completely that the man of to-day is a totally different being from the man of seven years ago and should not be held responsible for his earlier opinions and acts, we may conclude that he would have encouraged about seven revolutions in taste between his day and ours.

Happy men are usually lazy; they do not have to find distraction in work or sport; they have no internal disquiet to allay; and so, if mentally active, they prefer to fulfil themselves in conversation and contemplation, if mentally inactive they prefer to be comatose. Wilde's mental activity was only equalled by his physical laziness. In a country where games and sports are thought necessary to salvation, his indifference to them outraged his contemporaries. "Football is all very well as a game for rough girls, but it is hardly suitable for delicate boys," he informed a pompous schoolmaster. And when asked at a country-house whether he ever took any exercise at all, he replied "I am afraid I play no outdoor games, except . . . yes . . . except dominoes. I have sometimes played dominoes outside French cafés." His favourite form of exercise was to lie on a sofa, thinking, or to sit at a table, talking. "One's real life is so often the life that one does not lead," he wrote when still in his twenties, and certainly he lived his real life in the imagination. After chatting for hours with a friend, he suddenly said "I ought not to be doing this. I ought to be putting black upon white—black upon white." But he did not really think so, his opinion being that hard work was simply the refuge of people who had nothing better to do. He had a poor view of industry, in his case the technical drudgery of putting black upon white, and he derided the notion that the acquisition of knowledge was valuable in itself or that there was something healthy and virtuous in physical toil. "The mind of the thoroughly well-informed man is a dreadful thing," he declared. "It is like a bric-a-brac shop, all monsters and dust, with everything priced above its proper value." "Examinations are pure humbug from beginning to end. If a man is a gentleman he knows quite enough, and if he is not a gentleman whatever he knows is bad for him." People were so industrious, he said, that they were absolutely stupid. "The sure way of knowing nothing about life is to try to make oneself useful." And two years in prison did not shake his view: "To chop wood with any advantage to oneself or profit to others, one should not be able to describe the process . . . The natural life is the unconscious life . . . If I spend my future life reading Baudelaire in a café, I shall be leading a more natural life than if I take to hedger's work or plant cacao in mud-swamps." Except when he suffered from a rush of words to the pen, and gravely catalogued the names of inanimate objects from other people's books because they came well off the tongue and looked agreeable in print, his writings display a pleasing otiosity. "How exquisite these single daffodils are!" says one of the young talkers in *Intentions*. "They seem to be made of amber and cool ivory. They are like Greek things of the best period." A more industrious and less imaginative writer would have taken more trouble over the period.

Along with his laziness went a love of luxury. His nature was apolaustic, and the things he enjoyed were usually expensive. "We live in an age when unnecessary things are our only necessities," he claimed. A connoisseur of wine and food, and loving the best of both, he could yet be contented with inexpensive meals when cash was short, if the cooking was good and the cellar not indifferent; he could even adapt himself to rough fare in uncomfortable surroundings if the company was exhilarating, just as he would laugh at bad jokes when good ones were lacking, so strong was his wish to please and his love of pleasure. He rarely complained of the food set before him, though Sir Bernard Partridge tells me of "a little dinner in Tite Street with Oscar and his wife—he and I were going on to the Lyric Club afterwards. A chicken was brought in: Oscar took up the carvers and tried to cut a wing; laid them down again wearily, and said 'Constance, why do you give me these . . . pedestrians . . . to eat?'" One dish only he found quite unpalatable. He was lunching with Lord Alfred Douglas at some second-rate restaurant in Torquay. "A nice piece of cod?" suggested the waiter. "I hardly think cod is a very nice fish, is it?" said Wilde; then, seeing that the waiter was pained, he hurried on "Oh, no doubt the cod is a splendid swimmer, admirable for swimming purposes, but not for eating." The waiter, appreciating the joke, was mollified. Referring one day to Kipling's *Captains Courageous*, which describes a lad's adventures among the cod fishers off the Banks of Newfoundland, Wilde said "I really don't know why an author should write a book about codfishing . . . but perhaps," he added ruminatively, "it is because I never eat cod."

Until he began to make a lot of money with his plays he used often to patronise the Florence Restaurant in Rupert Street, where dinner could be had for 2*s*. Other favourite resorts, funds permitting, were Kettner's and the Café Royal; and at one time he was frequently to be seen at a public house called "The Crown" in Charing Cross Road, where Lionel Johnson, Ernest Dowson, Stewart Headlam, George Moore, Charles Conder and other youthful spirits met together after visiting a theatre or music hall. But when his financial condition lightened, his bills became heavier. Once he felt called upon to explain his indulgence: "When I am in trouble, eating is the only thing that consoles me. Indeed, when I am in really great trouble, as anyone who knows me intimately will tell you, I refuse everything except food and drink," which was received so well that he reserved it for a play. "Late suppers are the only thing my doctor allows me," was another explanation. He did not approve of drunkenness, and when asked during the Queensberry case whether his guests ever drank too much he replied "I should not limit their consumption, but I should consider it extremely vulgar for anyone to take too much wine at table." Another passage from his cross-examination is of interest here:

Carson: Do you drink champagne yourself?

Wilde: Yes; iced champagne is a favourite drink of mine—strongly against my doctor's orders.

Carson: Never mind your doctor's orders.

Wilde: I never do.

His feeling with regard to eating and drinking was summed up when "Enough is as good as a feast" was quoted by someone. "Moderation is a fatal thing," said he. "Enough is as bad as a meal. More than enough is as good as a feast."

Another indulgence was cigarette-smoking. Sherard reports that in Tite Street he used to carry a box of cigarettes with him from room to room, and that the box was the size of a large biscuit-tin. Their price rose with his income, but regardless of cost he never smoked them more than half-way through. He smoked in bed, and he smoked in his bath, inhaling and exhaling with quiet contentment. It seems that the more cigarettes he smoked the less of them he smoked, for Nellie Melba once counted six cases, gold, silver and leather, which he produced from different pockets, the reason for so many receptacles being that he would take two puffs of each cigarette, throw it away, and light another five minutes later; which perhaps explains his aphorism: "A cigarette is the perfect type of a perfect pleasure. It is exquisite, and it leaves one unsatisfied. What more can one want?"

More expensive still was his taste for hansom cabs. He never walked if he could help it, and he liked to keep a cab in constant attendance, though he could only afford to do so on special occasions until the production of his first modern comedy:

Carson: Is Park Walk about ten minutes walk from Tite Street?

Wilde: I don't know. I never walk.

Carson: I suppose when you pay visits you always take a cab?

Wilde: Always.

Carson: And if you visited you would leave the cab outside?

Wilde: If it were a good cab.

It is needless to add that Wilde was very popular with cabbies, who knew that they would not have to leave the West End of London and could count on regular meals and generous tips when he was their passenger. After his editorial experience he seldom went far from the fashionable quarter of the town. "I live in the East End because there the people don't wear masks," explained Olive Schreiner. "And I live in the West End because there they do," explained Oscar Wilde. As for life in the country, "they get up early because they have so much to do, and go to bed early because they have so little to think about," he complained. "There has not been a scandal in the neighbourhood since the time of Queen Elizabeth, and consequently they all fall asleep after dinner."

His liking for the good things of life, coupled with his romantic outlook, will account for what many have called his snobbery. "Every Irishman loves an aristocrat," says Oliver St. John Gogarty, who admits that he dearly loves a lord. This affection for the peerage is not peculiar to Irishmen, though the inhabitants of bullied, conquered and occupied countries are especially prone to it. There was not, however, a particle of sycophancy in Wilde's attitude to the English nobility, which was due to his love of great names that had resounded through history, to his fondness for luxury, spacious living, indolence, good manners and good cooking. Walking through the lofty rooms of the Duke of Westminster's London house one day, he made a magnificent gesture and said to Le Gallienne "Ah, Richard! this is how a gentleman should live." This aspect is emphasised by the reply W. B. Yeats made to Hugh Kingsmill, who had asked whether Wilde was a snob: "No, I would not say that. England is a strange country to the Irish. To Wilde the aristocrats of England were like the nobles of Bagdad." (Yeats pronounced it "Bahgdahd.") In his naif way Wilde dramatised the dukes and earls and marquises and their female counterparts with whom he was acquainted, throwing a romantic halo about them and seeing them as poetic creations. This required a great deal of imagination, but his childish side enabled him to bring it off. Unfortunately, as we shall hear, the unreal picture he formed in his mind was to be a leading factor in his downfall; but until he allowed his imagination to run away with him, his humour was constantly breaking into his dream.

It must be remembered that he was thoroughly spoilt by the aristocracy. He frequently stayed at Clumber with the Duke of Newcastle, and was a welcome visitor at the town and country houses of half the nobility. At the height of his vogue "To meet Mr. Oscar Wilde" was put on the most exclusive invitation cards. But this did not prevent him from saying, and from printing in a novel as well as a play, "The 'Peerage' is the one book a young man about town should know thoroughly, and it is the best thing in fiction the English have ever done." Lord Alfred Douglas assures us that Wilde was "entirely natural, and said, utterly without fear or 'respect of persons,' exactly what he thought or meant to express on any given occasion." To take two examples. He was talking to somebody at a big social crush when a noble quidnunc came up behind him, slapped him on the back and said "Why, Oscar, you are getting fatter and fatter!" Without turning round Wilde replied "And you are getting ruder and ruder," and continued his conversation. Explaining his inability to keep an appointment at some lordly establishment, he wrote "I am prevented from coming owing to a subsequent engagement." He never boasted of his acquaintanceship with princes or peers, though often spoke of his friendship with great writers, and would far rather have dined with Morris than with a marquis. It was his romantic nature, not his sense of values, that obliged him, whenever he gave an unmistakable self-portrait in his works, to raise himself to the peerage, becoming Lord Henry Wotton in *Dorian Gray*, Lord Illingworth in *A Woman of No Importance*, and Lord Goring in *An Ideal Husband*. When a friend twitted him over the number of titled characters in his plays, he did not defend his practice but merely said "You would permit at least a Colonial Knight? . . . I think you must allow me a Colonial Knight in my next play."

There was one displeasing side to his innocent love of rank: he attached an exaggerated importance to his own conception of how people ought to behave, and even lectured those who did not live up to it. Good manners, which imply a consideration for the feelings of others, are the cement which holds society together and makes social intercourse possible; they are the mark of a civilized people, and Wilde was quite justified in thinking them more important than good morals. But he should have known that good manners oblige a man not to take notice of bad manners. When anyone in his company behaved in an indecorous manner, or displayed what in his eyes was ill-breeding, he was usually ready with a reproof, and even went so far as to correct a man's pronunciation. Vincent O'Sullivan recounts the rather painful episode of Wilde telling a young Frenchman that he was eating oysters in the wrong way. Although Wilde tried to smooth the matter over, the boy was upset and did not enjoy his meal. But as this happened after Wilde's release from prison, it is charitable to suppose that he was recalling the days when he dined with people who knew how to eat oysters,

and merely wished to remind others of his past. That he could tolerate behaviour repugnant to him was shown when Charles Conder, drunk at the
time, bared his arm and plunged a pin up to the head in a muscle, repeating
the performance on his leg, without evincing any concern. "How interested
Baudelaire would have been!" was Wilde's sole comment.

Shaw accuses Wilde of snobbery in the worse sense: of writing about T. P.
O'Connor "with deliberate, studied, wounding insolence, with his Merrion
Square Protestant pretentiousness in full cry against the Catholic," and further
of declaiming against the vulgarity of the British journalist in a manner
that displayed "the odious class feeling that is itself the vilest vulgarity." As
usual with Shaw's estimates of human beings, whether favourable or unfavourable, it is advisable to hear the other side. O'Connor published some
verses in *The Sunday Sun*, attributing them to Wilde, who wrote to deny
that they were his. Instead of apologising for his error, O'Connor excused
himself on the ground that the verses might have been some of Wilde's
early work. Naturally incensed, Wilde wrote to *The Pall Mall Gazette* complaining of the treatment accorded him. Under the circumstances there was
nothing in his letters that should have aroused the indignation of anyone,
except perhaps O'Connor, who got what he deserved. There was also no
"odious class feeling" behind Wilde's attack on British journalists. From
the beginning to the end of his public life he was sneered at and insulted by
the greater part of the press, *Punch* being the worst offender. He did not
seem to mind; and what he said of the newspapers would have been echoed
by every intelligent person of his time, irrespective of class:

"Journalism justifies its own existence by the great Darwinian principle
of the survival of the vulgarest."

"Instead of monopolising the seat of judgment, journalism should be apologising in the dock."

"The newspapers chronicle with degrading avidity the sins of the second-
rate, and with the conscientiousness of the illiterate give us accurate and
prosaic details of the doings of people of absolutely no interest whatever."

"What is behind the leading-article but prejudice, stupidity, cant and
twaddle?"

"In old days men had the rack. Now they have the press."

"In centuries before ours the public nailed the ears of journalists to the
pump. That was quite hideous. In this century journalists have nailed their
own ears to the keyhole. That is much worse."

As a matter of sober fact, no man was ever more free from malice than
Wilde, who could satirise a species but never an individual. The only man

of genius in English literary history who can be compared with him in this respect is Sydney Smith. Even Henry Fielding, on the whole the finest character among our men of letters, must be excluded on account of his Richardson and Walpole lampoons. Wholly lacking in rancour himself, Wilde never understood the envy and hatred that talent feels for genius, and appears to have regarded the examples that came to his notice as among the unaccountable freaks of human nature, sad if slightly comical. Sherard says that he spoke of his enemies, those who had pursued him with venom and helped to encompass his downfall, with tolerance, serenity and condonation, and that "he never had one bitter word for the many friends who betrayed him." He did not even return good for evil with the object of humiliating the man who had maltreated him and of raising himself in his own or the other's esteem: he was simply a kind-hearted human being, in whom there was no spite. One day he was grossly insulted in a London club by a journalist, who later appealed to him for help. He sent a considerable sum of money. O'Sullivan heard of this action from a man who did not like Wilde but knew of the case.

His generosity whether giving his time, his trouble, his ideas or his money, was only limited by mental prostration and financial exhaustion. Although he said "Young people nowadays imagine that money is everything . . . and when they grow older they know it," he never invested a penny in his life and gave money, if he had some to give, to anyone who asked for it. As one would expect, cash with him took the place of coloured counters with children. Sending a checque to William Rothenstein, he wrote: "Enclosed is an absurdly coloured thing, which foolish bankers take in exchange and for which they give, in reckless moments, gold, both yellow and red." He had no liking for professional philanthropy, and used to tell a story about a certain man who spent twenty years of his life trying to get some grievance redressed or some unjust law altered: "Finally he succeeded, and nothing could exceed his disappointment. He had absolutely nothing to do, almost died of *ennui*, and became a confirmed misanthrope." Lord Goring in *An Ideal Husband* says to someone who has given a deal of money to public charities "Dear me! what a lot of harm you must have done!" Mrs. Cheveley in the same play remarks "Philanthropy seems to me to have become simply the refuge of people who wish to annoy their fellow-creatures." Elsewhere Wilde affirms "Charity creates a multitude of sins," and, dealing with the nature of charitymongers, "People are so fond of giving away what they do not want themselves, that charity is largely on the increase."

His own generosity was unadvertised and personal. When Ouida's books

went out of fashion and the authoress could get no money to pay her rent
and her fare back to Florence, she applied for assistance to the people who had
once lionised her. "But rich people never lend money," said Wilde, who
managed somehow to raise what was needed. A young solicitor of his acquaintance was deeply in love, wanted to get married, and blurted it all
out to Wilde. "How much would you actually need in order to marry Marjorie?" asked Wilde. "A hundred and fifty pounds. Then I could take a
tiny flat and work. She is earning her own living." Wilde, who had just
received some royalties on his first modern comedy, sat down promptly and
wrote a checque for the sum, saying as he handed it to the solicitor "Go *at
once* and marry her, and bring her to our house at Worthing for your honey-
moon." The couple did not forget, and Marjorie was one of the only two
women who met him immediately on his release from prison. Ada Leverson,
who relates this story, says that "Oscar was the most generous man I have
ever met, and he showed his kindness always in the most graceful way." She
even asserts that he rather resented any friend who was not in actual need
of help, and she repeats what many others have stated: that there was no
trouble he would not take to advance a friend's interest, though he was
much too lazy to make efforts for himself. Charles Ricketts tells us that
Wilde secured work for him as a designer of books and bindings from suc-
cessive publishers; and if half of what one has heard and read is true, it would
seem that when he was not giving people ideas he was getting them jobs.
Beggars did not appeal to him in vain, though the advice which once accompanied his help might, if followed, have seriously reduced the recipient's
takings. A beggar accosted him in the Haymarket, and backed his appeal
for alms with the assurance that he had no work to do and no bread to eat.
"Work!" exclaimed Wilde. "Why should you want to work? And bread!
Why should you eat bread?" He paused, put his hand on the man's shoulder,
and continued in a friendly manner: "Now if you had come to me and said
that you had work to do, but you couldn't dream of working, and that you
had bread to eat, but couldn't think of eating bread, I would have given you
two shillings and sixpence." A pause. "As it is, I give you half-a-crown."

His sympathy with others and interest in their affairs was part of his rich,
gay, generous, life-loving nature. "There is always luncheon at 1 o'clock at
the Café Royal," he said to A. E. W. Mason, who told me that Wilde had
probably realised the value to him, not only of advice, but of a square meal.
Mason remembers H. B. Irving and his brother Laurence at those lunches,
and remembers too that Wilde listened eagerly to what they all had to say,
offering criticism here, encouragement there, and flattering his juniors by

seeking their advice on difficult points in his own work. He appeared to take as much interest in them as they did themselves, and he gave his close attention to the story Mason was then writing, his first, *A Romance of Wastdale,* which was about a brother and sister. "No," said Wilde, "that won't do. Everything in life has its symbol. Passion has its flower; and affection between a brother and a sister has its symbol too. But, my dear fellow, it is cold boiled mutton." Mason dropped the brother and sister. Richard Le Gallienne was equally impressed by Wilde's interest in his poems; William Rothenstein was enchanted by the way in which Wilde perceived his aim and brought out what was latent in him; W. B. Yeats could not help being pleased when Wilde said that he told stories like Homer; Elizabeth Robins, on her arrival in England, was taken in hand by Wilde, who became her adviser, introduced her to theatre managers, and cheered her at every difficult moment in her early career, though at the time he was sought after by every fashionable hostess in London. The tale of his kindness and sympathetic consideration for struggling artists only ended with his life. And we may say of his interest in others that if it was sincerely felt it displayed a nice nature; if insincerely felt, a nicer nature. But it was part of his joy in life, part of the experience of living which he never found dull, and part of his imagination. He once said of a famous actress who, after a tragic domestic life, had married a fool, "She thought that, because he was stupid, he would be kindly, when, of course, kindliness requires imagination and intellect."

In addition to his understanding of their aims and sympathy with their doings, the younger men were fascinated by his impromptus, such as: "Whatever was good enough for our fathers is not good enough for us." "I can believe anything, provided that it is quite incredible." "We are not sent into the world to air our moral prejudices." "If you want to mar a nature, you have merely to reform it." "Sound English common sense—the inherited stupidity of the race." "To be natural is such a very difficult pose to keep up." "I love acting. It is so much more real than life." They liked still more his deflation of the current conception of selfishness, from which they had suffered: "Selfishness is not living as one wishes to live, it is asking others to live as one wishes to live. And unselfishness is letting other people's lives alone, not interfering with them." It was agreeable, too, to be told that "Self-sacrifice ought to be put down by law. It demoralises those for whom the sacrifice is made. They always go to the bad." Above all they enjoyed his praise when they had made a success. One of his sayings ran "Anybody can sympathise with the sufferings of a friend, but it requires a very fine nature —it requires, in fact, the nature of a true individualist—to sympathise with a friend's success." Such indeed was his own nature, and the unfeigned pleasure he took in the success of others was perhaps his rarest attribute.

It was as natural for him to praise people as to take joy in their triumphs, and, unless provoked by hostility or boorish manners, he could not bring himself to say anything harsh. "You certainly tell of marvellous things in a marvellous way," he wrote to Marie Corelli about one of her novels, which was the truth, if not the whole truth. He was thoughtful for others in all sorts of ways. Two observant women ("Michael Field") saw him with his wife in a box at a performance of Ibsen's *The Master Builder*. "Oscar seems to exhale Paris," they noted, "and this atmosphere makes one feel easy and gay to look at him. He watches the stage impassively but with intentness. Our claps help his and those of a few others to bring the curtain up at the end of Act 4." The play can hardly have aroused his enthusiasm, but he knew that an extra "curtain" would encourage the actors, so he went on applauding; just as, after lunch at the Café Royal, he would send for the chef to compliment him on some dish. Withal he had a childlike love of being liked, receiving as much pleasure from praise as he experienced in giving it. In the course of his trial he confessed that he was "enormously fond of praise and admiration." He thought praise from anyone delightful, though the praise of literary people was usually tainted with criticism, and of the young men outside his own class whose company he kept he frankly confessed. "I like to be liked. I liked their society simply because I like to be lionised."

Yet his friends, though they loved him, did not lionise him. Let us see what effect he had on some of them before passing on to two who must be noticed more particularly at this stage of his life. Most of his acquaintances came under the spell of his extraordinary personality, says Richard Le Gallienne, and even those who did not care for him were amazed by his gifts: for example, Sir Henry Newbolt, who heard him in '87 holding forth at a function attended by all the bigwigs in politics and society, Gladstone and Lord Acton among them. Wilde, surrounded by a group of women, was speaking of the splendours of the lesser-known Elizabethan and Jacobean dramatists. "His quotations seemed to me to bear out all that he claimed for them," writes Newbolt, "and I noted the names that I might study them at my leisure. But when I searched the plays afterwards I found not a word of any of the lines . . . My feeling was chiefly one of almost awed surprise at his wonderful powers—the imitations were so perfect and so striking in themselves as to be worthy of the forged names he appended to them." William Morris was not the only man who, when dying, could bear to see no one but Oscar Wilde. The British Ambassador in Paris, Lord Lytton ("Owen

Meredith"), was consoled in his last days by Wilde, who sat by his bedside holding his hand almost up to the end, and was the sole person outside his family whom he wished to see. They became great friends during the last year of Lytton's life, and Wilde was much distressed when he died. The kind of solace Wilde could impart is suggested by one of the two female authors known as "Michael Field": "What I like about him is the sense of bien-être, of comfort, he conveys to the brain. All that a woman does to a man by her presence on the hearth, or by the tea-table, he does to the brain—neither lulling it nor stimulating it—introducing about it a climate of happiness, so that it is twice itself, freed from the depression of fragility or chill . . ." Charles Ricketts thought him "the kindliest and most generous of men I ever met and the most richly endowed in intellect. . . . In intellect and humanity he is the largest type I have come across. Other greater men of my time were great in some one thing, not large in their very texture." This will explain how he was able to transform people's mental outlook, to change their melancholy to joy, to renovate them spiritually and physically. He was, strictly speaking, a healer: the virtue of happiness in him passed into others. Without any apparent effort, says Lord Alfred Douglas, he exerted an enchantment which transmuted the ordinary things of life, investing them with strangeness and glamour: "One met him, feeling depressed, and in five minutes he had altered the whole aspect of the situation and everything became *couleur de rose*. To repeat the process involved an infinite amount of wit and humour, profundity of thought and deep insight." Vincent O'Sullivan admits to having known people he had liked better than Wilde, "but never one it was such a happiness to see or be going to see. It was rather like the emotion of going to hear some Schubert music, some Schumann, well sung, well played." Robert Sherard was more moved by mountains than by music: "One felt an enthusiasm for the man as one listened to him, the kind of enthusiasm that one experiences for Nature at the spectacle of some grand piece of scenery, some light on sea or land. One was lifted out of oneself."

Two instances of Wilde's healing powers have been given, though dozens must have remained unrecorded. One day Graham Robertson had a violent toothache, accompanied by such a bad cold that he could not visit the dentist, who was coming to him instead. Aching and sneezing, Robertson was waiting for the dentist's arrival when Wilde was announced:

"You're not pleased to see me."

"The person does not exist whom I should be pleased to see. I hate everybody and wish they were dead."

"Just so." Wilde sat down comfortably.

"I said that no one but the dentist was to be admitted; but that's a new man and I suppose he thought——"

"*What* did he think?" Wilde seemed genuinely moved. D'you mean he thought that I—I——?" Robertson nodded affirmatively. "But—but I don't *look* like a dentist, do I?"

"Oh, I don't know. Perhaps in the half-light you might pass——"

"Don't! It's awful! I feel as if I *were* a dentist. Let's talk about something else."

Then, says Graham Robertson, a really wonderful thing happened. Oscar could not bear sick people, but he started talking and telling stories so brilliantly that for an hour and a half Robertson laughed without stopping, and when the real dentist arrived he had no toothache and no cold left, having laughed them both away.

The second case is even more remarkable, for Oscar shrank from sorrow as well as sickness. It is from the pen of Mrs. H. M. Swanwick, sister to Walter Sickert:

"When my father died in 1885 my mother nearly went mad with grief. She shut herself up, refusing to see her friends in a dumb despair.

"One afternoon Oscar called: I told him of her desperate state, and he said he must see her. She stubbornly refused, and I went back to him to say I could not prevail on her. 'But she must see me,' he replied. 'She must. Tell her I shall stay here till she does.' Back I went, and for a few minutes my mother sat, crying and wringing her hands, and saying 'I can't. Send him away.' Then she arose and went into the room where he was waiting, crying as she went. I saw Oscar take both her hands and draw her to a chair, beside which he set his own; then I left them alone. He stayed a long time, and before he went I heard my mother laughing.

"When he had gone she was a woman transformed. He had made her talk; had asked questions about my father's last illness and allowed her to unburden her heart of those torturing memories. Gradually he had talked of my father, of his music, of the possibilities of a memorial exhibition of his pictures. Then, she didn't know how, he had begun to tell her all sorts of things which he contrived to make interesting and amusing. 'And then I laughed,' she said. 'I thought I should never laugh again.'

"I should not have been surprised if, after my father's death, Oscar had not been near us for a while. But he not only came, he exercised all his gifts, his insight, his patience, his wit, to draw the poison from the wound of a woman not young, not socially important; a woman who had been hospitable to him and for whom he felt a simple affection."

Oscar Wilde's most intimate friend, who probably understood and sympathised with him more than anyone else, was Robert Ross. They met in the late eighties. Ross, the son of a Canadian lawyer whose money had disappeared in an unlucky investment, spent a few terms at Cambridge, and lived thenceforth on an allowance from his mother, plus a little which he earned by occasional articles for high-class reviews. He was a small, slight, attractive man, with an affectionate, impulsive nature, and considerable charm of manner. People took to him at once; and as he had the art of flattering them without appearing to do so, his circle of acquaintance rapidly widened. He was shrewd in the assessment of characteristics, knew how far to go with one man, how to ingratiate himself with another, and whether this person or that was worth cultivating. He was an extremely agreeable, and sometimes witty, companion. Acquaintances found him restful or stimulating, according to their needs, and he had the valuable quality of inspiring both men and women with the desire to help him, with satisfactory financial results. In conversation his touch was light; his criticisms were neat without being too pointed, his appreciations warm without being too effusive, his reminiscences entertaining without being too veracious. Always unassuming, he played up to those he wished to impress and made them feel that they were very good fellows, and, in retrospect, that he was a very good fellow too. His chief interest was in painting, and he became known as a very good judge of it, running a shop and eventually being appointed Assessor of Picture Valuations to the Board of Trade; but this was some years after Wilde's death. The desire to please, which was strong in both of them, though perhaps from different motives, ripened their friendship, and they were soon "Oscar" and "Robbie" to one another. They had another taste in common which will appear in due course; but for the moment it is only necessary to say that a talk with Ross stimulated Wilde to write one of his duologues in *Intentions*, and that their natures coalesced, Wilde's imagination being complemented by Ross's shrewdness. They remained close friends to the end; and Ross became Wilde's literary executor.

One would have to stretch the meaning of the term "friendship" in order to cover the relationship between Wilde and Frank Harris; but as, with the exception of Sherard, Harris was the only man who wrote a full-length biography of Oscar from personal knowledge of his subject, he earns a place in Wilde's story. He had none of the pliability and adaptability of Ross: nothing could turn him from his strenuous, blatant, truculent, independent and undependable course, except hard cash, spot cash, and plenty of it. Against Ross's subtlety he appeared obvious, but there was some cunning in his obviousness. He described himself as Welsh and born in Wales, also as Irish and born in Ireland, and he finished up as an American Etonian, or, if an Etonian was present to check the assertion, as an American Rugbean. "No one but a salamander would risk the stake for the accuracy of a single statement in Harris's autobiography," writes Hugh Kingsmill in his fascinating Life of Harris; but we know for a fact that much of his early life was passed in America and that he studied for a year at Kansas University. He returned to England with a cowboy's outlook on life, tempered by the classics, and in time became editor of *The Evening News* and then of *The Fortnightly Review*. He married a wealthy widow with a house in Park Lane, and his future career as a Conservative politician seemed assured. But everything went wrong, possibly because Harris himself was never quite right in his surroundings, and after a few years he found himself away from Park Lane, away from his wife, far away from the Front Bench of the House of Commons, and in control of *The Saturday Review*. He met Oscar Wilde in the middle eighties. At first Wilde disliked him, which must have been evident to Harris, because in describing their early encounters he reversed the rôles and made it appear that it was he who disliked Wilde. Then they met at a dinner-party, where Harris told how a prize-fighter had taken on a mob single-handed, his description being vivid enough to gain Wilde's praise. After that they were on friendly terms; but Wilde could never have felt quite at ease with Harris, whose personal appearance was improbable, whose social manners were peculiar, whose deep resonant voice could drown an orchestra, and whose language sometimes made a bargee's seem polite; whereas Wilde never used a word that could not have been spoken in a drawing-room, and detested brag and bluster as much as he dreaded boredom. One is not surprised, then, to learn from William Rothenstein that Harris was responsible for the only unkind thing he ever heard Wilde say. It was at a dinner-party given by Harris at the Café Royal. The guests included Max Beerbohm, Aubrey Beardsley and Robert Ross. The conversation was monopolised by Harris, who told a seemingly interminable story which was an expansion and paraphrase of a tale by Anatole France. "What a charming story, Frank," said Oscar when at last the end came, adding thoughtfully after a pause, "Anatole France would have spoiled that story." Undeterred Harris went on to speak of his social successes, and of all the grand houses he had stayed at. Oscar, who had reached the limit of boredom, cut in "Yes, dear Frank, we believe you—you have dined in every house in London, *once*."

In fact Harris must frequently have made Wilde feel extremely uncomfortable. "I do not know what a football scrimmage is," said he, "but I imagine it must be very like a conversation with Frank Harris"; and if it had not been for Harris's open admiration of him, and sincere delight in his company, their meetings would have been more restricted. But he was a godsend to Harris, who, beneath all his clamour and worldly ambition and sharp practice, had a flair for literary distinction and a liking for those who had gained it; and we need not question the sincerity of his final tribute to Wilde: "I have known no more charming, no more quickening, no more delightful spirit . . . I do not believe that in all the realms of death there is a more fascinating or delightful companion." His debt to Wilde was considerable. He had a very assertive, not to say aggressive, personality, and Wilde gave him as good an opinion of himself as he tried to have, brought out the best in him, and made him feel twice the man he was. Several of Wilde's apologues have appeared in a volume of short stories called *Unpath'd Waters* by Harris, who doubtless remembered Oscar's remark, "To be suggestive for fiction is to be more important than a fact," and, taking the tip, founded his chief work of fiction on the life of Wilde. Apart from inspiring him in this way, and giving him countless hours of priceless entertainment, Wilde, considered objectively as a personality, never impinged on Harris at all, and the conversations he records between Wilde and himself are simply the conversations of Harris with himself, one Harris adopting a different viewpoint partly for the sake of argument but principally that he might bring the word "Confessions" into the title of his book. All the same he probably liked and admired Wilde more than any man he met, and treated him well, as we shall hear, when it suited his purpose.

Rapidly running through Wilde's well-known contemporaries who had little or no part in his story but whose attitude to him or his to them is known, we find that George Meredith and Henry James had a low opinion of his talents, but this may have been due to the fact that unpopular novelists are usually envious of popular playwrights. Wilde thought highly of Meredith, whom he called an incomparable novelist, but his summary of Meredith's qualities was more likely to have remained in the novelist's memory: "As a writer he has mastered everything, except language; as a novelist he can do everything, except tell a story; as an artist he is everything, except articulate." We have already heard what Wilde thought of Swinburne: there is no record of what Swinburne thought of Wilde, who however made one or two amusing comments on Swinburne's housemate, Theodore Watts-Dunton, a famous critic of the time: "You know, Watts is a solicitor, and the business of a solicitor is to conceal crime. Swinburne's genius has been killed, and Watts is doing his best to conceal it." "I have suddenly realised why

Watts is an authority on the sonnet: the sonnet of course is made of six and eight." (In those days the advice of a solicitor cost 6s. 8d.). A criticism Wilde passed on James Payn, editor of *The Cornhill Magazine* and writer of romantic novels, is worth quoting because of its aptness to so much modern fiction. As one turns over the pages of a novel by James Payn, he wrote, "the suspense of the author becomes almost unbearable." Wilde was intrigued by the personality of Max Beerbohm, then in his early twenties, and said "The gods have bestowed on Max the gift of perpetual old age." He also asked Ada Leverson "When you are alone with him, Sphinx, does he take off his face and reveal his mask?" Max Beerbohm has justified this query by restricting his opinion of Wilde to caricature, the only form of art in which malice can pass for good humour.

It is broadly true to say that Wilde was not popular with literary people, and that his astonishing conversational gifts were thoroughly appreciated only in social and political circles, where he was recognized as the most brilliant talker of the age, despite such outspoken comments on the politicians as: "The Lords Temporal say nothing, the Lords Spiritual have nothing to say, and the House of Commons has nothing to say and says it." "In modern life nothing produces such an effect as a good platitude. It makes the whole world kin." "In England a man who can't talk morality twice a week to a large, popular, immoral audience is quite over as a serious politician. There would be nothing left for him as a profession except Botany or the Church." Some of his fellow-authors really hated Wilde, but they kept the feeling to themselves until it was safe to show it. George Moore was the most distinguished of these haters, though there was never any secret about his feeling, which was cordially reciprocated by Wilde. The fact that they were Irish may have had a lot to do with it, for the Irish dislike one another with fervour. But these two were as dissimilar in temperament as Shaw and Wilde, as Moore and Shaw. To note the more obvious contrasts, Moore was mean in his habits, coarse in his language, and narrow in his interests. Wilde was generous in his habits, refined in his language, and wide in his interests. Moore painfully acquired his knowledge and style. Wilde gained his knowledge and style by instinct. Everything came easily to Wilde, particularly success with women. Nothing came easily to Moore, least of all success with women. During the brief periods when they were on speaking terms, Wilde was revolted by Moore's excremental terminology; and when asked by someone whether he knew Moore, replied "I know him so well that I haven't spoken to him for ten years." One of Moore's novels, *Esther Waters,* drew this from him: "He leads his readers to the latrine and locks them in."

Another, *Evelyn Innes*, which deals with operas and singers, drew this: "I hear it has to be played on the piano." Also this: "Moore conducts his musical education in public." In short he neither liked Moore nor admired his work. "Great antipathy shows secret affinity," he once pronounced. "Then you have an affinity to George Moore?" he was asked. "No; but perhaps to Zola. Still, I hope not." Moore's emotions on the subject of Wilde were almost inarticulate. One evening he and Ernest Rhys caught sight of Oscar in a theatre bar. "That man will be eaten by worms," Moore hissed with venom. Women loved Wilde, almost to a woman, but one of them hated him: Lady Colin Campbell, who referred to him as "that great white caterpillar." It is possible, however, that some kind friend had reported Oscar's comment on the novel which she wrote after her divorce-case, when, following a merciless cross-examination, she had managed to clear herself: "Lady Colin has exhausted all her powers of imagination in the witness-box."

The one character in which it is almost impossible to visualise Wilde is that of a family man. He was not made for the home, least of all a Victorian one. Clearly he did his best to be a dutiful husband, and Yeats found him one day closeted with a missionary, who did not mind his native parishioners running about nude on week-days but wished to see them clothed at divine worship on Sundays. Wilde's fame as an art-critic had penetrated to Central Africa, and, doubtless at his wife's request, he was giving his advice on the various-coloured smocks with which the missionary had covered the floor, discussing the pros and cons of each with pontifical gravity. The impression Rothenstein carried away from Tite Street was that Wilde and his wife were on affectionate terms, but that there was something wistful and a little sad about Constance. She seems to have been rather sorry for her husband, in the way a mother is sorry for a wayward son. She could not understand why he should resent her mild censure when he had indulged in some extravagance of thought or behaviour; but the very gentleness of her reproofs made them more difficult to bear than if they had been accompanied by crockery, and his irritation found expression in an epigram: "The only way a woman can ever reform a man is by boring him so completely that he loses all possible interest in life." He was well aware of his failure to live up to her ideals, and confessed as much to Nellie Melba when talking about his two sons: "I was telling them stories last night of little boys who were naughty and who made their mother cry, and what dreadful things would happen to them unless they became better; and do you know what one of them answered? He asked me what punishment could be reserved for naughty papas, who did not come home till the early morning, and made mother cry far more?"

He delighted in his children, and as he amused them with strange stories they thought him a perfect papa. He was equally popular with the children of his friends. We hear from Mrs. Swanwick that he talked poetical non-sense and kept up mock-serious conversations with them, punctuated with roars of laughter. "I have never known any grown person who laughed so whole-heartedly and who made such mellow music of it . . . His laughter I shall hear till I die." He loved to buy things for his little boys, taking part in the discussions leading to each purchase with a judicial solemnity that suggested deliberations involving the fate of nations. In choosing a Noah's Ark for one of them, he weighed the merits of the different exhibits with episcopal ceremoniousness, and having made his decision the shopman was on the point of wrapping it up when Wilde raised his hand: "Stop! I have not yet tasted Noah's head." Not always were his efforts to entertain his sons successful. "It is the duty of every father to write fairy tales for his children," he informed Richard Le Gallienne; "but the mind of a child is a great mystery. It is incalculable, and who shall divine it, or bring to it its own peculiar delights? You humbly spread before it the treasures of your imagina-tion, and they are as dross. For example, a day or two ago Cyril yonder came to me with the question, 'Father, do you ever dream?' 'Why, of course, my darling. It is the first duty of a gentleman to dream.' 'And what do you dream of?' asked Cyril with a child's disgusting appetite for facts. Then I, believing of course that something picturesque would be expected of me, spoke of magnificent things: 'What do I dream of? Oh, I dream of dragons with gold and silver scales, and scarlet flames coming out of their mouths, of eagles with eyes made of diamonds that can see over the whole world at once, of lions with yellow manes, and voices like thunder, of elephants with little houses on their backs, and tigers and zebras with barred and spotted coats. . . .' So I laboured on with my fancy, till, observing that Cyril was entirely unimpressed, and indeed quite undisguisedly bored, I came to a humiliating stop, and, turning to him, I said: 'But tell me, what do you dream of, Cyril?' His answer was like a divine revelation: 'I dream of *pigs*,' he said."

Wilde left the religious instruction of his boys in the hands of their mother, which was sensible of him. As we shall find when we come to his parables, his guidance in such matters might have got the lads into trouble with the divinity master when they went to school. Asked by Arthur Balfour what his religion was, he replied "Well, you know, I don't think I have any. I

am an Irish Protestant." His attraction to the Roman Faith was purely
aesthetic, and theological squabbles bored him to silence. He was strongly
drawn to the personality of Jesus Christ, of whom however he was thinking
when he said "A thing is not necessarily true because a man dies for it"; and
though a lifelong lover of The Song of Solomon, his general view of the
Bible was mixed: "When I think of all the harm that book has done, I
despair of ever writing anything to equal it." He felt that there was something
to be said for Nero's persecution of the early Christians: "You know, Nero
was obliged to do something. They were making him ridiculous. What he
thought was: 'Here everything was going on very well, when one day two
incredible creatures arrived from somewhere in the provinces. They are
called Peter and Paul, or some unheard-of names like that. Since their arrival life in Rome has become impossible. They collect crowds and block the
traffic with their miracles. It is really intolerable. I, the Emperor, have no
peace. When I get up in the morning and look out of the window, the first
thing I see is a miracle going on in the back garden.'" As for the later saints,
it is clear from a passage in *Intentions* that Wilde preferred sinners: "It is
well for our vanity that we slay the criminal, for if we suffered him to live
he might show us what we had gained by his crime. It is well for his peace
that the saint goes to his martyrdom. He is spared the sight of the horror
of his harvest." In lighter vein he remarked "The only difference between
the saint and the sinner is that every saint has a past, and every sinner a
future." He sympathised with the ritual of prayer, which he described as "a
compliment, a spiritual courtesy, which one may surely hope is appreciated in
the proper place"; but "Prayer must never be answered: if it is, it ceases to
be prayer and becomes a correspondence." He also took an indulgent view
of the behaviour of a certain princess who regularly communicated at the
12 o'clock mass at the Madeleine. As no one else ever did this, her solitary
performance was severely criticised, but Wilde said she was "quite right to
have a private interview with God." He was equally ready to support, not
only another man's right to his religious opinions, but his means of spreading
them. A. E. W. Mason tells me that he was sitting with Wilde and several
others in the Café Royal one day when the publisher Heinemann joined
them in an angry mood, because Richard Le Gallienne had taken a book of
his entitled *The Religion of a Literary Man* to another firm. "Fancy a literary
man pretending that he has some special brand of religion peculiar to himself! and fancy thinking it will be of interest to his readers!" exclaimed
Heinemann pettishly. Spacing his words carefully and nodding his head like
a mandarin with his knuckles to his teeth, Wilde observed: "My dear fellow,

of course Le Gallienne is quite right. How far you are behind the times! Surely you know that nowadays the religion of a literary man is an affair strictly between himself . . . and his public."

Wilde's religion, as with everyone who thinks at all, was the reflection of his mind, which was far too subtle to believe that there could be any such thing as absolute and universal truth, his individualism being so extreme that his attitude to the question could be summed up in the phrase: what is one man's truth is another man's lie. He knew that a religion is no more true because fifty billion people have believed in it than it is less true because the same number of people have disbelieved in it. "Art and Liberty seem to me more vital and more religious than any Creed," he once said. "The artist's view of life is the only possible one and should be applied to everything, above all to religion. Cavaliers and Puritans are interesting for their costumes, not their convictions." This was his real belief. He was a born pagan, and the enthusiasm of religious people was as tedious to him as their narrowness was deadening:

"One should never take sides in anything. Taking sides is the beginning of sincerity, and earnestness follows shortly afterwards, and the human being becomes a bore."

"To believe is very dull. To doubt is intensely engrossing. To be on the alert is to live; to be lulled into security is to die."

Lacking belief in religious superstition, he made up for it by believing in omens, sorcery, and so on. He refused to drive behind a white horse, once foretold some great misfortune because an old witch-woman had looked through the window of a restaurant at himself and a companion, and used to quote (or invent) rubbish from books of magic as if he thought there was something in it: for example, "If you carve a Cerberus upon an emerald, and put it in the oil of a lamp, and carry it into a room where your enemy is, two new heads will come upon his shoulders and all three devour one another." But all this was part of the drama of life, lending colour to otherwise commonplace happenings, part also of the boy in him who in that respect had not outgrown the phase when fairy-tales are more real than reality.

Perhaps his own life seemed to him the most wonderful of all fairy-tales, and he sometimes spoke of himself in the third person. Certainly no one ever suffered less from a sense of inferiority. "Could anything be more petty—a greater revelation of insignificance?" he asked Vincent O'Sullivan, after describing the scene made by a well-known poet because he had not been placed in a prominent position at some public dinner in Paris. "Now for me, the highest place is where I am myself." His sense of his own value went far beyond ordinary conceit: it was a placid acceptance of something that was not open to argument, something as obvious as the sun in the heavens. When a statesman said to him that the Macs had done everything and the O's nothing in nineteenth century England, he replied "You forget: there are O'Connell and O. Wilde." During his early attempts at recognition, however, the "O" did not satisfy him, for when an American entered his name in a club visitor's book as O. Wilde he protested: "O. Wilde! Who is O. Wilde? Nobody knows O. Wilde. But Oscar Wilde is a household word." He was too fearless, too honest and too idiosyncratic to cover up his egotism by associating it with some progressive cause, some supposedly self-effacing movement. His individualism was intense. "The only schools worth founding are schools without disciples," he stated, and while in prison he wrote "I am a born antinomian. I am one of those who are made for exceptions, not for laws." Yet he had to admit that in certain ways he resembled other people, and would talk amusedly of "that dreadful universal thing called human nature" and of the brotherhood of man being no mere poet's dream but "a most depressing and humiliating reality." Still, if he could not escape the ordinary emotions of humanity, he could at least rise in thought above the ordinary man. "Most people are other people," he declared. "Their thoughts are someone else's opinions, their lives a mimicry, their passions a quotation." And he would tell a story, which eventually became a blank-verse play called *A Florentine Tragedy*, only a fragment of which survives. This is the version of the tale as I heard it from Robert Ross:

"Most people love beauty because their neighbours love the same beauty. They admire strength because everyone does so. Very few among us have the courage openly to set up our own standard of values and abide by it. You remember what happened to the Merchant of Florence? No? Then I will tell you.

"He had married a girl who, it seemed to him, would fulfill all the requirements of a wife: she would mend his garments, attend to his house, and see that he was well fed. All of which she did. Their life together, like that of most married couples, was quite uneventful. Every day he went out to sell and to buy, and every evening he came home again, and ate his food, and talked of what he had done, and went to bed. The neighbours called theirs an ideal married life, and it would have continued so to the end if one day a young prince of the ruling family had not stopped to make a purchase at their house when the merchant was away from home. This prince, you see, had not been told whether the merchant's wife was comely or otherwise, so he was able to make up his own mind on the subject, and he thought that she was comely. He came again and again; and as the good woman had never been encouraged to relate her experiences at home after her husband had finished speaking of his bargains abroad, she never mentioned her visitor. But the prince's tales of gallant exploits held her enthralled; she found them so much more interesting than her husband's stories of purchase and sale; and gradually she came to feel contempt for the merchant, who seemed so weak and unadventurous compared with her dashing carefree prince.

"One day the merchant returned home earlier than usual and found the prince talking with his wife. He said that he was highly honoured that so distinguished a person should visit his humble dwelling; and thinking that the prince had come to buy his wares, he offered to display his best jewels and embroideries. But the prince showed no inclination to see them, and said that his steward would come in the morning and buy whatever the merchant wished to sell at his own terms. The merchant was astonished at such generous treatment, and said that in return he would give the prince whatever he asked. 'What if I asked for your wife?' questioned the prince. 'You joke, my lord,' replied the merchant. 'She is not worthy of your regard. She can cook and spin and keep the house; but that is all.' 'No, not all,' said the prince, 'for she is good to look upon.' Then the merchant spoke of his trade, but the prince did not heed him; of politics, but the prince did not hear. So he brought wine and asked the prince to drink with him. And now he surprised the secret of those two, for when the prince drank to his wife he caught the glance that passed between them, and he threw his cup to the ground. 'That is a fine sword of yours,' said he; 'yet though my own is rusty, I dare swear its steel is better tempered. Good my lord, do me the honour to test them.' The prince laughingly expressed his willingness, and they stood up to fight. At first it seemed they sparred in jest, but soon the swords flashed in earnest, and in a minute the prince was disarmed. 'Now for our daggers,' said the merchant, 'for one of us must die.' It was even so. The merchant threw the prince to the ground, and stabbed him in the throat. Then he arose and looked at his wife, who moved towards him with arms outstretched, half dazed with amazement and admiration. 'I did not know that you were brave and strong,' she said. 'I did not know that you were beautiful,' said he. And he took her in his arms."

CHAPTER TWELVE

THE WIT

SEVERAL writers of reminiscences dealing with the eighties and nineties suddenly come to life when Wilde enters their pages, and coin neat repartees at his expense; which suggests that he, like Falstaff, was not only witty himself but the cause of wit in others. There is no doubt that he did inspire many succeeding novelists, dramatists and talkers, whose epigrams may be described as Wilde and water. But memory is so treacherous, and we shall not be far out if we assume that in real life he won all his contests with wit, the memory of which rankled until the losers could pay him back in fiction. The enduring animosity of Whistler, due entirely to Wilde's superiority as a man, a talker and a wit, is sufficient proof that no one else had a dog's chance against Oscar when he cared to exert himself. We have already seen him winning Henley's reluctant praise; we have heard that Shaw was content to play second fiddle to him; we know that Carson, the cleverest cross-examiner of his day, was hopelessly outclassed by him on the intellectual plane; and all these, Whistler, Henley, Shaw and Carson, were born fighters, loving combat, while Wilde hated friction, loathed argument ("It is only the intellectually lost who ever argue," he said), and would head any list of famous Men of Inaction.

C. J. Holmes gives us a tantalising glimpse of one witty interchange between Wilde and Charles Ricketts at the latter's studio: "Ricketts, perched on the edge of the table, engaged Wilde in a long verbal combat. So swiftly came parry and *riposte*, that my slow brain could only follow the tongue-play several sentences behind, and cannot remember a word of what passed, except 'Oh, nonsense, Oscar!' from Ricketts, although it lives in memory as the most dazzling dialogue which I was ever privileged to hear." But the most satisfactory evidence of Wilde's superiority as a wit over all his contemporaries comes from Wilfred Scawen Blunt, who had met pretty well every famous artistic, social and political figure between 1870 and 1920. He was present on July 17th, 1894, at "a brilliant luncheon" given by Margot Asquith and her husband some two months after their marriage.

Wilde was then at the height of his social glory, says Blunt. "Of all those present, and they were most of them brilliant talkers, he was without comparison the most brilliant, and in a perverse mood he chose to cross swords with one after the other of them, overpowering each in turn with his wit, and making special fun of Asquith, his host that day, who only a few months later, as Home Secretary, was prosecuting him . . ." Another passage in Blunt's diary, written on hearing of Wilde's death, runs: "He was without exception the most brilliant talker I have ever come across, the most ready, the most witty, the most audacious . . . Nobody could pretend to outshine him, or even to shine at all in his company. Something of his wit is reflected in his plays, but very little. The fine society of London and especially the 'souls' ran after him because they knew he could always amuse them, and the pretty women allowed him great familiarities, though there was no question of love-making."

Wilde's wit was entirely effortless and spontaneous. He never influenced the conversation in any direction, and never attempted to dominate it: he just slipped into it, became a part of the general give-and-take. Whatever the theme, his wit was as ready as it was kindly. His heavy features became sensitive and alert, his face alive with gaiety; good-nature seemed to exude from him, pleasure to radiate from him, happiness to enfold him. Frivolity was the keynote to his wit. What other people took seriously he dealt with humorously; what they dismissed as trivial he treated with great solemnity. His favourite method of ridiculing conventional standards was to change a word or two in a proverb or cliché, and so add an aspect to truth. Here are some good examples of his conversational flings:

"Work is the curse of the drinking classes."

"One of those characteristic British faces that, once seen, are never remembered."

"Everyone should keep someone else's diary."

"It is always a silly thing to give advice, but to give good advice is absolutely fatal."

"I can resist everything except temptation."

"Duty is what one expects from others; it is not what one does oneself."

"Don't be led astray into the paths of virtue."

"You can't make people good by Act of Parliament—that is something."

"She has the remains of really remarkable ugliness."

"The English have a miraculous power of turning wine into water."

"Genius is born, not paid."

"Ouida loved Lord Lytton with a love that made his life a burden."

"I rely on you to misrepresent me."

"Whenever I think of my bad qualities at night, I go to sleep at once."

"He is old enough to know worse."

"Never buy a thing you don't want merely because it is dear."

"Consistency is the last refuge of the unimaginative."

"Whenever a man does a thoroughly stupid thing, it is always from the noblest motives."

"I am due at the club. It is the hour when we sleep there."

"Nothing is so dangerous as being too modern. One is apt to grow old-fashioned quite suddenly."

"He hasn't a single redeeming vice."

"Morality is simply the attitude we adopt towards people whom we personally dislike."

"I usually say what I really think. A great mistake nowadays. It makes one so liable to be misunderstood."

"It is only by not paying one's bills that one can hope to live in the memory of the commercial classes."

"For an artist to marry his model is as fatal as for a *gourmet* to marry his cook: the one gets no sittings, and the other no dinners."

"Her capacity for family affection is extraordinary. When her third husband died, her hair turned quite gold from grief."

"Nowadays most people die of a sort of creeping common sense, and discover when it is too late that the only things one never regrets are one's mistakes."

"I choose my friends for their good looks, my acquaintances for their good characters, and my enemies for their good intellects. A man cannot be too careful in the choice of his enemies."

Most of Wilde's best sayings were a mixture of fun and profundity, and when the fun predominated he would often preface the remark with a laugh or dismiss it with a gesture to suggest the degree of significance which he attached to it. Wit is the salt of wisdom, humour the preservative of thought, and the reason Wilde is still read with delight, while his masters in philosophy, Ruskin and Pater, are mainly studied in the places where dead languages are cherished, is due to his temperamental levity, which helped to make him, with the sole exception of Sydney Smith, the wittiest of humorists and the most humorous of wits. It was his opinion that "Seriousness is the only refuge of the shallow"; and he was undoubtedly right when he said: "Humanity takes itself too seriously. It is the world's original sin. If the caveman had known how to laugh, History would have been different." The great humorist raises common sense to poetry, lifts the burden of life, releases the spirit, imparts happiness, creates brotherhood, and cleanses the mind of cant, pretentiousness and conceit. He is the chief civilising force in humanity, the real democrat and equalitarian, detested and dreaded by tyrants and humbugs. "That idiot laughter!" cries Shakespeare's King John: "a passion hateful to my purposes." The great humourist is also the true seer, but as human beings have only listened to the saint or the charlatan they have not profited in a practical way by the vision of their jesters. We know what serious people have made of the world, but we shall never know what humorous people would make of it, because the world will never be intelligent enough to give them a chance, and they would be too intelligent to take it: which is just as it should be, for the holy spirit of Humour is partly dependent on the unholy stupidity of man.

Wilde's humour, which glistened with wit, played around every subject so happily and continuously that people would sit listening to him, spellbound, oblivious of time, for four or five hours, and then beg him not to stop. Unfortunately for us, it was all so enjoyable that no one was capable of recording what Nellie Melba called "that brilliant fiery-coloured chain of words." And so we must content ourselves with occasional links detached from the chain and preserved by some of his listeners as feeble specimens of the fascinating whole. His manner of speech heightened the comedy of the matter. Sometimes he would start speaking with the utmost solemnity, as though giving the whole of his mind to an important theme which required the gravest deliberation; then there would be a pause, as if he were searching for the exact words to do justice to the occasion; then would come the flash of phrase and the explosion of mirth. The following incidents illustrate this side of his humour.

After Coulson Kernahan had given an honest summary of his religious beliefs, Wilde said: "You are so evidently, so unmistakably sincere, and most of all so truthful, that . . . I can't believe a single word you say."

"It is a kind of genius to be twenty-one," he informed a youthful writer; and having delivered a eulogy on the glories of adolescence, he concluded with: "To win back my youth, there is nothing I would not do—nothing . . . except take exercise, get up early, or be a useful member of the community."

Hearing of the malicious attacks on his character made by an acquaintance, he began what he had to say in a tone of mingled grief and indignation: "It is perfectly monstrous, and quite heartless, the way people go about nowadays saying things against one behind one's back that are absolutely and entirely . . . true."

While waiting for the arrival of a cable which was to tell him of the success or otherwise of the New York production of *Lady Windermere's Fan*, a look of painful apprehension crossed his face as he said "This suspense is unbearable . . . I hope it will last." Which, together with several other remarks that were received with a roar of laughter, found its way into one of his plays.

One saying of his went so well that he repeated it on several subsequent occasions, and Mark Twain either heard it or heard of it, appropriated it, and spoilt it. This is the original version: "I never put off till to-morrow what I can possibly do . . . the day after."

It was related in an English paper that during his lecture tour in America he had been seen in Boston on an exceptionally fine day wearing a mackintosh and carrying an umbrella, and had given as a reason "I hear that it is raining in London this morning." Hoping that he had not been guilty of such an absurdity, Sherard asked him whether there was any truth in the story. Shaking his head mournfully, Wilde replied "A false report." "Ah, I thought so," said Sherard, much relieved. "Yes," Wilde continued in a distressed tone of voice, "I discovered later, and the discovery upset me a good deal, that the weather had been perfect in London that day . . . so my mackintosh and umbrella were really quite unnecessary." For some reason best known to himself Sherard never published this.

In the latter part of last century the scholarly critics of Shakespeare spent much time and wrote many articles on the question of whether Hamlet was really mad or only pretending to be. Wilde listened carefully to a lunch-time discussion, in which the case for and against Hamlet's lunacy was judiciously put, and his interruptions showed that he was genuinely interested. At last, with a burst of enthusiasm, he announced that he would write a book on this absorbing topic. Everyone was thrilled. "Yes," he said, his eyes gleaming with the fanaticism of a scholar on the brink of some momentous discovery, "and I have already found a title for my book." A Chorus of "Tell us: what is it?" Back came the answer: "*Are the Commentators on Hamlet Really Mad or Only Pretending to Be?*"

One day in Paris the talk centered upon the leading figures of the French Revolution, and the character of Marat was debated. One Frenchman said he was a genius, another that he was a gamin, a third that he was the spirit of the Revolution, a fourth that he was the spirit of evil, and so on. Someone turned to Wilde and asked for his opinion. "Poor fellow," he said dolefully: "What bad luck . . . for taking a bath just once in a way." He spoke of course in French, and this is the nearest English equivalent I can give.

His appearance could be as unexpected as his repartees. William Heine-mann, the publisher, once asked him to lunch with Gérard Harry, in the hope that he would write an introduction to Harry's translation of Maeter-linck's first play *Princesse Maleine*. He arrived with a gloomy expression on his face, dressed in deep mourning, and Harry tactfully hinted that he did not wish to bother Wilde at a period of bereavement. Wilde explained the cause of his desolation: "This day happens to be my birthday, and I am mourning, as I shall henceforth do on each of my anniversaries, the flight of one year of my youth into nothingness, the growing blight upon my sum-mer." As for the introduction, he said that he must wait for the necessary inspiration. He waited patiently, but it never came.

In quickness of repartee Wilde can have had few equals, in amiability of exchange none. Some examples have been preserved.

It was the fashion in his time for women to leave the dining-table before the men, who could then light their cigarettes. At one party, captivated by his talk, the women stayed too long, and it happened that a table-lamp began to smoulder. "Please put it out, Mr. Wilde: it's smoking," said the hostess. "Happy lamp," murmured Wilde.

Lord Avebury had published his list of the Hundred Best Books, and at a function where the views of celebrities were being canvassed Wilde was asked to compile a list of his hundred favourites. "I fear that would be impossible," said he. "But why?" "Because I have only written five."

A man who was present on the occasion told the following to Sir Bernard Partridge, who passed it on to me. Wilde was holding forth on the great suicides of history and claiming that all of them had committed their *felo de se* in the grand manner. "What about Judas Iscariot, Oscar?" asked someone. "Oh, Judas! I don't count him. After all he was merely a *nouveau riche*."

A youth was being informed that he, like everyone else, must begin at the bottom of the ladder, when Wilde cut in "No, begin at the top and sit upon it." On hearing that the lad was just going to Sandhurst, Wilde urged him to go to Oxford instead. "But I am going to be a soldier." "If you took a degree at Oxford, they would make you a colonel at once . . . at any rate in a West Indian regiment."

"Surely you remember knowing me in Manchester," said a man whom Wilde had failed to recognise. "Very possibly in Manchester I may know you again," was the reply. Another fellow, who greeted him with "Hullo, Oscar!" and a dig in the ribs, got this: "I don't know you by sight, but your manner is familiar." His apology for having apparently cut an old acquaintance was: "I didn't recognize you—I've changed a lot."

Puns were popular in the nineteenth century. Wilde was not addicted to them; but he made a good one at a wedding-party, when Lord Morris, who had a very strong Irish accent, was looking in vain for a shoe to throw after the young couple. "Why not throw your own brogue after them?" was Oscar's helpful suggestion.

Wilde was a master of satirical nonsense, the gravity of his measured utterance making his best efforts inexpressibly comical, though perhaps he never reached the sublime heights of Sydney Smith's imaginative outbursts, which actually prostrated people, making them ill with laughter. Fortunately we have something better than an echo of Wilde's nonsense in *The Importance of Being Earnest*; and here a few airy trifles from his table-talk must suffice:

"A well-tied tie is the first serious step in life."

"More women grow old nowadays through the faithfulness of their admirers than through anything else."

"When she is in a very smart gown, she looks like an *édition de luxe* of a wicked French novel meant specially for the English market."

"There is no secret of life. Life's aim, if it has one, is simply to be always looking for temptations. There are not nearly enough of them. I sometimes pass a whole day without coming across a single one. It is quite dreadful. It makes one so nervous about the future."

"Nothing is more painful to me than to come across virtue in a person in whom I have never expected its existence. It is like finding a needle in a bundle of hay. It pricks you. If we have virtue we should warn people of it."

"I know so many men in London whose only talent is for washing. I suppose that is why men of genius so seldom wash; they are afraid of being mistaken for men of talent only."

"Twenty years of romance make a woman look like a ruin; but twenty years of marriage make her something like a public building."

"It is sad. One half of the world does not believe in God, and the other half does not believe in me."

"No modern literary work of any worth has been produced in the English language by an English writer ... except of course Bradshaw."

"I would sooner lose a train by the ABC than catch it by Bradshaw."

"West Kensington is a district to which you drive until the horse drops dead, when the cabman gets down to make enquiries."

"Bayswater is a place where people always get lost, and where there are no guides."

"Robert gave Harry a terrible black eye, or Harry gave him one; I forget which, but I know they were great friends."

"She is without one good quality, she lacks the tiniest spark of decency, and she is quite the wickedest woman in London. I haven't a word to say in her favour . . . and she is one of my greatest friends."

Speaking of a wealthy foreigner, who welcomed to his house every artist with the least claim to notoriety, Wilde said: "He came to London with the intention of opening a *salon*, and he has succeeded in opening a saloon."

When in the early nineties England was on the verge of war with France, Wilde was asked what he thought about it. "We will not go to war with France," he replied, "because her prose is perfect."

Lord Alfred Douglas and Wilde were sitting one day in the study of Dr. Warren, President of Magdalen College, Oxford. "I am thinking of presenting a statue of myself to the College," said Wilde. The consternation on Warren's face changed to relief when he added "Yes, to stand in the 'quad' here . . . a colossal equestrian statue."

He greeted a new arrival at a reception by the Countess de Grey with the words "Oh, I'm so glad you've come! There are a hundred things I want not to say to you."

"What terrible weather we are having," said a highly intellectual and very solemn woman he was taking in to dinner. "Yes, but if it wasn't for the snow, how could we believe in the immortality of the soul?" he rejoined. "What an interesting question, Mr. Wilde! But tell me exactly what you mean." "I haven't the slightest idea."

"Pray come to this symposium," said Wilde to E. F. Benson. "Everything nowadays is settled by symposiums, and this one is to deal finally with the subject of bimetallism . . . of bimetallism between men and women."

Wilde, however, could be as profound as he pretended to be superficial, and his genius enabled him to compress into a sentence what another would extend to a book. "Experience," he said, "is a question of instinct about life," and he was born with this instinct. No one ever said so many acute things in the guise of paradox. By shifting the viewpoint, he forced his listeners to look at life from unaccustomed angles and enlarged the boundaries of Truth. Though he owed something to La Rochefoucauld, he went deeper. His remark "We think that we are generous because we credit our neighbour with the possession of those virtues that are likely to be a benefit to us" is more complete than La Rochefoucauld's "The gratitude of most men is but a secret desire of receiving greater benefits." And although it is generally true to say that every intelligent maxim-maker since his time has been indebted to La Rochefoucauld for his observation "Our virtues are most frequently but vices disguised," we may claim that Wilde was wittier, more penetrating and more comprehensive than the Frenchman. Desmond MacCarthy has picked out four of Wilde's sayings and noted that they contain the pith of other men's theories and teachings. These are the four:

"As one reads history . . . one is absolutely sickened, not by the crimes that the wicked have committed, but by the punishments that the good have inflicted; and a community is infinitely more brutalised by the habitual employment of punishment, than it is by the occasional occurrence of crime."

"Man is least himself when he talks in his own person. Give him a mask and he will tell you the truth."

"Conscience must be merged in instinct before we become fine."

"Nothing can cure the soul but the senses, just as nothing can cure the senses but the soul."

Half of Tolstoy's message is in the last part of the first quotation, says Desmond MacCarthy; Yeats's theory of artistic composition is in the second; the essence of Samuel Butler's ethics is in the third; and the upshot of Meredith's philosophy in his novels, as it concerns love, is in the fourth. We may add that the core of Freud's doctrine is in Wilde's statement: "Every impulse that we strive to strangle broods in the mind, and poisons us . . . The only way to get rid of a temptation is to yield to it." What follows, then, taken with what has already been quoted, would have made Wilde memorable as an aphorist if he had said and written nothing else:

"A cynic is a man who knows the price of everything and the value of nothing."

"The sentimentalist is always a cynic at heart. Indeed sentimentality is merely the Bank-holiday of cynicism."

"Conscience and cowardice are really the same things. Conscience is the trade-name of the firm."

"Each class preaches the importance of those virtues it need not exercise. The rich harp on the value of thrift, the idle grow eloquent over the dignity of labour."

"Young men want to be faithful, and are not; old men want to be faithless, and cannot."

"The tragedy of old age is not that one is old, but that one is young."

"There is a luxury in self-reproach. When we blame ourselves we feel that no one else has a right to blame us. It is the confession, not the priest, that gives us absolution."

"Nothing makes one so vain as being told that one is a sinner. Conscience makes egoists of us all."

"When a woman marries again it is because she detested her first husband. When a man marries again it is because he adored his first wife. Women try their luck; men risk theirs."

"Don't tell me that you have exhausted life. When a man says that one knows that Life has exhausted him."

"Science can never grapple with the irrational. That is why it has no future before it in this world."

"The reason that we like to think so well of others is that we are all afraid for ourselves. The basis of our optimism is sheer terror."

"The soul is born old, but grows young. That is the comedy of life. The body is born young, and grows old. That is life's tragedy."

"Each time one loves is the only time that one has ever loved. Difference of object does not alter singleness of passion. It merely intensifies it."

"Good resolutions are simply cheques that men draw on a bank where they have no account."

Most of the records of the childish controversies in the Victorian age can be boiled down to this passage by Wilde: "The English mind is always in a rage. The intellect of the race is wasted in the sordid and stupid quarrels of second-rate politicians or third-rate theologians . . . We are dominated by the fanatic, whose worst vice is his sincerity . . . There is no sin except stupidity." Another of his sayings should be remembered by the British people, for it warns them against a repetition of their behavior between the years 1919 and 1939: "There is only one thing worse than injustice, and that is justice without her sword in her hand. When right is not might it is evil."

Wilde was called upon to defend some of his aphorisms from the witness-box. In September '94 Frank Harris took over the editorship of *The Saturday Review* and asked Wilde for something that would give the paper a fillip. With his usual good nature, Wilde jotted down a list of *Phrases and Philosophies for the Use of the Young*, and was about to despatch it when another friend begged him for something to give a new magazine for Oxford undergraduates called *The Chameleon* an auspicious start-off. With his usual good nature, he handed the *Phrases and Philosophies* to his friend, not troubling to make any enquiry about the publication; after which he forgot all about it. But his memory received a severe jolt when Jerome K. Jerome in *To-day* drew attention to the objectionable character of certain contributions in the first number of *The Chameleon* (December 1894), especially a story called "The Priest and the Acolyte." Wilde, who no doubt sympathised with the subject of the story, thought the treatment deplorable, and protested against it, with the result that the magazine was withdrawn, the first number being also the last. But a few months later Carson did his best to identify Wilde with the publication of *The Chameleon*; and then it was made clear that he had had nothing whatever to do with it, but indeed had been instrumental in suppressing it, Carson shifted the attack to Wilde's own contribution, trying hard, and failing completely, to turn the *Phrases* into an indictment of their coiner:

Carson: "Religions die when they are proved to be true." Is that true? (Carson did not complete the quotation: "Science is the record of dead religions.")

Wilde: Yes; I hold that. It is a suggestion towards a philosophy of the absorption of religions by science, but it is too big a question to go into now.

Carson: Do you think that was a safe axiom to put forward for the philosophy of the young?

Wilde: Most stimulating.

Carson: "If one tells the truth one is sure, sooner or later, to be found out?"

Wilde: That is a pleasing paradox, but I do not set very high store on it as an axiom.

Carson: Is it good for the young?

Wilde: Anything is good for the young that stimulates thought, in whatever age.

Carson: Whether moral or immoral?

Wilde: There is no such thing as morality or immorality in thought. There is immoral emotion.

Carson: "Pleasure is the only thing one should live for?"

Wilde: I think that the realisation of oneself is the prime aim of life, and to realise oneself through pleasure is finer than to do so through pain. I am, on that point, entirely on the side of the ancients—the Greeks. It is a pagan idea.

Carson: "A truth ceases to be true when more than one person believes in it?"

Wilde: Perfectly. That would be my metaphysical definition of truth; something so personal that the same truth could never be appreciated by two minds.

Carson: "The condition of perfection is idleness?"

Wilde: Oh, yes, I think so. Half of it is true. The life of contemplation is the highest life.

Carson: "There is something tragic about the enormous number of young men there are in England at the present moment who start life with perfect profiles, and end by adopting some useful profession?"

Wilde: I should think that the young have enough sense of humour.

Strangely enough Carson did not question Wilde about another of his axioms: "Any preoccupation with ideas of what is right or wrong in conduct shows an arrested intellectual development." Or not strangely. Under the circumstances Carson may have felt that it applied to himself.

CHAPTER THIRTEEN

THE TALKER

THE man who in 1880 had satisfied his histrionic nature by adorning his body in remarkable apparel was in 1890 adorning his thoughts in astonishing language. He was still acting a part, but it was a part that absorbed his entire genius, and he had succeeded in producing a personality the like of which had never previously appeared before the public. What we must bear in mind is that it was a part after his own heart: he had built it up from the foundations of his character: it represented himself, his attitude to life, his delight in existence, his innate kindliness, his happy disposition, his love of showing-off. It was a part, we may say, performed by a child with the imagination of a poet, the intelligence of a wit, and the skill of an actor.

In addition to the creative ability necessary for such a purpose, he possessed the two indispensable qualifications for a talker who wishes to hold his audience: a prodigious memory and a beautiful voice. A good memory constitutes about seventy per cent of what commonly passes for genius. The politician who can confound his opponent's present attitude by recalling his past utterances goes far. The barrister who can quote forgotten statutes at the right moment, and has all the evidence in a case at his tongue's tip, need have no anxiety about his future. The writer who can remember a quarter of what he has read is in clover. Wilde had the uncanny faculty of reading both pages of a novel simultaneously, seeing them as one picture, and photographing them on his mind with such rapidity that he could read almost as fast as he could turn the pages, and afterwards tell the story and sketch the characters in detail from memory, improving both. Several people have testified to his remarkable gift, but the evidence of W. B. Maxwell is enough: We opened a book at the first page, laid it on the billiard-room table, and clustered round to watch him. It was, I think, the third volume of a three-volume novel. He turned the pages fast to begin with, then faster and faster, and a little slower towards the end of the book. We did not time him. But he could not have been more than three minutes. Closing the book with a smile he handed it back for us to study and then question him. He stood the examination without a single mistake." He not only had the full story at his command, says Maxwell, but he could quote whole passages from it verbatim.

No one will listen for long without impatience to a man whose manner of utterance is not as attractive as the matter; and in this respect Wilde had been royally endowed. Some people said that his was the "golden voice" of Sarah Bernhardt, and it is possible that he had trained it to resemble hers, for he accented certain words in her fashion and copied some of her tricks of speech. But the musical quality was his own, the general effect of his speech peculiar to himself. His voice has been described as "warm," "full," "bony," "mossy," "flexible," and "caressing." Desirous to obtain the impression of an expert in elocution, I applied to Franklin Dyall, who had appeared in the original production of *The Importance of Being Earnest* and is himself the possessor of a very fine voice. He tells me this: "Wilde's voice was of the brown velvet order—mellifluous—rounded—in a sense giving it a plummy quality—rather on the adenotic side—but practically pure 'cello—and very pleasing." He certainly made exquisite music of it, performing with it artistically as a musician performs on his instrument, conscious of its range, commanding its scale, causing it to sing, to linger, to rise and fall, with never a false note struck, all in perfect harmony with the spoken words. Thus he could make the slightest story sound delightful, and those who had heard him speak a parable found it cold and lifeless when they read it in print.

"He was probably the greatest self-consciously deliberate master of the Art of Conversation who has talked the English language," writes Desmond MacCarthy, and this would have been echoed by everyone who had heard him improvise for an hour or more. Even those who were violently prejudiced against him on account of his appearance, his affectations or his notoriety, surrendered completely to the allurement of his conversation; and this does not refer only to people with artistic or intellectual sympathies. Frank Harris tells a story for the truth of which I obtained the late Lord Grimthorpe's confirmation. Hearing that Wilde was at Leeds nearby, Grimthorpe asked him to lunch at Kirkstall Grange, where the party consisted of fox hunting Yorkshiremen. The moment Wilde was announced the sportsmen went to ground, reading papers with great intentness, earnestly consulting one another in corners, anxious above all things not to be introduced to the man who gazed at sunflowers, the object of Gilbert's satire and the ridicul of *Punch*. Wilde appeared not to notice their preoccupation and began talking to his host. In five minutes the papers were abandoned, the consultation ceased, and Wilde was surrounded by a listening and laughing party o boneheaded country-squires, all of whom begged Grimthorpe to let them meet the fascinating fellow again. This sort of thing was continually happening. When Wilde stayed with W. B. Maxwell's family at Bank in the New Forest he quickly converted the hostility of the county people who lunched with them to enthusiasm; and many a man who, like Sir Chartres Biron, had conceived a strong antipathy towards him, succumbed to his charm at a first meeting. George Moore, who loathed him, after hearing him hold a table entranced for several hours at a dinner given to the Princess of Monaco by Frank Harris, had to admit that there was nothing in life like Oscar's conversation, and cursed himself for having allowed seven years to pass by since their last meeting.

Nothing at all resembling his conversation had been heard before. The great talkers of the past were more limited in their appeal, too anxious to appropriate the conversation and steer it in the direction of their choice, and most of them were accused of grave social defects by someone or other. Dean Swift was caustic and inclined to be quarrelsome; Doctor Johnson was dogmatic and occasionally shouted people down; Coleridge was a pure monologist, unadaptable, and had no humour; Macaulay was too informative and self-assertive; Carlyle was verbose and denunciatory. Wilde's sole equal in the art of entertaining his hearers was Sydney Smith, the most spontaneously witty and amusing talker on record, who never bored his listeners, never preached, and never engrossed the conversation. But he had not the poetry and profundity of Wilde, whose affectations and exhibitionism were an essential part of his personality and of his technique as a talker. E. F. Benson says that he monopolised the conversation, but practically contradicts the assertion by adding "That monopoly was eagerly accorded him, for he talked superbly." What actually happened was that Wilde would begin by talking to his neighbour at a dinner-party when everyone was chatting away to someone else. The laughter provoked by what he said would attract the attention of those opposite, then those to the right and left of him, then those farther away, and so on all down and round the table, until at last everyone was listening spellbound to the talk of one man. The difference between him and the real monopolist was that he adjusted himself to his audience; he did not compel them to submit to his direction. The least comment or interruption by anyone would command his immediate attention and possibly start him off on a fresh subject. He watched his listeners closely, noted the smallest sign of restiveness, and promptly switched over to a new theme. He seemed to know by instinct whether people wanted to be amused or impressed, to talk or to listen. If they wanted to talk he brought them into the

conversation, and often made so much of what they said that by the time he
had finished with it they were delighted by their own brilliance or profundity. This unegotistical quality made him the most attractive of companions, for in the midst of his elaborate flights of eloquence he was always
ready to stop and hear someone else, paying equal attention to lord and com-
moner, child and adult, notability and nonentity. Moreover, he never talked
of his own affairs except to intimates, never laid down the law, never contradicted, never pretended to be an authority on anything (except, occasionally,
manners), was always pliant and considerate, would join heartily in a laugh
against himself, and gave the whole of his genius to supply the pleasure of
the moment, whether the company consisted of one or two friends or a large
and distinguished party. His tact in choosing exactly the right subject for the
people he met, and handling it in a manner perfectly adapted to their taste,
is illustrated by Shaw's description of their one successful encounter. The
story Oscar told of the young man who invented a theatre stall which economised space appealed to Shaw's keen interest in economics and statistics;
and as it reminded Shaw of some yarn by Mark Twain, he remained for the
rest of his life under the strange delusion that Wilde's humour resembled
Twain's. But in conversation Wilde was a master of many styles. He could
bring tears to the eyes of his audience, make them smile with joy, en-
rapture them with fantasy, enthral them with eloquence, tickle their intelli-
gences with wit, and send them into fits of laughter by exhibitions of farcical
humour or outrageous burlesque. So sure was he of his power that he described the process in *Dorian Gray*: "He played with the idea, and grew
wilful; tossed it into the air and transformed it; let it escape and recaptured
it; made it iridescent with fancy, and winged it with paradox . . . He was
brilliant, fantastic, irresponsible. He charmed his listeners out of themselves,
and they followed his pipe laughing."

  Much of the effect he produced was of course due to his own radiance of
spirit, his vitality and exuberance, his love of pleasure and giving pleasure,
his strange personality, his physical oddity; but not a little was also due to
his highly developed dramatic sense, and a studiously perfected technique.
Never hesitating to find a word, but sometimes pausing to make an effect, his
talk flowed steadily on, delivered in a solemn, almost portentous, style; and
the contrast between the sobriety of the utterance and the whimsicality of the
substance, the gravity of the manner and the trivality of the matter, was
overpoweringly comical. His serious stories, too, were frequently lit up with
flashes of humour, when his whole being would undergo transformation, the
heavy impassive face becoming eager and sensitive, the steady watchful eye

sparkling with merriment, the slow rhythmical oracular speech slipping easily into a pungent, vivid and arresting form. He enjoyed his own performances quite as much as his audience did, and his laugh was constant, whole-hearted and infectious. Occasionally it was noticed that he seemed surprised by his fabulous inventions, as if he were merely the mouthpiece or agent for some mystical power which had taken control of him, and then he gave the appearance of being intoxicated by his own words and almost bewildered by his own brilliance. Undoubtedly he was inspired throughout those amazing sessions when people did not know how long they had been silent and instead of being exhausted cried for more. But usually he was in complete command of himself, at peace with life, at ease with everyone, aware of his extravagance, amused by his poses, certain that others were equally amused, and "blowing bubbles of enjoyment" which arose from a sunny disposition and an unfailing gaiety of mind.

He felt that "Conversation should touch on everything, but should concentrate itself on nothing," and when talking he never allowed one mood to prevail, but went easily by imperceptible stages from comedy to tragedy, from satire to sentiment, from beauty to burlesque, each being pointed by a different inflexion of the voice, a movement of the eyes, a slight or elaborate gesture. He did not like the sort of bore who is here today and not gone tomorrow, with his mania for facts and information, his harping on right and wrong, his craze for accuracy. "Is that your own story or did you get it from the *Mercure de France*?" asked one of these public nuisances. "Very likely indeed, but I believe it came originally from the Dutch," rejoined Wilde. "I made up another too. Once upon a time . . ." An Irish throat specialist named George Stoker interrupted him in the full flow of his discourse with "That shows what a fat lot you know about it!" Oscar burst out laughing: "You are impossible, George!" He used to say that "Gossip is charming. History is merely gossip, but scandal is gossip made tedious by morality." And when someone spoke of Holbein's portrait of Anne of Cleves, whose ugliness had been too much for Henry VIII, he clarified his theory of history: "You believe she was really ugly? No, my dear boy, she was exquisite as we see her in the Louvre; but in the escort sent to bring her to England travelled also a beautiful young nobleman of whom she became passionately enamoured, and on the ship they became lovers. . . . What could be done? Discovery meant death. So she stained her face, and put uncouth clothes upon her body, till she seemed the monster Henry thought her. Now, you do not know what happened? Years passed, and one day when the king went hawking he heard a woman singing in an orchard close, and, rising in his stirrup to see who with lovely voice had entranced him, he beheld Anne of Cleves, young and beautiful, singing in the arms of her lover."

He seemed to have read everything, to have met everyone, and could always throw light on the nature of men and books. Laurence Housman first met him at the studio of Ricketts and Shannon, and afterwards recalled a fragment of his conversation: "Travellers in South America tell of a bird which, if seen by you unawares, flies to hide itself. But if it has seen you first, then, by keeping its eye on you, it imagines that it remains invisible, and nothing will induce it to retreat. The bird-trappers catch it quite easily merely by advancing backwards. Now that, surely, is true philosophy. The bird, having once made you the object of its contemplation, has every right to think (as Bishop Berkeley did, I believe) that you have no independent existence. You are what you are—the bird says, and the Bishop says—merely because they have made you a subject of thought; if they did not think of you, you would not exist. And who knows?—they may be right. For, try as we may, we cannot get behind the appearance of things to the reality. And the terrible reason may be that there is no reality in things apart from their appearances." Another fragment was preserved by Sherard, who noticed a man sitting alone at the Café Royal and asked who he was. "That is Frederick Sandys," said Wilde, adding sorrowfully that he had been dead for some years. Sherard proving sceptical, an explanation followed: "In his lifetime he was a great painter, a true artist. Then he died, but came back afterwards, and now he sits in the Café Royal all day and most of the night, drinking little glasses of brandy. What a pity it is that dead men will come back and persist in showing themselves, just to pretend that they are alive, when everybody knows the contrary!" On the other hand many people who were generally thought to be dead were, according to Wilde, not only alive but keenly interested in his own words. For instance, "Flaubert has just told me that he was lost in admiration when I recited to him these wonderful lines 'The land was dry and burnt up with heat. The people went to and fro over the plain, like flies crawling upon a disk of polished copper.'" Gautier, Baudelaire, Keats and Rossetti were among his ardent admirers, and those of his friends who seemed worthy of the confidence were treated to their spoken appreciations of his writings. Still more unexpected, though perhaps easier to swallow, Queen Victoria was watching his career with the closest interest and sympathy; indeed there were moments when she ran the risk of neglecting her Empire, so absorbed was she in his latest publication so enchanted with his last Prose Poem. This was all a part of his self-dramatisation, his enjoyment of play-acting, and these in turn were due to hi boyish hilarity and delight in ostentation. "But I must fly!" he would suddenly exclaim: "already I can hear the horses of Apollo pawing impatiently at the gate. I shall be late for lunch and disappoint my newest and dearest friend!" In time this projection of himself as the central figure in the drama of life, abetted by his unprecedented success as a playwright and raconteur became second-nature with him. "What do you think of my work, Mr. Wilde?" asked Hubert Crackanthorpe, whose volume of stories had recently appeared. "Your play, dear boy, your play," answered Wilde, who, after relating the episode to a friend, commented on it as if it had occurred to someone else: "The great dandy, who has just come in to get rid of a few minutes, and is going on to another party, saying indifferently while putting on his coat, 'Your play, dear boy, your play.'"

In exhibiting Wilde as a talker, I will begin with his late arrival at a luncheon-party as described partly by Beerbohm Tree to myself and partly by E. F. Benson in his autobiography, the fusion of the two accounts no doubt giving us an approximately accurate record of the story. After making his excuses, Wilde sat down and began to speak with the solemnity of a Prime Minister on the verge of war:

"I am, and have been for some time, extremely busy. I have undertaken to write the first volume of The People's Cheap Guinea Series of Great Thoughts, and the subject has occupied every minute I could spare from eating, drinking, and sleeping. My contribution to the Series will consist of a small volume of moral essays, which I am hopeful will be purchased by many wealthy persons of restricted means who wish to give their friends little tokens of ill-will at Christmastime. The Archbishop of Canterbury has kindly consented to write a preface expressing his earnest desire that these brief sermons, as I dare to call them, will carry their message of sorrow into many otherwise happy homes. The first essay, on which I am now engaged, deals with the Value of Presence of Mind, and is in the form of an anecdote . . . an incident from real life which was related to me by a well-known actor, still happily amongst us, who owes his very existence to a daring exhibition of coolness in the face of terrible danger. He was playing the chief part in a drama which had proved extremely popular in the West End of London. For months there had not been an empty seat in the house, and at every performance the queues for the pit and gallery stretched for miles: indeed they stretched as far as Hammersmith. (I ought to add that the play was being performed at Hammersmith.) One evening, at that tense moment when the poor flower-girl rejects with scorn the odious proposals of the wicked marquis, a huge cloud of smoke poured from the wings and the scenery was caught by great tongues of fire. Although the safety curtain was immediately lowered, the audience were terrified and dashed towards the exits. A hideous panic broke out, men shouting and pushing, women screaming and clutching. There was a serious danger that many of the weaker ones would be trampled to death; and in fact some skirts were soiled, several dress shirts were crumpled. At the height of the din the actor of whom I have spoken, who loves and is loved by the flower-girl in the play, came up through the orchestra door, took in the situation at a glance, scrambled on to the stage, stood erect with flashing eyes and upraised arm before the iron curtain, and in a voice which rang like a trumpet through the theatre commanded silence. The audience knew that voice well, and felt reassured: the panic subsided. He told them that there was no longer any danger from the fire, which was now completely under control, but that there was a very real danger from their own fear: their lives depended on keeping their heads: they must return to their seats at once. Feeling thoroughly ashamed of themselves, they did as they were bidden; and when the exits were clear and the seats occupied once more, the actor leapt lightly over the footlights into the stalls and vanished through the first convenient doorway. Then the auditorium filled with smoke; the flames raced in from every side; and not another soul left the place alive."

What amazed his friends more than anything else about Wilde was the readiness with which he invented stories to illustrate whatever subject was being discussed at the time. Richard Le Gallienne relates how, in speaking of Free Will as an illusion and of Destiny as inescapable, he improvised in this manner:

"Once upon a time there was a magnet, and in its close neighbourhood lived some steel filings. One day two or three little filings felt a sudden desire to go and visit the magnet, and they began to talk of what a pleasant thing it would be to do. Other filings nearby overheard their conversation, and they, too, became infected with the same desire. Still others joined them, till at last all the filings began to discuss the matter, and more and more their vague desire grew into an impulse. 'Why not go to-day?' said one of them; but others were of opinion that it would be better to wait until to-morrow. Meanwhile, without their having noticed it, they had been involuntarily moving nearer to the magnet, which lay there quite still, apparently taking no heed of them. And so they went on discussing, all the time insensibly drawing nearer to their neighbour; and the more they talked, the more they felt the impulse growing stronger, till the more impatient ones declared that they would go that day, whatever the rest did. Some were heard to say that

t was their duty to visit the magnet, and that they ought to have gone long
ago. And, while they talked, they moved always nearer and nearer, without
realising that they had moved. Then, at last, the impatient ones prevailed,
and, with one irresistible impulse, the whole body cried out, 'There is no use
waiting. We will go to-day. We will go now. We will go at once.' And then
in one unanimous mass they swept along, and in another moment were
clinging fast to the magnet on every side. Then the magnet smiled—for the
steel filings had no doubt at all but that they were paying that visit of their
own free will."

Perhaps Wilde's most lovable aspect was his constant desire to please and
amuse everyone with whom he came into contact: he did not reserve his
brilliance and charm for distinguished company or important individuals.
Out of the abundance of his spirit he gave lavishly to all and sundry.
Graham Robertson once found his mother listening to Oscar, who was
speaking in a very nice and feeling manner about his Aunt Jane. "I didn't
know you had an Aunt Jane," said Robertson. "No, I dare say not," returned Oscar sadly. "She was a very old lady. I hardly remember her myself.
But I am sure that I have often told you about Aunt Jane's ball." Robertson
declared that this was the first that he had ever heard of it; so Oscar made
good the omission; and as Robertson assures me that in those days he had a
wonderful memory and heard the story retold several times, we have here
an almost exact reproduction of Oscar's words:

"Poor Aunt Jane was very old, and very, very proud, and she lived all
alone in a splendid, desolate old house in County Tipperary. No neighbours
ever called on Aunt Jane, and, had they done so, she would not have been
pleased to see them. She would not have liked them to see the grass-grown
drives of the demesne, the house with its faded chintzes and suites of shuttered rooms, and herself, no longer a toast and a beauty, no more a power
in the countryside, but a lonely old woman who had outlived her day.

"And from year to year she sat alone in her twilight, knowing nothing of
what passed in the world without. But one winter even Aunt Jane became
aware of a stir in the air, a wave of excitement sweeping over the neighbourhood. The New people were coming into the New house on the hill and
were going to give a great Ball, the like of which had never been seen. The
Ryans were enormously rich—'Ryans?' said Aunt Jane. 'I don't know the
Ryans. Where do they come from?' Then the blow fell. The Ryans came
from nowhere in particular and were reported on good authority to be 'in
business.'

" 'But,' said Aunt Jane, 'what are the poor creatures thinking of? Who will go to their ball?' 'Everybody will go,' Aunt Jane was assured. 'Everybody has accepted. It will be a wonderful affair.'

"When Aunt Jane fully realised this, her wrath was terrible. This is what things had come to in the neighbourhood, then—and it was her fault. It had been for her to lead; she had brooded in her tent when she should have been up and doing battle. And then Aunt Jane made her great resolve. *She would give a Ball—a Ball the like of which had never been imagined: she would re-enter Society and show how a *grande dame* of the old school could entertain. If the County had so far forgotten itself, she herself would rescue it from these impertinent interlopers. And instantly she set to work. The old house was repainted, refurnished, the grounds replanted; the supper and the band were ordered from London and an army of waiters engaged. Everything should be of the best—there should be no question of cost. All should be paid for; Aunt Jane would devote the rest of her life to the paying. But now money was as nothing; she spent with both hands.

"At last the great night arrived. The demesne was lit for two miles with coloured lamps, the hall and staircase were gorgeous with flowers, the dancing-floor smooth and shining as a mirror.

"The bandsmen were in their places and bowed deeply as Aunt Jane, in splendid gown and blazing with diamonds, descended in state and stood at the ballroom door.

"There she waited. Time went on, the footmen in the hall, the waiters in the supper-room began to look at each other, the band tuned up two or three times to show its zeal; but no guests arrived.

"And Aunt Jane, in her beautiful gown, waited at the ballroom door. Eleven—twelve—half-past twelve.

"Aunt Jane swept a deep curtsy to the band. 'Pray go and have your supper,' she said. 'No one is coming.'

"Then she went upstairs and died. That is to say, she never again spoke a word and was dead in three days. And not for some considerable time after her death was it discovered that Aunt Jane had quite forgotten to send out any invitations."

Laurence Housman, in *Echo de Paris*, makes Wilde describe how he had spent a week-end at a duke's country-house entertaining guests, and how missing an early train on Monday morning, he had been compelled to return to the house for a while before another was due. The exhibition hours of the ducal family were over, says Wilde, and "It was a charnel house: the bones of its skeleton rattled; the ghosts gibbered and moaned. Time remained motionless. I was haunted. I could never go there again. I had seen what man is never meant to see—the sweeping up of the dust on which the footfall of departing pleasure has left its print. There for two days I had been creating my public ... The breath of life I had so laboriously breathed into their nostrils they were getting rid of again, returning to native clay ..." Though this is a perfectly truthful picture, Laurence Housman tells me that the incident was described to him "*not* by Oscar but by one of the family. Oscar missed his train and had to come back and wait for the next—and it was *he* who was the extinct volcano with all the fire gone out of him. He could no longer talk; he was played out; his powers of performance were over." He certainly had to pay for those luncheon-parties, dinner-parties, and week-ends. A famous actor is usually exhausted after performing a strenuous part; but Wilde gave two or three one-man shows daily, sometimes almost a non-stop performance, in an endless ever-changing repertoire, and had to make up his parts as he went along. He liked it; otherwise he would not have done it; but he must occasionally have wondered whether the dukes and duchesses were worth it.

At all events he was at his happiest among his friends and among artists, with whom, as he did not have to dazzle or impress them, he could be quite simple and unaffected. In their company a more serious note was struck, and he reserved his parables for them. Some of these apologues, most of which had a biblical flavour, and all of which owed something to the language of the Gospels or the Song of Solomon, were inspired by his interest in the character of Christ, self-identification with whom was a part of his histrionic nature, and appeared, after much re-touching by their author, in *The Fortnightly Review* for July '94 under the title of *Poems in Prose*. They were not improved by the final form he gave them for publication. Such earlier versions as we possess, reported by the friends to whom he told them, are less ornate and more impressive than the printed ones; and since no picture of him as a talker would be complete (or rather as complete as we can now make it) without some examples of this very characteristic feature of his conversation in sympathetic surroundings, the fables which follow are the spoken stories, not the written compositions.

Just as the musician thinks in sound, the sculptor in form, and the painter in colour, so did Wilde think in stories: his philosophy expressed itself naturally in parables, which arose spontaneously in his mind from the topic of the moment. Thus:

"What have you been doing since yesterday?" he asked André Gide. Gide told him.

"You really did that?"

"Yes."

"And you are speaking the truth?"

"Absolutely."

"Then why repeat it? You must see that it is not of the slightest importance ... There are two worlds. The one exists and is never talked about it is called the real world because there is no need to talk about it in order to see it. The other is the world of art: one must talk about that because otherwise it would not exist."

Wilde promptly emphasised his point with a story which he never published. Gide's version is not as satisfactory as this by Charles Ricketts:

"Now a certain man was greatly beloved by the people of his village, for when they gathered round him at dusk and questioned him, he would relate many strange things he had seen. He would say: 'I beheld three mermaids by the sea who combed their green hair with a golden comb.' And when they besought him to tell more, he answered 'By a hollow rock I spied a centaur; and, when his eyes met mine, he turned slowly to depart, gazing at me sadly over his shoulder.' And when they asked eagerly 'Tell us, what else have you seen?' he told them 'In a little copse a young faun played upon a lute to the dwellers in the woods who danced to his piping.' One day when he had left the village, as was his wont, three mermaids rose from the waves who combed their green hair with a comb of gold, and, when they had departed, a centaur peeped at him behind a hollow rock, and later, as he passed a little copse, he beheld a faun who played upon a pipe to the dwellers in the wood.

"That night, when the people of the village gathered at dusk, saying: 'Tell us, what have you seen to-day?' he answered them sadly 'To-day I have seen nothing.'"

Once invented, Wilde would often repeat his stories, trying them out in various guises, testing their effect on different people, until he had achieved the form that satisfied himself. "All art is at once surface and symbol," he would affirm, and his own tales point the truth of this. Here is one that he told in many ways, the least elaborate being the most effective:

"When Narcissus died the flowers of the field were stricken with grief and begged the river for drops of water that they might mourn for him. 'If all my drops of water were tears,' replied the river, 'I should not have enough to weep for Narcissus. I loved him.' 'How could you help loving Narcissus?' said the flowers: 'he was so beautiful.' 'Was he beautiful?' asked the river. 'Who should know that better than yourself?' said the flowers, 'for every day, lying on your bank, he mirrored his beauty in your waters ...' 'I love him,' murmured the river, 'because, when he hung over me, I saw the re-flection of my own beauty in his eyes.' "[1]

From every angle Jesus Christ appealed to Oscar Wilde. His character as a man and his assumption of godhead pleased Wilde's sense of dramatic contrast. Also they both thought and taught in stories, and both had a strong intuition of their tragic destiny; though in Oscar's case what started as an attitude became a conviction, the rôle changing to reality. One of his tales was the foundation of several later romances by men who heard him tell it or heard others repeat it. It was related in great detail, but only the barest skeleton has come down to us, unless in the writings of others. It describes how Jesus had recovered after the crucifixion, escaped from the tomb, returned to His trade, and lived on for many years, the only Man on earth aware of the legends retailed in His name, the false reports about Himself, and the central myth of Christianity. One day St. Paul visited the town where He worked, and He alone did not go to hear the preacher. Thereafter His fellow-carpenters noticed that for some unaccountable reason Jesus kept his hands covered ... Fortunately Wilde's brief spoken Jesus versions of two other stories which centre on Christ have been preserved:

"On the night when Jesus died, Joseph of Arimathea went down from Mount Calvary and came upon a young man weeping bitterly. And Joseph spoke to him: 'I know how great thy grief must be, for surely He was a just Man.' And the young man made answer: 'I am not weeping for Him but for myself. For I too have wrought miracles; I have turned water into wine, healed the sick, given sight to the blind, fed the multitude, cast out devils, caused the barren fig-tree to wither, and raised the dead. All that this Man did, I have done. And yet they have not crucified me.' "

"Christ came to the city and heard the sounds of great rejoicing. He entered a dwelling and saw a man lying drunk upon a couch. He touched him on the shoulder and asked 'Why do you waste your soul in drink?' The man looked up and answered 'I was a leper once, and you healed me. What else should I do?' He went further into the city and saw a youth following a harlot, and said to him 'Why do you look at this woman with eyes of lust?' The youth knew Him, and answered 'I was blind once, and you gave me sight. At what else should I look?' So He spoke to the woman: 'Why do you walk

---

[1] This, as well as the ensuing three stories, were given to me by Adela Schuster, to whom Wilde told them. I showed them to Robert Ross, who preferred the more flowery compositions published by Wilde. Many years later I showed them to Robert Sherard, who wished to add some flowers from his own memory. But I prefer these to any I have read: they are shorter and simpler than those in *Poems in Prose* and more direct than those remembered by André Gide.

in the way of sin?' And the woman replied 'You forgave my sins, and the way is pleasant.' And He passed out of the city, and saw an old man weeping by the wayside, and asked him why he wept. The old man answered 'Lord, I was dead, and you brought me back to life. What else can I do but weep?'"

One more of Wilde's *Poems in Prose*, perhaps his best, was related in a form so much superior to the printed parable that it must find a place here:

"And there was a great silence in the House of Judgment; and the soul of the man stood naked before God. And God opened the book to the man's life and said 'Surely thou hast been very evil. Since thou hast done all these things, even into hell will I send thee.' And the man cried out 'Thou canst not send me into hell.' And God said 'Wherefore can I not send thee into hell?' And the man answered 'Because in hell I have always lived.' And there was a great silence in the House of Judgment. And God said to the man 'Seeing that I may not send thee into hell, even into Heaven will I send thee.' And the man said 'Thou canst not send me into heaven.' And God said 'Wherefore can I not send thee into heaven?' And the man said 'Because I have never been able to imagine it.' And there was a great silence in the House of Judgment."

CHAPTER FOURTEEN

THE DRAMATIST

SIR BERNARD PARTRIDGE writes to me: "In the late eighties Oscar Barrett produced at the Lyceum a pantomime which broke away from tradition and reverted to the fanciful style of the old Planché extravaganzas, reducing the low comedy element to a minimum. Oscar Wilde, who was rather hard-up then, seemed to me the very man to make a success of this sort of thing, and I suggested to him that he ought to write a pantomime on these lines. He thought a moment, and then said 'Well, I'd write a pantomime to-morrow . . . if only they'd let me dramatise the Book of Revelations!'" But pantomime producers are seldom in search of novelty, and nothing came of it. Instead, George Alexander, the young and zealous actor who had just become manager of the St. James's Theatre, begged Wilde to write him a modern comedy. Wilde was quite agreeable, but nothing happened. In the belief that cash would evoke inspiration, Alexander then insisted that he should take £100 in advance of royalties. Wilde was extremely agreeable, took the money, spent it, and hoped for more, but did not write a line of the play, and whenever the two happened to meet chatted away with entire composure about anything except what the actor-manager was bursting to ask him. Alexander was that rare creature: an artist who was also a man of business, or perhaps it would be truer to say that he was a man of business who was also an artist. He felt sure that Wilde could write a first-rate play, and, what was much more to the point, he felt sure that Wilde could write a box-office success. The thought that so much cash and prestige depended on the industry of the most indolent author he had ever come across maddened him, and at last the explosion occurred. Some twenty years later Alexander recalled it for my benefit:

"When am I going to see that play?"

"My dear Alec, you may see any play you wish to see. You have only to go to the theatre where it is being performed, and I am sure they will give you admirable seats."

"You know perfectly well the play I mean."

"How can I know if you keep it secret?"

"The play you are writing for me."

"Oh, that! My dear Alec, it isn't written yet, so how can you possibly see it?"

"May I ask if you have started to write it?"

"Not with pen and ink . . . no . . . but it is all written in my head, and there I think we must leave it for the present."

"But don't you want to make money?"

"I much prefer money that is made for me . . . Ah, I was forgetting . . . yes . . . I suppose I shall have to do something. I owe you a hundred pounds."

"Oh, don't worry about that!"

"I don't."

He found it quite impossible to write a play during the fashionable season, so he waited till the late summer of that year (1891), when he wrestled with his theme in what he called a cottage near Lake Windermere. (It was probably a cottage of some twenty rooms.) All his plays were written when he was on holiday, and the names of the leading characters were usually taken from the places where he had stayed or in the neighbourhood. None of his plays took more than three or four weeks of actual work to polish off, though he sometimes lazily lingered over them: they were his scrapbooks into which he put bits he could recall from his own conversation. He had a poor opinion of contemporary dramatists. "It is the best play I ever slept through," he said of a piece by Arthur Pinero, and of another playwright: "There are three rules for writing plays. The first rule is not to write like Henry Arthur Jones; the second and third rules are the same." So he showed them how the job ought to be done, and in the autumn of '91 handed George Alexander *Lady Windermere's Fan*, which he described as "one of those modern drawing-room plays with pink lampshades." In one reading Alexander spotted a winner, and, thinking that Wilde would jump at the money, said he would be willing to buy the play outright for £1000. "I have so much confidence in your excellent judgment, my dear Alec, that I cannot but refuse your generous offer," was the unexpected reply. His confidence was wholly justified, for he made £7000 out of the original run.

The rehearsals did not go as smoothly as Alexander had anticipated. Wilde entertained views of his own which conflicted with the actor's, and stuck to them stubbornly. For example, at every rehearsal of Act 2 it was pointed out to him that the curtain could be brought down on something more effective than the usual dramatic outburst. He treated the suggestion with disdain, and Alexander was galled by his "damned Irish obstinacy." At last he consented to try a light ending, and rather to his annoyance found that it was a great improvement. Next, he declined to discuss the actor's plea that the audience should be let into the secret of Mrs. Erlynne's identity early in the play; though after the first night he took the advice of his friends, who said that the psychological interest of the second act would be greatly increased by the disclosure, and in a letter to the press admitted that Alexander had "strongly held and urged" this opinion before the production. The attitude he adopted to both of Alexander's suggestions reveals his essential juvenility: he enjoyed the unreal rhetoric of the dramatic "curtain," and he loved to "keep a secret" from the audience. Proof that he had not been pleased with the rehearsals was indirectly supplied in a letter which he wrote to *The Daily Telegraph* on the morning of the day which saw the first performance of his comedy. That paper had misreported a speech which he had made when taking the chair at a meeting of the Playgoers' Club. According to the published account, he had said that the stage was furnished with a set of puppets, but "What I really said was that the frame we call the stage was 'peopled with either living actors or moving puppets,' and I pointed out briefly, of necessity, that the personality of the actor is often a source of danger in the perfect presentation of a work of art. It may distort. It may lead astray. It may be a discord in the tone or symphony. For anybody can act. Most people in England do nothing else." He went on to say that "the actor's aim is, or should be, to convert his own accidental personality into the real and essential personality of the character he is called upon to personate." Then he hinted at the sort of trouble he had been having at rehearsals: "There are many advantages in puppets. They never argue. They have no crude views about art. They have no private lives. We are never bothered by accounts of their virtues, or bored by recitals of their vices; and when they are out of an engagement they never do good in public or save people from drowning, nor do they speak more than is set down for them. They recognise the presiding intellect of the dramatist, and have never been known to ask for their parts to be written up. They are admirably docile, and have no personalities at all. I saw lately, in Paris, a performance by certain puppets of Shakespeare's *Tempest* . . . Miranda was the mirage of Miranda, because an artist has so fashioned her; and Ariel was true Ariel, because so had she been made. Their gestures were quite sufficient, and the words that seemed to come from their little lips were spoken by poets who had beautiful voices. It was a delightful performance, and I remember it still with delight, though Miranda took no notice of the flowers I sent her after the curtain fell."

On the day before the production of his play Wilde asked Graham Robertson to go to a certain shop and order a green carnation, which he must wear at the first performance.

"A *green* carnation?"

"No, I know there's no such thing, but they grow them somehow at that shop. I want a lot of men to wear them to-morrow—it will annoy the public."

"But why annoy the public?"

"It likes to be annoyed. A young man on the stage[1] will wear a green carnation; people will stare at it and wonder. Then they will look round the house and see here and there more and more specks of mystic green. 'This must be some secret symbol,' they will say: 'what on earth can it mean?'"

"And what does it mean?"

"Nothing whatever, but that is just what nobody will guess."

Lady Windermere's Fan was produced at the St. James's Theatre on February 20th, 1892, with Alexander as "Lord Windermere" and Marion Terry as "Mrs. Erlynne," and there was no doubt of its success from the start. Nothing to compare with it had been seen on the English stage since Sheridan's *The School for Scandal*, about 120 years before. Between the acts of that first night Richard Le Gallienne went up to the theatre bar and found Wilde in the midst of a group of young admirers, over whom he towered head and shoulders. He left them for Le Gallienne.

"My dear Richard, where have you been? It seems as if we hadn't met for years. Now tell me what you have been doing? Ah, I remember ... Yes .. You have pained me deeply, Richard."

"I pained you! How?"

"You have brought out a new book since I saw you last."

"Well, what of it?"

"You have treated me very badly in your book, Richard."

"I treated you badly! You must be confusing my book with somebody else's. My last book was *The Religion of a Literary Man*. You can't have read it, or you wouldn't say I had treated you badly."

"That's the very book. I have read every word of it, and your treatment of me in that book is infamous and brutal. I couldn't have believed it of you, Richard—such friends as we have been too!"

"I treated you brutally in my *Religion of a Literary Man*! You must be dreaming! I never so much as mentioned you in it."

[1] Ben Webster in the part of Cecil Graham.

"Ah, Richard! that was just it."

After a roar of laughter, Wilde ordered drinks and said "But do tell me: what else have you been writing?" Le Gallienne replied that among other things he had been writing an essay on loving one's enemies. "That's a great theme!" exclaimed Oscar. "I should like to write on that too. For, do you know, all my life I have been looking for twelve men who didn't believe in me . . . and so far I have only found eleven." He found the twelfth some three years later.

Loud calls for "author" brought Wilde on to the stage after the last act, and he received a tremendous ovation. Holding a cigarette between his fingers, and smiling blandly, he addressed the audience. Though the episode has become a classic in theatrical history, the true text of his speech has so far been lacking. The dramatic critics were too indignant to be exact, and as Wilde himself gave several fanciful recitals of what he had said to people who had not been present, the reports that have been printed are contradictory and inaccurate. Luckily a member of the St. James's Theatre staff took it down in shorthand, and so George Alexander was able to tell me not only what Wilde said, but the actual words he stressed:

"Ladies and Gentlemen: I have enjoyed this evening *immensely*. The actors have given us a *charming* rendering of a *delightful* play, and your appreciation has been *most* intelligent. I congratulate you on the *great* success of your performance, which persuades me that you think *almost* as highly of the play as I do myself."

The audience enjoyed this as much as anything they had heard that night. Not so the critics, who thought the cigarette insulting and the speech offensive, and whose irritation with the author extended to his work. William Archer and W. B. Walkley, the two best dramatic critics of the day until the arrival of Bernard Shaw three years later, pointed out what was novel in the play; but the rest, headed by Clement Scott of *The Daily Telegraph*, refused to admire his wit on account of his "insolent effrontery." Or, possibly, a rumour had reached them that, in reply to someone's statement that all the dramatic critics could be bought, Wilde had said: "Perhaps you are right. But, judging from their appearance, most of them cannot be at all expensive." Brother Willie wrote a disparaging notice of the play, but this may have been because one of Oscar's remarks had been repeated to him: "Relations are a tedious lot of people who don't know how to live or when to die." Oscar was a little put out by Willie's hostility, but he was too busy enjoying himself to give it serious consideration. "After a good dinner one can forgive anybody, even one's own relations," he remarked.

The new comedy was the talk of the town, and the epigrams in it were quoted everywhere. "I suppose there are wittier men than the author of *Lady Windermere's Fan*," said the author of *Lady Windermere's Fan*, "but if so I have never met one." A friend stopped him in the street and asked how the play was going. "Capitally," he replied: "I am told that Royalty is turned away nightly." Such was the craze it created that Charles Brookfield and James Glover wrote a musical travesty of it entitled *The Poet and the Puppets*, in which Wilde was caricatured by name. On hearing this, he appealed to the licenser of plays and insisted that Brookfield should read the libretto to him. With his invariable good nature he punctuated the reading with such phrases as "Delightful!" "Charming, my old friends!" "Exquisite!" etc. He refused to let them use the name "Oscar" but raised no objection to "O'Flaherty," and, as he showed them to the door, he said "I feel, however, that I have been . . . well . . . Brookfield, what is the word? . . . what is the thing you call it in your delightfully epigrammatic stage English, eh? . . . Oh, yes! . . . delightfully spoofed!" The travesty appeared at the Comedy Theatre in May; and a month later Oscar Wilde was again in the news.

After finishing his comedy the previous autumn he had gone to Paris and had there written a one-act play based on an episode in the Gospels of Matthew and Mark. Flaubert had already decked the legend of Salome in impeccable prose and Wilde decided to write his drama in French. The story had been in his mind for some time, and over lunch one day he told it to some French writers in greater detail than usual. Then he returned to his lodgings at 29 Boulevard des Capucines, and, as a blank book happened to be lying on the table, he thought he might as well use it up by writing what he had just been speaking. "If the blank book had not been there on the table I should never have dreamed of doing it. I should not have sent out to buy one," he stated. No blank book can have caused more trouble in the history of art. He wrote with his usual speed and concentration, probably in English, and suddenly became aware that it was between ten and eleven at night. He went to get some food at the Grand Café nearby, and asked the leader of the orchestra to play something in harmony with his thoughts, which were centred on "a woman dancing with her bare feet in the blood of a man she has craved for and slain." The leader of the orchestra, perhaps accustomed to such thoughts, rose to the occasion, and, according to Wilde, played such terrifying music that the conversation in the restaurant ceased and the listeners "looked at each other with blanched faces." Read "slight surprise" for "blanched faces," and everything else in this story may be taken as true.

We do not know for certain whether that first draft was written in English or French, but we may suspect the former, because of the obvious influence of the Song of Solomon on some of the longer passages and because in the first flush of inspiration he would naturally write in English. Also we know that on October 27th, '91, after his return from Paris, George Curzon gave a breakfast-party at which Oscar said that he was writing a play in French to be acted at the Français, and that he was ambitious of being a French Academician. Everyone promised to go to the first performance, Curzon as Prime Minister.[1] This suggests that Wilde was then at work turning his play laboriously into French. More than the Bible, much more than Flaubert, his drama shows the influence of Maeterlinck, who was then being acclaimed as the Belgian Shakespeare, presumably on account of his total lack of resemblance to Shakespeare, and who wrote symbolical dramas, quite unlike anything that had previously been seen on the stage, with a rigid simplicity of language and a haunting balladic effect. It is perfectly clear that Wilde at first regarded his *Salomé* as a *jeu d'esprit*, as a slight parable which for some queer reason he had turned into a play, which for some equally queer reason he had turned into French; and in the company of friends he would parody it, quoting with a laugh: "Who are those wild beasts howling? They are the Jews discussing their religion," and stressing the absurdity of the phrase "And I will give you a flower, Narraboth, a little *green* flower," though Charles Ricketts assured him that some flowers really were green. Later, however, when Maeterlinck and other French writers praised it with enthusiasm, while the English critics condemned it with ferocity, he went to the opposite extreme and claimed that it was a poetic and dramatic masterpiece.

Having shown it to several Frenchmen, who made a few suggestions and corrections, some of which he adopted, he read it to Sarah Bernhardt at her request. She at once expressed a wish to play the leading part, and incidentally made two sage comments: "*Mais c'est héraldique; on dirait une fresque,*" and "*Le mot doit tomber comme une perle sur un disque de cristal; pas de mouvements rapides, des gestes stylisés.*" She determined to produce it in London and took the Palace Theatre for that purpose. Wilde was full of ideas. "I should like everyone on the stage to be in yellow," said he. Someone mentioned that the sky should be violet. "A violet sky . . . yes . . . I never thought of that. Certainly a violet sky . . . and then, in place of an

[1] Curzon and Wilde had been friends at Oxford, where they had spent many afternoons in Oscar's rooms "talking and thinking in Greek." Wilde prophesied a great career for Curzon, who in due time became Viceroy of India, but just missed being Prime Minister because Baldwin "popped in between the election and his hopes."

orchestra, braziers of perfume. Think: the scented clouds rising and partly veiling the stage from time to time . . . a new perfume for each motion." The rehearsals had been in progress for three weeks when, in June '92, the Lord Chamberlain, acting on an ancient law that had been passed to suppress Catholic mystery plays, refused his licence on the ground that the play introduced biblical characters. The success of Wilde's first play had gone to his head, and he behaved like a pampered infant to whom something has suddenly and inexplicably been denied. That it was his own fault added to his exasperation. He should have applied for a licence before Sarah Bernhardt began to make her plans, and he must have known that there was a grave risk of refusal. Sarah, who had not the least notion that anything stood in the way of her production, and would not have moved a step if she had, was highly indignant with the Censor, furious because she had wasted so much time, trouble and money, and angry with Wilde, who was already angry with himself, which made him doubly angry with everyone else. He went to a dinner at the Authors' Club and spoke on the subject. "He was full of indignation and unbosomed his troubles at great length," Eden Phillpotts writes to me; "then turned his back on the assembly and departed. It was an example of pure wounded egotism, without any thought of anything but his personal grievance. A plump, pale, heavy-jowled man in evening dress with violets in his buttonhole, and only one smarting thought in his mind. On his departure amusement rather than sympathy appeared to be indicated by those who had heard him. Had he adopted a different line of approach, his very genuine grievance with an idiotic attitude to art would have found everybody on his side, of course. But those who pity themselves so much are apt to lose the sympathy of their neighbours." He complained to friends and acquaintances that every single dramatic critic except Archer in *The World* had approved the Censor's action, and that not one actor had protested against what was really an insult to the stage, "not even Irving, who is always prating about the art of the actor." He amplified this in a published interview:

"The Censorship apparently regards the stage as the lowest of all the arts, and looks on acting as a vulgar thing. The painter is allowed to take his subjects where he chooses . . . the sculptor is equally free . . . And the writer, the poet—he also is quite free . . . But there is a Censorship over the stage and acting; and the basis of that Censorship is that, while vulgar subjects may be put on the stage and acted, while everything that is mean and low and shameful in life can be portrayed by actors, no actor is to be permitted to present under artistic conditions the great and ennobling subjects taken from the Bible. The insult in the suppression of *Salomé* is an insult to the stage as a form of art, and not to me . . ."

For the first time in his life he completely lost his sense of humour, and with it his sense of proportion, for he announced quite seriously in a Paris journal, *Le Gaulois*, that he intended to become a Frenchman:

"My resolution is deliberately taken. Since it is impossible to have a work of art performed in England, I shall transfer myself to another fatherland, of which I have long been enamoured . . . Here people are essentially anti-artistic and narrow-minded. . . . Of course I do not deny that Englishmen possess certain practical qualities; but, as I am an artist, these qualities are not those which I admire. Moreover, I am not at present an Englishman. I am an Irishman, which is by no means the same thing. No doubt I have English friends to whom I am deeply attached; but as to the English, I do not love them. There is a great deal of hypocrisy in England which you in France very justly find fault with. The typical Briton is Tartuffe seated in his shop behind the counter. There are numerous exceptions, but they only prove the rule."

Wilde's threat that he was about to change his nationality gave *Punch* a good subject for a cartoon, and incited William Watson to write some satirical lines, concerning which Oscar remarked: "There is not enough fire in William Watson's poetry to boil a tea-kettle." In a few weeks his humour returned to his rescue, and he altered his programme, for the anti-artistic and narrow-minded English were still crowding to see *Lady Windermere's Fan*; and, recognising that he had judged them harshly, he revised his opinion of the country, taking a wider and more indulgent view: "England is Caliban for nine months of the year, and Tartuffe for the other three."

The French version of *Salomé* was published in Paris in February '93. Exactly a year later an English translation appeared in London, and the critics got the opportunity for which they had been waiting, but whether they displayed more of Caliban or Tartuffe is a nice question. The publisher was John Lane, who brought out several of Wilde's books, and most of the works of the advanced literary movement of the nineties. He drove very hard bargains with his young authors, sometimes with the help of a good lunch at the Reform Club, a careful selection of wines enabling him to arrange contracts agreeable to himself. He told Richard Le Gallienne that, though he disliked Wilde personally, such was the magic of the man's voice and conversation that he was afraid of transacting any business with him, knowing that he would be charmed into getting the worst of the bargain. The cellar of the Reform Club being useless in the circumstances, his partner

Elkin Mathews was present whenever Wilde called to discuss business, and thus reinforced the firm did its best. On his part, Wilde did not like Lane, and, to put him in his place, named the valet in *The Importance of Being Earnest* after him.

At the author's request, Lord Alfred Douglas did an English translation from the French original. Wilde did not like it, and when Aubrey Beardsley, who claimed that he could make an ideal translation, begged to be allowed to do it, Wilde gave way. But he thoroughly disliked Beardsley's version and said he would rather use the one by Douglas, who thereupon gave him permission to make what alterations he pleased, but added that his own name as translator had better not appear if the text was not his. Wilde made some alterations, and dedicated the play in its English form to Douglas, whose name appeared as translator, though he never considered the published version as his work.

Meanwhile, Robert Ross had persuaded Wilde to let Aubrey Beardsley do the illustrations, which Wilde disliked almost as much as he had disliked the same artist's translation, saying to one friend "They are too Japanese, while my play is Byzantine," and to another "They are like the naughty scribbles a precocious schoolboy makes on the margins of his copybooks," and to a third "They are cruel and evil, and so like dear Aubrey, who has a face like a silver hatchet, with grass-green hair." He had some ground for complaint, as "dear Aubrey" had caricatured him in several of the drawings, and the animalistic quality of Beardsley's work did not suit the hieratic quality of Wilde's. People looked for evil in Beardsley's pictures, and having evil in themselves, they naturally found it; but Wilde's play suffered from the connection, because the positions of dramatist and draftsman were reversed, the play being used to illustrate the illustrations. The two did not like one another, possibly because in certain respects they were alike. Both were arrogant, disdaining criticism, despising the bourgeois. Beardsley copied Wilde's dandyism, and his remark that he had caught a cold by leaving the tassel off his cane shows that he was attracted to one form of Oscar's humour. Both were preoccupied with "sin," which resulted in Beardsley becoming a Roman Catholic, in Wilde becoming what he called "a pagan," what the world called "a sinner." But their differences were considerable. Beardsley thought of nothing but his art, was narrow in his interests, intolerant and unforgiving by nature. Though Wilde had given him the chance of his life in *Salomé*, he never forgot that his translation had been turned down; and when John Lane started *The Yellow Book* with Beardsley as illustrator, the antagonisms to Wilde of both publisher and artist was shown by his absence as a contributor.

This quarterly publication, the first number of which came out in April '94, has in some curious way become associated with the forward movement of the nineties in art and letters. It is supposed to have expressed the daring and rebellious spirit of youth, straining at the leash of Victorian respectability. It did nothing of the sort. It favoured no movement, it displayed no tendency. Among its early contributors were Henry James, George Saintsbury, Richard Garnett, Edmund Gosse, William Watson, Max Beerbohm, and suchlike innocuous literary tories. The only startling note was provided by Beardsley, who, however, was only permitted to alarm the readers for four numbers, after which William Watson informed the editor, Henry Harland, and the publisher, John Lane, that they must choose between his poems and Beardsley's illustrations. They did not hesitate for a moment, but came down handsomely on the side of poetry and respectability: Beardsley was sacked, and the fifth number, already in the press and containing more of his work, was withdrawn. *The Yellow Book* "turned grey in a single night" when Beardsley left it, and lingered on for nine more issues, feeble and reputable to the last. Arthur Symons, an unorthodox critic, left it too, and with Beardsley started *The Savoy* the following year. This ran for eight numbers, and might just as well have been called *The Beardsley*, for he was, if not the life and soul, at least the body and death of it.

Oscar did not care for *The Yellow Book*, calling it "horrid," "loathsome," "dull," "a great failure," and "not yellow at all." When Charles Ricketts praised it, he said "My dear boy, do not say nice false things about *The Yellow Book*. I bought it at the station, but before I had cut all the pages I threw it out of my carriage window. Suddenly the train stopped and the guard, opening the door, said 'Mr. Wilde, you have dropped *The Yellow Book*.' What was to be done? In the hansom, with the subtlety of the poet, I cunningly hid it under the cushions, and paid my fare . . . When came a loud knocking at the front door, and the cabby appearing, said 'Mr. Wilde, you have forgotten *The Yellow Book*.'" As for the illustrator, he made a remark similar to one that had already proved effective with Frank Harris: "Yes, dear Aubrey is always too Parisian; he cannot forget that he has been to Dieppe . . . once."

But *The Yellow Book* was still in the future when Herbert Beerbohm Tree asked Wilde if he might produce the successor to *Lady Windermere's Fan*. Tree, unlike Alexander, was more of an artist than a business-man, though in '92 he had already been the successful manager of the Haymarket Theatre for five years, and was to remain there for another five before building an imposing edifice for himself, Her Majesty's Theatre, just across the way. As an actor too he was the opposite of Alexander, who specialised in "straight," "romantic juvenile" and "gentleman" parts, performing them in a polished but uninspired manner ("He doesn't act on the stage: he behaves," said Wilde), while Tree was utterly unsuited to anything in that line and made his big success in "character" parts of a weird, fantastic, comic, macabre, machiavellian, sinister and sometimes repellent order. Although he had already played several "straight" parts in what can only be called a crooked manner, he was clearly not the actor for a witty and debonair aristocrat in a fashionable drawing-room comedy, and Wilde told him so. "As Herod in my *Salomé*, you would be admirable. As a peer of the realm in my latest dramatic device, pray forgive me if I do not see you." Tree, who gave him these details, was persistent, and at last Wilde, who had found Alexander a little trying, good-naturedly consented. It must here be stated that, after his unfortunate experience with Mary Anderson over *The Duchess of Padua*, Wilde never wrote a play with a definite actor or actress in view for any particular part, and in that respect he was being quite truthful, if a trifle pompous, when he said to Vincent O'Sullivan "I never write plays for anyone. I write plays to amuse myself. After, if people want to act in them, I sometimes allow them to do so."

Tree had known Wilde for some years and revelled in his wit and fancy in a way that was foreign to the temperament and beyond the intellectual scope of Alexander. Himself a personality of a rather exotic kind, an actor in private life who loved to amaze people and amuse them, a bit of a dandy and a *bon viveur*, Tree saw in Wilde all his own qualities magnified and perfected, plus a genius for self-expression which he lacked; and he would willingly have given all his success as an actor in exchange for Wilde's success as a talker. His good-nature, boyishness, light-heartedness and unenviousness responded to similar qualities in Wilde, and he told me that "Oscar was the greatest man I have ever known—and the greatest gentleman." As Tree had met pretty well every notability of his time, his tribute, like those of Ellen Terry, Wilfred Scawen Blunt and Charles Ricketts, is not without significance. Robert Sherard recalled for me an evening which he had spent in the company of Tree and Wilde: "Beerbohm Tree had a great liking for Oscar and a huge admiration for his genius. I was at a supper Tree gave at the Garrick Club to celebrate the election as a member of that club of Lord Edward Cecil, a supper at which *inter alios* the Duke of Newcastle, Corney Grain, Joseph Knight, Borthwick of *The Morning*

Post, and John Hare were present; and I remember how Oscar held everyone the whole night with his wit, but I cannot remember a single thing Tree said except that at five a.m. he was with us in the entrance with his auburn hair all tousled over his eyes suggesting a final jeroboam or a whiskey and soda or anything else you'd like—a jolly, kind hospitable man. As to what Oscar thought of him, he certainly never said anything disparaging about him, though I do not fancy that he vastly admired his acting. But he thought him what he was—a thoroughly good unphilistine chap. I have always loved Tree's memory in remembrance of his respect for Oscar."

A Woman of No Importance was written for the most part at Babbacombe, Torquay, in a house lent to the author by Lady Mount Temple for the summer season of '92. Tree was touring the provinces that autumn, and Wilde spent three days with him and his wife in Glasgow, talking, planning, laughing, eating and drinking—partridges, oysters and champagne, according to Mrs. Tree, who adds that, as soon as everything was settled and the play practically cast, "the glamour of him as a guest palled a little, and I remember how glad we were, Herbert and I, when some smart invitation recalled him." Or was it only "I" and not Herbert? Wives are not usually partial to male friends who absorb the interest of their husbands. The rehearsals went swimmingly, and Tree could hardly contain his admiration for an author who, when a portion of the script needed revision, "retired into a corner of the theater and shortly emerged with a completely new scene bristling with wit and epigram." A play by Henry Arthur Jones was in its last week at the theatre, and one morning a rehearsal of the new piece was interrupted by a terrific crash. Wilde was equal to the emergency: "Pray do not be alarmed, ladies and gentlemen. The crash you have just heard is merely some of Mr. Jones's dialogue that has fallen flat."

Wilde and the Trees, with their friends, made a lively luncheon-party most days at the Continental Hotel in Lower Regent Street, and Wilde told them the stories of plays he intended to write: *A Florentine Tragedy* and *La Sainte Courtisane.* One actor in the cast, Fred Terry, who was playing "Gerald Arbuthnot," resented the author's advice. He was acting the part as a man of the world, and Wilde wanted him to be a high-spirited youth. Terry did not agree, and became irritable:

"Oh, well, you know, Mr. Wilde, you can lead a horse to the water, but you can't make him drink."

"No, Terry. But you have a circus. In that circus is a ring. A horse enters the ring and approaches a trough of water. The ringmaster cracks his whip and says 'Drink!' and the horse drinks. That horse, Terry, is the actor."

"So, Mr. Wilde, you compare the stage to a circus?" said Terry angrily.

"Ah," came the bland reply, "yours was the metaphor."

Feeling that the situation could be eased by a friendly talk away from the theatre, Wilde invited himself to lunch at Terry's flat, and, finding that the actor loved the characters of Dickens, talked about them in a most discerning and enthusiastic manner. Admiration for Dickens always melted Terry, who by this means was quickly won over to Wilde's conception of "Gerald Arbuthnot" and agreed to play the part exactly as he wished.

"Well, Mr. Wilde," said Terry when the time came to separate, "it's been a very great pleasure for me to find another person who is fond of Dickens."

"Oh, my dear boy, I've never read a word of his in my life!" replied Wilde, who, having gained his point at the cost of an hour's undiluted Dickens, could not resist a final fling. He probably knew the novels of Dickens a good deal better than Terry did; though the effect of *The Old Curiosity Shop* on most Victorian readers must have passed him by, for a comment he made on it would not have amused the average Dickensian: "One must have a heart of stone to read the death of Little Nell without laughing."

On the whole Wilde got on very well with his actors, and with two exceptions, to be named later, all of them were fond of him. He was easygoing, helpful and considerate at rehearsals, though he found the exhibitions of vanity on the part of "stars" a little jarring at times, which led him to think that actors as a class should not know how to read or write but should learn the words they had to speak from the lips of the author. "Shun the experienced actor," he advised two women playwrights: "in poetic drama he is impossible. Choose graceful personalities—young actors and actresses who have charming voices—that is enough. The rest is in the hands of God and the poet." He once told an interviewer that "the exact relations between the actor and the dramatist are usually a little strained"; upon which the interviewer asked "Do you regard the actor as a creative artist?" and he replied "Certainly. Terribly creative—terribly creative." All the same he managed to get the best out of the older people by courtesy and flattery. Bernard Shaw provides evidence of this: "Mrs. Calvert, whose great final period as a stage old woman began with her appearance in my *Arms and The Man*, told me one day, when apologising for being, as she thought, a bad rehearser, that no author had ever been so nice to her except Mr. Wilde." From something Lewis Waller told me, Wilde seems to have been if anything too nice. Waller was a robust actor, ideally suited to heroic romantic rôles, and in course of time played Shakespeare's Hotspur and Henry V unsurpassably, with such splendour of declamation that anyone who saw him in them could never thereafter read the plays without seeing and hearing him again. Wilde perceived this quality long before it appeared in public, and in a later play gave him a chance to suggest it; but when Waller was chosen to act Tree's part in *A Woman of No Importance* for a tour of the provinces, Wilde had nothing to do with it, and only attended one rehearsal at Waller's urgent request. After it was over, and Wilde had complimented the entire company, Waller, who did not feel at all happy in his part, took him aside and asked:

"Have you any criticism to make?"

"None, my dear Lewis, none."

"I mean about any individual performance?"

"Why cavil at a part when the whole is so charming?" countered Wilde.

"Any criticism at all would be helpful."

"Nothing I might say could possibly improve such a finished representation."

"That may be taken in two ways," objected Waller.

"I won't quarrel over the number."

"Am I good in my part?" asked Waller desperately.

"Admirable."

"But does the part suit me?"

"You make it suit you."

"Please tell me what you think. I shall be grateful, and I can stand anything."

"I think you are so good," replied Wilde, "that no one except myself will know that the part was not written for you . . . But between ourselves, my dear fellow, I long to see you as Milton's Samson Agonistes. . . . Now come and have supper with me. I long for that too."

An interesting sidelight on Wilde's liberality is supplied by W. H. Leverton, for many years box-office manager of the Haymarket Theatre. Wilde, it appears, never asked for "complimentary" seats but always bought those for his friends and himself, insisting on special vouchers being written out for him on cardboard tickets. "If I go to Charing Cross station and pay a penny to go to Westminster, I get a nicer ticket than if I bought one of your ten-and-sixpenny stalls," he informed Tree. For the first night of his new play he demanded forty stalls in the best positions. Tree wanted to know who was going to sit in them. "Do you think, my dear Herbert, that I am going to submit the names of my friends for your approval?" asked Wilde in a lofty manner. Tree excused himself on the ground that some of Wilde's friends might already have seats marked out for them, and he did not wish these to be duplicated. After some discussion they reached a compromise.

A Woman of No Importance first appeared at the Theatre Royal, Haymarket, on April 19th, 1893, and repeated the success of *Lady Windermere's Fan*. The critics had complained that in the earlier comedy the action of the play had been held up while the characters delivered themselves of epigrams. But "English critics always confuse the action of a play with the incidents of a melodrama," said Wilde. "I wrote the first act of *A Woman of No Importance* in answer to the critics who said that *Lady Windermere's Fan* lacked action. In the act in question there was absolutely no action at all. It was a perfect act." The critics were duly irritated, and the audience were thoroughly exhilarated. They could have gone on listening for ever to the absent-minded "Lady Hunstanton," who says of "Lord Illingworth": "I was in hopes he would have married Lady Kelso. But I believe he said her family was too large. Or was it her feet? I forgot which." And the interchanges between "Lord Illingworth" and "Mrs. Allonby" kept the house in a state of animation:

> Lord Illingworth (*not wishing to follow the rest of the party indoors*): Yes, let us stay here. The Book of Life begins with a man and a woman in a garden.
> *Mrs. Allonby*: It ends with Revelations.

Thunderous applause and cries of "author" at the close of the play brought a large man, who was sitting in a box in full view of the audience, to his feet. In clear tones, which were heard in every part of the theatre, he announced: "Ladies and Gentlemen: I regret to inform you that Mr. Oscar Wilde is not in the house." As the speaker was Mr. Oscar Wilde, he was in a position to know. Much felicitation was in progress behind the scenes, and when Wilde joined the happy throng in Tree's dressing-room such words as "marvellous," "unique," "wonderful" and "great" were being bandied about. Author and actor congratulated each other. Then:

"I shall always regard you as the best critic of my plays," said Wilde fervently.

"But I have never criticised your plays," said Tree reproachfully.

"That's why," said Wilde complacently.

Tree had been unexpectedly good in the part of "Lord Illingworth," a character which represents one side of the dramatist's nature, and says many things that Wilde himself had not only spoken in the past but had already given to "Lord Henry Wotton" in *Dorian Gray*. The part had a strange effect on Tree, who came in time to identify himself with it, retaining to the end of his life, both in wit and manner, a distinct resemblance to the original.

Even at that time Wilde noted it: "Ah, every day dear Herbert becomes *de plus en plus Oscarisé*; it is a wonderful case of Nature imitating Art."

In February '93, just before starting rehearsals at the Haymarket, Wilde was again staying in Lady Mount Temple's house at Babbacombe, and wondering whether to write another play in his *Salomé* vein which he had already entitled *La Sainte Courtisane*. This was a favorite story, related by him to many people in varying styles, and at last, probably in '93, he began to put it into dramatic form, though it was never quite finished. Early in '95 Charles Ricketts asked him how it was progressing. He laughed: "Yes, yes, she continues to say wonderful things, but the Anchorite always remains mute. I admit her words are quite unanswerable. I think I shall have to indicate his replies by stars or asterisks." The play was an expansion of his theory, previously put forward in *The Portrait of Mr. W. H.*, that the moment you convince someone else of a truth you become sceptical of it yourself. The almost completed drama was entrusted to Ada Leverson at the time of Wilde's trial. She restored it to him in Paris in the year '97; whereupon he left the manuscript in a cab, and, when breaking the news to Ross, said that a cab was a very proper place for it. In 1911 I heard Tree tell the story which he had heard from Wilde several times; but as Wilde told it quite differently on each occasion Tree's version must be regarded as the bare plot of the fable, unilluminated by the quaint digressions and unadorned by the jewelled language of the narrator's fancy:

"It is true: when you convert someone else to your own faith, you cease to believe in it yourself. Have you not heard the story of Honorius the Hermit? He was a very good man who lived alone in a cave . . . perhaps it is necessary to live alone in a cave in order to be a very good man . . . and the daughter of a king came to seek him out. She had heard that he was pleasant to look upon, and that he had forsworn the world. But she did not believe that he would remain true to his oath if he beheld herself, for no man had been able to resist her. So she left the city and went forth into the desert to find this holy man; and being directed to his cave by some peasants who brought him food, she stood without and called him by his name. And after she had called him many times he came forth and demanded the reason for her summons. And she told him that she was daughter of a great king, and would make him a prince if he would come with her to Alexandria. But he did not regard her, and made answer that there was only one King, who had died upon the cross; and that there was only one love, the love of God; and he spoke with scorn of the body, and of earthly beauty, and of human passions and of the things of this world. And then he told the story of the

Son of God, who had lived and suffered as a man so that other men could
be made to understand God, and so to love God. And as he spoke his voice
grew tender, and pity took possession of him, and his eyes rested upon the
king's daughter, and he saw that she was very beautiful; and he had compassion on her; and he said that she must unburden her soul, which was
heavy with sin, and live henceforth as a servant of Him who had died for
her.

"So the king's daughter told him of her life in the great city, of the kings
and princes who had been her lovers, of the slaves who did her bidding, of
the men who had died for her, and of those whose death she had contrived;
of the magnificence of her palace, the costliness of her apparel, and the
splendour of her jewels. Nothing had been denied her, and she had denied
herself nothing. But now, after listening to Honorius the Hermit, she had
decided to abandon her life of luxury and lust, and to dedicate herself to
God.

"But while she was speaking, Honorius the Hermit began to yearn for the
joys that had not been his, and to perceive that without experience of the
pleasures one sacrifices, there is no sacrifice. And he lusted after the body
of the king's daughter. Then he said: 'I will come with you to Alexandria,
and together we shall taste of the Seven Sins.' 'Nay,' she answered, 'for I
know that what you told me of God and His Son was true. I know that my
life has been evil; and I will not go with you to Alexandria.' 'Then I shall
go alone,' said he. 'Farewell.' And he would not be persuaded.

"So the king's daughter, who had come to tempt the holy man and by him
had been converted, remained in the desert; while the holy man, who had
renounced this world until the king's daughter had revealed its delights,
journeyed to Alexandria."

At this point Wilde would pause, the story over; but if in the mood, he
would add: "She, I regret to say, died of starvation. He, I fear, died of debauchery. That is what comes of trying to convert people."

The extraordinary financial success of his two comedies had a most unfortunate effect on Oscar Wilde. "We need greater virtues to sustain good
than evil fortune," says La Rochefoucauld, and Wilde, emotionally unripened,
did not possess them. He behaved like a boy who has just been let out of
school with as much money as he wants, the run of the town, a latchkey, no
responsibilities, and no parental or magisterial prohibitions of any kind
whatever. Just as the boy would go from café to confectioner, swilling and
gorging to his stomach's content, so did Oscar spend most of his time between the Savoy Hotel, Kettner's, and the Café Royal, eating, drinking,

smoking, sleeping, talking; but, unlike the boy, watching himself and the pageant of life, commenting on himself and the people around him, with that richness of humour and acuteness of perception which sprang from his still-developing intellectual powers. "To become the spectator of one's own life is to escape the suffering of life," said he, and he continued to escape it until the boy-actor in him ousted the adult-spectator and insisted on taking the centre of the stage. When he spoke of "that inordinate passion for pleasure which is the secret of remaining young" he meant, without being altogether aware of it, that only the young have an inordinate passion for pleasure; and at the age of forty he luxuriated in the gratifications which he had coveted at the age of fourteen.

At first he enjoyed it all with his habitual gaiety, and an additional gusto due to freedom from financial care. A hansom cab, engaged for the day, called for him at about eleven in the morning. Dressed in a frock-coat, carrying a cane, and wearing a top-hat, he stepped into it and drove to a florist in Burlington Arcade, where he bought a large buttonhole for himself and a smaller one for his driver. Then there would be a call or two to pay, lunch at the Café Royal, and more calls. After dressing for dinner, which he would have at the Savoy or elsewhere, he might drop in to see an act of his play, confer an epigram on some acquaintance, and go to a party and a late supper. In March '93 he took rooms at the Savoy Hotel, and often spent the night there, explaining that he could not go home as he had forgotten the number of his house, and was not quite certain of the street, though he believed the district was Chelsea. Whenever the rooms were changed to suit his taste, he would tell a friend about his magnificent new suite, and the colossal weekly bill he had to pay, exactly like a youngster who is thrilled by some new possession and impressed by its cost. Nothing could persuade him to walk a step when a conveyance was handy. To ask him to walk when a hansom was within hail was like asking a boy to eat bread-and-butter when cake was on the table. Leaving 30 Upper Grosvenor Street one day, Wilfred Scawen Blunt suggested that they should stroll together as far as Grosvenor Square. "No, no," said Wilde, calling a passing hansom, "I *never* walk." Quite apart from his dislike of exercise, walking seemed to him a waste of money. Since the money was there to be spent, not to spend it was the same as wasting it. In that sense he never wasted money: he spent it all.

Though seldom much of a clubman, he was a member of the New Travellers' in Piccadilly and the Albemarle in Albemarle Street, and Allan Aynesworth tells me that Wilde used to visit the Lyric Club at the corner of Coventry Street: "Before many minutes of his society, all of us in the smoking-room were inclined to think the sun was shining and it was a summer's day, though outside east winds and hailstorms were prevailing. I can often picture him quite clearly with his large fur coat and big fur collar, a large cravat, a walking-stick mounted with some beautiful work of art, and with his twinkling eye always a picturesque character that seemed to radiate a joyous and gay outlook on life. A tonic to the more morose members of the club."

With money pouring in from his comedies, with invitations pouring in from the aristocracy, with the social and artistic world of London infected by the dialogue in his plays, with his name in everyone's mouth, Wilde had achieved his heart's desire. He was easily the most talked-of writer in Great Britain, and the newspapers chronicled his movements as if he were Royalty. We hear of him staying at 51 Friedrich's Promenade, Bad Homburg, in June '92, a favourite resort of the Prince of Wales, whose liking and admiration for him steadily increased. He was to be seen at Buckingham Palace garden-parties and at every big social event of the season; though he drew the line at race-meetings, perhaps because conversation was liable to be suspended while the horses were in action.

His fame crossed the Channel, and for once in a way Parisian society lionised a British writer. He was invited everywhere; the French newspapers were full of his sayings and doings; and the periodicals which specialised in fashions found the velvet and flowered satin waistcoats which he wore beneath his frock-coat rather "loud." Toulouse-Lautrec did a pastel of him, and William Rothenstein painted him wearing a red waistcoat against a background of gold. "It is a lovely landscape, my dear Will. When I sit to you again, you must do a real portrait," was Oscar's comment. "From cab to cab, from café to café, from *salon* to *salon*, he moved with the lazy gait of a stout man who is rather weary," reports Henri de Régnier. "He carried on his correspondence by means of telegrams, and his conversation by means of apologues. He passed from a luncheon with Monsieur Barrès to a dinner with Monsieur Moréas, for he was curious about all kinds of thoughts and manners of thinking . . . Nothing disturbed his stolid bearing, his smiling serenity, and his mocking beatitude." Whenever he spoke of his own works he said that the writing of his comedies was far too easy, and he only attached importance to *Dorian Gray* and *Salomé*, at both of which he had laboured. He did not sympathise with the anti-semitism which was making itself felt in certain sections of Parisian society; and although he described Jewish money-lenders as "gentlemen who breathe through *their* noses and make you pay through *yours*," he nevertheless thought that hostility to Jews was "vulgar and ungrateful: they are the only people who lend money."

He still preferred the society of artists to that of any other class, and was always ready to help those in need. Charles Conder, invariably hard-up, was hawking his painted fans round Paris and selling them for what he could get. "Dear Conder!" said Wilde. "With what exquisite subtlety he goes about persuading someone to give him a hundred francs for a fan, for which he was fully prepared to pay three hundred." It gave him pleasure to pretend that he had never made money out of his stories: "While the first editions of most classical authors are those coveted by bibliophiles, it is the second editions of my books that are the true rarities, and even the British Museum has not been able to secure copies of most of them." And when he discussed the publication of his next tale or poem, he said that there would be five hundred signed copies for particular friends, six copies for the general public, and one copy for America. He was now the recipient of so many letters that he frequently left them unopened unless he recognised the handwriting, and he never apologised for tardy answers on the score of work: "I am a wretch not to have answered sooner—but I have no excuse, so you will forgive me." One evening Wilde dined at a restaurant with a friend who was accompanied by his mistress, an excessively ugly woman who managed somehow to convert her defect into a distinction. Immediately she was introduced to Wilde she asked him: *"Dites-moi, monsieur, si je ne suis pas la femme la plus laide à Paris?"* For once in his life, said Wilde in recounting the story, he was able to please a woman merely by telling her the truth: *"Mais, madame, dans tout le monde!"* He was always at his happiest in Paris, and never left it without regret. "The great superiority of France over England," he declared, "is that in France every bourgeois wants to be an artist, whereas in England every artist wants to be a bourgeois." This is probably a rosy view of the French bourgeois, of whom Wilde knew as little as the average alien visitor, but it expressed his sense of feeling at home in France. "When one is content one is silent," he said, "and nowhere is one more content than at Paris." If the evidence of his friends is anything to go by, he was only silent when asleep; but here again the statement expressed his sense of being at peace in Paris.

Two years of this kind of life produced a personality very different from the one his friends had known in the eighties. "In this world there are only two tragedies," he had said before prosperity transformed him. "One is not getting what one wants, and the other is getting it. The last is much the worst, the last is a real tragedy." By 1894 he had got what he had wanted, and the tragedy had overtaken him. "I like persons better than principles, and I like persons with no principles better than anything else in the world," was another saying of the period before success enabled him to act upon it. Now he surrounded himself with a crowd of parasitic young disciples, who followed him about everywhere, singing his praises, repeating his sayings, eating and drinking at his expense, and receiving checques, cigarette-cases, tie-pins and what-not in return for their flattery and admiration. He took offence at criticism, and even resented honest advice. He displayed an abnormal arrogance, and his attitude to everyone who did not praise him or please him was lordly and disdainful. This was not the mere egoism of the artist, which, as Charles Ricketts acutely observed, "is less profound than the covert vanity of the plain man, who has done nothing and feels secure in his borrowed opinions." It was the megalomania of a dictator, closely resembling the absurd vanity of a spoilt child. As he became more prosperous, he became more preposterous, and the hatred of him which blazed forth in the spring of '95 and pursued him for the rest of his life was in some measure the product of the three years between *Lady Windermere's Fan* and *The Importance of Being Earnest*, when Society fawned on him, while secretly envious of his success, annoyed by his assumption and condescension, and enraged by his insolent independence of thought and behaviour.

"The basis of literary friendship is mixing the poisoned bowl," he once said, and this would partly account for the fact that he made few literary friendships; but the curious thing about Wilde is that in the nineties he had not a single literary friend of his own age whose intellectual stature and artistic accomplishment could compare for a moment with his, which suggests that he had come to see himself as a unique phenomenon, as one who stood apart from the literary world of his time, and was above criticism. True, he asked the advice of young authors, but this was an act of patronage, and such advice could only be tendered in a spirit of reverence for the master. Adulation was what he craved for and increasingly obtained from the young men who were either dazzled by his brilliance or delighted by his dinners. As for his contemporaries, he told them what they ought to think and never listened to their opinions or deigned to consider whether they had any. Meeting Conan Doyle in the street one day, he asked "Have you seen my latest play?" "No." "Ah, you must go. It is wonderful. It is genius." Doyle noticed the extraordinary change in him, and thought he had gone mad. Another incident could not have occurred a few years earlier, though its victim was a wealthy and objectionable foreigner who, according to Wilde, had come to London with the intention of founding a *salon* and had only succeeded in opening a saloon, and whose pastry, we learn from the same source, was preferable to his poetry. "It was on a Sunday afternoon," Allan Aynesworth tells me; "the rain was teeming down, and we were waiting in front of this man's residence for the door to be opened, as we had all been invited to lunch. There were six of us, if I remember aright: Arthur Cecil, Corney Grain, George Grossmith, Arthur Sullivan, Oscar Wilde and myself. The bell not being answered immediately, we were fortunate to be able to get some shelter under the umbrella of Corney Grain, whose huge proportions and umbrella to match enabled some of us to keep partly dry. When the bell was at last answered by the butler, Oscar Wilde stepped forward and said 'We want a table for six for lunch to-day.' The consternation on the butler's face can scarcely be imagined."

With the mental derangement or delusion from which Wilde suffered, there went a corresponding hardening and defiance of manner, while his physical appearance deteriorated, becoming coarse and bloated. He looked apoplectic, the veins stood out on his forehead, he breathed heavily, he seemed to exude good living, he was fat and unctuous. Worse still, he was bored. In 1894, though no new play of his had been produced that year, his income was £8000 (between thirty and forty thousand in 1945 purchasing power), and as he went from place to place he disengaged himself from his hansom cab with difficulty. He told W. B. Yeats that he tried to sleep away as much of his life as possible, leaving his bed at two or three in the afternoon, and spending the rest of the day at the Café Royal: "I have written the best short story in the world, and I repeat it to myself on getting out of bed and before every meal," and he recited the parable of how Christ had returned to the city and had seen the effect of his miracles in those he had cured.

The life he led was scarcely conducive to steady literary work, and between the autumns of '92 and '94 he only wrote one comedy, though he commenced, tinkered with, tired of and abandoned several others, and got *La Sainte Courtisane* into some sort of shape. We first hear of *An Ideal Husband* when he was staying at The Cottage, Goring-on-Thames, in June '93, but he only sketched out the first draft then, for he admitted to Charles Ricketts that he had done no work, explaining why: "The river-gods have lured me to devote myself to a Canadian canoe—in which I paddle about—it is curved like a flower." At the end of that year he was in Cairo, and in the spring of '94 he was staying at the Hôtel des Deux Mondes in Paris. Between continental trips and social engagements he managed to get most of the play on paper, and he completed it in chambers which he had taken at 10-11 St. James's Place. Frank Harris states that he had suggested the plot to Wilde. If so,

Sardou must have suggested it to Harris, as it is to be found in that play-wright's *Dora*. But plots are everyone's property, and Wilde himself, who could invent a dozen a day, attached no significance to them. Mrs. Bancroft once said to him that the leading situation in one of his comedies reminded her of the great scene in a play by Scribe. "Taken bodily from it, dear lady," he admitted. "Why not? Nobody reads nowadays." The originality of a writer is shown in his treatment of a story that may be as old as the hills, as the majority of stories are, and Wilde was the most individual British dramatist between Shakespeare and Shaw.

During Tree's absence in America the Haymarket Theatre had been taken by Lewis Waller and H. H. Morell, and Wilde, now more than ever incapable of enduring the advice and criticism of George Alexander, allowed Waller to produce his new play. Unfortunately, as it appeared in the sequel, the only two actors who really disliked him were in the cast, though he was blithely unaware of their hostility. Charles Hawtrey was chosen to play "Lord Goring," a character into which Wilde put a good deal of himself, a wit, a dandy, whose indolence, irresponsibility, and sound common sense reflect similar qualities in his creator. All his friends remarked that in spite of his frivolous attitude to life, his trifling air and lazy inconsequence, Wilde's advice in mundane affairs was singularly shrewd; and each of these charac-teristics is given to "Goring." We do not know why Hawtrey disliked Wilde, as he is silent on the subject in his volume of reminiscences, but we may suppose that it was merely a case of physical antipathy. With the other actor, Charles Brookfield, who played "Goring's" valet because, as he informed the author, he did not want to learn many of his lines, we must suppose more than that. It has been rumoured that Wilde once spoke to Brookfield about something he was wearing which he ought not to have been wearing, or about something he was not wearing that he ought to have been wearing; and as Brookfield's mother moved in aristocratic circles, his father had been a royal chaplain, and both of them were once the intimate friends of Thack-eray, he may have taken offence at a lesson in propriety from a man whom he probably regarded as an Irish upstart. But even that would not account for the venom and malignance he was later to display. Already, as we have seen, he had written a travesty of *Lady Windermere's Fan*, and this helps us to discern the real motive of his hatred. In conversation he was a most amusing man, but when he came to transfer his humour to paper he could only produce rubbish. His plays are the feeblest kind of farce, and their obvious puerility made him jealous of Wilde's easy achievement and envious of his success. The fact that Wilde had such a high opinion of himself, was quite incapable of feeling the spleen and malice of meaner natures, and had shown no spark of resentment when he was parodied in *The Poet and the Puppets*, drove Brookfield frantic; and by the time *An Ideal Husband* was being rehearsed Wilde had become an obsession in the mind of the vindictive mortal who detested him yet could not refuse a part in his comedy. Wilde's unconsciousness of the situation fed the fury that for a while threatened Brookfield's reason, and nothing could have exacerbated his condition more successfully than Wilde's imperturbability, which was exhibited in its most infuriating form at one of the rehearsals. Although the date of production was nine days ahead, Wilde, with a lack of consideration for everybody that he would not have shown two years earlier, insisted on a rehearsal being called for Christmas Day. Such a proceeding was quite unjustifiable, and the actors were incensed, but Wilde's reputation was such that if he had told them to sing their parts they would probably have done so. He tried their tempers still further by keeping them waiting on the bleak stage for over an hour on Christmas morning; and when at last he made an appearance, Brookfield alone had the temerity to indicate their discontent:

"Don't you keep Christmas, Oscar?"

"No, Brookfield; the only festival of the Church I keep is Septuagesima. Do you keep Septuagesima, Brookfield?"

"Not since I was a boy."

"Ah, be a boy again!"[1]

An Ideal Husband, with Lewis Waller as Sir Robert Chiltern, was first seen at the Theatre Royal, Haymarket, on January 3rd, 1895, and was an instantaneous success. The Prince of Wales was in a box, and after the last act congratulated the author, who said that he would have to cut some of the scenes, as the performance was too long. "Pray do not take out a single word," said the Prince. No one appealed to Wilde's laziness in vain.

The play shows a considerable advance in construction and characterisation on his two previous comedies, and makes one wonder, in view of his next work for the stage, whether he would have continued to develop his powers as a serious dramatist or surrendered to the call of his natural genius for satirical nonsense, of which there are clear signs when father and son exchange words in *An Ideal Husband*:

Lord Goring: Everybody one meets is a paradox nowadays. It is a great bore.
    It makes society so obvious.
Lord Caversham: Do you always really understand what you say, sir?
Lord Goring: Yes, father, if I listen attentively.

·   ·   ·   ·   ·   ·

[1] Vincent O'Sullivan, in relating this incident, omits Oscar's last sentence. I had the story from Waller.

Lord Caversham: ... Want to have a serious conversation with you, sir.

Lord Goring: My dear father! At this hour?

Lord Caversham: Well, sir, it is only ten o'clock. What is your objection to the hour? I think the hour is an admirable hour.

Lord Goring: Well, the fact is, father, this is not my day for talking seriously. I am very sorry, but it is not my day.

Lord Caversham: What do you mean, sir?

Lord Goring: During the Season, father, I only talk seriously on the first Tuesday in every month, from four to seven.

Lord Caversham: Well, make it Tuesday, sir, make it Tuesday.

Lord Goring: But it is after seven, father, and my doctor says I must not have any serious conversation after seven. It makes me talk in my sleep.

It is probable that he would have returned to the graver themes of his first three comedies, because, as we shall find, he had already roughed out a scenario for the play to follow *The Importance of Being Earnest,* and also because the enthusiasm aroused by the latter made him perversely desirous to exhibit his gifts in an opposite direction. In asking Ricketts and Shannon to come to the first night of *An Ideal Husband,* he confessed "It was written for ridiculous puppets to play, and the critics will say, 'Ah, here is Oscar unlike himself!'—though in reality I became engrossed in writing it, and it contains a great deal of the real Oscar." Which was perfectly true. To one who knows Wilde only through his works, it may seem that the dramatic and sentimental passages in his three serio-comedies were written with his tongue in his cheek. This was my own view for many years. But the close study of his personality necessitated by this biography has convinced me that the romantic sentiment in his plays was just as much a part of his nature as the wit and humour. He once read the last act of *A Woman of No Importance* to a party of friends, and, noting that they were all suitably impressed, said "I took that situation from *The Family Herald.*" Possibly he did, but he would not have done so if it had not appealed to him. "Out of ourselves we can never pass," he once wrote, "nor can there be in creation what in the creator was not." The sentimental scenes and speeches in his plays betray the stunted emotional growth of the dramatist; they are adolescent and conventional just as that side of his nature was adolescent and conventional. Once or twice his intelligence functions along with his feeling and explodes some rhetorical outburst; but usually the serious passages are carefully isolated from the comic and run away with the writer. The phrase in *A Woman of No Importance* which closes his most sustained and sentimental flight of eloquence, "Child of my shame, be still the child of my

shame," was for many years a humorous gag among actors, in close compe-
tition with "Dead! Dead! And never called me mother!" from *East Lynne*,
but Wilde probably saw nothing funny in it, and would have been rather
hurt if anybody had laughed at it. In those days nobody did; but the British
theatre had not then been taken in hand by Bernard Shaw, who became
a dramatic critic just in time to do justice to Wilde as a playwright in his
review of *An Ideal Husband*:

"Mr. Oscar Wilde's new play at the Haymarket is a dangerous subject,
because he has the property of making his critics dull. They laugh angrily
at his epigrams, like a child who is coaxed into being amused in the very
act of setting up a yell of rage and agony. They protest that the trick is
obvious, and that such epigrams can be turned out by the score by anyone
light-minded enough to condescend to such frivolity. As far as I can ascertain, I am the only person in London who cannot sit down and write an
Oscar Wilde play at will. The fact that his plays, though apparently lucrative, remain unique under these circumstances, says much for the self-denial
of our scribes. In a certain sense Mr. Wilde is to me our only thorough
playwright. He plays with everything: with wit, with philosophy, with
drama, with actors and audience, with the whole theatre. . . . "

Six days after the first performance of *An Ideal Husband*, an interview
with Wilde by Gilbert Burgess appeared in the *Sketch*. Omitting the questions he was asked, some of his answers must be quoted to show why those
critics and journalists who took themselves seriously, and such members of
the general public as were in a similar plight, did not feel affectionately disposed towards the speaker:

"For a man to be a dramatic critic is as foolish and inartistic as it would
be for a man to be a critic of epics or a pastoral critic or a critic of lyrics.
All modes of art are one, and the modes of the art that employs words as its
medium are quite indivisible. The result of the vulgar specialisation of
criticism is an elaborate scientific knowledge of the stage—almost as
elaborate as that of the stage carpenter and quite on a par with that of
the call-boy—combined with an entire incapacity to realise that a play is
a work of art or to receive any artistic impressions at all . . .

"The moment criticism exercises any influence, it ceases to be criticism.
The aim of the true critic is to try to chronicle his own moods, not to try
to correct the masterpieces of others . . .

"Real critics? Ah, how perfectly charming they would be! I am always
waiting for their arrival. An inaudible school would be nice . . .

"I do not write to please cliques. I write to please myself . . .

"I never reply to my critics. I have far too much time. But I think some day I will give a general answer in the form of a lecture, which I shall call 'Straight Talks to Old Men' . . .

"You ask me what is my feeling towards my audiences—towards the public. Which public? There are as many publics as there are personalities . . . I am not nervous on the night that I am producing a new play. I am exquisitely indifferent. My nervousness ends at the last dress rehearsal. I know then what effect my play, as presented upon the stage, has produced upon me. My interest in the play ends there, and I feel curiously envious of the public—they have such wonderfully fresh emotions in store for them . . . It is the public, not the play, that I desire to make a success . . . The public makes a success when it realises that a play is a work of art. On the three first nights I have had in London the public has been most successful, and, had the dimensions of the stage admitted of it, I would have called them before the curtain . . . The artist is always the munificent patron of the public. I am very fond of the public, and, personally, I always patronise the public very much . . .

"Several plays have been written lately that deal with the monstrous injustice of the social code of morality at the present time. It is indeed a burning shame that there should be one law for men and another law for women. I think there should be no law for anybody . . .

"Nobody else's work gives me any suggestion. It is only by entire isolation from everything that one can do any work. Idleness gives one the mood in which to write, isolation the conditions. Concentration on oneself recalls the new and wonderful world that one presents in the colour and cadence of words in movement.

"The journalist is always reminding the public of the existence of the artist. That is unnecessary of him. He is always reminding the artist of the existence of the public. That is indecent of him . . . Journalists record only what happens. What does it matter what happens? It is only the abiding things that are interesting, not the horrid incidents of everyday life. Creation for the joy of creation is the aim of the artist, and that is why the artist is a more divine type than the saint. . . .

"The only possible form of exercise is to talk, not to walk . . .

"I am sure that you must have a great future in literature before you . . . because you seem to be such a very bad interviewer. I feel sure that you must write poetry. I certainly like the colour of your necktie very much. Good-bye."

Wilde was as generous with his cash as with his conversation, and in the summer of '94 he had been so hard-up that he was forced to ask George Alexander to let him have £150 in advance of royalties on a play he had not yet started to write. If, when he had read it, Alexander thought the play too slight, he could have the £150 back again. Wilde admitted that he was extravagant, that he was incapable of living prudently, but that he was the only person who suffered the consequences. "I am so pressed for money that I don't know what to do . . . you have always been a good wise friend to me—so think what you can do." This is the first hint we have of *The Importance of Being Earnest*, which, as with so many of his works, underwent metamorphosis. At first the plot was far more complicated, dealing with a case of double identity, and was placed in the period of Sheridan. But the moment Wilde gave rein to his native genius, it burst through the style and costume of the eighteenth century and rioted in its own dimension.

In September he went with his family to Worthing, where, at The Haven, 5 Esplanade, he began and finished what he called his "somewhat farcical comedy" in three weeks, reporting to Alexander that it was an admirable play, "the best I have written." Having no money, he could not go up to town, so he sent it to Alexander, warning him that it ought really to be acted by Charles Wyndham or Hawtrey: "Of course the play is not suitable to you at all. You are a romantic actor . . . you would be sorry if you altered the definite artistic line of progress you have always followed at the St. James's." He wrote it with such ease, scarcely blotting a line, that he had plenty of time for other things, and in a letter to William Rothenstein, asking him to give sittings, recommendations, and advice to an actress named Marion Grey who wanted to earn money as a model, he said: "I am away by the seaside, bathing and sailing and amusing myself." One morning a plot for another play occurred to him, and feeling that he had failed Alexander over *The Importance of Being Earnest*, he scribbled it down hurriedly and posted it off the same day, telling the actor that it would make a very strong drama: "*I want the sheer passion of love to dominate everything.* No morbid self-sacrifice. No renunciation—a sheer flame of love between a man and a woman." As Wilde's scenario contains the entire plot and characters of a play called *Mr. and Mrs. Daventry* by Frank Harris, about which there was to be so much trouble and prevarication in the years to come, I summarise it here:

Act 1. A fashionable man of rank marries a simple girl, well-born but quite
   unused to the ways of the world. Boredom follows, and he asks a crowd
   of his smart friends down to their country-house telling his wife before-

hand how she is to behave, and suggesting that she should flirt with one of her old admirers, Gerald Lancing. All the guests except Gerald treat her with haughty indifference, and her husband flirts with Lady X, whom he arranges to meet in the drawing-room after everyone else has gone to bed.

Act 2. The guests, having said good-night, the wife, tired out, is half-asleep on the sofa of the drawing-room when the husband enters, and as he at once lowers the lights he does not see her. Lady X joins him and he locks the door. In the midst of their love-scene, Lord X knocks loudly, demanding to be let in. The wife, who has heard everything, saves the situation by turning up the lights, admitting Lord X, and explaining that they had all become so much interested in their talk that they had not noticed how late it was. Lord and Lady X go off to bed; the husband starts to explain; she repulses him; and he leaves her. Disturbed by the noise and wondering whether burglars are breaking in, Gerald arrives on the scene. The wife tells him what has happened; he is indignant, and makes it clear that he loves her.

Act 3. The wife visits Gerald at his rooms, and they confess their love for each other; but no sooner have they agreed to go off together than the husband calls. She waits in another room while the husband, "a gross sentimental materialist," begs Gerald to do his utmost to make his wife forgive him. Gerald decides to sacrifice himself, and says he will do what he can. When the husband has gone, the wife returns, and Gerald keeps his promise; but she scornfully refuses, and in the end persuades him to take her away.

Act. 4. They have been living together for three months. The husband has challenged Gerald to a duel. Gerald has accepted the challenge. The wife feels convinced that Gerald will not be killed. When he has left to decide the issue, the husband turns up and asks his wife to return to him. But the wife passionately affirms her love for Gerald, whose life, even at the cost of her husband's death, is all-important to her because he is the father of her child. The husband leaves. A shot is heard. Gerald returns, calling her husband a coward for not turning up at the duel. But she replies that her husband was no coward at the end, for he has killed himself. They cling to one another as the curtain descends.

Alexander decided at first that *The Importance of Being Ernest* was not in his line, and on Wilde's recommendation he sent it to Charles Wyndham, the best light-comedy actor of his day. But when Henry James's play *Guy Domville* failed at the St. James's Theatre in January '95, Alexander asked for the return of *Earnest*. Wyndham consented on the understanding that Wilde should write another play for him before writing another for Alexander; who agreed on condition that the scenario Wilde had sent him from Worthing should not be touched. These preliminaries settled, disagreements began. *Earnest* was originally in four acts. Alexander said that it should be in three. Wilde did not like to scrap any of his lines, which, after all, however easily conceived, had been indited with some effort. In telling me that Wilde had fought for nearly an hour to retain a scene, Alexander could only remember the end of their bout:

"Do you realise, Alec, what you are asking me to sacrifice?"

"You will be able to use it in another play."

"It may not fit into another play."

"What does that matter? You are clever enough to think of a hundred things just as good."

"Of course I am . . . a thousand if need be . . . but that is not the point. This scene that you feel is superfluous cost me terrible exhausting labour and heart-rending nerve-racking strain. You may not believe me, but I assure you on my honour that it must have taken fully five minutes to write."

The scene in question was one in which Algernon Moncrieff is arrested for debt, and in the light of Wilde's future a remark made by the solicitor has an ominous if comical significance: "Time presses, Mr. Moncrieff. We must present ourselves at Holloway Gaol at four o'clock. After that it is difficult to obtain admission."

Franklin Dyall, who played the part of Merriman, has given me several interesting particulars: "I can remember very clearly the first reading of the play—Wilde's delicious enjoyment of it—delicious is the only word—the actors' conceit that only they would appreciate it—it wouldn't get over to the public . . . I don't remember that Wilde interfered at all at rehearsal —or, if he did, it was privately, as it should be done, with the producer (G. A.). His attitude towards Alexander was that of one to a friend— open—free—and creating a very nice happy atmosphere in the theatre." That was how a member of the company saw it; but privately Wilde had a great deal to say to Alexander, who was agitated by the stream of suggestions and at length determined to put his foot down, telling Wilde that everything he wanted would be done, but preferably in his absence. "If you don't leave us alone, we'll never be ready; so go away like a good fellow and come back again for the first performance." Having recovered from this, Wilde said with prelatic solemnity: "My dear Alec, I have still one more thing to say to you and to Aynesworth. So if you will both of you come and have supper with me at the Albemarle Club to-night, I shall not trouble you again." Following a weary evening's rehearsal, Alexander, who was playing "John Worthing," and Allan Aynesworth, who was playing "Algernon Moncrieff," walked up St. James's Street to the Albemarle, both of them feeling tired, depressed and apprehensive. Wilde, in full evening dress, met them in the hall of the Club. He laid one hand on Alexander's shoulder, saying "My dear Alec," laid the other hand on Aynesworth's shoulder, saying "My dear Tony," and after an impressive pause went on: "I have only one thing to say to you. You are neither of you my favourite actor. We will now go in to supper."

Anxious lest *Earnest* might convert the press to a favourable view of his work, he gave an interview to Robert Ross, which appeared in *The St. James's Gazette* on January 18th:

"The old dramatic critics talk of having seen Macready," he said: "that must be a very painful memory. The middle-aged boast that they can recall *Diplomacy*: hardly a pleasant reminiscence . . . They should be pensioned off and only allowed to write on politics, or theology, or bimetallism, or some subject easier than art."

"How would you define ideal dramatic criticism?"

"As far as my work is concerned, unqualified appreciation."

"Have you heard it said that all the characters in your play (*An Ideal Husband*) talk as you do?"

"Rumours of that kind have reached me from time to time . . . My works are dominated by myself."

"Do you think the critics will understand your new play?" (*Earnest.*)

"I hope not."

"What sort of play are we to expect?"

"It is exquisitely trivial, a delicate bubble of fancy, and it has its philosophy."

"Its philosophy?"

"That we should treat all the trivial things of life seriously, and all the serious things of life with sincere and studied triviality."

After admitting that he had no leanings towards realism, he continued: "If a journalist is run over by a four-wheeler in the Strand, an incident I regret to say I have never witnessed, it suggests nothing to me from a dramatic point of view. Perhaps I am wrong; but the artist must have his limitations."

"Well," said Ross at the conclusion of the interview, "I have enjoyed myself immensely."

"I was sure you would. But tell me how you manage your interviews."

"Oh, Pitman."

"Is that your name? It's not a very *nice* name."

Leaving the actors and critics to their own thoughts, he went off with a

friend to Algiers, explaining his absence from London at such a moment
to Ada Leverson: "I begged my friend to let me stay to rehearse, but so
beautiful is his nature that he declined at once." Returning in time for the
dress rehearsal on February 12th, at the close of which he went on to the
stage and staggered the company by saying "Well, Alec, I suppose we must
start rehearsals for the play on Monday," he informed a press reporter, who
asked him whether he thought the play would be a success "My dear fellow,
you have got it wrong. The play *is* a success. The only question is whether
the first night's audience will be one." It was.

The Importance of Being Earnest started its career at the St. James's
Theatre on February 14th, 1895. Outside the worst snowstorm for years,
with a biting wind which drove the snow about in clouds of stinging
flakes, was making life difficult for the drivers of broughams, victorias,
hansoms, and other carriages which blocked King Street from end to end.
Inside all was bright and festive. The pretty bejewelled women wore sprays
of lilies, while many young men, who had arrived at the theatre with tall
ivory-topped ebony canes, wore lilies of the valley in their buttonholes,
white gloves with rows of black stitching on their hands, and very pointed
shoes on their feet. For a reason which will be apparent in the next chapter,
Wilde spent most of his time behind the scenes that night, though after the
second act he visited Ada Leverson's box, where Aubrey Beardsley and his
sister Mabel were sitting, and remarked to their hostess: "What a contrast the
two are! Mabel a daisy, Aubrey the most monstrous of orchids." He was
dressed in (what in his case always seemed to be) the depth of fashion:
his coat had a black velvet collar; he carried white gloves; a green scarab
ring adorned one of his fingers; a large bunch of seals on a black moiré
ribbon watch-chain hung from his white waistcoat; and, like the young men
in the stalls, he wore lilies of the valley in his buttonhole. Franklin Dyall is
my authority for Wilde's presence on the stage throughout the performance,
and for what follows: "As Merriman I only had a few lines to say, but one
of them got the biggest laugh of the play: 'Mr. Ernest Worthing has just
driven over from the station. He has brought his luggage with him.' This
was received with the loudest and most sustained laugh that I have ever
experienced, culminating in a round of applause; and as I came off Wilde
said to me: 'I'm so glad you got that laugh. It shows they have followed
the plot.' There is nothing much else that I remember except his remark
about taking a call. He said 'I don't think I shall take a call to-night. You
see, I took one only last month at the Haymarket, and one feels so much
like *a German band*.' I don't know why, but it made me laugh, and I

have a mental laugh now when I think of it." The reception of the play was phenomenal. "In my fifty-three years of acting, I never remember a greater triumph than the first night of *The Importance of Being Earnest*," Allan Aynesworth assures me. "The audience rose in their seats and cheered and cheered again." After it was all over Wilde went up to the long room leading to Alexander's sanctum. "Well, what did you think of it?" asked the actor, bubbling over with pleasure. "My dear Alec, it was charming, quite charming," replied Wilde, nodding his head in the ponderous manner peculiar to him. "And, do you know, from time to time I was reminded of a play I once wrote myself called *The Importance of Being Earnest*." But some years later, in a letter to Louis Wilkinson, he said that his "fanciful, absurd comedy, written when I was playing with that tiger, Life," had been "delightfully acted."

The critics, though they tried hard to find fault with it, had to admit that it was extremely funny, and the two who had always treated Wilde as a dramatist of distinction gave it unqualified praise. "Believe me, it is with no ironic intention that I declare Mr. Oscar Wilde to have 'found himself,' at last, as an artist in sheer nonsense . . . there is no discordant note of seriousness. It is of nonsense all compact, and better nonsense, I think, our stage has not seen . . . The laughter it excites is absolutely free from bitter afterthought." (A. B. Walkley in *The Speaker*.) "It is delightful to see, it sends wave after wave of laughter curling and foaming round the theatre . . . an absolutely wilful expression of an irrepressibly witty personality . . . 'farce' is far too gross and commonplace a word to apply to such an iridescent filament of fantasy." (William Archer in *The World*.) A relatively new dramatic critic, given the job by an enterprising editor because he had scarcely ever seen a play and so would bring an entirely fresh mind to his work, had obviously seen too many plays by this time: "To the dramatic critic especially, who leads a dismal life, it came with a flavour of rare holiday . . . It is all very funny, and Mr. Oscar Wilde has decorated a humour that is Gilbertian with innumerable spangles of wit that is all his own. We must congratulate him unreservedly on a delightful revival of theatrical satire." (H. G. Wells in *The Pall Mall Gazette*.) But there was one discordant note, which came from an unexpected quarter. "It amused me, of course," wrote Bernard Shaw in *The Saturday Review*; "but unless comedy touches me as well as amuses me, it leaves me with a sense of having wasted my evening." And he made it plain in his article that *Earnest* had failed to touch him. The fact that he was present on the second night, when the players were suffering from the usual reaction after the excitement of the first and the comedy fell rather flat, may have had something to do with his disappointment; but he never altered his opinion. Three acts of laughter for laughter's sake was no laughing matter for him.

Wilde pretended to be rather vexed by the chorus of adulation. "There are two ways of disliking my plays," he said; "one way is to dislike them, the other is to prefer *Earnest*." But this epigram had been rather over-worked, for he had used it in connection with art and poetry: "There are two ways of disliking art; one way is to dislike it, the other is to like it rationally." And: "There are two ways of disliking poetry; one way is to dislike it, the other is to read Pope." Actually he was as pleased as Punch. Two of his plays were running in the West End of London at the same time, both of them huge successes, and each quite different from the other. Furthermore, no play in living memory had been received by intelligent audiences with such continuous and hilarious laughter as was *Earnest* at every performance, and when the curtain fell on each act the applause was felt to be much more for the author than for the actors.[1] Nevertheless the performances of the two chief male characters were worthy of the play, and have never been equalled since; the reason being that later impersonators of "Jack" and "Algy" have not realised the vital importance of being earnest in their parts. They have been either studiously affected or consciously comical, instead of being realistic and serious, and the fun of the play on the stage depends on the simple sincerity and perfect gravity of the players. Once let the audience feel that the actors are enjoying the joke, or are performing their parts in an artificial manner as if they did not really believe in them, and the humour of the thing evaporates. George Alexander and Allan Aynes-worth did not make this mistake, and I have never heard such persistent and delighted laughter in a place of entertainment as on the seven or eight occasions when I witnessed the 1909-10 revival of *Earnest* at the St. James's Theatre.

In an earlier chapter it was remarked that the perfect fusion of the immature emotional side of Wilde's nature with the over-mature intellectual side produced a masterpiece. *The Importance of Being Earnest* is that master-

[1] Yet, for a cause unconnected with its merits, the first run was a financial failure, Alexander as manager losing £289 8. 4. He revived it in 1902, but the time was not yet ripe. Its first chance came in 1909, when it ran for eleven months, with Alexander and Aynesworth in their original parts, Alexander making a net profit of £21,942—his third largest profit during a 28 years management of the St. James's Theatre, beating even *The Second Mrs. Tanqueray* and being beaten by *His House in Order* and *Bella Donna*, all of which, however, had the advantage of highly successful runs on their first appearance. He used *Earnest* as a stop-gap on several occasions between the 1909-10 revival and his death in 1918. (See *Sir George Alexander and the St. James's Theatre*, by A. E. W. Mason, 1935.)

piece. It could only have been written by one in whom boyishness and braininess were combined to an extraordinary degree. With his three serio-comedies Wilde may be compared with Sheridan, though *The School for Scandal* remains by far our best comedy of manners. But with *Earnest* he stands alone. It comes in no category. To call it a farcical comedy is obvious but fatuous. It is like no farce and no comedy and no farcical comedy on earth. It follows no rules and makes its own laws as it goes along. One cannot even call it perfect of its kind, because there is no kind. It is *sui generis*, perfect of itself, and the quintessence of Oscar. It ridicules every-thing that human beings take seriously: birth, baptism, love, marriage, death, burial, illegitimacy and respectability; yet so light-heartedly and so absurdly that only a humourless clergyman could take offence at it. Wilde called it "A Trivial Comedy for Serious People," and said: "The first act is ingenious, the second beautiful, the third abominably clever." All of it is ingenious, all of it is abominably clever, and the whole is beautiful because perfection is beauty. Many people, with Shaw, have complained that it is not some-thing else, not serious enough, not touching, not like life, not a dozen other things. But Wilde did not wish to move people, except to laughter. He set out to provide a dish that would be pleasing to the palate and joyfully digested; and the unique trifle he served up for us has become a classic.

CHAPTER FIFTEEN

THE DRAMA

ALTHOUGH they had drifted far apart by the beginning of 1895, Oscar and his wife were still on outwardly affectionate terms. During the period of his prosperity they were to be seen together at the first performance of new plays, and, though she never enjoyed the experience, Constance continued to appear on special occasions in striking clothes of her husband's design. Mrs. Belloc-Lowndes sends me this: "I remember a private view at the Grosvenor Gallery, which she attended in a green and black suit and hat which recalled coloured engravings of eighteenth-century highwaymen. It made a considerable sensation, for instead of looking at the pictures most of the women present were eagerly asking each other whether they had yet seen Mrs. Oscar Wilde." On his side Oscar made a point of attending his wife's weekly receptions: "The drawing-room would be filled Sunday after Sunday with a crowd of interesting and amusing people," continues Mrs. Belloc-Lowndes, "and to my thinking Oscar was by far the most interesting and amusing of those there. Unlike many men celebrated for their wit, he was just as delightful, and took just as much trouble to entertain and cheer his guests in his own house, as he did in those of other people. To me an agreeable addition to those gatherings was the presence of the two little boys, Cyril and Vyvyan. With regard to their children, the Wildes followed the French habit of having them present when they had visitors, instead of keeping them well out of sight, as was then the English custom. Both boys had pretty manners, the younger possessing some of his mother's charm. I remember better the elder of the two, who was later distinguished for his remarkable ability, and who was killed early in the 1914-18 war, for he used to hang delightedly on his father's words . . . The last time I was in their house I was one of a small party at dinner, where the guest of honour was the fiancée of a clergyman attached to Old Chelsea Church. We were only six, and I remember thinking in my heart of hearts, that surely Oscar must feel somewhat bored. But if so, he gave no sign of it, and, as was always the case wherever he happened to be, he poured out a stream of brilliant paradoxical talk to the delight of his guests." Constance kept an autograph book, from which we learn the names of some of her visitors: Ruskin, Whistler, Swinburne, Browning, Meredith, Sargent, G. F. Watts, Sir Edwin Arnold, Mark Twain, Oliver Wendell Holmes, Henry Irving, Ellen Terry, Sarah Bernhardt, Walter Crane, T. P. O'Connor, John Bright, A. J. Balfour, etc. Very much against her will, Constance was regarded as an authority on dress and decoration, and in November '94 an interview with her appeared in *To-day*, wherein she did her best to live up to the reputation which her husband had created for her.

Curiously enough, in view of what was to come, the first estrangement between Oscar and his wife was caused by his friendship with a woman. Part of his attractiveness to women was due to the fact that, while delighting in their society, they were not physically necessary to him. "The real Don Juan," he told Vincent O'Sullivan, "is not the vulgar person who goes about making love to all the women he meets, and what novelists call 'seducing' them. The real Don Juan is the man who says to women, 'Go away! I don't want you. You interfere with my life. I can do without you.' Swift was the real Don Juan. Two women died for him." His own friendships with women were surprisingly warm and enduring; and one of them, a famous demi-mondaine of the time named Bibidie Leonard, he used to visit frequently at her house in York Terrace, Regent's Park. It seems that her affairs with other men made him feel jealous, or as jealous as it was in his nature to feel, and he used to declare that she had taught him more than any other woman. "No, she was not in the least immoral," he explained to a friend. "Immoral women are rarely attractive. What made her quite irresistible was that she was unmoral." The discovery by Constance of his visits to Bibidie brought on the unavoidable domestic heat, described by Shakespeare as "the hourly shot of angry eyes," followed by the usual inventions and excuses, succeeded by the inevitable coolness. But it was impossible to be angry or disdainful with Oscar for long, and the episode was soon forgiven. "Women love us for our defects," said he. "If we have enough of them they will forgive us everything, even our intellects." But Constance was completely unaware of the main defect in his nature, and when it was made known to her at the time of his arrest she was bewildered and incredulous; though one remark she let slip proves that their relationship had been strained from the beginning of his success as a playwright: "He has been mad the last three years."

It was in the late eighties that Wilde became a practising pederast. We are told by people who study this kind of thing that in the lives of many adolescents there is a period when attraction to their own and the other sex is about equal, and during which their sexual bent may be decided by chance. Whether or not this is true, Wilde, at any rate, remained bi-sexual for a prolonged period, becoming homosexual from the time when he gave way to that side of his nature. To anyone who had known him well or studied his personality closely, there can have been nothing surprising in the revelation of his sexual nature, for the emotional life of a man is bound up with his sexual life, and, as we have seen, there had been no development of his emotional nature. It might have been an undergraduate who wrote of "Dorian Gray." "There were moments when he looked on evil simply as a mode through which he could realise his conception of the beautiful." And there is something quaintly naïf and melodramatic about his attitude to the pathological freakishness which he had just begun to indulge: "There are moments, psychologists tell us, when the passion for sin, or for what the world calls sin, so dominates a nature, that every fibre of the body, as every cell of the brain, seems to be instinct with fearful impulses. Men and women at such moments lose the freedom of their will. They move to their terrible end as automatons move. Choice is taken from them, and conscience is either killed, or, if it lives at all, lives but to give rebellion its fascination, and disobedience its charm. For all sins, as theologians weary not of reminding us, are sins of disobedience. When that high spirit, that morning star of evil, fell from heaven, it was as a rebel that he fell."

Wilde's later description of what had happened to him, written in prison, again sounds the note of drama so dear to juvenile minds: "I let myself be lured into long spells of senseless and sensual ease. I amused myself with being a *flâneur*, a dandy, a man of fashion. I surrounded myself with the smaller natures and the meaner minds . . . Tired of being on the heights, I deliberately went to the depths in the search for new sensations. What the paradox was to me in the sphere of thought, perversity became to me in the sphere of passion. Desire, at the end, was a malady, or a madness, or both." He had allowed himself to be "lured into the imperfect world of coarse uncompleted passion, of appetite without distinction, desire without limit, and formless greed." Fortune had so turned his head, he confessed, that he fancied he could do whatever he chose; and even from the darkness of his cell he spoke of certain associates of that period in the manner of a boy who has enjoyed himself hugely during an escapade: "Clibborn and Atkins were wonderful in their infamous war against life. To entertain them was an astounding adventure."

There are occasions when it is difficult to think of Wilde as a responsible person at all, when he seems more like a schoolboy than a rational adult. One feels that he was far more attracted to the idea of doing something outrageous than desirous of fulfilling his nature; and one wonders whether the homosexual strain in him would ever have shown itself if he had not been allured by the concept of "sin," if there had been no danger attached to it, if it had not seemed to him daring, peculiar, decadent, perverse, rebellious, and even aristocratic. Nowadays his tendency no longer being considered either wicked or extraordinary, he might have shocked those who share it by proclaiming himself uncompromisingly heterosexual. There was too a strange innocence or unknowingness in his most questionable behaviour, of which an example must be given. But first a word about his associates.

An Old Marlburian named Alfred Taylor had rooms in Little College Street, just behind Westminster Abbey. He was a young man who combined an amateur interest in the arts with a professional interest in social introductions. His rooms were furnished and decorated in a tasteful and comfortable manner; the walls were hung with heavy green draperies; the scent of incense lingered in the air; daylight was usually excluded; and the lamps discreetly shaded, cast a dim light on the thick rugs. At first sight a visitor would guess Taylor to be catholic and democratic in his choice of friends, for men who had obviously been to a public school or university mixed with younger men who might have been their grooms or valets, and the accents of Mayfair and the Mile End Road mingled together in seeming equality. Briefly, Taylor was a pleasant and cultured fellow who happened also to be a pimp; and, though he may not have known it, some of his less genteel clients were blackmailers.

Wilde was a constant visitor to these rooms,[1] and Taylor introduced him to several of the young men, who, to their amazement and no doubt discomfort, soon found themselves dining at such places as the Savoy Hotel and Kettner's and listening to a stream of talk which must have made them wonder whether the wine had gone to their heads. This of course appealed to Wilde's keen sense of contrast, his love of astonishing some people and shocking others; but so innocent or obtuse was he that it never occurred to him that he was doing anything out of the ordinary when he invited a schoolboy admirer of his own class named Stuart Young, aged 15, to dine with him and one of Alfred Taylor's young men at the Savoy. Eleven

---

[1] Asked at his trial whether the street was in rather a rough neighborhood, Wilde replied: "Perhaps. It was very near the Houses of Parliament."

years afterwards Young recalled the occasion: "There was present besides myself and Wilde a young man of about twenty whom he introduced as 'Freddy Atkins.' He seemed to be somewhat embarrassed by our conversation, for with my serious precociousness I insisted upon discussing art and literature. Wilde must have found me vastly amusing, and I was in the seventh heaven of delight. I well remember his remark: 'I am feeling quite refreshed by you, Jackie. If only I had a boy of your calibre near me oftener, I might be a better man.'" So far, so bad. But worse was to follow, for when next they met Wilde took the lad with him to Taylor's rooms, solely for the purpose—and of this there is no shadow of doubt—of letting him enjoy an hour or two's talk on art and literature in congenial surroundings; just as a more orthodox senior would have taken a boy to the Tower of London or Madame Tussaud's Wax-works. On both occasions Wilde's action, since it was quite harmless in effect and intention, must be regarded as that of one whose innocence approaches imbecility.

A man who flaunts his peculiarities in the eyes of the world must not complain if the world notices them, and certain folk who had been proud of Oscar's acquaintance in the past began to cold-shoulder him, thus disproving his assertion that "if you pretend to be good the world takes you very seriously, but if you pretend to be bad it doesn't. Such is the astounding stupidity of optimism." Occasionally his well-wishers remonstrated with him, but they received no encouragement. One of them, an ambitious young American dramatist named Clyde Fitch, who owed his intellectual inspiration to Oscar's works and had been greatly encouraged by the older man's praise, took his courage in both hands and mentioned the nasty rumours that were being circulated. Wilde, who had given Fitch a lift in his hansom, lightly dismissed the subject with an epigram. But Fitch would not be silenced and demanded a straight answer to the charges. Wilde refused to discuss the topic, and at length called to the driver "Stop to let this man out! I invited him for a drive, but he is not a gentleman." When the occasion demanded it Wilde never lacked pluck. One evening after dinner Robert Ross took him and several other friends to the Hogarth Club. Immediately they entered the smoking-room an old member got up and left in a pointed manner. Other members rose to follow; but Oscar sized up the situation quickly, strode over to one of those about to leave, and haughtily addressed him: "How dare you insult a member of your own club! I am Mr. Ross's guest. An insult to me is an insult to him. I insist on your apologising to Mr. Ross." The member was driven to pretend that no insult had been intended, and they all returned to their seats.

Though no one except his intimate friends was aware of it in the nineties, Robert Ross was also a pederast. I met him once in 1916 and liked him very much, but had no notion of his sexual proclivity until his one-time secretary Christopher Millard informed me of it some years after his death. Wilde kept his friends in moral-tight compartments. Robert Sherard, Frank Harris and their like knew nothing of the Oscar known to Robert Ross, Reginald Turner and their like. As the last-named was one of Wilde's closest friends, the little I have been able to learn of him[1] may be recorded here. He was the illegitimate son of a well-known and wealthy newspaper proprietor, who had two children by a Frenchwoman, Frank Lawson and Reginald Turner, as well as other children by other women. His method was to allow £100 a year for the keep of each of his offspring up to the age of twelve, when, after an interview, he would settle a considerable sum on those he liked. On the whole he was a good "natural" father, for even the children he did not like were given a fair start in life. In due time Frank Lawson came up for inspection, passed with flying colours, and was enriched; but Reginald Turner was not so lucky, his father dying before he could qualify for the donation. However, Frank was a generous fellow, and an income of five or six hundred pounds a year was passed on to Reginald, who inherited a lot more at the death of his elder brother. Turner became a barrister, though he never practised; and towards the end of Oscar's life he left England, frightened away by a law case in which, through the skill of his counsel, he had been cleared of a charge resembling that brought against Wilde. He settled down in Florence, where he wrote a number of third-rate novels. (I speak from hearsay, not having read a word of them myself.) Everyone thought him a witty and delightful fellow, and that he was excellent company is proved by his wide circle of friends.

It is possible that Wilde would have lived to a respectable age and received a knighthood from the friend who afterwards became King Edward VII if, in an unfortunate moment for both of them, he had not been introduced to Lord Alfred Douglas. One day in 1891 Lionel Johnson, the poet, took Douglas to call on Wilde in Tite Street. They were almost instantaneously attracted to one another, Douglas being fascinated by Wilde's conversation, Wilde being fascinated by Douglas's personal appearance and historic name. They had tea in the small writing-room on the ground floor facing the street, and before Douglas left he was taken upstairs to be introduced to Constance. Wilde asked him to dine at the Albemarle Club, and their friendship began. It ripened rapidly, and in time became what Douglas

[1] From Lord Alfred Douglas.

describes as an "infatuation" on both sides. More than thirty years after Wilde's death Douglas wrote that he was "the most wonderful man I ever met," and was "so far beyond the ordinary 'good talker' that I have never been able to discover anyone who was in the same class with him or even remotely approached it. . . . He did succeed in weaving spells. One sat and listened to him enthralled." Douglas also tells us that Wilde was "most kind and hospitable, and generally sweet-tempered . . . In those days my greatest pleasure was to be with him . . . I really was crazy about the man . . ." And in his autobiography (1929) he confesses: "The truth is that I really adored him . . . There was nothing I would not have done for him. It is a mere commonplace of truth to say that I would gladly have died for him, or gone to prison in his stead." Wilde, for his part, was quite carried away by Douglas, to whom he wrote letters of extravagant devotion and admiration, though the attraction in this case was more sensual than spiritual. Douglas was an aristocrat, and Wilde romanticised aristocrats; Douglas was a budding poet, and Wilde loved poets; Douglas was excessively good-looking, and Wilde worshipped physical beauty. All the same, Wilde knew lots of aristocrats, many poets, and any number of good-looking people, and it is safe to say that he could have resisted the possessor of one or even two of these qualifications; but a combination of all three floored him, and Douglas became his ideal.

At the time of their first meeting Douglas was aged twenty-one, and had been two years at Oxford. He was the third son of the eighth Marquis of Queensberry, and lived with his mother, who had divorced his father. All his friends called him "Bosie," a variation of "boysie" which his mother had named him as a baby. By nature he was generous, outspoken, loyal to his friends, a terror to his enemies, high-spirited, wilful and independent. But he had been thoroughly spoilt by his mother, whose indulgence had brought out what was worst in his character: self-love, self-pity, arrogance, and a violent temper, which exploded when he could not have his own way. He responded quickly to kindness, but reacted fiercely against any sign of hostility or the least attempt to dominate him. A lover of sport, he was also a lover of literature, and when not hunting or shooting or playing games he was reading Shakespeare and the poets or listening to music. He had turned out a certain amount of humorous verse while at Winchester, but started to write serious poetry in his first year at Magdalen.

The obsession being reciprocal, Wilde and he saw a great deal of each other, and when apart they corresponded regularly. For a period in their relationship there were what Douglas describes as "familiarities" between

them, which never went beyond "the usual schoolboy nonsense." Douglas
stayed with Wilde and his wife when they were at Babbacombe, at a
farmhouse which they took near Cromer, at Goring-on-Thames, where
Constance left them for some weeks, and finally at Worthing. Wilde
stayed with Douglas twice at 34 High Street, Oxford, and again at his
mother's house near Bracknell in Berkshire. They visited Paris, Florence and
Algiers together, and their friendship was a theme for discussion wherever
gossipmongers gathered together. It was also a subject for scandal. Wilde's
reputation being impaired by the strange guests he entertained at the Savoy
and elsewhere, and Douglas's father stepped on the scene.

The Marquis of Queensberry was, we may charitably assume, a madman:
that is to say, he wanted the world to be run according to the Queensberry
rules; and when its inhabitants showed no inclination to suit his convenience,
he lost his temper. As a boy he spent seven years in the Navy, inheriting
the title at the age of nineteen. He was a fine horseman, riding his own
horses in the Grand National on several occasions, and very keen on
hunting, being Master of the Worcestershire Foxhounds for two years,
and a fearless rider with the Quorn and Cottesmore. In the course of his
life he managed to squander some £400,000, over half the estate which he
inherited, and to gain a reputation with the man in the street by winning
the amateur light-weight boxing championship and by compiling the rules
of boxing known as his. At some West End play he got up and denounced
the opinions of a certain character, declaring that all right-minded people,
including himself, were atheists. He was extremely combative, self-assertive,
prejudiced, and conceited, and would go to any lengths to revenge what
he construed as an insult. Indifference to his views drove him frantic; and
as he bored people with his atheistical opinions on every possible occasion,
he was frequently driven frantic. He may have been liked by his horses
and dogs, with whom he spent far more time than with his wife and
children, but no one else cared for him, and most of his acquaintances were
frightened of him. On the rare occasions when he was at home he bullied
his wife and neglected his children, but nearly all his time was spent elsewhere, and Douglas says that as a boy he scarcely ever saw his father. Once
the entire family were turned out of their home near Ascot at twenty-four
hours' notice because Queensberry wished to bring a party of friends which
included his mistress. His wife bore with his brutal behaviour for twenty
years; but when he proposed that his mistress should come along and that
the three of them should live together, the breaking-point was reached,
and in 1887 she divorced him. Her troubles, however, were not yet over.

The sums he was compelled to pay her by the Scottish courts were never sent at the right time, and twice a year she had to threaten legal proceedings before he would hand them over. Thus the payments were always delayed, and by this means, aided by a stream of abusive letters, he continued to persecute her. It may be added that his second marriage was annulled within six months of its celebration.

Three of his sons suffered from his savage temperament. The eldest, Lord Drumlanrig, was private secretary to Lord Rosebery, Foreign Minister in Gladstone's Government, who recommended him for an English peerage. Queensberry, a Scottish peer, had no right to a seat in the House of Lords merely on that account; but he had been elected by his fellow-peers to sit there as one of the sixteen who represented the rest; and this he did until one day he refused to take the oath, describing the ceremony as "Christian tomfoolery"; after which he went about cursing his fellow-peers for not re-electing him. Drumlanrig declined the offered peerage because he knew that his father would be enraged if he had a seat in the House of Lords while Queensberry himself had not. Gladstone and Rosebery suggested that he should confer with his father on the point. Queensberry at once said that he was delighted by the honour done to his son, who, however, not wishing to take any risks, asked his father to express his pleasure in writing. Queensberry consented, wrote to Gladstone, and Drumlanrig became Lord Kelhead; within a month of which Queensberry began to despatch insulting letters about his son's elevation to Rosebery, Gladstone and the Queen, threatening to horsewhip the former, whom he followed to Homburg for the purpose and prowled around the hotel at which Rosebery was staying with a dog-whip, possibly because he had not brought a horse. An appeal was made to the Prince of Wales, who calmed him down and persuaded him to abandon the project.

The second son, Lord Douglas of Hawick, fared no better. He married a clergyman's daughter, for which he was abused and insulted by Queensberry, who, knowing nothing whatever about them, made extremely offensive remarks concerning his wife and her family, and refused to have anything to do with him or to see his children. Later on Queensberry wrote obscene letters to this daughter-in-law, and when father and son met in the street blows were exchanged, with the result that they were taken to a police court and "bound over to keep the peace." After that Queensberry deprived his son of all financial aid, never spoke to him again, and spat at him when in a filial mood he visited his father on his deathbed.

Queensberry's treatment of his third son, Lord Alfred Douglas, is part of

our story. It began by his telling the young fellow that Wilde was not a fit
companion for him, and that their association must cease. As Douglas was of
age, and his father had practically ignored his existence up to then; and as,
moreover, he had no intention of letting anyone choose his friends for him,
he firmly but respectfully declined to take the advice of his parent, who at
first dismissed him as a fool and a baby, and not long afterwards threatened
to dock his allowance. Their correspondence had reached the stage at which
each was beginning to introduce matters unrelated to the point at issue
when one day Queensberry went to the Café Royal and sat down not far
from where Wilde and Douglas were lunching. Douglas at once went
over and begged him to join them. A flat refusal was followed by a sulky
acquiescence, and Queensberry was introduced to Wilde. Inside ten minutes
the man who had come to their table with loathing and contempt in his
heart was laughing with delight, and before the lunch was over Wilde had
done what no one else had ever succeeded in doing: he had, says Douglas,
charmed Queensberry into pleasant and happy conversation, and led him
right out of the bog of argument in which he always landed himself when
discussing religion. They sat talking till past four, and Queensberry was so
completely captivated that he wrote to his son withdrawing everything he
had said against Wilde, and adding that Lord de Grey had assured him
that Wilde was a friend of his and his wife's, was "perfectly all right," a
man of genius and a marvellous talker. Queensberry finished the letter with
a compliment that he would have thought twice before paying a great
boxer or jockey: "I don't wonder you are so fond of him; he is a wonderful man."

Unfortunately Wilde could not live with the Marquis and so prevent
him from relapsing into Queensberry. At the end of two months he was
normal again, and his son received a letter in which he repeated everything
he had said against Wilde prior to their meeting, and declared that
unless Douglas swore never to see the man again his allowance would be
stopped. That put the son's back up, and in reply he questioned his father's
right to interfere, refused positively to obey him, and said that if he was
mean enough to stop the allowance he could go ahead and do it. Queensberry
went ahead and did it. But the stoppage of the allowance did not stop
their correspondence, which became extremely acrimonious, and at last
Queensberry wrote a letter beginning "Alfred," containing a flood of false
accusations and a cataract of abuse, and ending "Your disgusted so-called
father"; which inspired his son to send him a telegram: "What a funny
little man you are!" This did not help to smooth things over, and Queens-

perry foamed at the pen, commencing another letter "You miserable Creature," going on to lament that he had committed a crime in bringing "such a creature into the world," and concluding with the solacing reflection that his son had probably not been begotten by himself, in which case the crime was not his.

During this breezy interchange of sentiments Queensberry was stamping round the West End of London vowing vengeance against Wilde, defaming his character, and threatening to shoot, thrash, assault, fight, ruin, disgrace, or otherwise incommode him. As time went on the subject of Wilde went to his head, taking the place previously occupied there by Christianity, though he identified the man with Satan, not with Jesus; and at last, having simmered for a year, he boiled over and dashed into action. Accompanied by a prize-fighter, the "screaming scarlet Marquis," as Wilde used to speak of him, called at No. 16 Tite Street. The two boxing "stars" were shown into the library by the seventeen-year-old footman, who was small in stature and tremblingly nervous at the sight of the ex-champion and his fellow-bruiser. Wilde got up and stood by the fireplace to receive his visitors, quite capable of taking on half a dozen of such between the puffs of a cigarette, and having no more physical fear of Queensberry than if he had been a tame rabbit.

"Sit down!" barked the Marquis.

"I do not allow anyone to talk like that to me in my house or anywhere else," said Wilde calmly. "I suppose you have come to apologise for the statement you made about my wife and myself in letters you wrote to your son. I should have the right any day to prosecute you for writing such a letter." (Queensberry had written to Douglas that he had heard on good authority that Mrs. Wilde was petitioning to divorce her husband for unnatural practices.)

"It was privileged, as it was written to my son."

"But how dare you say such things about your son and me?"

"You *were* kicked out of the Savoy Hotel at a moment's notice for your disgusting conduct."

"That is a lie!"

"And you have taken furnished rooms for him in Piccadilly."

"Somebody has been telling you an absurd set of lies about your son and me. I have not done anything of the kind."

The other stuck to his guns, so Wilde warned him:

"Lord Queensberry, do you seriously accuse your son and me of improper conduct?"

"I don't say you are it, but you look it and you pose it, which is just
as bad. If I catch you and my son together again in any public restaurant,
I will thrash you."

"I don't know what the Queensberry rules are, but the Oscar Wilde rule
is to shoot at sight. Leave my house at once."

"It's a disgusting scandal!" yelled the sportsman, amazed by the unexpected attitude of his opponent, and, like all bullies, cowed when his bluff
was called.

"If it is so, you are the author of the scandal and no one else."

Wilde had rung for his servant, who now appeared, and nearly fainted
when his master said:

"This is the Marquis of Queensberry, the most infamous brute in London.
You are never to allow him to enter my house again. Now," he went on,
opening the door for his uninvited guests: "get out!"

And the screaming scarlet Marquis left hurriedly, the professional pugilist
treading on his heels. It was a great pity that Queensberry did not carry out
his threat and try to thrash Wilde, because if he had done so Wilde would
have reduced him to pulp and got off with a nominal sentence for man-
slaughter.

Following this incident the correspondence between father and son was
resumed, the former affirming his intention of thrashing his son if ever he
found him with Wilde in a public restaurant, the latter thoughtfully supplying the date, place and hour at which he and Wilde would be found together at public restaurants. After a while Queensberry began to return his
son's letters unopened, upon which Douglas wrote a post card saying that
he had made a point of appearing with Wilde at the Berkeley, Willis's
Rooms, the Café Royal, and other places, and that he would continue to do
so, "but if you try to assault me, I shall defend myself with a loaded revolver,
which I always carry; and if I shoot you or if he shoots you, we shall be completely justified, as we shall be acting in self-defence against a violent and
dangerous rough, and I think if you were dead many people would not
miss you." Having failed to carry out his threats, though provided with
every opportunity to do so, Queensberry had to stop making them; but he
did not abandon hope of reprisals, and to save him from having fits his
acquaintances kept off the topic of Oscar Wilde.

The Marquis temporarily disposed of, Wilde next had to deal with blackmailers. He had written a number of fanciful, extravagant and artificially
expressed letters, which he called prose poems, to Douglas, and certain
phrases in them would have startled anyone unacquainted with the Eliza-

bethan sonneteers. For example: ". . . it is a marvel that those red rose-leaf lips of yours should be made no less for the madness of music and song than for the madness of kissing. Your slim-gilt soul walks between passion and poetry. I know Hyacinthus, whom Apollo loved so madly, was you in Greek days . . . when do you go to Salisbury? Do go there to cool your hands in the grey twilight of Gothic things . . ." Some of these letters had been stolen from Douglas's coat-pocket, and it occurred to the thieves or their accomplices that the writer might be willing to purchase them. In order to show that they meant business, a copy of the letter just quoted was sent to Tree, who was then rehearsing *A Woman of No Importance*. Tree promptly handed it to Wilde, with the remark that the sentiments expressed in it were open to misconstruction; but Wilde explained that it was a prose poem, and if put into verse might be printed in such a respectable anthology as the Golden Treasury. "Yes, but it is not in verse," objected Tree. "That no doubt explains why it is not in the Golden Treasury," answered Wilde. On the first night of Tree's production one of the blackmailers named Allen caught Wilde at the stage-door of the Haymarket Theatre and offered him the original letter for ten pounds. "Ten pounds!" exclaimed Wilde. "You have no appreciation of literature. If you had asked me for fifty pounds, I might have given it you." While Allen was wondering whether it was too late to raise the price, Wilde set his mind at rest: "Besides, I have a copy of that letter, and the original is of no use to me. I look upon it as a work of art. I should have desired to possess it; but as you were good enough to send a copy to Mr. Tree, who naturally knew I should wish to have it and so passed it on to me with, I am sure, deep regret that he could not keep such a lovely thing himself, I no longer want the original. Good-night."

Some days later another man called on Wilde at Tite Street, and in view of his usual attitude to blackmailers there is no reason to doubt his description of what took place, which he gave to Tree, and Tree gave to me:

"Would you like to have all those letters you wrote to Lord Alfred? I've got them here."

"If they are all as perfect as the one of which some kind person sent a copy to Mr. Tree, I should certainly like to have them. But why not continue your admirable practice of sending copies? Then I should not need the originals."

"How much will you give?"

"One cannot estimate their value in money. The price of beauty is above rubies."

"Well, you can have them for thirty pounds."

"Why do you want thirty pounds?"

"I want to go to America and make a fresh start."

"A strange design, but not . . . if you will pardon the reflection . . . not original . . . Columbus thought of it before you. I hope you will be more fortunate than he, and miss the continent on your way."

"Here they are," said the man, producing the letters, which Wilde glanced at casually, and then wrote a cheque, handing it to him with the words:

"You are willing to give me the letters, and I am willing to pay for your journey to America. That is a pleasant and amicable arrangement. Good-bye; and the best advice I can give you for the new life you propose to lead is that on the day you land in America . . . you sail for England."

The fellow was so much in sympathy with Wilde's view that he never went to America at all. After his departure Wilde looked through his letters more carefully, and found that the one of which Tree had handed him a copy was not amongst them; but he dismissed the subject from his mind until one night Allen came to his house with the original of the missing letter. Wilde repeated more or less what he had said before, but this time Allen stood his ground, remarking: "A curious construction could be put on that letter."

"Art is seldom intelligible to the working classes," said Wilde.

"A man has offered me sixty pounds for it."

"If you take my advice you will go to him at once and sell it for sixty pounds. I myself have never received so large a sum for any prose work of that length. But I am glad to find that there is someone in England who will pay such a high price for any letter of mine."

"The man is out of town."

"He will come back," said Wilde encouragingly. "I assure you, on my word of honour, that I shall pay nothing for that letter."

Allen then appealed for help, saying that he was penniless.

"Well, I can't guarantee your cab expenses," remarked Wilde; but taking pity on the fellow he gave him ten shillings and saw him out.

An hour or so later another of the gang named Clibborn was shown in, and Wilde became irritable:

"I can't be bothered any more about that letter," he cried. "I don't care tuppence about it."

But the newcomer said that he had been told to give the letter back.

"Give it back? Why does he give it back to me?"

"Well, he says that you were kind to him, and that there is no use trying to rent [1] you, as you only laugh at us."

---

[1] Blackmail.

Wilde glanced at the letter, which had been much soiled by its passage from hand to hand, and said "I think it quite unpardonable that better care was not taken of an original work of mine." Then, parting with another ten shillings, he remarked "I am afraid you are leading a wonderfully wicked life." "There's good and bad in every one of us," returned Clibborn.

In spite of these transactions, several more of Wilde's letters to Douglas, as well as copies of the ones he had bought back, found their way into the hands of Queensberry, sending up his blood-pressure without quickening his sense of poetry.

There was no truth in the assertion that Wilde had been asked to leave the Savoy Hotel; but from October '93 to the end of March '94 he was occupying chambers at 10-11 St. James's Place, in order to obtain more privacy than a hotel could give him, and he continued to lunch or dine at the Savoy whenever he pleased. He and Douglas were constantly to be seen together, and the world at large would have remained in ignorance of anything except that a playwright and a peer had contracted an intimate friendship but for the fact that in September '94 a book entitled *The Green Carnation* was published anonymously. It was written by Robert Hichens, who had just become music critic to *The World* in succession to Bernard Shaw. Earlier that year Lord Alfred Douglas had been staying with Lord and Lady Cromer at the British Agency in Cairo, and had gone up the Nile with Reginald Turner, E. F. Benson and Robert Hichens. At that time Hichens had not met Wilde, about whom he heard a great deal from Douglas, and *The Green Carnation* was practically the outcome of their talks together at Luxor, supplemented by later meetings with Wilde.

"Esmé Amarinth" in the book is quite an amusing caricature of Wilde, many of whose remarks are quoted, slightly distorted to make them appear more absurd than they actually were. The duologues in *Intentions* are cleverly parodied, and the character of "Mrs. Windsor" is a pretty good imitation of the Duchess of Berwick in *Lady Windermere's Fan*. To give a few examples. "Esmé Amarinth," when he reaches the country, exclaims: "Thank heaven there are no nightingales to ruin the music of the stillness with their well-meant but ill-produced voices!" He also declares that "Nothing is so unattractive as goodness, except, perhaps, a sane mind in a sane body." And he is quoted as having coined the phrase: "The arsenic flower of an exquisite life." "Mrs. Windsor" is even more Wildean: "The train has been punctual for once in its life. How shocked the directors would be if they knew it, but, of course, it will be kept from them." She reports that someone's mother "lives at Canterbury, where she does a lot of good among the rich. They say she actually converted one of the canons to a belief in the Thirty-nine Articles after he had preached against them . . . in the Cathedral." And she complains that clergymen "who have nothing to say always do preach long sermons, don't they? They keep hoping they will have something to say presently, I suppose." Hichens clearly perceived the resemblance between Wilde and Sydney Smith. "I love drinking Bovril in secret: it seems like a vice" recalls Sydney's remark about the heterodox Brahmin "who, I am credibly informed, eats beefsteaks in private!" When "Amarinth" and the party "all got up early as a mark of respect to the country air," they must have remembered that Sydney had once done the same. And when Hichens writes of "Amarinth" "He had made a name for himself by declaring that he was pleased with the Equator and desired its further acquaintance," we are reminded of Sydney's criticism of Jeffrey: "Why, you will scarcely credit it, but, strictly between ourselves, it is not more than a week ago that I heard him speak disrespectfully of the Equator!" Which may also have been the origin of Wilde's "disappointment" with the Atlantic, for, as Hichens says of "Amarinth," "He had ruined the reputation of more than one eminently respectable ocean which had previously been received everywhere."

The Green Carnation was read and discussed far more widely than *Dorian Gray* had been, and people began to wonder all sorts of things. It was hinted in one paper that Wilde himself had written it, but he contradicted the rumour from Worthing on October 1st: "I invented that magnificent flower. But with the middle-class and mediocre book that usurps its strangely beautiful name I have, I need hardly say, nothing whatsoever to do. The flower is a work of art. The book is not." All the same he confessed to Ada Leverson "Robert Hichens I did not think capable of anything so clever. It is such a bore about journalists, they are so very clever." Needless to say, the book raised Queensberry's temperature and nearly brought on a seizure. Douglas had spent three or four months with Wilde at The Cottage, Goring-on-Thames, in the middle of '93, and now, in the autumn of '94, they were together again at Worthing; and all that Queensberry could do was to fume impotently. He would not even have extracted pleasure from the fact that the two quarrelled while staying at Brighton, whither they went in October from Worthing, because their separation would only have baulked him of his revenge. They put up at the Grand Hotel, Brighton, and then Wilde took rooms at 20 King's Road. Each nursed the other through an attack of influenza, and tempers became a little frayed in the process. But they soon made it up, and in January '95, while *Earnest* was being rehearsed, they went off to Algiers. When Queensberry heard of this latest expedition, he was livid with fury, and his insanity took a curious form, as we shall presently hear.

In the course of their holiday in North Africa, Wilde and Douglas met André Gide: that "egotist without an ego," as Wilde called him. Gide's description of what happened in Algiers and Blidah was subjected to a ruthless analysis by Robert Sherard, who proved conclusively that the statements about Wilde and Douglas in Gide's book *Si le Grain Ne Meurt* are wholly false. Douglas also called them "a mass of lies and misrepresentations," while another of Wilde's most intimate friends, Reginald Turner, declared that "Anything so preposterously untrue has never been written . . . The whole thing is fantastic." We must therefore regard Gide's account of their visit solely as a problem for the pathologist who is studying the mental condition of Gide. But many years before he produced that book, he had written several articles on Wilde, in one of which he had briefly described their meeting in Algiers without the sensational and incredible details which he later conceived. Parts of the article we may certainly accept as authentic, for one of Wilde's remarks was repeated to other people—"I have put all my genius into my life; I have only put my talent into my works"—while the following reveals the man as he came more and more to see himself, a figure of tragedy moving steadily towards his doom: "My special duty is to plunge madly into amusement . . . No, not happiness. Certainly not happiness . . . Pleasure . . . One must always set one's heart upon the most tragic . . . My friends are extraordinary; they beg me to be careful. Careful? But can I be careful? That would be a backward step. I must go on as far as possible. I cannot go much further. Something is bound to happen . . . something else." "Do you know the risk you are running?" asked Gide. "It is best never to know," answered Wilde. But he did know, for several old acquaintances were beginning to avoid him, and on at least one occasion he was extremely indignant when a man whom he had looked upon as a friend, showed a disinclination for his society.

Returning to London alone from Algiers, he heard from someone that Queensberry had booked a seat at the St. James's Theatre for the first night of *The Importance of Being Earnest* with the object of creating a disturbance. George Alexander, duly warned, cancelled the booking; but Queensberry was not the man to be put off as easily as that, and he arrived in time for the performance carrying what Sherard calls "a phallic bouquet," namely a large bunch of carrots and turnips, which he intended to hurl at the author when he took a call at the end of the play. Two stalwarts were ready for the Marquis, who was politely but resolutely refused admission.

He slipped round to the gallery entrance, but was again headed off; to the pit, with no better luck. Undaunted he tried the stage-door, but every emergency had been provided for, and he was ejected. This will explain Wilde's presence at the back of the stage throughout the evening; there was no guarantee that Queensberry would not get in disguised as a policeman, and for the sake of the management the author was discreet. However, the weather was not favourable to fresh tactics, and the baffled Marquis had had enough of it: he went away to brood over his wrongs and revolve a new plan to set them right. The morning's papers, describing the rapturous success of *Earnest*, incited him to frenzy; and three days later, to be precise at 4:30 p. m. on February 18th, he called with a witness at the Albemarle Club, produced a visiting card, wrote on it "To Oscar Wilde posing as a somdomite" (his rage no doubt being responsible for the spelling), handed it to the hall porter with the words "Give that to Oscar Wilde," and departed. After which he continued in a state of feverish disquietude for twelve days.

Meanwhile, with the shouts of the first-night audience echoing in his ears, Wilde went off on a round of country-house visits, fulfilling his last engagements as an entertainer of the British upper classes. He was back by the end of February, and on the afternoon of the 28 he called to see Ricketts and Shannon at their new residence in Beaufort Street, Chelsea. Often in the past he had spent an evening in their studio at the Vale, a cul-de-sac off the King's Road, saying to a fellow who once accompanied him "I am taking you to the one house in London where you will never be bored," and there he would sit for hours listening to their views on art, talking away himself, and quite content with a supper of beer and eggs. When, after his imprisonment, he heard from William Rothenstein that Ricketts and Shannon were rising in the world, he said "Ah, I suppose when you go there to supper they give you *fresh* eggs now."

Ricketts was alone when Wilde called on the 28th February, working in a long low gloomy room lit by a single lamp. "In response to loud knocking I opened the front door," Ricketts reports, "my eyes still half-covered by the vizor or guard engravers use. Wilde stood in the mist which flooded the street." They had not met for some time, and had seen little of each other since Wilde's success as a playwright. "My dear Ricketts, you look like a conspirator with a mask. May I come in? Or are you an alchemist turning wood blocks into gold? I can see your glass or crucible. Tell me now of your magic practices." For once they did not seem at ease together, and for a while the conversation consisted of polite enquiries. Then Ricketts referred to Wilde's plays. "Yes, I live in a world of puppets who do not understand, and yet would play with the strings . . . But why this darkness? This place is like a tomb." Ricketts lit two candles. "My dear fellow, how could you leave the Vale for this dull, dark house? Tell me now about yourself: Why this change?" Ricketts explained that he was setting up as a printer and publisher, and intended to bring out editions of the lesser-known poets, such as Vaughan, Suckling, Herbert, Crashaw, as well as the classics. Instantly Wilde manifested the keenest interest: "You must of course bring out a Chatterton. Rossetti was right; Chatterton was the founder of our romantic school." He quoted some lines and said "These might be by Keats. Naturally you will publish the Sonnets; one has to find them in hideous editions edited by men who handle Shakespeare as they would consols, or any other business investments." He paused, then added "You must print my *Portrait of Mr. W. H.*" This was an awkward moment for Ricketts, who had previously, at the author's request, done an imaginative portrait of Will Hughes for a frontispiece to the book which Wilde had written, an expansion of the original essay; so he explained that he was starting in business with a total capital of £1000, that all he could do at first was to issue Milton, Blake, Keats, etc., in limited editions, but that if successful he would follow an edition of the Sonnets with Wilde's book. Apparently his explanation was lost on his visitor: "I see, my dear Ricketts, even your charming picture of Willie Hughes has not convinced you! . . . I must work upon the thing again; it is still short for book form. But why do I say this, as if size meant anything? Think of the ocean: how dull! and of a pearl, which can be perfect." He laughed quietly. "Have you noticed how annoyed pigs become if you do not cast pearls before them? We must talk about all this later." He got up and strolled about the room as if trying to pick on some other topic.

Ricketts felt uncomfortable. Had Wilde taken his purely business explanation to mean a lack of enthusiasm for *The Portrait of Mr. W. H.*? Wilde had helped him greatly in the past, and he did not wish to appear thankless or discourteous. But the moment had gone, and Wilde was now talking of the theatre and of some absurd comment in the press. A little later he left, and Ricketts watched his form disappearing in the mist. There had been constraint in their conversation; something seemed to have come between them; the old friendly feeling had vanished; the supper of beer and eggs was a thing of the past. Soon afterwards Shannon came in, and reported that he had just met Wilde in the King's Road: "He stopped me and said charming things about you and your publishing his *Mr. W. H.* I thought he looked tired and preoccupied. We waited in the fog for a hansom to pass, near a shop with sausage rolls and pork pies lit by gas. Wilde became quite funny and said suddenly 'What curious things people will sometimes eat! . . . I suppose they must be hungry.' A cab passed, and, hailing it, he named a club near Piccadilly."

The club was the Albemarle, where he arrived at 5 o'clock, and where the hall porter handed him an envelope, within which was the card Queensberry had left ten days before. Surprised by the nature of the proceeding, the hall porter had made a note of the date and hour of Queensberry's call. Wilde wanted to know if he had looked at the card, and he admitted that he had but that he did not understand it. No one else had seen it, he assured Wilde, and he had put it in an envelope at once. Wilde should have emulated the man's discretion, and left the Marquis to cool his heels indefinitely. Instead he drove to the Avondale Hotel in Piccadilly, whence he despatched a note to Robert Ross asking him to call there at 11.30 the same night. "I don't see anything now but a criminal prosecution," he wrote; "my whole life seems ruined by this man. The tower of ivory is assailed by the foul thing. On the sand is my life spilt. I don't know what to do." The words suggest the sensations of a small boy watching the destruction of his sand-castle on the seashore with a mixture of awe and glee. The result of their conference was a visit the following morning to Ross's solicitor, Charles Humphreys, who wanted to know, before undertaking the case, if there was any truth in the libel. Upon Wilde's assurance that there was not, Humphreys agreed to act for him. On March 1st Wilde applied for a warrant; the Marquis was arrested and charged at Marlborough Street Police Court on March 2nd, the case being adjourned for a week. On March 9th Wilde, accompanied by Lord Alfred Douglas and his brother Lord Douglas of Hawick, drove to the court in a carriage and pair. The magistrate directed Lord Alfred to leave the court at once. The evidence was then given, and it became clear that the Defence had nothing serious to bring against Wilde except some letters which he had written to Douglas. Queensberry was duly committed for trial, being released on bail at £500.

Immediately following the police court proceedings Humphreys went down to the Temple to ask Sir Edward Clarke if he would lead for the Prosecution at the trial. Clarke had won a very high position as a barrister, achieved as much by personal integrity as by forensic ability, and had occupied the position of Solicitor-General for six years. He was above all things reliable, a man who could be trusted to make the best of a good case, and a man who would always be fair to the other side. He did not undertake cases unless he could believe in the innocence or rectitude of those for whom he appeared, and in the course of his life he sacrificed much by advising people against litigation. If he had been approached in the first instance, there is no doubt whatever that he would have advised Wilde to tear up Queensberry's card and forget all about it, for he realised that, even if successful, Wilde's reputation would suffer, and his innate puritanism was wholly against such a case, which involved the public exhibition of at least one family skeleton. However, the proceedings had started by the time he was asked to take part in them, and all that he could do was to satisfy himself that the man for whom he had been requested to act was innocent. He asked Humphreys to bring Wilde to his chambers, where he made his position clear: "I can only accept this brief, Mr. Wilde, if you can assure me on your honour as an English gentleman that there is not and never has been any foundation for the charges that are made against you." Wilde solemnly declared, presumably on his honour as an Irish gentleman, that the charges were absolutely false and groundless. Clarke then accepted the brief. At this point we must remember that, as far as Wilde knew, the Defence had nothing to bring against him except his written work, such as *Dorian Gray*, and several of his letters to Douglas; and he felt quite confident that when Edward Carson, counsel for the Defence, who had been at Trinity College, Dublin, with him, cross-examined him on his literary productions he could more than hold his own. Having set the law in motion, he light-heartedly left London with Douglas for Monte Carlo.

During their absence Queensberry was not idle. His declared object was to save his son, and he now set out to ruin his son, his real object being the satisfaction of his maniacal thirst for revenge on anyone who had thwarted his will, and the operation of his hatred over as wide a field as possible. With the help of a private detective, he began to collect evidence, rushing hither and thither in a flurry of excitement, buttonholing this man, examining that, and offering bribes to anyone who was perjurable in the interests of public morality. Male and female prostitutes were surprised to find how popular they had suddenly become. Men who expected nothing in return were apparently delighted to meet them and stand them expensive drinks, merely for the pleasure of their company; and they felt flattered when it was assumed that they were sufficiently intimate with a popular dramatist to be able to pass on information concerning his habits. But nothing of value was obtained by these means; and if it had not been for the obliging action of a less popular dramatist named Charles Brookfield, the Defence would have been in a bad way. "Brooks," as he was affectionately called by his friends, enlisted under Queensberry's flag, not for money but for pure love of the thing, and not only put the detective in touch with a female who stated that her profession had suffered from Wilde's activities, and who knew the haunts of his accomplices, but suborned a commissionaire at the Haymarket Theatre to give the addresses of Wilde's blackmailing associates. When, long afterwards, Wilde was told what his fellow-dramatist had done, all he said was "How absurd of Brookfield!"

In this way a handy little gang of male prostitutes and blackmailers was partly frightened, partly cajoled and partly bribed into giving evidence against Wilde, who, on his return to London shortly before the trial, spent a day with Douglas at his solicitor's office studying Queensberry's plea of justification, which gave a list of witnesses for the Defence together with the charges to be substantiated. This opened his eyes to the seriousness of his position, but did not alter his course.

The question why he ever embarked on such a course, and why he maintained it after recognising the danger, has troubled many people, and no satisfying answer has yet been given. The explanation is to be found in his nature. We have already seen how from his earliest days he had dramatised himself and his career, his histrionic capacity being a part of that emotional life which never reached maturity. Gradually the performance had become so much a part of his being that he was convinced of its reality, seeing himself at first as a symbolic figure climbing slowly to the heights of success, and at last, when he had tasted the fruits of victory, as a symbolic figure plunging suddenly to the depths of failure. The story of Jesus intensified the make-belief, and he saw himself in the rôle of Christ, the shouts of his first-night audiences being his hosannas, with Calvary to come. Now if it had been put to him exactly as here written, his intelligence would have ridiculed the picture; but unfortunately, whenever called upon to act either in reality or in the imagination, his intelligence became an uncertain quantity, and the actor was left in possession of the stage. Further, he had been corrupted by applause and success; he was suffering from swelled head; and in his action against Queensberry we seem to see two conflicting characters: the one hurrying towards an inescapable destiny, the other marching with assurance towards a victory that would crown his previous triumphs. A third element entered into the drama: he was embroiled in the family quarrel of an historic house: he stood between a lord and a marquis in the eternal conflict of youth with age. Had his friend's name been Smith, whose father was a "mister," things would not have come to this pass, and he might have been deprived of his downfall. For, primarily, the motive that drove him onward, consciously or unconsciously, was the feeling that his life would not be complete without disaster and tragedy, and that he must plumb the depths as he had scaled the heights. "It is what we fear that happens to us," he once said, and his admission after the event—"I admit I lost my head. I was bewildered, incapable of judgment"—is proof that he was acting throughout almost automatically, the slave of his own imagination, playing the part that had become second-nature to him. In his comedy, *An Ideal Husband*, he was clearly envisaging his own catastrophe: "Think of their loathsome joy," says one of the characters, referring to the behaviour of the newspapers should the scandal of Sir Robert Chiltern's career become public property, "of the delight they would have in dragging you down, of the mud and mire they would plunge you in. Think of the hypocrite with his greasy smile penning his leading article, and arranging the foulness of the public placard." In trying to excuse his conduct, Chiltern speaks of the "men who, each one of them, have worse secrets in their own lives," and Goring replies "That is the reason they are so pleased to find out other people's secrets. It distracts public attention from their own." These passages are an exact prediction of what happened in Wilde's case.

There was another influence at work egging him on to combat, though for the reasons already given he was merely being pushed in the direction he wished to take. This was Lord Alfred Douglas, who, long before his father left the opprobrious card at the Albemarle Club, had urged Wilde to take proceedings against Queensberry on the strength of the libels contained in the letters which the Marquis had written to his son. If Wilde had done this, writes Douglas, the libeller "would not have had a leg to stand on. The evidence which my father got later took a long time to collect, and could not have been available at the time when he first started his attack." After Wilde had been moved to action, Douglas thought he had made a grave mistake in not consulting George Lewis, who, besides being a personal friend, was the only solicitor who would have given him proper advice. But as that error could not be rectified, Douglas not only encouraged Wilde to proceed but related the whole story of Queensberry's persecution of his family to Sir Edward Clarke, wrote it all out as a basis for the brief Humphreys was preparing, and assured Clarke that "if he would call me as a witness at the beginning of the case, *before* Wilde, we could create so much feeling and prejudice against my father that no jury would give him a verdict . . . I told Clarke that if he did not put me in the witness-box we might just as well throw up the case at once." Clarke replied that he intended to start off with a deadly attack on Queensberry for his conduct to his family. "Yes, but will you promise faithfully to put me in the box?" asked Douglas. "I promise you I will," said Clarke; "you shall go into the box immediately after my opening speech."

Convinced that Wilde would win if only they could discredit Queensberry at the outset, Douglas put up £360 towards the cost of the case, got his family to rally round, and, as he said, "screwed Oscar up to the 'sticking place.'" There were moments when Wilde relented, when he perceived the absurdity of the action from his own point of view, but his attitude was never seriously shaken, and one word from Douglas was sufficient to buoy him up. He still believed that he would win on the literary issue, and arranged to meet Frank Harris one day at the Café Royal with the intention of asking him to go into the witness-box and testify to the sound morality of *Dorian Gray*. Bernard Shaw, who was present, has recorded the incident, and Douglas joined them while they were talking. Harris told Wilde flatly that he had not an earthly chance of winning the case, that the highest testimonials to his writings would be useless, that no jury would give a verdict against a father trying to protect his son, that the case would be decided on the evidence which the Defence had collected, and that the best thing he could do was to write a letter to the press explaining that he had made a mistake in bringing the action, and then to go abroad until the fuss had blown over. Douglas, who knew exactly how and why his father was "protecting" him, knew too that Queensberry's persecution would not stop until he was in his grave, and felt certain that a full exposure of the man's infamous conduct to his family would decide the matter, promptly got up, told Harris that his advice showed he was no friend of Oscar's, and walked out. Wilde followed his example, after remarking that Harris was failing him in his hour of need, and that he now knew who his real friends were. Harris thought that Wilde was weakly submitting to the will of Douglas. But therein he displayed ignorance of Wilde's nature. "Nobody in the wide world could persuade him to do what he did not want to do," says Vincent O'Sullivan, and our analysis shows that he was acting under the influence of a mystical concept.

Two nights before the trial began Wilde dined with his wife and Douglas at a restaurant, and then the three of them went on to a box at the St. James's Theatre, where *Earnest* was running to packed houses. Constance could scarcely have enjoyed herself. "She was very much agitated," Douglas writes, "and when I said good-night to her at the door of the theatre she had tears in her eyes." They never met again. Oscar was in an airy mood. Between the acts he paid a visit to George Alexander, who told me what passed between them.

"I don't think you ought to have come to the theatre at such a time," said Alexander. "People will consider it in bad taste."

"Are you going to accuse everyone in the theatre of bad taste for seeing my play at such a time?" asked Wilde laughing. "I would consider it in bad taste if they went to anyone else's play."

"Do be serious."

"Then you mustn't be funny."

"Will you take a bit of advice?"

"Certainly . . . if it is advice that I wish to take."

"Why don't you withdraw from the case and go abroad?"

"Everyone wants me to go abroad. I have just been abroad. And now I have come home again. One can't keep on going abroad, unless one is a missionary, or, what comes to the same thing, a commercial traveller. But make your mind easy, my dear Alec. I have consulted Mrs. Robinson, the palmist, and she assures me that I shall win."

"Do you really believe in palmists?"

"Always . . . when they prophesy nice things."

"When do they ever prophesy anything else?"

"Never. If they did no one would believe in them, and the poor creatures must earn a living somehow."

"Oh, you're impossible!"

"No, not impossible, my dear fellow . . . Improbable . . . yes . . . I grant you improbable."

Alexander gave it up, and Wilde returned to his box, where he laughed heartily all through the last act.

The Queensberry trial commenced at the Old Bailey on April 3rd, 1895. Sir Edward Clarke's opening speech would have been admirable if, as Douglas says, his client had been the Archbishop of Canterbury; but as it largely consisted of praise for Wilde's literary achievements, and as he did not follow it up by asking in a modified form the questions which were to be expected in cross-examination, he would have done better if he had abandoned the case before it began. Clarke's failure to show up Queensberry and then to put Douglas in the witness-box, as he had promised to do, decided the verdict. It must be admitted in his favour that he believed implicitly in Wilde's oath of innocence, and he thought he could win on the single issue. But he must have known, when he read the plea of justification, that Wilde was not quite as innocent as he had protested; and it was therefore his duty to exhibit Queensberry as one who had justifiably earned the detestation of his family, and whose solicitude for his son was sheer hypocrisy. Clearly something had happened to make him change his mind. But

what? It is improbable that we shall ever know for certain, though we can
make a reasonable guess. An absolutely upright man, Clarke was nevertheless amenable to the social atmosphere around him, and it must have been
conveyed to him by interested people, obliquely enough to leave him unconscious of being influenced, that the scandal and odium following on the
exposure of the head of a leading aristocratic family would do incalculable
harm to Society. As a godly man and a pillar of the established order, it
may further have been hinted to him that, whether innocent or guilty,
Wilde was an undesirable personage, whose standing was of small account
compared with that of a well-known sportsman who was also a marquis.
In some such fashion Clarke had been moved to alter his conduct of the
case ("for who so firm that cannot be seduced?") and in effect, though of
this he was entirely unaware, to sacrifice his client's only chance.

Carson began by cross-examining Wilde on *Dorian Gray* and the *Phrases
and Philosophies for the Use of the Young*, their interchanges having been
given in previous chapters. Next there was a passage between them relating
to the letter, already quoted, that Wilde had written to Douglas. "I think it
is a beautiful letter," said Wilde. "It is a poem. I was not writing an ordinary letter. You might as well cross-examine me as to whether *King Lear*
or a sonnet of Shakespeare was proper."

"Apart from art, Mr. Wilde?"

"I cannot answer apart from art."

"Suppose a man who was not an artist had written this letter, would you
say it was a proper letter?"

"A man who was not an artist could not have written that letter."

"Why?"

"Because nobody but an artist could write it. He certainly could not write
the language unless he were a man of letters."

"I can suggest, for the sake of your reputation, that there is nothing very
wonderful in this 'red rose-leaf lips of yours.'"

"A great deal depends upon the way it is read."

"'Your slim-gilt soul walks between passion and poetry.' Is that a
beautiful phrase?"

"Not as you read it, Mr. Carson. You read it very badly."

"Have you often written in the same style as this?"

"I don't repeat myself in style."

After reading another letter from Wilde to Douglas, Carson asked: "Is
that an ordinary letter?"

"Everything I write is extraordinary," Wilde retorted. "I do not pose as
being ordinary, great heavens!"

Then there were questions about a young man named Alphonse Conway, whom Wilde had met at Worthing.

"He sold newspapers at the kiosque on the pier?" queried Carson.

"No, I never heard that up to that time his only occupation was selling newspapers. It is the first I have heard of his connection with literature."

"Was his conversation literary?"

"On the contrary, quite simple and easily understood. He had been to school, where naturally he had not learned much."

Wilde came through the first day's ordeal triumphantly, having scored off Carson at every move in the game. Meeting the actor, Charles Goodhart, in Piccadilly Circus, he seemed to be in high spirits. Goodhart did not like to touch on a subject that was being advertised on every placard within sight and shouted by every paper vendor in the neighbourhood, so he made a remark about the weather. Then said Wilde "You've heard of my case, I suppose?" "Oh—er—yes," returned Charles nervously. "I'm sure I wish you the—er—best of luck—and—er—" but Wilde spared his feelings: "Don't distress yourself. All is well. The working classes are with me . . . to a boy."

The next day Wilde was cross-examined on his knowledge of Alfred Taylor and his friendships with young men. As he afterwards described all his answers on such subjects as "absurd and silly perjuries," it is unnecessary to give them. Besides, the history of his homosexual amours is no more interesting than the average man's visits to a brothel: passion is significant, evacuation is not. One remark he made is worth preserving because it was true of himself generally, though it was by no means the whole truth in regard to the young man whose relations with him were under discussion. "What is there in common between you and Charlie Parker?" probed Carson, and Wilde made answer "I like people who are young, bright, happy, careless and original. I do not like them sensible, and I do not like them old. I don't like social distinctions of any kind, and the mere fact of youth is so wonderful to me that I would sooner talk to a young man for half an hour than be cross-examined by an elderly Q.C." Carson subjected Wilde to a devastating cross-examination, and Clarke's re-examination did not help matters. When the court rose at the end of the second day's hearing, Carson was in the middle of his opening speech for the Defence, and before a single witness on Queensberry's side had been called it was generally felt that the Prosecution had failed.

When on the third day it became clear from Carson's speech that the Defence were going to prove justification by calling witnesses, whose evidence would show that Taylor had procured them for a certain purpose, and whose exact relations with Wilde would be described, Clarke left the court and advised Wilde to drop the case, since, if it went on to the end, and the jury found the accusations true, the judge would order his arrest. Wilde thanked Clarke for his advice and agreed to act upon it. In the hope that he would leave the country, Clarke then said that he need not be present in court while the announcement was being made; and Mathews, a junior counsel, hinted that they would keep the case going in order to give him time to clear out; but he refused to go. Carson was still speaking when Clarke returned and asked the judge if he might have a few words with the counsel for the Defence. Following a short conversation between himself and Carson, he rose and addressed the judge: "Having regard to what has been referred to by my learned friend in respect of the matters connected with the literature and the letters, I feel we could not resist a verdict of Not Guilty in this case—Not Guilty with reference to the word 'posing.' In these circumstances I hope you will think I am not going beyond the bounds of my duty, and that I am doing something to save, to prevent, what would be a most horrible task, however it might close, if I now interpose and say on behalf of Mr. Oscar Wilde that I would ask to withdraw from the prosecution." Skilled in the interpretation of legal terminology, the learned counsel for the Defence understood this to mean that his client's plea of justification had been proved; the judge supported him; and the jury, defrauded of the sensations which they had been led to anticipate, angrily added to their verdict the statement that Queensberry's action had been "for the public benefit." The Marquis was the hero of the hour, being loudly cheered as he left the dock, and enjoying a further demonstration of public approval when he reached the street. Incidentally, it is of interest to record that Charles Brookfield and Charles Hawtrey, both of whom had been acting for over a hundred nights in Wilde's play *An Ideal Husband*, gave a dinner to Queensberry to celebrate his victory. As sportsmen they were naturally delighted with the success of their hunt through the West End stews, and overjoyed at the thought that they had brought their quarry to earth. Although Wilde's own folly had enabled them to do it, Queensberry and Brookfield could congratulate themselves unreservedly on having wrecked the career of a genius. Few people in history could boast as much, and their dinner-party must have been most gratifying to both of them. Some years later Brookfield was appointed Censor of plays, the authorities no doubt feeling that such a high sense of moral responsibility as his should not go unrewarded.

Wilde drove from the Old Bailey to the Holborn Viaduct Hotel, where a room had been reserved for lunch, and where he was shortly joined by

Robert Ross, Lord Alfred Douglas and Lord Douglas of Hawick. While
there he wrote a letter to the *Evening News*:

"It would have been impossible for me to have proved my case without
putting Lord Alfred Douglas in the witness-box against his father. Lord Alfred
Douglas was extremely anxious to go into the box, but I would not let him
do so. Rather than put him into so painful a position, I determined to retire
from the case, and to bear on my own shoulders whatever ignominy and shame
might result from my prosecuting Lord Queensberry."

Lunch over, Wilde drove to the Cadogan Hotel in Sloane Street, where
Douglas had rooms. There he was repeatedly urged by his friends to leave
for Dover and Calais, but he kept saying "It is too late" and "The train has
gone." Douglas's cousin, George Wyndham, sent a message begging Wilde
to leave the country; but nothing could move him. He sat in a chair drinking hock and seltzer, saying little, waiting for the stroke of fate, his face
expressionless. At his request Ross went to break the news to Constance,
who burst into tears, and, though quite unable to realise what had happened, added her entreaty to that of his friends: "Poor Oscar! Poor Oscar!
I hope he is going abroad." With the help of Lady Wilde she left Tite
Street that evening.

Frank Harris imagines that Wilde's inaction on April 5th bears out the
wholly fictitious portrait of a weak-willed, easily-influenced effeminate which
Harris gives in his book. The very opposite is the truth. Despite the plead-
ings of all his friends, Wilde remained. Having little sense of reality, he
could not imagine what was in store for him, and, if partially paralysed
by the shock, he was half-hypnotised by the picture of himself as one pre-
destined to suffer.

Meanwhile Charles Russell, solicitor for Queensberry, sent the statements
of all the witnesses Carson had intended to call to the Director of Public
Prosecutions. The Home Secretary, H. H. Asquith, had a conference with
the Attorney-General and the Solicitor-General, whereat it was determined
that a warrant for Wilde's arrest should be executed; and at some time
between seven and eight o'clock that evening the police called at the Cadogan Hotel and knocked at the door of Room 53.

"Mr. Wilde, I believe?"

"Yes?"

"We are police officers and hold a warrant for your arrest."

"Oh, really?" He seemed relieved.

"I must ask you to accompany us to the police station."

Wilde got up, a little unsteadily, put on his overcoat, took his hat and gloves, and followed them out. They drove in a four-wheeler, via Scotland Yard, to Bow Street. Robert Sherard once asked Wilde, in view of his superstition on the subject, whether the cab horse that drove him from the Cadogan was white. "I was too much interested to notice," said Wilde, having chatted away on all sorts of topics with the detectives, who thought him a most amiable gentleman. At Bow Street the charges were read out to him, after which he was taken to a cell, where press reporters were allowed to peer at him through the grille, and where he paced to and fro all night, unable to sleep. Next day he was removed to Holloway Gaol.

His friends had been active all this while. Douglas, who had been absent when Wilde was arrested, having gone down to the House of Commons to find out from his cousin George Wyndham whether there would be a prosecution, went at once to Bow Street with the intention of bailing Wilde out, but found that it was impossible. Ross had gone to Tite Street to get some clothes for Oscar, found the house deserted except for Alfred the man-servant, and with his help burst open the bedroom door which Constance had locked. But when he got to Bow Street, outside which a mob was howling obscenities, he found that he could not see Wilde or leave the clothes for him. Returning to Tite Street, he forced the library door and took away some letters and manuscripts. After that both he and Turner thought it would be advisable to leave the country. They crossed to Calais, where they stayed at the Terminus Hotel.

When the news of Wilde's arrest reached Sir Edward Clarke the following morning, he wrote at once to Humphreys offering to defend Wilde at his trial for nothing. Humphreys replied on the same day that Wilde had expressed "his deepest gratitude for your very kind offer, which he most gladly accepts." A few other people acted as human beings at this juncture, and their names should be remembered. Ernest and Ada Leverson and Adela Schuster offered any help within their power, and Mrs. Bernard Beere, who had acted "Mrs. Arbuthnot" in *A Woman of No Importance*, wrote in a similar strain. Wilde's one comfort in Holloway Prison was the daily visit of Alfred Douglas, who describes the way in which they were allowed to speak to one another for fifteen minutes: "The visitor goes into a box rather like the box in a pawnshop . . . There is a whole row of these boxes, each occupied by a visitor, and opposite, facing each visitor, is the prisoner whom he is visiting. The two sides of visitors and prisoners are separated by a corridor about a yard in width, and a warder paces up and down the corridor . . . The visitor and the prisoner have to shout to make

their voices heard above the voices of the other prisoners and visitors . . .
Poor Oscar was rather deaf. He could hardly hear what I said in the babel.
He looked at me with tears running down his cheeks and I looked at him.
Such as it was, as he told me in nearly every letter he wrote . . . this interview was the only bright spot in the day." He was kindly treated by the
warders, but he had no books, could not smoke, and slept badly. Douglas
was with him in the intervals of his appearances at Bow Street Police Court,
when Sir Edward Clarke again let his client down by failing to cross-
examine the witnesses, and on April 19th Wilde and Taylor were committed
for trial. Taylor of course had been rounded up immediately after the
collapse of the Queensberry case: the rooms at 13 Little College Street had
been raided, many incriminating documents found there, and Taylor was
given the option of being prosecuted or of acting as evidence against Wilde.
He chose the former: yet Marlborough did not glory in her son. The other
witnesses against Wilde were given the same option, but they preferred
perjury to prison. Thus it came about that Taylor and Wilde were charged
with conspiracy, and they were jointly tried.

What Wilde found most distressing during those weeks in Holloway
Prison were the interviews with his solicitor. Looking back on the past,
some eighteen months later, he honestly confessed that he did not regret his
association with the young men whose evidence had sent him to gaol, but
"what is loathsome to me is the memory of interminable visits paid by me to
the solicitor Humphreys, when in the ghastly glare of a bleak room I would
sit with a serious face telling serious lies to a bald man till I really groaned
and yawned with ennui." Perhaps, if he had been able to witness what was
going on in the world outside the prison walls, he might even have reconciled himself to Humphreys.

It was not a pleasant sight. The Victorians were busily engaged in a very
ancient pastime at which they were adept. They knew better than any
previous age how to

> Compound for sins they were inclined to
> By damning those they had no mind to.

They damned Wilde with such vigour and thoroughness that, on this
evidence alone, they must be considered the most vicious age in history.
By the fury of their condemnation they stand condemned. Nothing on the
same scale had ever happened before, though Macaulay has an interesting
passage on Byron which shows that the British people were always liable
to spasms of immoral indignation:

"We know no spectacle so ridiculous as the British public in one of its periodical fits of morality. In general, elopements, divorces, and family quarrels, pass with little notice. We read the scandal, talk about it for a day, and forget it. But once in six or seven years our virtue becomes outrageous. We cannot suffer the laws of religion and decency to be violated. We must make a stand against vice. We must teach libertines that the English people appreciate the importance of domestic ties. Accordingly some unfortunate man, in no respect more depraved than hundreds whose offences have been treated with lenity, is singled out as an expiatory sacrifice. If he has children, they are to be taken from him. If he has a profession, he is to be driven from it. He is cut by the higher orders, and hissed by the lower. He is, in truth, a sort of whipping-boy, by whose vicarious agonies all the other transgressors of the same class are, it is supposed, sufficiently chastised. We reflect very complacently on our own severity, and compare with great pride the high standard of morals established in England with the Parisian laxity. At length our anger is satiated. Our victim is ruined and heartbroken. And our virtue goes quietly to sleep for seven years more.... The obloquy which Byron had to endure was such as might well have shaken a more constant mind. The newspapers were filled with lampoons. The theatres shook with execrations. He was excluded from circles where he had lately been the observed of all observers. All those creeping things that riot in the decay of nobler natures hastened to their repast; and they were right; they did after their kind. It is not every day that the savage envy of aspiring dunces is gratified by the agonies of such a spirit, and the degradation of such a name."

The treatment of Byron, however, was Christian compared with that accorded to Wilde, who suffered from living in a more putrid period. "He will never lift his head again," said the art critic Gleeson White, "for he has against him all men of infamous life." The first people to display their infamy were the journalists, who not only justified the worst that Wilde had ever said about them but went much further than he could have conceived possible. To read the paragraphs and leading articles that were turned out day after day between the Queensberry case and the trial of Wilde, at a time when the accused was still technically innocent of offence, is to realise that Shakespeare's view of human beings as expressed through the mouth of Timon of Athens was a charitable one.

Resulting from this exhibition, a nation-wide prejudice was created against Wilde, and the police court magistrate, Sir John Bridge, refused to allow him bail, which meant that he was unable to collect evidence or to raise money at a time when both were vital to him. His creditors at once obtained judgment against him, an execution was put into his house, a sale of his possessions was held there on April 24th, and nearly everything went for a song, though some of his personal belongings were bought by friends and eventually restored to him. Thus the man who a few weeks before was earning an income of several thousands a year was made bankrupt for just over a thousand. Taking their cue from the press, a rabble of thieves and sensation-mongers crowded the house, broke into rooms, burst open drawers, stole manuscripts and anything else they could get away with; and at last the disorder and rowdiness became so great that the police were called in. Normally Wilde's belongings would have fetched four times the amount demanded by his creditors; but the behaviour of the newspapers and the action of the magistrate ruined him. Among other manuscripts stolen at the sale were the complete form of *A Florentine Tragedy, The Duchess of Padua* (of which a prompt copy existed), and the enlarged version of *The Portrait of Mr. W. H.*, which had been returned by the publisher on the day that the Queensberry case took an unpleasant turn.

The publisher was John Lane, who was on a visit to New York at the time. He was, as we know, not fond of Wilde, and it was now safe to disclose his real feelings. The fact that he had been only too glad to publish Wilde's works when the author's reputation was at its height did not deter him from stopping their sale and withdrawing every copy from circulation the moment it was advisable to do so; and he spent some days in feverish activity, despatching cables and writing letters to put himself right with the world and to deny that he had introduced Wilde to a youth named Shelley, who had been employed by him and was mentioned as a witness in the case.

Nothing on earth could rouse Wilde to resentment. He thought Brookfield's behaviour "absurd," Lane's "childish," and Alexander's "ridiculous." It is certainly not easy nowadays to apprehend the peculiarly Victorian brand of humbug which the latter exhibited. From April 6th till May 8th, when it was withdrawn, *The Importance of Being Earnest* was advertised on the placards and in the programmes of the St. James's Theatre as, presumably, a work of divine origin or supernatural conception; for the author's name was obliterated by slips of paper on the placards and blocked out on the programmes. Apologists for the actor-manager have declared that he did this in the interests of Wilde, the removal of whose name being the only alternative to the removal of his play; in other words, that Alexander believed people would only go to see the play if they did not know who had written it. But the author of *Earnest* was much more famous than any of his works, and there was scarcely a playgoer in the metropolis who did not know that George Alexander was acting in an Oscar Wilde comedy at the

St. James's Theatre; so the only possible explanation of the manager's conduct is that he thought people would still enjoy the play if they were not
shocked by seeing the words "Oscar Wilde" attached to it; which means
that the Victorians were quite willing to laugh so long as they could pretend
that their laughter was not due to the man who had provoked it; and Alexander pandered to their hypocrisy. It has been asserted that he did so because
he wished to help the author financially. Since this also signified helping
the manager financially, we need not challenge the assertion.

Another manager, Charles Wyndham, showed a different spirit. The last
nights of *An Ideal Husband* had been announced at the Haymarket before
the Queensberry action, as Tree wanted the theatre on his return from
America. But the play was doing so well that Waller had arranged to
transfer it to Charles Wyndham's theatre, the Criterion. For the final performance at the Haymarket, April 6th, Waller ordered slips of paper to be
pasted over Wilde's name, probably after consultation with Alexander. Both
of them, by the way, had been asked by Douglas that day to go bail for
Wilde; both had refused; and, as it happened, the application for bail was
turned down shortly after. When Wyndham got to hear of the slip-of-paper
policy, he absolutely declined to let Waller bring the play to the Criterion
unless the author's name appeared on all bills, placards and programmes, his
reason being that he would not allow a theatre of his to be the means of
affronting a man on his trial. Waller was compelled to accept this condition,
and *An Ideal Husband* continued its run for a fortnight at the Criterion,
from the 13th to the 27th of April. Judged by Victorian standards, Wyndham
was clearly eccentric.

In the state of public feeling created by the press nearly everyone who had
known Wilde, or was in any way attracted to his sexual peculiarity, took
fright. The railways and steamers that trafficked with the continent suddenly
had to cope with a sort of holiday rush out of season. People who had received letters from him, or to whom he had given manuscripts, burnt them;
while those who had written to him demanded the return of their letters.
Among others the Acton family delivered his correspondence to the flames;
and Edward Burne-Jones, who had liked Wilde very much and had exchanged letters with him over many years, sent an urgent request for the
return of everything he had written. Robert Ross, in complying, asked that
Wilde's letters to the painter should be restored, but was curtly informed
that they had all been destroyed. As Burne-Jones also put Swinburne's
letters on the fire, it seems that the first half of his surname was singularly
appropriate.

The scandal affected every section of the community wherein Caliban and Tartuffe had the time of their lives. For the lower classes it was a sort of "Roman holiday." What they believed to be an aristocrat had been flung to the legal lions; bawdy jokes were bandied about in the streets; and any man who had long hair or wore an eyeglass or dressed too well or spoke in a refined manner or carried a noticeable bunch of flowers was liable to have "Oscar" yelled at him and to attract the unwelcome attention of every loafer and passer-by in the vicinity. One gentleman, stung by the gibe and unable to proceed with that unconscious aloofness so necessary to the occasion, stopped to expostulate, but was moved on by the police to the derisive cheers and displeasing comments of the jovial onlookers.

The middle classes behaved as if they had been publicly insulted. They said little, but from the expression on their faces it was clear that something was on their minds and that they supported extreme measures whatever the circumstances. Broadly speaking they felt that art was largely responsible for what the world had come to. They had read the accounts of the case, and Wilde's repartees under cross-examination had roused their distrust. Wit to them was a sign of insincerity, poetry a synonym for perversion, cleverness a form of wickedness. They had always said . . . but as they had said it so often we need not repeat it. Instead we will quote Wilde's comment, some three years later, on the attitude of such folk: "I never came across anyone in whom the moral sense was dominant who was not heartless, cruel, vindictive, log-stupid, and entirely lacking in the smallest sense of humanity. Moral people, as they are termed, are simple beasts. I would sooner have fifty unnatural vices than one unnatural virtue."

As for the upper classes, we learn from Sherard that "a lady who belongs to the highest English nobility" wrote to him that "the ordinary run of English society *hated* Oscar." Their hatred was due primarily to his intellectual superiority, but without doubt his essay *The Soul of Man Under Socialism* had made matters much worse; while the satire in his plays, his self-esteem, and the fact that they could not do without him, nor snub him, nor discompose him in the least degree, but had to bear his sometimes insolently independent witticisms with smiling faces which concealed seething resentment, did not make it easier for them to put up with him. A feeling of self-annoyance gave a keener edge to their anger. There is but one step from popular success to popular obloquy. The moment a man who has been petted and spoilt trips over the law and falls from favour, he receives no mercy. Those who once praised him feel that he has betrayed them, and hurt vanity more than anything else makes them kick him when he is down.

Such was the prevailing insanity that Wilde's children had to be removed from their school, presumably because they might have contaminated the other boys, and the epidemic spread to France. Robert Sherard, then in Paris, received a letter from Wilde begging him to call on Sarah Bernhardt, who had promised to produce *Salomé* at her own theatre, and ask her to buy the play outright for three or four hundred pounds, as the author was in dire need of money for his defence. Sherard's reception by the actress left him speechless with gratitude; she wept tears over the distress of her dear kind friend Oscar; her voice trembled with emotion as she spoke of him; and though she could not produce or purchase *Salomé* at the moment, she would be only too pleased to help him with a loan. "What I can do I will— the utmost—out of friendship for a great artist, who is also a man of good heart, and who, I am sure, is suffering most unjustly." Sherard, who had been reading nothing but denunciations of him in the Paris press and hearing nothing but execrations of him by English and American residents, was deeply moved by her compassion and promise of help, and at once despatched a telegram to Oscar with the good news that funds would soon be sent and that Sarah had spoken of him with sympathy and affection. Calling at her house on the day she had arranged that he should receive the money, he was told that she was out, would not be back that afternoon, and had left no message for him. The same thing happened the day after, and the day after that. He went in search of her, and eventually found her at a *salon* talking prettily to a crowd of admirers about pottery. Contriving at length to attract her attention, she smiled winningly and fixed another appointment at her house. He kept it, only to be told that she was engaged and hoped he would come again the following day; but she was an elusive lady, and he was informed at his next visit that she was working at her sculpture with a model, that he need not call again, and that she would write to him. She never wrote; and when he sent a letter praying for a few lines from her secretary, so that he could show it to their friend whose hopes had been kindled by the promise of assistance, she did not reply. After reading Sherard's report, Oscar's sole comment on her behaviour was "I suppose Sarah is hopeless; but your chivalrous friendship—your fine chivalrous friendship—is worth more than all the money in the world." Though prudent enough in her attitude to Wilde, the famous actress was extremely imprudent in not buying *Salomé*; for within ten years her three or four hundred pounds would have turned into thirty or forty thousand pounds, and she must have experienced moments of remorse at the thought of it. Her refusal was serious for him, for although Clarke was giving his services for nothing there were solicitors, junior counsel and so on to be paid, and, what certainly worried him more than anything, his mother to be supported. His wife could keep herself and their children on her own income.

Just before the trial Sir Edward Clarke advised Lord Alfred Douglas to leave the country for his friend's sake. Douglas would not move until Wilde had begged him to go; then he went to the Terminus Hotel, Calais, whence, half way through the trial, he wired Clarke some information which, though compromising to himself, would help Wilde, and again asked to be called as a witness. This brought a rebuke from the solicitors, who described his telegram as "most improper," said that Clarke had been much upset by it, and told him not to interfere again.

The trial opened at the Old Bailey before Justice Charles on April 26th, and lasted five days. Wilde was indicted under an act that had only been passed ten years before, and which did not exist in any other civilised country. The clause dealing with his offence had been added by Henry Labouchere, not, as Harris thinks, with the object of reducing the act to absurdity, but with the intention of increasing its gravity. Wilde pleaded Not Guilty, concerning which we may quote Bernard Shaw: "Wilde could plead Not Guilty with perfect sincerity, and indeed could not honestly put in any other plea. Guilty or not guilty is a question not of fact but of morals: the prisoner who pleads Not Guilty is not alleging that he did this or did not do that: he is affirming that what he did does not involve any guilt on his part." In a way it is a pity that Wilde did not stand up to his accusers and assert his innocence in the light of his own nature. It would have been a more dignified proceeding than a denial of the charges backed by "absurd and silly perjuries." Years earlier he had discussed the divorce case which wrecked the political career of Sir Charles Dilke with W. E. F. Britten, the artist. "People are so foolish in always denying the truth of these charges," he said. "I want to see the man who will face the judge in the Divorce Court, and not only confess but express his complete satisfaction with the experiment. As for the British public, they are always liable to stand on their hind legs and bray aloud that they are a moral people. Regarding poor Dilke, monstrous as it may appear, you can take it from me that not only will he be hounded from Society, but he will be cut by every lady in London and also by most of the men." Human nature being what it was, his own no less than other people's, he did not act on his excellent precept when he should have done, though there were special reasons in favour of such a course. The prejudice created against him by the press, the tainted evidence of the witnesses, the injustice with which he had been treated by the police court magistrate, the sale of his possessions, the desertion of many people whom he thought he could rely on: everything pointed to the fact that he would not receive a fair trial, and so he might just as well have been hanged for a sheep as a lamb, and gone to prison as a martyr instead of a liar.

We need not dwell on the trial beyond remarking that Clarke tried to get the charge of conspiracy between Wilde and Taylor dropped on the ground that, if it were maintained, the defendants could not be called as witnesses; that the judge refused, which meant that the evidence against Taylor, which was often not evidence against Wilde, influenced the minds of the jury against the latter; that Clarke managed to discredit a great deal of the evidence for the Prosecution, and got one witness dismissed from the box for perjury; that he secured an acquittal on the conspiracy charge; and that the trial ended with a disagreement of the jury. Throughout the hearing Wilde seemed to be weary and apathetic; there was no fight in him at all, though at one moment he pulled himself together and showed what he might have done if his spirit had not been numbed by the weeks in Holloway Gaol and the mental anguish through which he had passed. He was being cross-examined on the subject of two poems which Lord Alfred Douglas had contributed to *The Chameleon*; and with reference to a line in one of them he was asked by the prosecuting counsel, C. F. Gill, "What is the 'Love that dare not speak its name'?" His answer drew loud applause and a few hisses from the gallery of the court, the outburst being sternly checked by the judge:

"The 'Love that dare not speak its name' in this century is such a great affection of an elder for a younger man as there was between David and Jonathan, such as Plato made the very basis of his philosophy, and such as you find in the sonnets of Michael Angelo and Shakespeare. It is that deep, spiritual affection that is as pure as it is perfect. It dictates and pervades great works of art like those of Shakespeare and Michael Angelo, and those two letters of mine, such as they are. It is in this century misunderstood, so much misunderstood that it may be described as the 'Love that dare not speak its name,' and on account of it I am placed where I am now. It is beautiful, it is fine, it is the noblest form of affection. There is nothing unnatural about it. It is intellectual, and it repeatedly exists between an elder and a younger man, when the elder man has intellect, and the younger man has all the joy, hope and glamour of life before him. That it should be so the world does not understand. The world mocks at it, and sometimes puts one in the pillory for it."

On May 1st, following the disagreement and discharge of the jury, Clarke immediately applied for bail on behalf of Wilde, but the judge refused to allow it; and Gill announced that the case would be tried again, which made it clear that the Home Secretary and his legal advisers had already determined to get a conviction if humanly possible, and the law officers set about the job with exceptional diligence. Application for bail to a judge in chambers, who had no option in the matter, resulted in Wilde's release on May 7th. The amount of the bail was fixed at £5000, Wilde himself being responsible for half that sum, Lord Douglas of Hawick and the Rev. Stewart Headlam being sureties for the other half. Actually Headlam ran no financial risk, as his fellow-surety promised to be answerable for £1800, the balance of £700 being put up by Earnest Leverson, a well-to-do business man. But as Headlam's action was that of a Christian, he naturally incurred the grave risk of offending the large majority of Christians. He had founded a Christian-Socialist movement called the Guild of St. Matthew. As a result of his activities he had been "silenced" by his ecclesiastical superiors, but he was always liable to break out in a fresh place. He had only met Wilde twice, and his action was solely due to the fact that he considered the case was being prejudged. He hesitated at first, knowing that people would think he had done it for the sake of notoriety. "I knew quite well that this action of mine would with many people damage my already damaged reputation, and that it would sadly try some of my best friends, whom I had already tried a good deal," he wrote in an unfinished account of his life. This forecast proved correct. The first sign of the coming storm was the flight of his housemaid. Next he lost an old friend, Henry Norman, and became temporarily estranged from H. W. Massingham. A keen co-worker on Headlam's Guild, the Rev. J. G. Adderly, resigned therefrom. Another parson, C. L. Marson, brought the matter up at a public meeting and did his best, but failed, to arouse hostility against Headlam, who was threatened with stoning at his house in Upper Bedford Place. "Isn't this the man that went bail for the notorious convict, Wilde?" shouted someone at a School Board election meeting, months after Wilde had been sentenced. Headlam jumped up and heatedly retorted "Yes, I am the man, and by the laws of England everyone is reckoned innocent until he is proved guilty. And I would do it again to-morrow." Thunders of applause, and ejection of a heckler.

Wilde had a fortnight's freedom between the trials. Upon his release he drove straight to the Midland Hotel, St. Pancras, accompanied by Lord Douglas of Hawick. Two rooms had been engaged for him, and they had just sat down to dinner when the manager burst into the room. "You are Oscar Wilde, I believe." "I am." "You must leave at once." The screaming scarlet Marquis was responsible. He had arranged to have Wilde followed, and hired a gang of roughs to make certain that his victim should have no-where to lay his head. Wilde went from one hotel to another, even journeying to such remote suburbs as Kilburn and Notting Hill, which he had read about in books though never seen; but not being expert in the craft of entering by one door and leaving by another or otherwise baffling pursuit, he was ordered out of each within a few minutes of his arrival. By about midnight the roughs were beginning to feel the effects of hospitality at so many places of call and lost touch with Wilde, who, deadbeat, arrived at his mother's house in Chelsea, No. 146 (now 87) Oakley Street, shortly before 1 o'clock. His elder brother heard a faint knock on the front door, opened it, and was astonished to see Oscar. "Give me shelter, Willie. Let me lie on the floor or I shall die in the streets." He staggered in and slumped into a chair. Willie, who was also a trifle unsteady on his legs, though from a dif-ferent cause, afterwards described his brother's arrival: "He came tapping with his beak against the window-pane, and fell down on my threshold like a wounded stag."

This was Willie's hour. His famous brother, fortune's darling, Society's pet, who had taken a lofty line with him, and had occasionally hinted dis-like of his drunken habits and disreputable friends, was now at his mercy; and he was not the sort of person to let bygones be bygones. "Thank God my vices are decent!" was one of his pleasantries, and he constantly said things to hurt Oscar, who was made to feel acutely uncomfortable, though never resentful. A certain family pride altered Willie's tone in conversation with other people. "Oscar was *not* a man of bad character," he once informed Bernard Shaw: "you could have trusted him with a woman anywhere." When Oscar got to hear of Willie's efforts in his behalf, he was in despair: "He tells me that he is defending me all over London. My poor dear brother could compromise a steam-engine." W. B. Yeats called at the house in Oakley Street one day with letters of sympathy from people in Ireland. "Who are you? What do you want?" demanded Willie. Following an explanation, he continued "Do these letters urge him to run away? Every friend he has is urging him to, but we have made up our minds that he must stay and take his chance." Willie babbled on incoherently, his eyes filling with tears of whisky and self-pity: "He could escape. Oh yes, he could escape. There is a yacht in the Thames, and five thousand pounds to pay his bail—well, not exactly in the Thames, but there is a yacht. Oh yes, he could escape, even if I had to inflate a balloon in the backyard with my own hand; but he has resolved to stay, to face it out, to stand the music like Christ. . . . It is his vanity that has brought all this disgrace upon him. They swung incense before him . . . they swung it before his heart." Willie went on repeating to everyone who called and to everyone he met "Oscar is an Irish Gentleman: he will stay to face the music"; and, lest the chief actor should forget his lines, to Oscar himself "You are an Irish gentleman: you must stay to face the music." Lady Wilde was responsible for Willie's attitude. By some curious process of thought, she had managed to convince herself that Ireland was defying the universe in the person of her second-born, to whom she said: "If you stay, even if you go to prison, you will always be my son; it will make no difference to my affection; but if you go I will never speak to you again."

Everyone else who cared for him tried to make him go. Robert Sherard, who came over from Paris at the request of friends in order to take Wilde away for a few days from his depressing surroundings, urged him to leave the country, but he would not consider it. "I could not bear life if I were to flee," he said. "I cannot see myself slinking about the continent, a fugitive from justice." Sherard describes the room in which Wilde received him: "It was a poorly furnished room, in great disorder. He was lying on a small camp-bedstead in a corner between the fireplace and the wall, and in a glass on a mantelpiece was an arum lily, sere and yellow, which drooped lamentably down over his head. His face was flushed and swollen, his voice was broken, he was a man altogether collapsed." One of the first things that Wilde said was "Why have you brought me no poison from Paris?" The sound of the phrase pleased him, and he repeated ". . . poison from Paris." Sherard got a little peevish when the same question was put to him several days in succession, and at last he told Wilde exactly how to make prussic acid, knowing perfectly well that he had not the remotest intention of committing suicide. An extremely sympathetic observer, Sherard nevertheless could not help noticing that Oscar was actually enjoying the new part that had been thrust upon him, was making the most of a great tragic rôle. Unaccountable though it seemed to Sherard, this evidence squares with our picture of the man and explains why he would not listen to his friends when they urged flight. True, his mother's attitude would have influenced him against running away if he had felt inclined to do so, but the self-portrait of a figure of Fate never left him now. Circumstances had merely precipitated the catastrophe, which had always been inevitable. To quit the centre of the stage and vanish into the wings was not only against his nature: it was against the nature of things: what had been decreed must come to pass.

But his friends were as keen to get him away as he felt destined to stay.

Lord Alfred Douglas, whose daily letters to Wilde throughout this period made life bearable for him, wrote to his brother, the chief surety, begging him to tell Oscar that he was at liberty to leave. Though the loss would have crippled him at that moment, his brother replied "If there is even a chance of conviction, in God's name let him go." But nothing that Douglas could say would make Wilde stir. Frank Harris also did his best. He entered the Oakley Street house one morning in a breezy way and said "I have come to take you out, Oscar. You musn't mope here all day." Willie wanted to know where they were going. "To the Café Royal, if he'll come." Sherard, who was present, exclaimed "That's fine of you, Harris!" But Wilde would not go there: "It wouldn't be seemly for me to defy public opinion," he said. Harris took him instead to Pagani's in Great Portland Street, where they had a private room and where, according to Harris, Wilde broke the news that he was not wholly innocent of the charges brought against him. A later scene between them, which is given in detail by Harris, must be rejected in detail by us. We should feel quite confident that the whole of it owed more to Harris's fancy than to his "notes" if we were not equally confident that his "notes" existed only in his fancy. Harris was too busy a man, too much interested in himself and not enough interested in other people, ever to make notes of conversations unless money transactions were involved. Nevertheless there is evidence to show that he really did offer to secure a yacht for Wilde's escape if the latter were willing to bolt; which is the one grain of truth in a scene that Harris invented some fifteen years later in order to appease his own vanity by exposing Wilde as a weakling, his notion of a strong man being one who, when faced with the consequences of his own actions, promptly absconds.

Sherard gives us a few glimpses of life in the dismal home of Willie and Lady Wilde. One day he brought Ernest Dowson along for an hour or two, which pleased Oscar. Another evening a veiled lady came in a cab and left a horseshoe with a bouquet of violets and the words "For Luck" on the card attached. Sherard did not know who she was, but I have heard on good authority that she was Ellen Terry. Wilde suffered from constant thirst, and Sherard went out again and again to fetch lemonade and soda water and claret from a grocer's shop nearby. Oscar appeared to be stunned by the tragedy, for he looked dazed, sighed frequently, and spoke hardly at all. Sherard was probably not an invigorating influence, for Wilde suggested selling the few books in his possession to order to pay his friend's return fare to France, though the latter's poverty was the excuse for his suggestion.

During the brief breathing-space between his trials, two Jewesses behaved

as Christians are supposed to behave. One rescued him from want, the other
from Willie. Adela Schuster, to whom Wilde refers in his letters as "the
lady of Wimbledon," heard of his bankruptcy, and wrote to ask if she might
be his banker. He replied that he had no money for his defence and nothing
to give his mother, whom he had always helped to support. Upon which a
cheque for £1000 was sent him with the assurance that it was a wholly
inadequate recognition of the pleasure his conversation had given her. That
indeed is how everyone who gave him money after his downfall should have
regarded their gifts: as token payments for something that was quite beyond
price. Deliverance also came from Ada Leverson, a clever journalist whom
Oscar called "The Sphinx." She visited Oakley Street, realised how wretched
he was there, and asked him to stay with her husband and herself in Court-
field Gardens. But first they summoned their servants together, and Ernest
Leverson spoke to them: "You most of you know Mr. Wilde and have waited
upon him. You know now the dreadful thing that has happened to him; you
know of what he is accused; you know that he is out on bail. Now your mistress and I would like him to come and stay with us here until he is a free
man again, but before inviting him I feel it right to ask you to tell me with
frankness whether you think you will be able to make him comfortable . . ."
There was a pause, during which the butler and cook exchanged glances.
The butler cleared his throat and pronounced the verdict: "Well, sir—sir and
madam—speaking for myself and I think for the rest of us—well, sir, we've
most of us read the case, but we know Mr. Wilde, and we have always been
proud to wait on him, and proud we shall still be, sir, if I may make so bold—
we'll all of us do all we can to make the poor gentleman comfortable." In
case the butler was taking too much upon himself, Leverson offered any of
them who wished to go a month's wages; but the butler had gauged the
position accurately, and not one of them left. Only the coachman was not
present, the Leversons fearing that he would gossip in public houses; so
they sent him away for a holiday. The rest promised to keep the secret, which
if divulged would almost certainly have resulted in damage to the Leversons'
property, not to mention their reputation.

Ada Leverson then went to fetch Oscar in a hired brougham, and he was
inexpressibly relieved to get away. The nursery floor, consisting of two large
rooms, one small one and a bathroom, was given up to him. He asked her to
leave the children's toys where they were: a rocking-horse, dolls' houses,
golliwogs and so forth; and in a room where rabbits and other animals
sported on a blue and white dado he received his friends and talked with
his solicitors. To save the Leversons any embarassment, he never left his

floor till 6 in the evening, breakfast, luncheon and tea being sent up to him. But punctually at 6 he went downstairs, carefully dressed for dinner, a flower in his buttonhole, his hair waved by an old hairdresser who called daily for the purpose. He still wished to resemble the bust of Nero in the Louvre. From 6 to 8 he talked to Ada Leverson in the drawing-room, walking up and down, smoking cigarettes, never once mentioning his troubles, delightful as ever. One thing he said lingered in her memory:

"After the first glass of absinthe you see things as you wish they were. After the second you see them as they are not. Finally you see things as they really are, and that is the most horrible thing in the world."

"How d'you mean?"

"I mean disassociated. Take a top hat. You think you see it as it really is. But you don't, because you associate it with other things and ideas. If you had never heard of one before, and suddenly saw it alone, you'd be frightened or you'd laugh. That is the effect absinthe has, and that is why it drives men mad. Three nights I sat up all night drinking absinthe, and thinking that I was singularly clear-headed and sane. The waiter came in and began watering the sawdust. The most wonderful flowers, tulips, lilies and roses, sprang up, and made a garden of the café. 'Don't you see them?' I said to him. 'Mais non, monsieur, il n'y a rien.'"

It was not a very happy illustration of his thesis, but he was not the man to stick to his thesis if something more picturesque occurred to him.

One day Oscar's wife came, and they were alone for two hours, at the end of which she left in tears. She had brought an urgent message from her lawyer imploring him to leave the country before his next trial, which would unquestionably ruin him. She might just as well have tried to influence a rock: he was immovable, backing his obstinacy with the statement that his mother had told him it would be dishonourable to go. Hearing the reason of Constance's visit, Ada Leverson wrote him a note praying him to follow his wife's advice. When he went down for dinner that evening, he returned her note with the words "That is not like you, Sphinx," and went on to talk of books. Constance, by the way, had found a home with Lady Mount Temple, who invited Oscar to visit her between the trials. She was a saintly person who thought ill of no one, and, having nothing to be ashamed of, did not need the cloak of moral indignation.

On May 19th, the night before his second trial commenced, Wilde asked his hostess to put a sleeping-draught on the mantelpiece of his bedroom. He did not intend to take it, he said, but its mere presence would have a magical effect. The following morning she stood in the hall to see him off, as he was staying in Oakley Street for the duration of the trial. He turned to her suddenly before going out, and his voice faltered for the first time: "If the worst comes to the worst, Sphinx, you'll write me?" Then he stepped into the little brougham which she had hired for him, and drove away with his friend More Adey.

Every civilised human being will agree that the government of that day made a grave error in prosecuting Oscar Wilde at all. In view of the sensation which he had created, he should have been told to leave the country. But either the authorities lost their heads owing to the outcry in the press, or they really believed that a moral purge was necessary and would be achieved by a legal conviction; which implies either that they were very weak or that they were very foolish. By instituting a second trial, however, they are exposed as vindictive. Their only excuse is that they were frightened. During the evidence given in the Queensberry case and at the first trial of Wilde several names were mysteriously written down on pieces of paper, read by the judge, passed to the jury, and muttered over but never spoken aloud. This gave rise to the suspicion that names of important people were being suppressed; and so it came about that when, for instance, a leading politician took a holiday abroad for his health, the worst construction was put upon his absence. The obvious way of dealing with such a situation was to disclose the names that had been written down, or, better still, to let rumours have their way for a season until the next scandal disseminated a fresh crop. But neither course appealed to the Home Office, and we are forced to conclude that malevolence against Wilde was the main motive behind the government's procedure. Our conclusion is strongly supported by the fact that the Solicitor-General, Sir Frank Lockwood, was sent down to the Old Bailey to lead for the Prosecution, which he conducted with the utmost ferocity. His antagonism was unrestrained, and, as a journalist wrote in *To-day*, he "fought like a tiger," being reproved for his bitter partisanship by Sir Edward Clarke. To make certain of getting a conviction, he availed himself of the right to the last word as Law Officer of the Crown, a right which Clarke had never once claimed throughout his six years as Solicitor-General.

That the action of the government in ordering a second trial was considered unfair in the legal profession is shown by the efforts of Edward Carson, who was utterly out of sympathy with Wilde and very hostile to him in the Queensberry case. He did his best to influence the Solicitor-General against a further prosecution. "Poor Wilde has suffered a great deal, Sir Frank. Cannot you let up on the fellow now?" he asked. "I dare not do so," Lockwood replied. "If I did so it would be said all over the world that we dropped the case owing to the names mentioned in the Marquis of Queensberry's letters." He might have added that one of the names mentioned was a relation of his own; but we have already seen that the official excuse covered a malignant purpose; and though it is true that Lockwood dealt with the rumours by having all the hitherto suppressed names mentioned in court, it is equally true that his handling of the case showed clearly that the prosecution had become a persecution.

The second trial of Oscar Wilde began on May 20th at the Old Bailey before Justice Wills. As the charge of conspiracy had been dropped, Sir Edward Clarke applied that the cases of Wilde and Taylor should be taken separately. The judge agreed; but Clarke's request that Wilde should be tried first was refused, the Prosecution desiring to make the evidence against Taylor and his certain conviction create a still greater prejudice against Wilde. After Taylor had been found guilty, the sentence being postponed, Wilde took his place in the dock. The male witnesses for the Crown, who had originally been bribed by Queensberry for their evidence, had been well rehearsed, well clothed, well fed, well housed and well looked after in the interval. They were paid for their attendance at the court and carefully guarded from any influence that was likely to make them reconsider their stories. By profession they were prostitutes, blackmailers, extortioners and swindlers, described by the judge as belonging to a gang of the vilest type, and most of them were ultimately arrested in the performance of some branch of their business and sent to prison. The female witnesses were hysterical servant girls, whose evidence, said the judge, was not fit to hang a dog on. Clarke had no difficulty in disposing of what may be called the "respectable" evidence; and we must not forget that Wilde was acquitted of the charge of debauching youth and corrupting innocence, and that he was convicted solely on the evidence of accomplices who had the choice of witnessing against him or of standing in the dock with him.

The trial dragged on for four days. Stewart Headlam called for Wilde at Oakley Street every morning, accompanied him to the court, and took him back every evening. His stay with the Leversons had done him good, and his bearing throughout the final ordeal was calm and dignified. London was placarded with his name, and Sherard remarked one evening "Well, you have got your name before the public at last." He laughingly replied "Nobody can pretend now not to have heard of it." His last evening was spent in making arrangements for his mother in case he did not return. Everything of value that he had brought with him to Oakley Street had been pawned or sold by Willie, including the scarab ring which he had worn for so many years, but the few trifles still in his possession were at his request distributed as keepsakes to his friends by Willie's wife. He went to bed early that night, after bidding farewell to each of his friends.

His demeanour in court on May 25th was impressive. He appeared to dominate the scene, almost as if he had become the symbolic figure of his imagination. "Intellectually speaking he stood head and shoulders above the judge who tried him and the counsel who prosecuted him," said one observer, while another likened him to a wounded lion being worried by a pack of mongrel terriers. The judge's summing-up was what is commonly called impartial. That is to say, it analysed the evidence with care, showing what should be accepted and what rejected, but it made much of the evidence that told against Wilde and little of the evidence that told in his favour. The jury retired at 3:30 in the afternoon and were absent for two and a half hours, when they returned with a verdict of "Guilty" on all counts except one. In sentencing Wilde and Taylor to two years hard labour, Justice Wills made a speech in which cruelty, stupidity, hypocrisy and mendacity were nicely blended, the sort of speech that Shakespeare had in mind when he wrote:

> but man, proud man
> Drest in a little brief authority,
> *Most ignorant of what he's most assured,*
> His glassy essence, like an angry ape,
> Plays such fantastic tricks before high heaven
> As make the angels weep.

The blow, partly expected because in his fancy it had been preordained, was not the less a terrible shock when it descended. While Taylor took it with seeming indifference, Wilde reeled under it, and caught at the rail of the dock to steady himself. His eyes stared with horror, his face flushed, and in a husky voice he asked; "And I? May I say nothing, my lord?" The judge signed to the warders, who touched Wilde on the shoulder; and he, after one agonised look round the court, disappeared from view.

Sherard gives the impression that as he left the Old Bailey the entire street was filled with men and women dancing with joy at the fall of an aristocrat. Harris beats this by saying that the scene was as soul-defiling as anything witnessed in the French Revolution. Sherard, torn between rage and misery, exaggerated; while Harris follows Sherard's account closely enough to convince us that he was not there. What actually happened was that about a dozen female prostitutes were merrily kicking up their heels at the prospect of a trade-revival. " 'E'll 'ave 'is 'air cut reg'lar *now*!" cried one of them, and they all laughed harshly. Though scarcely an edifying spectacle, we may say in their favour that the harlots had not been so well brought up as the many righteous people who were quite as pleased but dared not dance for joy.

CHAPTER SIXTEEN

THE IMPENITENT

WITH that previsional sense of his tragic destiny which is expressed in so many of his works, Wilde makes one of the characters in *Lady Windermere's Fan* say: "Misfortunes one can endure—they come from outside, they are accidents. But to suffer for one's own faults—ah!—there is the sting of life." It was the knowledge that he had brought all his troubles upon himself that made the early months of imprisonment so agonising. Not given to self-pity at any time, it would have helped him greatly if he could have indulged in that emotion now, but there was no conceivable ground for it: his martyrdom was gratuitous, self-inflicted and quite meaningless, and he suffered the torments of one who cannot reasonably complain of his sufferings. If he had defied the law, he might have felt heroic; if he had been persecuted from the start, he might have felt victimised. But he could neither brace himself with the conviction of having done right, nor solace himself with the consciousness of having been wronged.

For a man of his gregarious and sybaritic nature prison-life was unrelieved horror. English gaols in those days, whatever they may be now, were mere torture-houses, producing crime and lunacy in equal measure. Oscar's first six months were spent in Wandsworth Prison, where he could scarcely breath in the fetid air of his cell and was at first quite unable to eat the food, the mere sight and smell of which made him vomit. When hunger at last forced him to eat, he suffered from diarrhoea and became so weak that he could hardly stand. In spite of exhaustion he could not sleep on his plank bed, and at nights he suffered from the wildest delusions. He had not yet learnt how to speak to the other convicts during their daily exercise without moving his lips, and one day he heard a man behind him say "I am sorry for you; it is harder for the likes of you than it is for the likes of us." He replied "No, my friend, we all suffer alike." The feeling of sympathy thus imparted warmed him, and every day a few words passed between them until a warder saw his lips moving, reported them both to the Governor, and he had to undergo the terrible experience of solitary confinement in complete darkness for twenty-four hours on bread and water, compared with which the crank-turning which made every bone in his body ache, and the oakum-picking which made his fingers numb with pain, were pleasant pastimes. He was spared none of the cruelties and indignities which un-imaginative human beings wreak upon those who fall into their power; and as one who belonged to a different social class from the other prisoners, he was the special victim of that pettiness and spite which the majority of those who have been subjected to authority display whenever they have a chance to exercise it.

The chaplain was as foolish, the doctor as brutal, as the warders. "Mr. Wilde," said the former, "did you have morning prayers in your house?" "I am sorry . . . I fear not." "You see where you are now." He might have replied that the parson at least should have been grateful, since the omission of morning prayers in so many homes provided him with a job. But the expression on the chaplain's face was unaccommodating. One Sunday morning Wilde felt so ill that he could not lift himself from his bed. The doctor came, charged him with malingering, and said that he would be punished if he did not get up. Though he fell over once or twice while making the effort, he managed somehow to get his clothes on, and went to chapel, where he fainted on his feet and in falling injured his ear, which ached and bled for many months and never properly recovered from the accident. He returned to consciousness in the prison infirmary, where he was treated well and en-joyed the luxury of clean sheets and good bread and butter. Another chap-lain, Dr. Morrison, who had been dismissed for writing articles denouncing the prison system but was reinstated on the discovery that he was right, came to Wandsworth after Wilde had been there a short time and had several long talks with him. Once Morrison used the word "patience," and Wilde burst out "I could be patient, for patience is a virtue. It is not patience, it is apathy you want here, and apathy is a vice." Throughout the whole period he spent in Wandsworth not an hour passed that he did not long for death.

Sherard went to see him in August '95. The interview took place in a vaulted room, where they were separated from each other by two rows of iron bars, a warder standing in the passage between them. Wilde had just been granted the privilege of one book a week, and he told Sherard that he had been reading Pater and Newman. "I noticed that his hands were dis-figured, and that his nails were broken and bleeding," says Sherard; "also that his head and face were untidy with growth of hair." The friends and relations of Constance Wilde had been urging her to obtain a divorce, but Sherard felt that this would be the last straw, and at length managed to persuade her to visit Oscar. She went in September, and was horrified by the conditions imposed upon visitors. "When I go again, I am to get at the Home Secretary through Mr. Haldane and try and get a room to see him in and touch him again," she told Sherard, to whom she also declared her intention of making a home for Oscar after his release. When Sherard next visited Wandsworth he was partly, if unintentionally, responsible for the attitude which Wilde soon adopted towards Douglas, and which was to have a curious result.

Douglas had spent the summer of '95 at Capri, and on his return to Paris in the autumn he was invited by the *Mercure de France* to contribute an article on Wilde, giving his version of what had happened. Convinced that the truth would do much to rehabilitate his friend in France, he wrote the article, which contained many extracts from the letters which Oscar had written to him from Holloway Prison and while staying with the Leversons. These letters were, says Douglas, the most sincere and moving things that Wilde ever wrote, and might have altered many people's opinion of him: nothing but good could have come of their publication. But when Sherard heard of what was happening from the man who translated the article, he told Wilde that Douglas was going to publish all his letters in a newspaper, which suggested to Wilde that his most intimate feelings and affairs were about to be blazoned to the world, and he authorised Sherard to prevent it. The moment Douglas heard that Oscar objected to his letters being published, he withdrew the article, and at a later date destroyed the letters. Sherard had been misinformed as to the nature of the article, and should have asked to see it before speaking to Oscar on the subject. His well-meant but overzealous action had a most unfortunate sequel, as we shall learn.

In the meantime R. B. Haldane, who was serving on the Prison Commission under the chairmanship of Sir Evelyn Ruggles-Brise, had written to ask Dr. Morrison what could be done for Wilde. Haldane had met Wilde in the days of his social success, and, having more imagination than most politicians, had been "haunted by the idea of what this highly sensitive man was probably suffering under ordinary prison treatment." He had therefore visited Wilde in Holloway Gaol, and finding that the only book he could obtain was Bunyan's *Pilgrim's Progress*, which did not satisfy him, had sent him several other works. Afterwards he went to see him at Wandsworth; and when the chaplain reported that Wilde was ill in the infirmary, Haldane managed to arrange his transfer to Reading Gaol, which was considered relatively healthy. An incident on the way to Reading has been described by Wilde. Already he had endured several railway journeys in humiliating conditions when being taken to and from the Bankruptcy Court. On one of these occasions he stood on a station platform, handcuffed to two other convicts, in a steady drizzle of rain, depression sitting heavily on the warders no less than their charges. "Sir," said Wilde to one of the warders, no doubt to cheer him up, "if this is the way Queen Victoria treats her convicts, she doesn't deserve to have any." But the episode on the way to Reading was not of a nature to arouse mirth, except among the sportsmen who took part in it:

"On November 13th, 1895, I was brought down here from London. From two o'clock till half-past two on that day I had to stand on the centre platform of Clapham Junction in convict dress, and handcuffed, for the world to look at. I had been taken out of the hospital ward without a moment's notice being given to me. Of all possible objects I was the most grotesque. When people saw me they laughed. Each train as it came up swelled the audience. Nothing could exceed their amusement. That was, of course, before they knew who I was. As soon as they had been informed they laughed still more. For half an hour I stood there in the grey November rain surrounded by a jeering mob. For a year after that was done to me I wept every day at the same hour and for the same space of time."

The Governor of Reading Gaol for the first eight months of his incarceration there was Colonel Isaacson, described by Robert Ross as "a perfect monster," by those who suffered under him as something unprintable, by Wilde as "unimaginative." Like all people who believe in punishment, he was vindictive and sadistic by nature, modelling himself on the God of his fathers as depicted in the Old Testament. Wilde was frequently punished by him for trivial offences, and would have been thoroughly brutalised in the process but for the humanising effect of converse with his fellow-convicts. He soon learnt how to speak without moving his lips; and as the prisoners did not take their exercise in the same order every day, he gradually got to know most of them, finding out their names and histories, and arranging with Ross or some other friend that those who needed it should have sums of money waiting for them at a post office on their release.

Wilde's cell was the third on the third landing of "C" block: hence he was known as C.3.3. At first his occupation was oakum-picking, but he made little progress at it, and, on the strange assumption that an author should know something about the making of books, he was for a while employed as a binder. However, he soon managed to disillusion the authorities on that point, and eventually became schoolmaster's orderly, which meant that he could take charge of books and distribute them to the other prisoners, a task which he failed to accomplish satisfactorily. But this was in the last phase of his captivity, after Isaacson's departure, and as there was no less arduous job in the prison he held it until his release. Under Isaacson he broke down in health and spent some time in the infirmary. His friends, who were allowed to visit him four times a year, got to know of it, and attempts were made to have his sentence reduced. A few people had already drawn up petitions for his liberation. Bernard Shaw, remembering that Oscar had been the only distinguished signatory to his memorial for the reprieve of the Chicago anarchists, was one of them; but as he could only get Stewart Head-lam to put his name to the document, he abandoned the project. Several young Frenchmen of letters tried to persuade Zola to sign an appeal to Queen Victoria, but he refused. Frank Harris approached George Meredith, whose name at the head of a petition would have meant much, but he declined to help. Although Wilde had harmed no one but himself, not a single prominent man in any country could be persuaded to save him a day's torture by signing a paper. Justice Wills had described the case as the worst in his experience, and as he was never certified insane we may conclude that nearly all his famous contemporaries agreed with him.

It is pleasant to record that at least two University dons behaved in a civilised manner. Robert Yelverton Tyrrell, Regius Professor of Greek at Trinity College, Dublin, was the only man Harris could get to sign his petition; while Frederick York Powell, Regius Professor of Modern History at Oxford, signed another. Greatly to his credit Harris went to see Sir Evelyn Ruggles-Brise, who as Chairman of the Prison Commission was helping on many humane reforms; and though Harris did not behave as he relates in his book, he did something more characteristic and more honourable to himself: he walked up and down the office angrily inveighing against the idea that a man could be imprisoned for Oscar's fault at all. Ruggles-Brise informed the Home Office that one or two petitions were on the way, and asked that Wilde's mental and physical condition should be taken into account. Two officials were sent down to Reading Gaol, learned that Wilde was in the infirmary, and were taken to the door through which they could observe him without being seen. Oscar has been exhibited in this biography to little purpose if the reader cannot guess what the officials saw. He was sitting on the side of his bed surrounded by the other patients, who were shouting their delight at the stories he was telling them. As always in the exercise of his astonishing gift, he seemed radiant with health, bursting with high spirits, and as happy as a sand-boy. It was evident to the onlookers that prison-life was doing him a world of good, and the people who were trying to get sig-

natures for their petitions were informed in September '96 that there were
no grounds, medical or otherwise, to justify mitigation of the sentence. Oscar
had heard that his friends were doing their best for him, and when the news
was broken he was in despair. "The refusal to commute my sentence has
been like a blow from a leaden sword," he wrote. "I am dazed with a dull
sense of pain." Yet when Haldane paid him a visit he did not seem completely downcast, for on being pressed to use his leisure by writing some
considerable work he replied "I am preparing a small volume of table epigrams." It was through Haldane, backed by Ruggles-Brise, that he was
allowed the books he wanted, as well as writing material; and, best of all,
their influence resulted in the removal of Isaacson to Lewes Gaol, his place
being taken in July '96 by "that good kind fellow Major Nelson," as Oscar
spoke of him.

Reading Gaol may have been healthier than Wandsworth, but in Isaacson's
time existence there was just as unpleasant, the warders quite as ruthless, and
the convicts lived under a reign of terror. It was a frightful revelation to
Wilde, who had never related what he had read in books to the facts of contemporary life, and had suffered from the not uncommon delusion that
human beings were improving. Prison completed an education that had begun
when he was arrested, and he never recovered from the experience. His will-
power was broken with the shattering of his self-respect, which was largely
dependent on his respect for others, an attitude he could no longer maintain
when their behaviour had shown them unworthy of anything but contempt.
The first effect of the shock to his mental system was noted by Ross and
Sherard when they visited him in May '96. Sherard was in a truculent mood,
and, Ross reports, "seemed anxious that the third person in the railway carriage should know on what mission we were bent." Their interview took
place in an undignified setting. Wilde was in a sort of rabbit-hutch, and the
light was feeble. Sherard describes him as "altogether crushed down," while
Ross says that he had become "temporarily *silly*. That is the mildest word that
will describe my meaning." He seemed to be talking to himself while they
were giving him the kind of news in which he would normally have taken an
interest. "He said he had nothing to say and wanted to hear *us* talk," which,
as Ross remarks, was "very unlike Oscar." Streaks of grey and white showed
in his hair, a bald patch on the crown of his head, and he asked them whether
they thought his brain seemed all right. "They treat me cruelly," he added
in a low voice. Ross had the impression that he was wasting and pining away,
and felt that he might die at any moment.

Three months before their visit, on February 3rd, '96, Oscar's mother had died. "No one knew how deeply I loved and honoured her," he wrote, but the actor in him spoilt the simple sincerity of that statement by building up the effect: "Never even in the most perfect days of my development as an artist could I have found words fit to bear so august a burden, or to move with sufficient stateliness of music through the purple pageant of my incommunicable woe." His wife had gone to stay with the Ranee of Sarawak near Genoa, and though she was ill at the time she endured the fatigue and discomfort of the journey home in order that he should hear from her, not from a stranger, the news of his mother's death. He was much moved by her kindness, and in a letter to Ross about a month later he said "I feel that I have brought such unhappiness on her and such wrong on my children that I have no right to go against her wishes in anything. She was gentle and good to me here when she came to see me. I have full trust in her." Having failed to induce her to obtain a divorce, her family had tried hard to make her agree to a legal separation, and at length she had consented; but she wished to make a settlement on her husband, who told Ross that he would sanction her terms whatever they were. Before leaving prison he signed the deed of separation, giving her the custody of the children, and receiving from her £150 a year on condition that he did not live with Lord Alfred Douglas. He felt the loss of his children acutely: "That is, and always will remain to me, a source of infinite distress, of infinite pain, of grief without end or limit."

In March '96 *Salomé* was seen on the stage for the first time. It was produced by Lugne-Poë at the Théâtre de L'Oeuvre in Paris, and was well-received by audience and critics. Wilde expressed what he could feel of gratification: "It is something that at a time of disgrace and shame I should be still regarded as an artist: I wish I could feel more pleasure: but I seem dead to all emotion except those of anguish and despair." Ross's letters were comforting; they kept him in touch with the world of art; they were both amusing and informative, telling him what he wanted to know in a witty conversational way. While Isaacson was Governor he never had enough books and was not allowed those of his choice. More Adey sent him some volumes of the Greek and Latin poets, but reading them brought on headaches. With the arrival of Major Nelson, however, life for him was completely changed no longer did he have to pick oakum or suffer solitary confinement; books that he had asked for were sent by his friends; he read Dante; he studied German ("Indeed, this seems to be the proper place for such study," he remarked); he wrote letters; he was allowed a light in his cell as late as he wished; he could talk with the other prisoners; and the warders were much kinder. As a result of this humane treatment his longing for death soon changed to a longing for life, and his main concern became the financial provision for his future; so much so that when, as he thought, Ross and other friends failed to display a business sense in dealing with his affairs, he got very irritable and wrote pages of complaint.

Visitors were now allowed more often than before, and he would write to ask them to "my next At Home." To one, who wanted to know how he had managed to survive the horrors of Isaacson's régime, he replied "I was buoyed up with a sense of guilt." Frank Harris, Robert Ross, More Adey, Robert Sherard, Charles Ricketts and several others went to see him; but he would only receive friends, and even some of those were excluded. From the books of reminiscences dealing with that period the uninstructed reader may be led to suppose that the Great Western Railway ran special excursions to accommodate all the people who wished to call at Reading Gaol; but when the books were written Wilde had become world-famous, and his circle of intimates had increased to such an extent that most of their faces would have been unfamiliar to him.

His real friends at this time were in prison with him, several warders and many convicts occupying his thoughts more than occasional visitors from the outside world. To one warder he happened to say that the chaplain and the doctor, who saw him occasionally, bored him with their uninteresting conversation. "If you find the conversation of these educated men uninterest-ing, what must you find mine?" asked the warder. "I like to talk with people who have some originality, whether educated or not," he replied: "I detest the commonplace, the practical, and the stereotyped." He had discovered that the sympathy of the policemen "who in their homely, rough way strove to comfort me on my journeys to and from the Bankruptcy Court under conditions of terrible mental distress" was strangely consoling; and the kindness of the warders who had charge of him after the coming of Major Nelson was of the same quality. He took a genuine interest in their hobbies, and they consulted him over newspaper competitions, his advice sometimes resulting in prizes of half-a-guinea or a guinea. "You don't know that since I have been here I have won a silver tea-service and a grand piano," he in-formed Ross. Talking between warders and convicts was officially forbidden but the rule was not strictly adhered to after Isaacson left. One warder had leanings toward literature, and though Wilde was only too ready to impart knowledge it may be doubted whether the man found it helpful. For example:

"Excuse me, sir, but Charles Dickens, sir: would he be considered a great writer now, sir?"

"Oh, yes, a great writer indeed: you see he is no longer alive."

"Yes, I understand, sir. Being dead he would be a great writer, sir . . . Now, sir, John Strange Winter, sir: would you tell me what you think of him, sir?"

"A charming lady, he is a charming lady; but I would rather talk to her than read his books."

"Thank you, sir. I did not know he was a lady, sir . . . Excuse me, sir, but Marie Corelli: would she be considered a great writer, sir?"

This, said Wilde in recounting the incident, was more than he could bear, and putting his hand on the man's shoulder he said gravely "Now don't think I've anything against her *moral* character, but from the way she writes *she ought to be here*."

"You say so, sir, you say so," said the warder, amazed but not doubting the accuracy of the information.

That some of them became much attached to him is shown by the following incident. One morning he woke up feeling very ill, and the warder on duty went to make him some hot beef-tea, an action that would have got him into serious trouble if discovered. On the way back to Wilde's cell the hot bottle slipped between his shirt and skin, and just at that moment he was summoned by the Chief Warder. Throughout their conversation he was in agony, the hot bottle pressing against his skin and becoming hotter and hotter every minute until he nearly howled with pain. At last he got away and described the experience to Wilde, who burst out laughing. The man was annoyed at having his sufferings treated as a joke, marched out and banged the door. An hour later he returned with breakfast, and Wilde looked suitably contrite, saying he would not touch the meal until he was forgiven.

"Not even the cocoa?" asked the warder.

"Not even the cocoa."

"Well, rather than starve you, I'll forgive you."

"And supposing I laugh again?"

"I shan't forgive you again."

The next morning Wilde handed him a humorously written "Apology" with the words "Here is something which is not of much value now, but probably will be if you keep it long enough."

A warder named Martin was particularly nice to Wilde, bringing him biscuits, newspapers, etc., and was the means whereby he was able to make life easier for other prisoners. There are in existence scraps of paper on which messages were scribbled to Martin asking him to find out the address of one man, to take a message to another, to get the name of a third, and so on, always with the object of helping them with advice or money. Some children were in prison for poaching rabbits, and Wilde was greatly agitated. He asked whether he could pay the fine and set them at liberty: "Please, dear friend, do this for me. I must get them out. Think what a thing for me it would be to be able to help three little children. If I can do this by paying the fine tell the children that they are to be released to-morrow by a friend and ask them to be happy and not to tell anyone." Martin managed to arrange it, and the children were freed. Several of the warders and not a few of the convicts were financially assisted by Wilde after his release; they crossed the Channel to see him, and he kept in touch with them by correspondence until his death.

His mere presence was a tonic to many of them, for he was able to enjoy the things which, by contrast with their lot, would have intensified the misery of others, such as the sunshine or the sight of sparrows hopping about the stone-paved yard where the prisoners took their exercise. He was often seen to smile: at his fellow-convicts, at warders who had spoken nicely to him. But when anyone was punished for a breach of rules he was wretched, and the sight of children or lunatics within the gaol distressed him to tears, while a case of flogging affected him almost to hysteria. From the moment he was permitted to receive books from friends his happiness returned and small inconveniences no longer worried him. Asked if he did not feel humiliated at having to wash his cell out every morning, he answered "Not in the least. I consider no one too good to do his own work." He began to read Goethe's *Faust*, and, thinking another prisoner would be interested to hear that it was a great work of art, wrote to tell him so one Sunday, adding "The silly chaplain, bleating from the reading-desk and bawling from the pulpit, makes me sick with rage, but I enjoyed the lovely sunlight." He formed a poor opinion of the chaplains at Holloway, Wandsworth and Reading, and said to a convict who had confessed that his religious belief was wavering: "People fashion their God after their own understanding. They make their God first and worship him afterwards. I should advise you however to postpone coming to any conclusion at present; and if you should happen to die in the meantime, you will stand a much better chance, should a future exist, than some of these braying parsons." To another convict, who was afraid of ghosts and thought the prison must be haunted by them, he said: "Not necessarily so. You see, prisons have no ancient traditions to keep up. You must go to some castle to see ghosts, where they are inherited along with the family jewels." Once he happened to mention to a poor prisoner that he had no money with which to face the future. The man said that he had £5 in the savings bank, and offered the sum to Wilde, who of course refused it.

"You'll miss my £5 when you wake up one morning and find yourself without a breakfast," warned the man.

"I hope that it will never come to that, but if it does I promise to write to you for your £5, and I will buy a sandwich with it."

"And a cigar?" asked the man laughing.

"The amount would scarcely run to that; but should there be anything over, I'll buy a postage stamp and write an acknowledgment."

Although he wrote in Reading Gaol "Those who have much are always greedy, those who have little always share," he did not have to go to prison to learn that truth. His own impulse, whether rich or poor, was always to share, and he wanted his fellow-sufferers to experience his enjoyment of good books, asking Ross to get novels by Stevenson, Thackeray, Jane Austen, Stanley Weyman and Anthony Hope, which he would pay for and give to the prison library. He could not bear the thought of having no books of his own when he was free again, and he wondered whether his friends would give him some, the authors he favoured being Flaubert, Stevenson, Baudelaire, Maeterlinck, Dumas *père*, Keats, Marlowe, Chatterton, Anatole France, Gautier, Dante and all Dante literature, Goethe and all Goethe literature.

Yet the pleasure of reading the books of his choice was not so keen as the pleasure of being able to write once more; and he settled down to the composition of a long letter to Lord Alfred Douglas, portions of which were published in 1905 (with additions in 1908) by his literary executor, Robert Ross, who gave it the title of *De Profundis*, though Wilde called it *Epistola: In Carcere Et Vinculis*. The letter is a revelation of all that is feeblest in the writer. Excellent as parts of it are, and written with all the sincerity of which he was capable, the work is emotionally unconvincing, simply because Wilde, whenever he became serious about himself, became theatrical. The good passages are those where his intelligence is in the ascendant or where he is reporting an incident like the one at Clapham Junction. He did not really think, as he fancied he did, that the secret of life was revealed through suffering, that truth was taught by sorrow, and that humility was a divine attribute. This was an effective attitude to adopt, and he adopted it because it was effective; but it did not express his real nature, and was but a temporary reaction to circumstances, an admission that life had wounded him, his egotism making him wish to believe that, as he had been made to suffer, there was something nobler in sorrow than in joy, in humility than in pride, just as the egotist who is temperamentally wretched likes to think that there is something finer in misery than in happiness. But when Wilde put aside the tragic rôle which he played with such zest, and gave rein to his intelligence, he realised that he had not altered in the least, and that if anything prison had intensified his individuality:

"At every single moment of one's life one is what one is going to be no less than what one has been."

"To regret one's own experiences is to arrest one's own development."

"I don't regret for a single moment having lived for pleasure. I did it to the full, as one should do everything that one does."

"I am far more of an individualist than ever I was. Nothing seems to me of the smallest value except what one gets out of oneself. My nature is seeking a fresh mode of self-realisation." (Or, in other words, being an actor, he was studying a new part.)

"My ruin came not from too great individualism of life, but from too little. The one disgraceful, unpardonable, and to all time contemptible action of my life, was to allow myself to appeal to society for help and protection."

As in the past, so for the future, he admitted no external sanction or command. Neither religion nor morality could help him; he was a born agnostic, and had to find his way by his inner light: "Only that is spiritual which makes its own form." God had created a world for each separate human being, "and in that world, which is within us, one should seek to live." Concerning his so-called guilt, he thought it "a bestial infamy" that he should have been sent to prison "for offences that in all civilised countries are questions of pathology and medical treatment"; while reason told him that the laws whereby he was convicted and the system under which he suffered were wrong and unjust. He did not mean to change his conduct because he knew that he could not change himself: "To me reformations in morals are as meaningless and vulgar as Reformations in theology. But while to propose to be a better man is a piece of unscientific cant, to have become a deeper man is the privilege of those who have suffered. And such I think I have become."

In the first fifteen months of his imprisonment he had been compelled for lack of more attractive literature, to read the Bible, and had sketched out in his mind two plays, which he intended to write in the style of *Salomé*: one dealt with Pharaoh, the other with Ahab and Jezebel (which he pronounced "Isabel"). In after years he used to tell the stories of both very impressively, though he never wrote them. It was however the personality of Jesus that appealed to him more than anything else in the Bible, and now more than ever before he saw himself in the character of Christ, whom he describes as the supreme romantic type, the greatest of artists, and the first and most complete individualist in history. "To turn an interesting thief into a tedious honest man was not his aim. He would have thought little of the Prisoners Aid Society and other modern movements of the kind." As with all estimates of Christ, the views put forward by Wilde reveal much more of the writer than of the subject, and we learn from them that his own condemnation and sufferings had completed the parallel with Jesus which for many years he had instinctively drawn. It followed that, as with Christ, there had to be a Judas among his disciples, one who, however dissimilar the motives, caused him to be betrayed to the authorities; and Lord Alfred Douglas was cast for the part. Although Wilde's intelligence made him write "I must say to myself that I ruined myself, and that nobody great or small can be ruined except by his own hand," his histrionic nature demanded a villain for the drama of which he was the hero; and a great deal of the long letter which he wrote to the young man whom he had professed to love was devoted to a fanciful record of their friendship.

We cannot say for certain when it occurred to Wilde that the hero of his prosperity would make the ideal villain of his adversity, but it must have happened near the time when Sherard spoke to him about the letters which Douglas was going to quote in an article, and unquestionably Sherard's exaggeration did much to embitter Wilde in his then frame of mind. But something more was needed to complete the transposition of the leading characters, and Robert Ross supplied it. What follows is wholly inferential, but no other explanation covers all the facts. Ross had known Wilde several years longer than Douglas, and was intensely jealous when Douglas supplanted him in Wilde's affection. The enforced separation of the two gave him an opportunity to re-establish himself as Wilde's most intimate friend, and he made the best of it. He probably told Wilde that Douglas was enjoying himself in Italy, that he was showing Wilde's letters to everybody, and that he had completely forgotten the man for whose ruin he had been primarily responsible. In the state of remorse and despair to which Wilde had been reduced, it is easy to see how galled he must have been at every mention of Douglas's light-heartedness, how the least hint must have magnified the contrast between Douglas's freedom and his own bondage; and at last he told Ross to ask for the return of the letters he had written to Douglas, and, in the event of his own death, to destroy them, adding that, if he survived prison, he would destroy them himself. "They must not be in existence," he wrote. Some ten months after Wilde's conviction Ross informed Douglas that Oscar had turned against him, had spoken of him with bitterness and dislike, and had demanded the return of the letters. Douglas felt sure that Wilde's attitude was due to his present sufferings, and replied to Ross in these terms: "When he comes out of prison, if he chooses to say he does not want my friendship, and that he wants his letters back, he can do so with his own mouth; but in the meanwhile I am not taking any advice or any messages from you, nor shall I give you any of Oscar's letters, and you can mind your own damned business and leave me to mind mine." It is unlikely, after this, that Ross painted Douglas in a more favourable light whenever he visited Reading Gaol, and there is evidence to show that he was partly responsible for the arrangement whereby Oscar's income from his wife would be stopped if he joined Douglas after his release.

Thus, apart from Wilde's own desire to find a Judas for his drama, at least one of his friends was more than willing to help him in the search; and by the time he came to write his Epistle to Douglas the whole story had formed itself in his remarkably fertile mind, commencing with the theory that he had allowed himself to be "taunted into taking action against Queensberry," that he had suffered himself "to be thrust into a trap," and forgetting that Douglas was not with him when he started the action, and that he had discussed the question with Ross, whose solicitor he had consulted. Having convinced himself that Douglas had been his evil spirit in the Queensberry affair, he experienced no difficulty in tracing his gradual demoralisation to the same malign source, and reeled off a string of accusations, all of which, if true, were self-condemnatory.

For nearly three years—so runs his story—Douglas had been by his side except at rare intervals. Throughout that period he had kept the young man in luxury, buying him whatever he wanted, and even paying his gambling debts. In return for these benefits, Douglas had created horrible scenes, "long resentful moods of sullen silence" alternating with "sudden fits of almost epileptic rage," in one of which he had come near to murdering his friend. This had at last worn Wilde out: "It was the triumph of the smaller over the bigger nature." Douglas had ruined him both ethically and artistically, his conversation centering upon one topic, which Wilde eventually found monotonous, his companionship, in which there was no charm, preventing Wilde from writing plays. Several times a year Wilde had ended their friendship, only renewing it after tearful entreaties, pitiful appeals and threats of suicide. Hatred, Wilde asserted, was the chief emotion in Douglas's character; his brain was undeveloped, his imagination dead, his heart unborn; he had gambled with Wilde's life as he had gambled with his money, "carelessly, recklessly, indifferent to the consequences"; he was in reality Wilde's enemy, such an enemy as no man ever had, utterly unworthy of the affection lavished upon him; and he had completed Wilde's ruin in less than three years. But in the full swing of his indictment, Wilde's sense of drama converts Douglas into an instrument of Fate: "It makes me feel sometimes as if you yourself had been merely a puppet worked by some secret and unseen hand to bring terrible events to a terrible issue."

We need not dwell on this extraordinary document, in which the tortured imagination of a man in duress exaggerated trifling incidents into momentous events, beyond noting that Douglas and Wilde had quarrelled acrimoniously on several occasions. The former was self-willed, the latter obstinate, and when self-will meets obstinacy there is usually friction. For the rest, the state of mind in which Wilde wrote is discerned by himself, when he refers to the changing, uncertain moods of his letter, "its scorn and bitterness, its aspirations and its failure to realise those aspirations"; and in telling Ross about it he indicates the spirit in which it should be read: "I need not remind *you* how fluid a thing thought is with me—with us all —and of what an evanescent substance are our emotions made." For nearly two years, he said, "I had within me a growing burden of bitterness, much of which I have now got rid of." The temptation to ease themselves of bitterness by making others responsible for their sufferings is one which human beings can rarely resist.

Ross was instructed to have the letter typed, so that several copies could be made: "I assure you that the typewriting machine, when played with expression, is not more annoying than the piano when played by a sister or near relation." Ross, as his literary executor, must have control of all his works: "The deficit that their sale will produce may be lodged to the credit of Cyril and Vyvyan." On the day of his release Wilde handed the manuscript to Ross, who, instead of sending it to Douglas after copies had been taken, kept it, and published the less personal passages five years after Wilde's death. Douglas remained in ignorance of the fact that *De Profundis* consisted of extracts from a letter addressed to himself until the personal parts were read aloud in court and used as evidence against him in 1913, Wilde never having referred to it during their association after he came out of prison. But the story of how Ross tried to discredit Douglas, and of how Douglas succeeded in discrediting Ross, has no place in a biography of

Wilde. It may be read in *The Autobiography of Lord Alfred Douglas* (1929).

Having discharged his bitterness in the manner described, Wilde's main concern was the provision for his future. The letter to Douglas was finished by March '97, and on April 7th Frank Harris paid a visit to Reading Gaol. Harris was in a jubilant and generous mood. He had just made twenty odd thousand pounds in South Africa (only the people who had lost it could tell us how) and had applied for leave to see Wilde on "financial business." He had come, he proclaimed, to place his cheque-book at his friend's disposal. Naturally Wilde was much moved by such kindness, and could scarcely speak his gratitude for the £500 which Harris promised him. But a cheque-book is not quite the same thing as a signed cheque, and Harris can scarcely have reached Paddington station before the difference occurred to him. Within four days he sent a message to Wilde by More Adey, saying how sorry he was that he could not manage it after all. Wilde was deeply chagrined, and in a letter to More Adey said that "Frank Harris has no feelings. It is the secret of his success. Just as the fact that he thinks that other people have none either is the secret of the failure that lies in wait for him somewhere on the way of life," which proved to be an accurate forecast of Harris's future. A hint of Wilde's disappointment must have reached Harris, who sent some clothes to him on his release, together with a cheque that looked as much like £500 as possible, the second cipher being missing.

All Wilde's friends who could afford it subscribed to a fund which would give him several months of leisure after his imprisonment: amongst others, Adela Schuster, the Leversons, Ross, Adey and Charles Ricketts. The last-named contributed £100, though he could ill afford it, and three days before Oscar regained his freedom went to see him in the company of Ross and Adey. He had to wait while the others discussed with their friend certain details about clothes, where he wanted or did not want to go on leaving prison, etc., and Ricketts heard afterwards that Oscar had been refractory, unreasonable and impatient on these points, though everything had been talked over and agreed upon some time before; but of this there was no sign when Ricketts entered the room, where an inspector and two warders stood against the wall, and where Oscar sat at a green baize table looking wonderfully well and in excellent spirits. After a cordial greeting, Oscar said laughingly:

"Both my dear friends would wish me to retire to a monastery . . . Why not La Trappe? . . . or worse still, some dim country place in England:

I believe it was Twyford . . . They speak of Venice later with its silence and dead waterways. No, I have had enough of silence!"

"But, Oscar, is not Venice, with its beauty and stillness, the very place for work and privacy? There you could see your friends if . . ."

"No! . . . Privacy! work! my dear Ricketts. I wish to look at life, not to become a monument for tourists . . ."

They talked of the French production of *Salomé*, and Ricketts asked whether he had thought of a new play.

"A play! the Theatre!" exclaimed Wilde. "My dear boy, what folly was mine! I held the future of the English stage in the hollow of my hand, to make or mar. To-day, in London, who would produce a work of mine?"

Ricketts reported that *Lady Windermere's Fan* had recently been done at Richmond, that Ellen Terry had praised him, and that Henry Irving had expressed his sympathy.

"I must return to literature, and you must print *The Portrait of Mr. W. H.*," said Wilde. "I know it needs retouching, though one of my early masterpieces. Your picture, Ross tells me, has vanished; it was not in the sale; but you must design me another wonderful frontispiece."

"My dear Oscar, of course I will publish a book of yours, but for the moment let it be some other work, your *Sainte Courtisane*, for instance."

"Alas! she no longer says marvellous things; the robbers have buried her white body and carried away her jewels . . . Yes, perhaps you are right . . . *Mr. W. H.* might be imprudent . . . the English public would have to read Shakespeare's Sonnets."

"Why not the play about Pharaoh?" suggested Ross.

"Yes, of course, the King is tremendous when he cries to Moses 'Praise be to thy God, O prophet, for he has slain my only enemy, my son!' . . . But I must have books about Egypt, full of the names of beautiful things, rare and curious meat for the feast, not the mere flesh-pots the Jews regretted. At night, in the cold . . . when I felt hungry . . . I have often thought of fantastic feasts . . . Yes, I have sometimes been cold and hungry . . . cold is worse than hunger . . . in time one gets used to this . . . but many of my warders have been friends . . . Don't mention this; it might lead to trouble. . . . Knowing that I had not enough food, they have brought me curious things to eat, Scotch scones, meat pies and sausage rolls, believing that a hungry man can eat anything, just as the British throw Bibles to bears." He laughed; and their interview was at an end.

It was only from friends that Wilde heard of the outside world, but Major Nelson made a point of keeping him up to date whenever they happened to meet. Part of the Governor's duty was to inform prisoners of the deaths of their relations; and in telling Wilde that his aunt had passed away, Nelson thought he would like to hear the latest news in the art world: "It may interest you to know that Mr. Poynter has been made President of the Royal Academy." Wilde replied cheerfully "I am grateful to you for your kindness in telling me about my poor aunt," paused, and went on sadly "but perhaps you might have broken Poynter to me more gently." A few days before his departure Nelson told him that some Americans had called to offer a large sum of money for the story of his prison experiences. Wilde put on his dignified air: "I cannot understand, sir, that such proposals should be made to a gentleman."

In order to disappoint any of Queensberry's friends who might be travelling down to receive him, Wilde left Reading Gaol the evening before he was due to be released, drove in a closed carriage to an inconspicuous station a few miles up the line, and took the train to Paddington. The warders who accompanied him were in plain clothes, like himself. They went to Pentonville Prison, to which he had been taken before going to Wandsworth, and from there, in the early morning of May 19th, 1897, he walked into freedom. Stewart Headlam, whose Christian-Socialist Guild had lost many members since he went bail for Wilde, had promised to meet him when he came out, and with Ross was waiting for him in a brougham. Driving down the Euston Road they saw a newspaper placard with the anticipatory announcement "Release of Oscar Wilde." They reached Headlam's house, 31 Upper Bedford Place, Bloomsbury, before 6 o'clock in the morning, and Wilde enjoyed his first cup of coffee for two years. He talked much of Dante and for Headlam's guidance wrote down the best way to study him and the best books to read. He had not yet decided where he wished to go; but he was quite determined not to accept Frank Harris's invitation to accompany him on a driving-tour through France. "To be with him would be like a perpetual football match," said he. Ada and Ernest Leverson and one or two other friends called to see him. Their anxiety not to display their feelings embarrassed them, but the moment Oscar entered the room into which they had been shown he put them at their ease. "He came in with the dignity of a king returning from exile," says Ada Leverson. His first words were "Sphinx, how marvellous of you to know exactly the right hat to wear at seven o'clock in the morning to meet a friend who has been away! You can't have got up: you must have sat up." He talked, he laughed, he smoked, he wore a flower in his buttonhole; he bridged the two years' gap. Suddenly he spoke of religion, saying that he looked on all the different faiths as colleges in a great university, but that Roman Catholicism was the greatest and most romantic of them all. Then he wrote a letter to a Roman Catholic Retreat, asking if he might retire there for six months, and sent it off by cab. While waiting for the answer he walked up and down talking of a dozen things, two of which stuck in Ada Leverson's memory:

(Of Major Nelson) "The dear Governor! Such a delightful man, and his wife is charming. I spent happy hours in their garden, and they asked me to spend the summer with them. They thought I was the gardener." He laughed. "Unusual, I think? But I don't feel I can. I feel I want a change of scene."

(Of the journey from Reading to Pentonville) "Do you know one of the punishments that happen to people who have been 'away'? They are not allowed to read *The Daily Chronicle*! Coming along, I begged to be allowed to read it in the train. 'No!' Then I suggested I might be allowed to read it upside down. This they consented to allow, and I read *The Daily Chronicle* upside down all the way, and never enjoyed it so much. It's really the only way to read newspapers."

When the messenger returned with the reply to his letter, his friends dared not look at him while he read it. His request was refused: they could not accept him on a momentary impulse: he must think it over for at least a year. But they need not have given him a year: an hour was more than enough. After yielding to his emotions and sobbing for a while, he quickly passed in imagination from cloister to café, cheered up, and arranged with Robert Ross to leave at once for Dieppe. They started for Victoria station at about noon, and stopped on the way at Hatchards bookshop in Piccadilly, where someone recognised him. He left hurriedly, and a few hours later saw the chalk cliffs of England for the last time.

CHAPTER SEVENTEEN

THE EXILE

WILDE'S punishment continued after his release from gaol, and his post-prison behaviour should only be judged by those who, possessing his sensibility, have also experienced two years hard labour and the ignominy of an outcast who was perpetually affronted and hounded.

He arrived at Dieppe in the company of Robert Ross and Reginald Turner. They put up at the Hôtel Sandwich, Wilde having assumed a different name "to prevent postmen having fits." Yet the alias of his choice was sufficient to arouse curiosity: Sebastian Melmoth, the Christian name recalling a well-known martyr, the surname being taken from a novel by C. R. Maturin, his mother's uncle, called *Melmoth the Wanderer*. Naturally he enjoyed appearing under a stage-name for the fresh part he was about to play, and he reported to Ada Leverson that "Reggie Turner is staying here under the name 'Robert Ross,' Robbie under the name 'Reginald Turner.' It is better they should not use their own names." He had some £800 to draw upon, and they passed a hilarious week. A crowd of young poets and students came from Paris to welcome him, and he entertained them sumptuously at the Café des Tribunaux, where they enjoyed such a boisterous evening that he was warned by the Sub-Prefect against similar orgies. At first the French were inclined to sympathise with him, their attitude being not so much pro-Wilde as anti-English; but when their wealthy British and American visitors evinced hostility, they pocketed their patriotism with their cash and showed him less respect.

In those days Dieppe was a popular resort for artists, some of whom, including Charles Conder, Walter Sickert and Jacques-Emile Blanche, felt uncomfortable when Wilde arrived and kept out of his way. But the more respectable English residents and visitors were not content with a neutral position, and made it their business to insult him, either by leaving a café when he entered it or by complaining of his presence to the proprietor, who, in order not to lose his customers, would request Wilde to leave. After all, as Macaulay wrote of Byron, "it is not every day that the savage envy of aspiring dunces is gratified by the agonies of such a spirit," and for the rest of his life Wilde was exposed to what Charles Ricketts described as "the bitterness of those who cannot forgive their victim the wrong they have done." This bitterness, this savage envy, broke out on many occasions, and though Wilde made light of it in the company of friends it added to the burden of past suffering. Once, when some people had behaved rudely, a Norwegian landscape painter named Fritz Thaulow walked up to him and said in a clear voice which everyone in the restaurant could hear "Mr. Wilde, my wife and I would feel honoured to have you dine with us *en famille* this evening." Wilde went, and there he met Conder, who had been avoiding him but who now renewed their old friendship. The Thaulows lived in an opulent house, the Villa des Orchidées, in the Faubourg de la Barre. They were generous folk, sympathising with all who were ill-treated by the world or were otherwise unfortunate. No sooner had they got to know Wilde, who often visited them in the coming weeks, than they invited the Mayor of Dieppe, the presidents of the city council and the chamber of commerce, to a reception in celebration of the distinguished Irishman's arrival in France, fresh from an English prison. It is not recorded whether those gentlemen accepted the invitation, but it was not the class of function at which they would have jumped. Arthur Stannard and his wife were also kind to Oscar while he was staying at Dieppe and in the neighbourhood. Mrs. Stannard ("John Strange Winter"), who was disgusted at the way in which people who had once boasted of knowing him now cut or insulted him, asked him frequently to meals at her house and was often seen in his company out-of-doors. But Dieppe was not populated by Thaulows and Stannards, and after about ten days of it Oscar decided to leave for a village on the coast some nine miles away where no one would know him. Before settling down there he sent a letter to *The Daily Chronicle*, which appeared in the issue of May 28th. Warder Martin, whose kindness to him had lightened his last weeks at Reading Gaol, had been dismissed for giving biscuits to a child; and he wrote to plead for Martin and to protest against the barbarous treatment of children and lunatics in prison. The humanising influence in prison, he stated, came from the prisoners, the dehumanising influence from the officials.

On May 31st we find him comfortably installed at the Hôtel de la Plage, Berneval-sur-Mer. Here he had the two best rooms, the only other resident being an old gentleman who went to bed at eight every evening because there was nothing else to do. His sitting-room was soon crowded with books and decorated with pictures and flowers, and on a pedestal in one of the corners stood "a pretty Gothic Virgin," symbolising his present aspirations, just as the Hermes in Tite Street had symbolised his pagan past, each representing the changing acts in his variegated drama. His new belief was that the life he had led before going to prison, a life of appetite, cynicism, sensuality and sloth, had restricted him as an artist, and his requirements now were simple: just enough money to live on and to write, good health, peace and quiet, a few friends, much solitude, books, flowers, the sea, the sunshine and the dawn. He had, he thought, completely broken with the past, and when André Gide, who went to see him, asked whether he had known at Algiers what was in store for him, he replied: "Oh, naturally, of course I knew that there would be a catastrophe, either that or something else: I was expecting it . . . to go any further was impossible, and that state of things could not last . . . there had to be some end to it . . . Prison has completely changed me. I was relying on it for that . . . My life is like a work of art. An artist never begins the same work twice, or else it shows that he has not succeeded. My life before prison was as successful as possible. Now all that is finished and done with." Such was his feeling at the moment, and if he had made a contradictory statement twenty-four hours later it would not have affected the sincerity of his words to Gide; for he was so constituted that he could play Hamlet at a matinée and Falstaff at an evening performance with equal assurance and conviction. As it happened, he sustained the new rôle for nearly three months.

Friends who saw him at Berneval said that he had never looked better. Prison-life had removed his superfluous fat: he was strong, healthy and energetic. He rose at 7.30 in the morning, went to bed at 10, swam vigorously in the sea, and walked a great deal. "I adore this place. The whole country is lovely, and full of forest and deep meadow," he wrote. The landlord of the hotel was delighted with him: "If I had only three guests like Monsieur Melmoss, I should have a good season." His compliments charmed the chef, whom he called "an artist of great distinction," one who walked in the evening by the sea in order to get ideas for the next day's dishes. The custom house officers discovered a new interest in life when he gave them the novels of Dumas *père*. His love of Dumas perplexed his friends. How can a man who admires Flaubert, Gautier, Baudelaire and Pater, really enjoy *The Three Musketeers*? they wanted to know. But they had not his appetite for life in all its manifestations, and it never occurred to them that the boy who likes exotic things may also like exciting things. He was soon the most popular man in Berneval. The priest offered him a permanent seat in the choir, and the children of the place were in ecstasies when he gave them a

treat to celebrate Queen Victoria's Diamond Jubilee. About forty of them
sat down to a feast of strawberries and cream, biscuits, cakes and tea, and
Wilde himself waited on them. Afterwards they cheered him, shouting
"*Vivent Monsieur Melmoth et la Reine d' Angleterre!*" The villagers adopted
this salutation, and at odd moments during his residence amongst them
greeted him with it, much to the amazement of his visitors. One wonders
what *la Reine d' Angleterre* would have thought. He had an enormous
admiration for Queen Victoria, whose picture was on a wall in his room
at Berneval: "Every poet should gaze at the portrait of his Queen all day
long," he announced, and a year before his death he told Vincent O'Sullivan
that "The three women I have most admired are Queen Victoria, Sarah
Bernhardt and Lily Langtry," adding with a laugh "I would have married
any one of them with pleasure." The first had great dignity, the second a
lovely voice, the third a perfect figure. Clearly he did not demand spiritual
qualities in a wife.

Within a day or two of his arrival at Berneval he had made up his mind
that he wished to live there for ever, and was planning the building of a
châlet. A few hours later he saw one that had already been built, obviously
for no one but himself, and he decided that he must take it at once, the
yearly rental being £32. A writing-room, a dining-room, three bedrooms,
servants' rooms, a large balcony, and a superb view: what more could a
man desire? While living in it he could superintendent the erection of his
permanent home, which he wanted to be like some old English farm-house,
"like, I regret to say, Shakespeare's house." He wrote enthusiastically about
all his plans to Ross, who acted henceforth as his treasurer and through
whom his allowance from his wife was paid; but Ross, knowing that his
enthusiasms were often short-lived and that his generosity only ended with
his cash, guessed that as soon as he had a house of his own he would invite
everyone he met and liked to stay with him, and advised caution. Oscar
replied that his visitors would have to pay for their meals at the hotel,
and would be charged not only for accommodation at the Châlet but for *lots*
of extras, such as candles, baths, hot water, etc. If they did not take the
extras, of course they would be charged more, as at all the good hotels: Bath,
25 centimes; no bath, 50 centimes. Cigarettes in bedroom, 10 centimes a
cigarette; no cigarettes in bedroom, 20 centimes a cigarette. Ross gave way,
and Oscar took possession of the Châlet Bourgeat, still having his chief meals
at the hotel. He had to depend on Ross for everything, especially the payment of his "debts of honour" to fellow-convicts on their release; and when
one of them did not call for the £2 which had been left for him at the

post office, Wilde asked Ross to buy a Waterbury watch with the money: "I have no clock or watch, and the sun is always hours in advance. I rely on the unreliable moon."

In June he tried to finish *A Florentine Tragedy*, but was not in the mood. In July and August he wrote the greater part of *The Ballad of Reading Gaol* at the Châlet Bourgeat, his labours being constantly intermitted by visits of friends and trips to Dieppe. William Rothenstein, Charles Conder, Ernest Dowson and Dal Young stayed with him, and the latter offered him £700 to pay for the building of a house; but he hardly knew Young at the time, thought the offer quixotic, and refused it. Charles Wyndham, the actor, travelled to Berneval in order to commission the adaptation of some French play to the English stage, and paid him a handsome cheque in advance of royalties. This was pure kindness on the part of Wyndham, who knew perfectly well that the work would never be done and only mentioned it in order to spare Wilde the discomfort of accepting a money-gift. Another proposal, by the editor of *Le Journal*, that he should write a weekly causerie on literary topics, was rejected by him on the ground that people would merely read his articles out of morbid curiosity. But whether money was coming in or not, it was always going out. Wilde suffered from Falstaff's chief complaint: consumption of the purse, and, like Falstaff, could find no remedy for it. Any hard-up story sent his hand to his pocket. He heard that Ernest Dowson was in difficulties with his landlord at the Hôtel du Château at Arques-la-Bataille, went there at once, paid the bill, brought Dowson to Berneval as his guest, lent him money, and kept him until he could keep himself.[1] Dowson showed his gratitude in a curious way. He suggested that Wilde should acquire "a more wholesome taste" in the sex line, and strongly advised a visit to some Dieppe brothel. Wilde obliged, but the experiment was not encouraging, and he told Dowson that it was "the first these ten years, and it will be the last. It was like cold mutton." However, there was a bright side to everything, and in return for his acquiescence he asked Dowson to "tell it in England, for it will entirely restore my character." W. B. Yeats, in his autobiography, gives a version of this episode with fantastic elaborations by himself. Wilde kept his word and remained homosexual in his habits for the rest of his life.

A little more of Wilde's humanity and a little less of formal Christianity would have prevented Aubrey Beardsley from behaving as he did. He became a Roman Catholic in March '97 and was doing his best to obliterate his

[1] Later on, when financially embarrassed, Wilde had to dun Dowson for the return of the loan.

pagan adolescence. In July of that year he went to Dieppe and put up at the Hôtel Sandwich, whence he wrote to his brother that he might be leaving at any moment as "some rather unpleasant people come here. . . . I fear some undesirable complications may arise if I stay." When he saw Wilde approaching on the quay, he slipped up a side street, and in other ways managed to avoid a meeting. Wilde was fully conscious of his tactics, and felt indignant, but could think of nothing worse to say than "It was *lâche* of Aubrey." But Beardsley maintained his hostility to the end, writing in December '97 from Mentone to Leonard Smithers that he would edit and contribute to *The Peacock*, a quarterly which Smithers hoped to launch, "If it is *quite agreed that Oscar Wilde contributes nothing to the magazine, anonymously, pseudonymously, or otherwise* . . ." The quarterly never appeared, and Beardsley died three months later at the age of 25.

Wilde's favourite restaurant in Dieppe was the Café Suisse (Angle des Arcades, 17 & 19, Grande Rue, 1 & 3) and he was sitting outside it with a noisy crowd of acquaintances, looking very conspicuous in a Basque *béret*, when Sherard saw him for the first time since Reading Gaol. Sherard and Ross stayed with him at the Châlet Bourgeat in August. They visited the pretty villages in the neighbourhood, and Oscar was in excellent form. On one of their walks he remarked that a sense of approaching disaster had always haunted him, but he would not discuss his life in gaol, saying to Sherard, who asked him some question about it, "Now, Robert, don't be morbid." In fact he seemed to have been unaffected by his years of suffering except for a trick he had contracted of rearranging things on a table or elsewhere if they appeared to him out of order. "I had to keep everything in my cell in its exact place," he explained, "and if I neglected this even in the slightest, I was punished, and the punishment was so horrible to me that I often started up in my sleep to feel if each thing was where the regulations would have it, and not an inch either to the right or the left. And the terror haunts me still, and involuntarily my fingers make order where anything is disarranged." His robust physical condition was exemplified one morning when they went out to bathe. A cabin had been built for him on the beach, and Sherard tried vainly to open the door which had been jammed. Wilde came up, burst the door open with a push that nearly knocked the cabin over, and, except for the door, all was well. Sherard noticed a man hanging about the Châlet and wanted to know what he was doing. "I fancy he is a detective in the pay of Queensberry," said Oscar. "I am sorry for him. It must be tedious work. I have sometimes thought of talking to him and trying to cheer him up, for he has a sad countenance; but then, you see, the romance of secrecy would be gone, and I am sure he has nothing else to live for. *Chacun son métier*. Poor fellow!"

As the summer days shortened he began to get bored, and once he showed it in a most uncharacteristic manner. A woman who had asked him to lunch at Dieppe harped on the cheapness of living abroad, an aspect of existence that did not appeal to him. She went on for some time and at length began to praise her claret which she had bought at a bargain price: one franc a bottle. Wilde solemnly sipped the wine, put down his glass, and said "You were overcharged." This was a bad sign, and his letters show that he was wearying of a place at which, two months before, he had expressed a wish to pass the remainder of his life. "With freedom, flowers, books, and the moon, who could not be perfectly happy?" he had written in prison, and so he had thought at the time; but his nature craved companionship and conversation, and now he could not bear to be alone with his thoughts. The effort of writing *The Ballad of Reading Gaol* exhausted him, and he felt that he would never be able to start a new play. "I am not in the mood to do the work I want, and I fear I never shall be. The intense energy of creation has been kicked out of me. I don't care now to struggle to get back what, when I had it, gave me little pleasure." Towards the end of August the wind blew and the rain poured down; no friends came to see him, and he was sick of solitude. He called the weather "too British for anything" and owned "I simply cannot stand Berneval. I nearly committed suicide there last Thursday—I was so bored."

It was at this point that Lord Alfred Douglas re-entered his life. Constance Wilde, her advisers and Robert Ross, were determined to keep the two apart; but Douglas naturally wanted to know whether his friend had turned against him, as reported by Ross, and soon after Oscar's arrival in France wrote to ask if it were true. From Oscar's reply Douglas guessed that his feelings were unchanged, but that other people were standing in the way of their meeting. They exchanged more letters, and it became clear that Oscar had not altered in the least. But they did not see one another again until, prompted by her friends or relations, Constance wrote a very unpleasant letter to Oscar. The arrangement had been that husband and wife should not meet until a year's freedom had shown that he was a reformed character. But he was most anxious to see his children again, and when oppressed by the thought of a winter spent alone in Berneval he wrote to ask his wife to lessen the time of his probation. Her answer, obviously dictated by her advisers, incensed him. It consisted of a string of "condi-

tions," which he was compelled to accept before she would consider a reunion. One of her conditions was that he must never see Douglas again:
the rest have not been made known. Being the man he was, such a letter
could have but one effect, no doubt foreseen by her advisers: he promptly
arranged a meeting with Douglas. It took place at Rouen in August. "Poor
Oscar cried when I met him at the station," Douglas recalls. "We walked
about all day arm in arm, or hand in hand, and were perfectly happy."
Wilde talked as only he could talk—

> Till mean things put on beauty like a dress
> And all the world was an enchanted place,

as Douglas was to write of him later. They stayed a night at the Hôtel de
la Poste, where, Douglas being known, he could not pass under an assumed
name, much to the disappointment of Oscar, who extracted considerable
pleasure from incognitos and had looked forward to meeting Douglas either
as "Le Chevalier de la Fleur-de-lys" or as "Jonquil du Vallon." The next
day Wilde returned to Berneval, and Douglas to Paris, having arranged to
join each other at Naples the following month.

Half way through September Wilde broke the news to Ross, who was
extremely angry and wrote to point out the consequences of his action. In
reply Wilde excused himself on the ground that it was his one hope of self-
realisation in life and art, and further that the world had forced it on him,
his loneliness at Berneval during the last month having been insupportable.
On his way through Paris he lunched with Vincent O'Sullivan, to whom
he spoke of his difficulties, finishing up with the remark "I am not telling
all this to you because I want advice. I have thought it all out, and I would
not take advice from anyone." He then said he would start for Italy that
night if only he had the money. O'Sullivan went to his bank and handed
Wilde the amount he required, afterwards reflecting "It is one of the few
things I look back on with satisfaction. It is not every day that one has the
chance of relieving the anxiety of a genius and a hero." Wilde met Douglas
on the train between Paris and Italy, and their first fortnight was spent at
the Hôtel Royal in Naples, where they ran up a bill of £68 which Douglas
paid some weeks later. They went on to the Villa Giudici at Posilipo, where
they worked and amused themselves. Wilde was busy writing more verses
for *The Ballad of Reading Gaol*, and Douglas produced some of his best
poetry there. Though they kept a cook, a maid, and two boys to wait on
them, they managed to live on about 10s. a day. Marble steps led down to
the sea from their terrace, and they bathed regularly. Rats were the only

drawback to the place, and these were soon eliminated by a professional rat-catcher, though Wilde insisted that they had been charmed away by an old witch who "burned odours and muttered incantations." In addition to Douglas's £8 a week from his mother, and Wilde's £3 a week from his wife, Oscar received £100 from Dal Young, whose offer to build a house at Berneval had been refused. Young was a composer, and wanted a libretto for an opera: *Daphnis and Chloe*. Wilde and Douglas started on it, but Wilde's sole contribution was one lyric. Young got the £100 back with interest some years later, as did everyone else who advanced money to Wilde for work he never wrote.[1]

Their life at the Villa Giudici came to an abrupt end. Wilde's solicitor informed him that, as he had gone back to Douglas, his income would be discontinued; while Douglas's mother threatened to stop his allowance if they did not separate. Douglas put up a fight, but his mother was resolute, and the two friends agreed that as they could not live on poetry they had better part. As a matter of fact, they were both rather relieved. Except for the first two or three weeks the reunion had not been successful; they had quarrelled several times, and were beginning to get on one another's nerves. Douglas stuck it out loyally, because he would not cause Oscar pain, but he confided to his mother that he had "lost that supreme desire for his society which I had before, and which made a sort of aching void when he was not with me . . . If I hadn't rejoined him and lived with him for two months, I should *never* have got over the longing for him." Having discovered that Oscar did not mind his leaving, but was if anything comforted by the prospect, he begged his mother for £200, which he handed to Oscar, paid the rent of the Villa for three months, and left for Rome, writing to his mother on December 7th that Oscar had behaved perfectly to him: "He has been sweet and gentle and will always remain to me as a type of what a gentleman and a friend should be." There is not the least doubt that Wilde recognised the necessity of their separation, and did not blame Douglas for going. Yet within a week or two he was writing a letter to Robert Ross, the tone of which was due partly to a desire to propitiate Ross, but chiefly to a desire to see himself as one doomed to betrayal, the central figure in a drama of

[1] From the moment when Reinhardt made his reputation as a producer with *Salomé* at the Kleines Theatre, Berlin, Wilde became a European figure, and his works began to sell like roasted chestnuts in over a dozen languages. His bankruptcy was soon annulled, all his debts were paid, and by 1908 his estate was in a flourishing condition. Up to the 1939 war he was more widely read on the continents of Europe and Asia than any writer in English except Shakespeare. Of late years Shaw has been catching him up, and it is now a neck-to-neck race between them for second place.

woe. In this letter he portrays Douglas for the second time as Judas. Having
enticed him from Berneval with promises of a home and a carefree life, he
says, Douglas deserted him the moment there was a money-shortage. "It
is the most bitter experience of a bitter life," he sums up. He probably believed
every word of this at the moment of writing, because his solitude at the
Villa after Douglas's departure depressed him, and he was in a state of
mind when reproaches come more easily from the pen than praises. But
the letter must be regarded solely as a scene in the epic of Oscar, not as a
record of fact, and his decision never to see Douglas again was reversed from
the moment he saw Douglas again.

He did not stay at Posilipo for more than a week, but went to Sicily. On
his return he found that all his clothes had been stolen by a servant. This,
together with a bout of influenza and a sense of loneliness, made him quit
the Villa for Naples, where he stayed at 51 Santa Lucia. Eleanore Duse was
acting there at the time, and he went to see her many times. He sent her
Salomé, begging her to do it some day. She admired it but did not see herself
in the part. He ran across Vincent O'Sullivan, and one evening they sat
together in a restaurant near the theatre. After the show the place was invaded by a fashionable crowd, many of whom stared at Wilde out of curiosity. He left at once, O'Sullivan following him. A beggar accosted them;
Wilde gave him something; and O'Sullivan heard him murmur in English
"You wretched man, why do you beg when pity is dead?"

Meanwhile he had been trying to get money out of Leonard Smithers
for *The Ballad of Reading Gaol*. Ross had approached John Lane and several
other publishers, but none of them would touch it: Smithers alone displayed
enthusiasm, but then he was quite unlike any other publisher in London. He
was a Sheffield man who started life as a solicitor, continued it as a bookseller,
and ended it as a publisher. When Lane dropped Beardsley, Arthur Symons
got Smithers to issue *The Savoy*, and to interest himself in the works of the
young poets and artists whom the well-established publishers would not look
at. For a considerable time Smithers earned a living on the sale of pornog-
raphy, and that he never toned down into a respectable man of business
is shown by his threat to put a notice in his Bond Street window: "Smut is
cheap to-day." He boasted that he would publish anything that other firms
dared not, and his method of pushing his publications was as furtive as his
way of selling questionable books. His private life was unconventional, like
his business. There were usually several mistresses hanging around, as well
as a wife or so, and as he was a deep drinker and a drug-taker it is plain that
he had surprised a secret which many men have vainly longed to discover:

how to mix drink, women and drugs satisfactorily. Yet his appearance was
by no means lusty; he was pasty-faced, with pale hair, shifty eyes, and the
general look of one who would benefit from a good bath and a square meal.
Beardsley was his god, and he brought out some of that artist's best work,
including *The Rape of the Lock*; but his ambition was to have a best-seller,
and when at last it came his way in the shape of Wilde's *Ballad* he was taken
completely unawares and was quite unable to cope with such a novel situation.
It was also a cause of his undoing, for on the strength of his success he moved
to a shop in Bond Street and began to go steadily down the hill, reaching
the bottom in the early years of the present century, when he died of a self-
administered overdose of drugs in the presence of a drunken wife and a
drunken mistress.

  It seems that Smithers did not favour the principle of paying an advance
on royalties, for on October 2nd, '97 we find Wilde asking for, in fact demanding, twenty pounds: "In case you have not yet grasped the idea that an
advance of £20 on my poem is really a thing that I have a perfect right to
expect on business grounds, pray do so at once. Application to you for a
personal loan may, and I have no doubt will, follow later on, but up to the
present time our relations have been merely the usual business ones of poet
and publisher, with the usual complete victory for the latter . . . I also—such
is the generosity of my nature—send enclosed four more verses of great
power and romantic-realistic suggestion, twenty-four lines in all, each worth
a guinea in any of the market-places for poetry . . ." The four verses Wilde
sent from Naples are those beginning "For oak and elm have pleasant leaves"
and ending "His sightless soul may stray." For a while he toyed with the
idea of having the poem published in a newspaper. It was too long for *The
Daily Chronicle*, and Frank Harris had been "so offensive to me and about
me that I do not think negotiation possible with him." Harris was annoyed
that Wilde had declined to join him on a driving-tour through France after
he had broken his promise of £500: so *The Saturday Review* was out of
the question. "My idea is *Reynolds's*," wrote Wilde to Smithers, ". . . it cir-
culates among the criminal classes—to which I now belong—so I shall be
read by my peers—a new experience for me." But the newspapers were
frightened of his name, and he decided that anonymity was essential, if
for no other reason than that "the public like an open secret. Half the success of Marie Corelli is due to the no doubt unfounded rumour that she
is a woman." Ill-health, loneliness, and what he called "general *ennui* with a
tragi-comedy of an existence," made him talk of suicide, "but I want to see
my poem out before I take steps," and of course he would reconsider the

question if Smithers came to Naples and gave him a good dinner. In any case he wanted to pass the proofs before doing anything drastic: "I should not like to die without seeing my poem as good as I can make a poem whose subject is all wrong and whose treatment too personal." His estimate of *The Ballad* varied. Once he said that "some of the verses are awfully good," also "I *do* think the whole affair realised—and that is triumph." But it was utterly opposed to all his theories about art, and he had to admit "I am not sure that I like it myself. But catastrophes in life bring about catastrophes in art." What he thought of catastrophe was the first and last appearance of emotional reality in his work. The sufferings of others, far more than his own, called forth his pity. He had as little conscious cruelty in himself as it is possible for a human being to have, and he had been shocked to the soul by the hideous cruelties he had witnessed in prison. His sympathy with the victims resulted in the most poignant ballad in the English language. Critics have noted that the poem owes something to Coleridge's *Ancient Mariner,* to Hood's *Eugene Aram*, and to Housman's *A Shropshire Lad*, a copy of which was sent him by the author when he came out of gaol. But though it is uneven work, and contains verses that are precious and artificial, the general effect is fine enough to cancel all debts to others, and he never approached elsewhere the power and feeling in the best verses. Take these for proof:

(*The night before the execution*)

> Right in we went, with soul intent
>   On Death and Dread and Doom:
> The hangman, with his little bag,
>   Went shuffling through the gloom:
> And each man trembled as he crept
>   Into his numbered tomb.

.   .   .   .

(*The next morning*)

> At six o'clock we cleaned our cells,
>   At seven all was still,
> But the sough and swing of a mighty wing
>   The prison seemed to fill,
> For the Lord of Death with icy breath
>   Had entered in to kill.

.   .   -   .

(The execution)

And as one sees most fearful things
   In the crystal of a dream,
We saw the greasy hempen rope
   Hooked to the blackened beam,
And heard the prayer the hangman's snare
   Strangled into a scream.

And all the woe that moved him so
   That he gave that bitter cry,
And the wild regrets, and the bloody sweats,
   None knew so well as I:
For he who lives more lives than one
   More deaths than one must die.

     .   .   .   .

(Comment)

They hanged him as a beast is hanged:
   They did not even toll
A requiem that might have brought
   Rest to his startled soul,
But hurriedly they took him out,
   And hid him in a hole.

     .   .   .   .

(Consolation)

Yet all is well; he has but passed
   To life's appointed bourne:
And alien tears will fill for him
   Pity's long-broken urn,
For his mourners will be outcast men,
   And outcasts always mourn.

     .   .   .   .

And he of the swollen purple throat,
   And the stark and staring eyes,
Waits for the holy hand that took
   The Thief to Paradise;
And a broken and a contrite heart
   The Lord will not despise.

     .   .   .   .

The Ballad of Reading Gaol by C.3.3. was published in February '98 by
Leonard Smithers, six editions being issued in three months. But as each
edition only consisted of a thousand or twelve hundred copies, and as
Smithers brought it out with the caution he always displayed when dealing
with some unmentionable work, Wilde accused him of being "so fond of
suppressed books that he is suppressing his own." It was very favourably
reviewed in the press, Arthur Symons writing the best appreciation. Wilde
had never cared for the work of Symons, but now felt he must reconsider
its value, which he did by assuming that Symons was not a man but a firm:
"I have written to my solicitor to enquire about shares in Symons Ltd.
Naturally in mass productions of that kind you can never be certain of the
quality. But I think one might risk some shares in Symons." W. E. Henley
wrote a spiteful attack in *The Outlook,* but when Smithers wanted to reply
to it Wilde advised him not to: "What does it matter? He is simply jealous
. . . Besides, there are only two forms of writers in England, the unread and
the unreadable. Henley belongs to the former class." As usual Wilde bore
no resentment, and when Vincent O'Sullivan referred to Henley's article
he merely remarked: "Henley owes me seven-and-six. The other day I read
a review of his praising a novel by somebody called Mary Cholmondeley. I
bought the book, and before I had read very far I came on this sentence: 'The
birds were singing on every twig and on every little twiglet' Now, you
know, when an artist comes on a sentence like that in a book it is impossible
for him to go on reading it. So I consider that Henley owes me seven-and-
six." An undergraduate wrote to criticise the opening line of *The Ballad,*
saying that the soldier who was hanged did not wear a scarlet coat because
he was in the "Blues," a regiment of the Guards which wears a blue tunic.
Wilde replied that it would have been impossible to open his poem

> He did not wear his azure coat,
> For blood and wine are blue.

There were two or three more carping criticisms; but one would have to be
God to please all tastes, and even He would probably displease Satan.

As soon as Wilde could raise the money he left Naples for Paris in the
early part of '98. On March 24th his second letter on Prison Reform was
published by *The Daily Chronicle.* In it he said that it was useless to send
more inspectors round the prisons, as had been suggested, for they merely
went to see that the senseless and brutal rules were carried out. He referred
to the insufficient and inedible food, which always produced diarrhoea, the
filthy insanitary conditions in which the prisoners lived, and the punishment

of insomnia inflicted on all by the plank beds. He protested against the wretched books which convicts were given to read, the solitary confinement, the absence of all humanising influences, the interviews with friends when one was "exhibited like an ape in a cage," and the fact that they were only allowed to write letters four times a year. He described prison chaplains as well-meaning but silly men. "Once every six weeks or so a key turns in the lock of one's cell door, and the chaplain enters. One stands, of course, at attention. He asks one whether one has been reading the Bible. One answers 'yes' or 'no,' as the case may be. He then quotes a few texts, and goes out, and locks the door. Sometimes he leaves a tract." The letter ends with the statement that "the first and perhaps the most difficult task is to humanise the governors of prisons, to civilise the warders, and to Christianise the chaplains."

On April 7th, '98 Constance Wilde died at Genoa. Oscar told Douglas that on the night she died "I dreamed she came here to see me and I kept on saying 'Go away, go away, leave me in peace.'" Next day he heard by telegram that she had taken him at his word. With her went his last chance of seeing his children again, and we can understand why a talk with Smithers upset him. "He is rather dreadful," reported Oscar. "I suppose many of us are rather dreadful now, and do not realise to what we have come. But the other night he was speaking to me of his son, and we wept together." Dreadful or not, he quite enjoyed the company of Smithers, to whom he once addressed this request: "Write to me that you have given up your idea of coming to Paris—then your arrival will be a surprise."

For the first few weeks of his sojourn in Paris, Wilde stayed at the Hôtel de Nice; then he moved to another house in the same street: Hôtel d'Alsace, 13 Rue des Beaux-Arts, which, with some intervals, was henceforward to be his place of residence. He wished to take and furnish a flat or rooms off the Champs Elysées, and wrote to Ross at some length on the subject, complaining of the insanitary condition of his hotel, and objecting to furnished rooms on the ground that one could be turned out of them at a moment's notice, whereas "in unfurnished rooms one can do as one chooses." He suggested that Ross should open a subscription for "the sweet sinner of England," out of which he could take a flat, and started to make plans on the principle that "People who count their chickens before they are hatched act very wisely: because chickens run about so absurdly that it is impossible to count them accurately." Having had one experience of Oscar settling down for life at Berneval, Ross was not eager to have another, even though there was a greater likelihood of permanence at Paris, and the project was dropped.

Needless to say, Ross was always being asked to send Oscar's monthly allowance before the date on which it was due, the request being backed on one occasion by the assurance that if the checque did not arrive when anticipated "I am afraid I shall be obliged to telegraph to you daily." In addition to cash payments Ross sometimes sent Oscar a new suit, made by his London tailor Doré. Blue was the colour always chosen by the wearer, who intimated that he was growing stouter: "A rather painful fact, apparent to all, must now be disclosed. Pray mention it to no one but Doré—and break it to him gently." Doré did not interpret the hint generously enough, because the trousers were too tight round the waist, which Wilde attributed to the fact that he rarely had good dinners: "Nothing fattens so much as a dinner at 1 fr. 50."

It was fortunate for Wilde at this stage of his life that he took what he termed a passionate interest in humanity. He was never bored except when lonely, and it was difficult to feel lonely in Paris, with its shifting scenes and general air of gaiety. He loved the crowds, the traffic, the cabarets, the churches, the quays, the boulevards, the gardens, and "the unspeakable books" which he bought in the Palais Royal and read in his hotel. After a breakfast which consisted of a cutlet and a couple of eggs, he usually spent the rest of the day in cafés, never in his hotel "except when I am confined to the house by a sharp attack of penury." A favourite place was Pousset's, 14 Boulevard des Italiens, where he met writers and painters and musicians. Often he visited the *Quartier Latin* with some French poet and talked about art for hours together. He dined at unpretentious restaurants for two or three francs, "and we were all very gay on *vin ordinaire*—after all, the only proper intoxication is conversation." He had not yet reached the stage when anyone's society is better than no one's, and occasionally declined an invitation to lunch, "feigning temporary good health as my excuse." But he was more accommodating when someone begged to be allowed to pay a part of his hotel bill, "a request that I did not think it right to refuse." Maeterlinck was anxious for a meeting, and Wilde dined with him and Georgette Leblanc, then the prima donna of the Opéra Comique, in their pretty little house near the Bois de Boulogne. Frank Harris visited Paris in the late spring and was "most hospitable and nice," Wilde dining with him nearly every evening, once at Maire's where "the bill was terrific." Despite his poverty, and the insults of English and American visitors, which made him wonder "what would have happened to those in pain if, instead of Christ, there had been a Christian," he was still the best of company, and created laughter wherever he went. "Laughter," he announced, "is the primaeval attitude towards life —a mode of approach that survives only in artists and criminals."

In June '98 Dupoirier, the landlord of his hotel, became fretful about the payment of his bill, and to relieve his mind Wilde went with a friend to an inn, L'Idée, Le Perreux, Nogent-sur-Marne, where credit was available. Returning to Paris, he reported that the English were very unpopular, "as all those who are over here under Cook's direction are thoroughly respectable. There is much indignation on the boulevards. I try to convince them that they are our worst specimens, but it is a difficult task." A heat-wave emptied Paris that summer: "Even the criminal classes have gone to the seaside, and the gendarmes yawn and regret their enforced idleness. Giving wrong directions to the English tourists is the only thing that consoles them." In August he stayed with Rothenstein and Conder at the Hôtel de l'Ecu, Chanmerières-sur-Marne, where he rowed a lot and bathed twice a day. By now he had come to the conclusion that he was finished as an artist: "Something is killed in me. I feel no desire to write—I am unconscious of power. Of course my first year in prison destroyed me body and soul. It could not have been otherwise." But as Smithers wanted to publish *The Importance of Being Earnest* and *An Ideal Husband*, he corrected the proofs of the former, asking Ross to look at his "woulds" and "shoulds," his "wills" and "shalls," as he felt sure they were all wrong. Harris was at St. Cloud in the autumn, and they frequently breakfasted and dined together. Harris had just sold *The Saturday Review* and had bought a hotel at Monaco; and he wanted Oscar to spend the winter with him at La Napoule, near Cannes. This time Oscar raised no objection, though he was a little apprehensive: "Frank insists on my being always at high intellectual pressure—it is most exhausting—but when we arrive at Napoule I am going to break the news to him—now an open secret —that I have softening of the brain—and cannot always be a genius."

Consumption of the purse having reached the galloping stage, Wilde tried various dodges to get his allowance out of Ross well in advance. In one letter he said that the innkeeper at Nogent had threatened to sell his clothes if the bill were not paid. Ross reminded him that the same thing had happened a few weeks earlier, and he owned up: "I am so sorry about my excuse —I had forgotten I had used Nogent before—it shows the utter collapse of my imagination—and rather distresses me." But Harris was very kind and could usually be depended on for a few hundred francs at the conclusion of a good dinner: after all, each meal meant for him several hours of unalloyed entertainment such as he could find nowhere else in the world. In December Oscar was lunching and dining at Frank's expense every day at Durand's,

Oscar arriving at 1 and 8, Frank at 2:30 and 9:15, the former making this comment: "No one should make unpunctuality a formal rule, and degrade it to a virtue, but I have admirable, though lonely, meals." The British Embassy folk patronised Durand's, and it gave Harris not a little pleasure to note their disapproval of his guest.

Wilde travelled alone to La Napoule and settled down at the Hôtel des Bains about the third week in December. He spent Xmas day by himself. On December 26th he was sauntering by the sea when George Alexander rode past on a bicycle: "He gave me a crooked, sickly smile, and hurried on without stopping. How absurd and mean of him!" Thus the two most important "confessions" in Frank Harris's Life of Wilde must be dismissed as fabulous. Harris tells us that he travelled to La Napoule with Wilde, adding several circumstantial details, such as their meeting at the Gare de Lyon on a Sunday evening, the number of empty bottles on the table of the buffet where Wilde had dined, the depression of Wilde, who had clearly been crying, Harris's attempts to cheer him up, the discovery of the cause, their long argument in the train on the relative merits of boy-love and girl-love, their glimpse of Avignon, where they alighted in their pyjamas and overcoats to stretch their legs on the platform and drink a bowl of coffee, their discussion as to where they should go on reaching Marseilles, though this had been settled weeks before, their arrival at La Napoule, the dishes they had for breakfast, and how they spent their first day. Harris then implies that several weeks elapsed before Oscar came in one day, "very red and excited and more angry than I had ever seen him," to break the news that he had just been cut by George Alexander, which started them off on a lengthy disputation in which Wilde defended his sexual tendency. We now know that Harris did not arrive at La Napoule until January, at least a week after the Alexander incident. From Wilde's letters to Ross we cannot say positively that Harris was there until February 2nd but we know for certain that he had not turned up by January 2nd. It does not follow from this that Harris never discussed sex questions with Wilde; indeed, knowing Harris, we may feel pretty certain that he did. But it does follow that a man who invents so many details in what is supposed to be a record of fact cannot be trusted at any point in his narrative unless supported by outside testimony. Our doubt as to the truth of these "confessions" is strengthened by the fact that they are not spoken in Wilde's manner, and by our knowledge that he hated argument; and we may feel sure that, if he ever mentioned the subject to Harris at all, he dealt with it in a very different style. Since Harris knew Wilde well, it may seem strange that he should have given us these fictional talks; but we must remember that in his prime as an editor and a financier it never struck him that he would one day have to earn a living by writing "portraits" of the people he had met or entertained in his palmy period. When that time came his memory was failing, and in any case he had not been sufficiently interested in anyone but himself to remember the sayings and characteristics of others; so he carelessly read what had been written about them to get the background approximately right, invented the rest, and trusted to luck. While at La Napoule he was far more interested in the book he was writing on Shakespeare and the hotel he was running at Monaco than in Wilde, and we cannot rely on a word of the account he gives of their holiday together. To take one more instance, although nearly every episode is demonstrably apocryphal. He had not forgotten Wilde's remark that he had stayed at every big house in England—once. To square matters, he now invents a scene in which he overhears Wilde shouting from one room to a fellow in another a character-sketch of Harris himself, who is charged with pretending to have a good position in society and with being proud to meet such people as Arthur Balfour. This gives Harris an opportunity of saying in parenthesis that he made no such pretence and that he was not proud of meeting Balfour; it also enables him to say that on the previous evening Wilde had boringly held forth on the great houses he had stayed at and the great people he had known, the sort of thing Wilde never did but the very thing Harris had done on a certain occasion at the Café Royal.

To return to our history: on the day that Alexander cut Wilde a fellow named Harold Mellor cycled from Cannes to spend the night at the Hôtel des Bains. He had been over several times before; Wilde had taken to him; he was fascinated by Wilde's conversation; and henceforth they saw a lot of one another. Wilde liked La Napoule, which was engirdled by pines, and he loitered beneath the trees inhaling their scent, or basked on the beach in the sun. Sometimes he visited Nice, once to see Sarah Bernhardt in *La Tosca*. After the performance he went round to her dressing-room: "She embraced me and wept—and I wept—and the whole evening was wonderful." He witnessed the *Bataille des Fleurs* at Cannes, and would have gone there more often if the place had not been so popular with the English wealthy classes. When Harris at length turned up they did not spend much time together, because Harris was writing his Shakespeare book and going for long walks and attending to his hotel, while Oscar was "earnestly idling" and making himself agreeable to the fishing population of the district, of whom he wrote that they had "the same freedom from morals as the Neapolitans—they are very nice." During February he heard that the press had ignored the pub-

lication of *Earnest*, even though "The Author of *Lady Windermere's Fan*"
was substituted for his name on the title-page, and he begged Ross "If you
hear anything nice said about the play, write it to me: if not, invent it."

Mellor had a house at Gland on Lake Geneva, and asked Wilde to stay
with him. As this would mean free meals, and conceivably champagne, he
accepted the invitation, leaving La Napoule towards the end of February
and visiting Genoa on the way, so as to make a pilgrimage to his wife's
grave. "It was very tragic seeing her name carved on a tomb . . . my name not
mentioned of course . . . I brought some flowers—I was deeply affected—
with a sense, also, of the uselessness of all regrets. Nothing could have been
otherwise—and life is a very terrible thing." This was written some days later
in a subdued frame of mind, and gives no indication of his actual behaviour.
He drove out to the cemetery from Genoa in a little ramshackle green cab,
and gave way to a paroxysm of grief and remorse at the graveside, where
he sobbed and prayed, and strewed crimson roses on the earth, and vowed
eternal fidelity to the memory of Constance, his strongest emotion having
been expressed by himself in a youthful ballade:

> O mother, you know I loved her true!
> O mother, hath one grave room for two?

Utterly overcome by his feelings, exhausted and weeping, he drove away.
But sorrow could not hold him for long, and it vanished as quickly as it
had come: a mood of hilarity, recklessness and irresponsibility seized him;
he had a riotous time, particularly at a small inn on the quay, Albergo di
Firenze, "rather *mal-famée* but cheap"; and . . . the cab was not dismissed
for several days.

He spent the whole of March at Gland. Mellor's villa was prettily situated
on the edge of the Lake among pines, and the view of the Savoy mountains
on the opposite side pleased Wilde, who wrote to Louis Wilkinson that
Mont Blanc "at sunset flushes like a rose: with shame perhaps at the prev-
alence of tourists: he has lost all his terrors; spinsters climb him now: and
his snows are not virgin any more." Occasionally he crossed the Lake on a
petroleum launch to visit the Savoy villages; and sometimes he was to be
seen on a bicycle, a form of motion he did not find agreeable. Still less
agreeable was the society of Harold Mellor, who was thrifty and taciturn,
making no attempt to entertain his guest or help him to feel welcome. Though
well off and possessing a good cellar, he gave Wilde "the most horrid Swiss
vin ordinaire" at dinner, and "in the evening he reads *The Times* or sleeps—
both audibly." After a while they met only at meals, and Wilde stayed on

simply because he was hard-up: "I regard the place as a Swiss Pension, where there is no weekly bill." His dislike of Mellor extended to the country and its inhabitants. Switzerland, he declared, had produced nothing but theologians and waiters. The Swiss were ugly, shapeless, colourless, like cavemen: "their cattle have more expression." In short the atmosphere was not favourable to composition, which perhaps was a blessing, and the only work he did at Gland was to correct the proofs of *An Ideal Husband*, which Smithers brought out later in the year. His brother died on March 13th at the age of 46. He was sorry for Willie's widow, and would have made over to her a third of the small Irish property which became his on the death of his brother, but his creditors took the lot. As to Willie, "between him and me there had been, as you know, wide chasms for many years. *Requiescat in Pace*."

Life in Mellor's company became intolerable—"I never disliked anyone so thoroughly"—the moment he received his next monthly allowance he left for Genoa, writing to Ross from the Café du Nord at Geneva on April 1st that Mellor had wept at his departure, implored him not to go, and apologised for his own behaviour which was due to hereditary insanity. But not even the promise of champagne would have tempted Wilde to stay, and his joy in getting away was such that he included Mellor in a general amnesty. "I believe," he mused while sitting in the Geneva café, "that at the holy season of Easter one is supposed to forgive all one's friends . . ." The *ennui* of Gland was succeeded by the boredom of Santa Marguerita, Ligure, near Genoa, from which he was rescued by Ross and brought to Paris at the beginning of May, 1899. His visit to Gland had taught him a bitter lesson: "I used to rely on my personality—now I know that my personality really rested on the fiction of *position*—having lost position, I find my personality of no avail." Yet this was not true, for his position had been won by his personality. The fact is that his discomfort at Gland was due entirely to his host. Knowing nothing of Mellor except what we glean from Wilde's letters, we must take a lenient view of him, merely observing that, like most of his fellow-creatures, he was not at his best at home.

CHAPTER EIGHTEEN

THE END

NOT wishing to increase the bill he already owed at the Hôtel d'Alsace, Wilde considerately put up at the Hôtel de la Neva in Rue Montigny on his return to Paris; but finding that credit was even more restricted there, he moved on to the Hôtel Marsollier in Rue Marsollier. He was glad to be back in Paris, where he was made much of by several young poets. At a café in Montmartre where they congregated he was "received with *great* honour—and everyone was presented to me: I was not allowed to pay for my bocks, and the chasseur begged for my autograph in his album . . ." He dined one night with a friend at the Café de la Paix, and saw Ada Rehan, the actress, and Augustin Daly, her producer, at another table. Some time afterwards Ada told Graham Robertson what had happened:

"I didn't know what to do. Mr. and Mrs. Daly were with me and I could not tell how they would feel about it. You never *do* know with men when they are going to feel very proper and when they are not."

"And was Mr. Daly feeling proper?" enquired Robertson.

"No, he wasn't. It was such a relief! If I could not have bowed I should have cried. So Mr. Wilde came over and sat with us, and talked so charmingly—it was just like old times—we had a lovely evening."

Oscar refers to the meeting in one of his letters, and says that Ada's hair had turned quite white: "I accused her at once of dyeing her hair white—she was delighted." They asked him to write a play for them, but a few days later, on June 7th, '99, Daly suddenly died. Let Ada continue: "Arrangements had to be made and Mrs. Daly was not equal to taking them in hand. I seemed to be all alone and so confused and frightened. And then Oscar Wilde came to me and was more good and helpful than I can tell you—just like a very kind brother. I shall always think of him as he was to me through those few dreadful days."

The summer heat in Paris, aided no doubt by the warmth of his landlord over the settlement of an account, drove Wilde to Fontainebleau for fresh air and easy credit; and we have a snapshot of him there by Sir Peter Chalmers Mitchell, who was taking coffee one afternoon with two English friends, a stockbroker and a publisher, outside a café near the palace gates when Wilde sat down at a table nearby. The two Englishmen at once got up and left, after remarking that Wilde was probably staying there under a false name and that the hotel should be warned. Mitchell's attitude did not harmonise with that of the stockbroker and publisher. He went over to Wilde's table, raised his hat and began a conversation:

"Mr. Wilde, I don't suppose you remember me, but a long time ago Ion Thynne introduced me to you at the Café Royal."

"Ion Thynne. Yes! Isn't he dead?"

"I think so. It is years since I've heard anything of him. Robbie Ross is a friend of mine."

"Ah! Robbie, with the face of Puck and the heart of an angel. Would you care to sit with me?" Mitchell sat. "Of course I remember you. We talked and talked, and I asked you how to get rid of the body. I used you in *Dorian Gray,* but I don't think you would be easy to blackmail. Ion! In the days when I made phrases I called Ion 'exquisitely corrupt.'"

They talked for more than two hours, on crimes and punishments, on the management of gaols in England, on poems and poets, and on science. "I wish to record the impression for which I was least prepared," writes Chalmers Mitchell. "Oscar Wilde was a man of very wide information and interests, and of commanding intelligence." When Mitchell got up to go he asked Wilde to dinner that night. "No," replied Wilde. "Your friends would not stand it. I am going back to my little inn where they don't know me. Good-bye. Thank you."

To the landlord of the Hôtel Marsollier came at this moment an opportunity denied to the majority of his kind; he had the chance of immortalising himself by giving Wilde reasonable credit. But he had the soul of a tradesman, bartered his immortality for a hundred francs, and forced Wilde to leave. Another landlord, Jean Dupoirier of the Hôtel d'Alsace, to whom Wilde was already in debt, met him in the street, discovered that he was homeless and moneyless, told him to return to No. 13 Rue des Beaux-Arts, called at the Marsollier, paid Wilde's bill, rescued his property which had been distrained by the nameless landlord, brought it back to the Hôtel d'Alsace, extended Wilde's credit, and won his own immortality. At about the time this removal was being effected Sherard made his last attempt to reform Wilde. They met one evening by accident, and, after being very sentimental over their long friendship, Sherard began to abuse Wilde's friends in unprintable language. Wilde checked him sternly, and they parted in anger. But Sherard felt he had a mission to perform, and followed Wilde. Another explosion on his part ended in another separation. He made a third attempt the same evening, when Wilde accused him of egotism, of thinking solely of his own pleasure. "Were those dreadful journeys to Reading and Wandsworth pleasant?" Sherard burst out. "My God, Robert! and do you think it was pleasant for me to be in those places?" countered Wilde. This was unanswerable, and Sherard abandoned his efforts to remould Wilde's nature nearer to his heart's desire.

Late in September '99 Wilde dined with Laurence Housman, Robert Ross, Henri Davray and another friend; and twenty-four years later Housman published *Echo de Paris*, which is in part a reconstruction of Wilde's conversation at that meeting. I was most anxious to quote such passages from it as were definitely Wilde's, and Laurence Housman was kind enough to tell me exactly what he had created as a "likeness" of Wilde's general talk, and what, to the best of his memory, he had accurately reported. The following passages are therefore vouched for by Housman as being Wilde's in substance, and as nearly as possible his in manner:

"I told you that I was going to write something: I tell everybody that. It is a thing one can repeat each day, meaning to do it the next. But in my heart—that chamber of dead echoes—I know that I never shall. It is enough that the stories have been invented, that they actually exist; that I have been able, in my own mind, to give them the form which they demand."

"It is much easier for a Scotsman to be a genius than to be an artist. Mr. Gladstone, I believe, claimed to be a Scotsman whenever he stood for a Scottish constituency or spoke to a Scottish audience. The butter-scotch flavour of it makes me believe it was true. There was no art in that; and yet how truly typical! It was always so successful. . . . Your Scotsman believes only in success. How can a man, who regards success as the goal of life, be a true artist. God saved the genius of Robert Burns to poetry by driving him through drink to failure. Think what an appalling figure in literature a successful Burns would have been! He was already trying to write poems in polite English, which was about as ludicrous as for a polite Englishman to try to write poetry in the dialect of Burns. Riotous living and dying saved him from that last degradation of smug prosperity which threatened him."

"But do you mean no artists are successful?" asked Housman.

"Incidentally; never intentionally. If they are, they remain incomplete. The artist's mission is to live the complete life: success, as an episode (which is all it can be); failure, as the real, the final end. Death, analysed to its resultant atoms—what is it but the vindication of failure: the getting rid for ever of powers, desires, appetites, which have been a lifelong embarrassment? The poet's noblest verse, the dramatist's greatest scene, deal always with death; because the highest function of the artist is to make perceived the beauty of failure."

(*On Carlyle*) "In his prime he wrote his greatest work—the history of a failure—the French Revolution. The time came when, with all his powers matured, he stood equipped for the writing of his supreme masterpiece. There was no need to look far afield for a subject: it stood obvious awaiting him. After his French Revolution he should have written the life of Napoleon—the greatest success, the greatest failure that the world has ever known. He would have done it magnificently. What a spectacle for the world: the Man of Destiny receiving from the son of humble Scottish peasants his right measure of immortality! But because Carlyle was a Scotsman, he would not take for his hero the man whose life ended in failure; he could not bring himself to face the débâcle of Waterloo, the enduring ignominy and defeat of St. Helena. Had he been true to his art, he would have realised that St. Helena was the greatest theme of all—for an artist, the most completely significant in the whole of modern history. But because he had the soul of a Scotsman, because he worshipped success, he looked for his hero, and found him in that most mean and despicable character, Frederick the Great: a man to whom heaven had given the powers of a supreme genius, and hell the soul of a commercial traveller with that unavailing itch for cultural gentility which Voltaire has exposed for us. On that mean theme he wrote his most voluminous work . . . You smile at me, Robbie, but believe me, in my own ruin I have found out this truth. The artist must live the complete life, must accept it as it comes and stands like an angel before him, with its drawn and two-edged sword. Great success, great failure—only so shall the artist see himself as he is, and through himself see others; only so shall he learn (as the artist must learn) the true meaning behind the appearance of things material, of life in general, and—more terrible still—the meaning of his own soul."

Another passage in *Echo de Paris*, though not warranted by Laurence Housman, is nevertheless so characteristic of Wilde in his then mood that I believe the chronicler remembered it better than he afterwards thought:

"As I sit here and look back, I realise that I have lived the complete life necessary to the artist: I have had great success, I have had great failure. I have learned the value of each; and I know now that failure means more—always must mean more than success. Why, then, should I complain? I do not mean that a certain infirmity of the flesh, or weakness of the will, would

not make me prefer that this should have happened to one of my friends—
to one of you—rather than to myself; but admitting that, I still recognise
that I have only at last come to the complete life which every artist must
experience in order to join beauty to truth."

Vincent O'Sullivan tells us that in his last years the two figures whom
Wilde was readiest to talk about were Napoleon and Jesus Christ: the hero
chained to a rock, the god crucified; both failures in the eyes of men; for
"there is something vulgar in all success" and "the greatest men fail—or seem
to the world to have failed." That was how Wilde saw himself after his fall,
and in the stories of Napoleon and Jesus he could picture the drama of his
own life, for he too had been imprisoned and reviled, despised and rejected
of men. "If terrible sufferings courageously borne, the enduring of dire injustice and reviling without complaint, be matter of saintliness, then Wilde
was a saint," says O'Sullivan. He was punished by his spiritual and intellectual inferiors for what was itself a punishment, a mental malady that hurt
no one but himself, and he was treated as a moral leper to the day of his
death. At a word from some American or Englishman, barmen would refuse
to serve him drinks, restaurant proprietors would ask him to leave, hotel
managers would turn him out, barbers would decline to shave him, respectable fathers would clutch their children to their sides as he passed by. Many
men who had known all about his sexual oddity in the days of his success,
and had been proud of his acquaintance then, now disowned him and either
cut or avoided him. The English and Americans were his chief traducers
and tormentors, but every self-important French writer kept out of his way,
vicious little paragraphs about him appeared at regular intervals in the French
press, and only the younger and more rebellious spirits were to be seen in
his company. Wilde bore it all with extraordinary gentleness and good nature,
never indulging in recriminations, never expressing a sense of injury. The
worst thing he ever did in his life was to accuse Lord Alfred Douglas of
having ruined and deserted him, which, as we have seen, was not malice
but melodrama, and in the last years of his life he was on perfectly friendly
terms with Douglas. He could not feel revengeful against the English, who
pursued their crusade against him with unrelenting malignance; and when
the South African war broke out in the autumn of '99, the Irishman Wilde
was entirely pro-British, while the American Whistler was wholly pro-Boer.

Now and again, it is true, Wilde played for sympathy, but it was for the
sake of the drama to be extracted from his position, not out of self-pity.
Douglas touches on this in his account of Wilde as a talker during the last
phase: "It was part of his pose to luxuriate a little in the details of his tragic

circumstances. He harrowed the feelings of many of those whom he came across; words of woe poured from his lips; he painted an image of himself, destitute, abandoned, starving even (I have heard him use the word after a very good dinner at Paillard's); as he proceeded he was caught by the pathos of his own words, his beautiful voice trembled with emotion, his eyes swam with tears; and then suddenly, by a swift, indescribably brilliant, whimsical touch, a swallow-wing flash on the waters of eloquence, the tone changed and rippled with laughter, bringing with it his audience, relieved, delighted, and bubbling into uncontrollable merriment."

Like all actors, his nature demanded the stimulus of applause, and that is mainly the reason why he ceased to write. What he missed most was his audience: the pretty fashionable women who had thronged to hear him talk and whose appreciation had inspired his plays. "I have had my hand on the moon. What is the use of trying to rise a little way from the ground?" he said. He could see nothing ahead of him, nothing to be attained that was worth attainment. His recently published plays had been boycotted by the press, and for him there was no pleasure in writing what was received in silence. So he talked, and talked better than ever, and was satisfied now with the plaudits of a few friends round a table, since he could no longer dominate a *salon* or arouse the enthusiasm of a theatre. With his humorous outlook and happy temperament, he had always lived in the present; and in his later years he could quickly forget his tragedy in the joy of conversation, and the pleasure he derived from those "external things of life" which in prison had seemed to him so unimportant.

Early in 1900 Harold Mellor, feeling no doubt that his hospitality the previous March had left something to be desired, invited Wilde to Italy in the coming spring, offering him £50 for expenses, and actually induced him to pay another visit to Gland, tempting him with the prospect of rides in a curious vehicle called "an automobile," which Mellor had just purchased. Having announced to Ross that he was friends with Mellor again, "below zero of course," he went off to Gland, where he stayed for ten days, finding Mellor "almost as neurasthenic as I am" but enjoying the automobile, which constantly broke down: "They, like all machines, are more wilful than animals—nervous, irritable, strange things," and he thought of writing an article on "nerves in the inorganic world."

The thought of Rome was very pleasing, and this time, he decided, he would really become a Catholic, "though I fear that if I went before the Holy Father with a blossoming rod it would turn at once into an umbrella or something dreadful of that kind." They started for Italy early in April, staying eight days in Palermo, which Wilde thought "the most beautifully situated town in the world." Every day he went to the Cathedral, being shown all over it by a youthful Seminarist: "At first my young friend gave *me* information: but on the third day I gave information to him, and rewrote History as usual . . ." In spite of his incognito, the university students soon got to know who he was, and they turned up daily at the café to hear him talk: "To their great delight I always denied my identity." After spending three days at Naples, they reached Rome on Holy Thursday, Mellor leaving on Saturday, Wilde staying on for several weeks. "To the terror of the Papal Court," he appeared in the front rank of the pilgrims at the Vatican on Easter Sunday, and received the blessing of the Pope. "I was deeply impressed, and my walking-stick showed signs of budding; would have budded indeed, only at the door of the chapel it was taken from me . . ." For some time he had been suffering from what he believed to be mussel-poisoning, and for five months had been treated by a Jewish doctor in Paris, his condition becoming steadily worse. But the rash mysteriously disappeared after the Papal blessing, and a French artist whom he met at Rome promised to celebrate the event by painting a votive tablet: "The only difficulty is the treatment of the mussels—they are not decorative, except the shells, and I didn't eat the shells." Finding that the Vatican gardens were open to the Bohemian and Portuguese pilgrims, "I at once spoke both languages fluently, explained that my English dress was a form of penance," obtained admission, and "wandered in exquisite melancholy for an hour." He never missed an opportunity of seeing the Pope, received the Papal blessing seven times, and considered himself a thoroughgoing papist. "I have not seen the Holy Father since Thursday—but am bearing up wonderfully well," he informed Robert Ross, to whom he also imparted a painful piece of news: "You know the terrible, the awe-inspiring effect that Royalty has on me: well, I was outside the Café Nazionale taking iced coffee with galato—a most delightful drink —when the King drove past. I at once stood up, and made him a low bow, with hat doffed—to the admiration of some Italian officers at the next table: it was only when the King had passed that I remembered that I was *Papista* and *nerissimo*! I was greatly upset: however I hope the Vatican won't hear about it."

But in two or three weeks the novelty had faded; and although he was able to say "I would give more than words can paint to be no longer outside the Fold," he wrote to one friend that he was surrounded by "emblems of a religion whose efficacy lies in your faith and nowhere else," to another that "I cannot stand Christians because they are never Catholics, and I cannot stand Catholics because they are never Christians—otherwise I am at one with the Indivisible Church," and he assumed that the great Gothic and Renaissance revivals of architecture were due to the fact "that God found he could only live in temples made by hands: in the heart of man he could not live . . ." Dissatisfied with the Faith, he took up photography, at which he became so good that in moments of depression he felt that he was a born photographer. Tiring of churches, he tried cows, and discovered with pleasure that "cows are very fond of being photographed, and, unlike architecture, don't move." Rome was as usual crowded with Americans, "who go about with depressing industry, looking at everything and seeing nothing," and he was not sorry to leave it in the middle of May: "Life seems to be slipping from me. Events do not loom half as large as they once did. Age is not yet with me but its shadow is in the doorway." He left for Naples, went by boat to Genoa, and thence to Paris, having determined to spend the next winter in Rome, which he thought "the only city of the Soul."

"There is only one thing in the world worse than being talked about, and that is not being talked about," he had written in *Dorian Gray*, and he was now feeling the truth of this saying, as also of his statement that in the modern world tragedy was dressed in comedy, the great realities becoming commonplace or grotesque, though this, he admitted, had "probably always been true about actual life. It is said that all martyrdoms seemed mean to the looker on." His own martyrdom has been made to look much meaner than it really was. It has pleased many people to picture Wilde in his last days as a shabby, shuffling, cadging, drunken, loafer, either because they felt flattered by the comparison, or because they disliked him, or because they enjoyed preaching a moral sermon, or because it made a good story, or because they dreamt it. Childish vanity is the cause of most lies that people tell about others, but we need not trouble to disentangle the motives here. Two cases may be picked out from the fictional rubbish that has passed for candid reminiscence in the last forty years.

According to herself, Nellie Melba, the famous singer, was walking in the streets of Paris one morning in 1898, "when there lurched round the corner a tall shabby man, his collar turned up to his neck, a hunted look in his eyes." The man stopped her, announced himself as Oscar Wilde, and without the least preamble asked her for money. She, noble soul, "could hardly bear to look at him, not from hatred but from shame and pity." She emptied her purse and handed him ten louis. He "almost snatched it," and without a muttered word of thanks vanished, presumably without lurching. All we need say is that Wilde, whose attitude to women was chivalrous to a degree that would nowadays be considered affected, did not borrow money from them, and was scrupulously careful, after his downfall, never to speak to any of the famous women he had once known unless they made the first step, as with Ada Rehan, Sarah Bernhardt, and a few others. It happens that at about the time when the Melba meeting was supposed to have taken place he met a man to whom he had once lent money; and when Ross asked whether he had suggested repayment of the loan, he replied that he had not: "Gentlemanly feelings linger in the most improbable places . . . If I could have the feelings appropriate to my position—or rather my lack of position— it would be better for me—but while natures alter, what is artificial is permanent always."

The second case is quite as untrue, with a touch of burlesque to make it more piquant. We read in the Life of Lord Carson by Edward Majoribanks that the hero of that work was walking one wet day through Paris, and was about to cross the street when the driver of a cab almost ran him over and splashed him with mud. Stepping back quickly to the pavement, he knocked someone down, turned to apologise, and recognised "the haggard, painted features of Oscar Wilde," who was obligingly lying in the gutter. Carson begged his pardon, and, we are to assume, left him in the gutter. Whether this is Carson's invention or not will probably remain a mystery, but everyone knows what happens when a motor car collides with a tank. Wilde was the tank. Apart from that, it can be confidently stated with regard to these and similar stories that Wilde never put paint on his face, except when he was lecturing in America, never had a hunted nor a haggard look, was never shabbily dressed, did not shuffle, could carry his drink without staggering, and would have stood firm against the shock of anything short of a bull. All these stories remind one of the pump and the drag of Oxford: they are picturesque; they seem appropriate; but they are not true. He was invariably well-dressed, well-shaved, self-assured, and imposing. It was said that his father, Sir William Wilde, was so patriotic that he carried the soil of his country about on his person. Oscar's patriotism never went to that length, and he was always as clean as soap and water could make him.

The number of people who helped him financially has grown considerably since his time, and one wonders why he did not set up as a sort of Monte Cristo instead of touching everyone he met for the price of a drink. But there is no doubt that some of his friends treated him generously, if not with his generosity. In dealing with this aspect of the man we must remember that he had no money-sense at all, and just as he had shared with others when he was in funds, so did he expect others to share with him when their luck was in. All his life he had given with both hands, and he felt disturbed when cash was doled out to him with one hand. His friends cannot be blamed, for they were not millionaires, and they knew that money slipped through his fingers like water, that £50 given him on Monday had usually disappeared by Saturday. Thus he passed through long periods of chill penury, interspersed by short periods of cordial prosperity. "I have been a king, and now I want to be a beggar," he said with his usual flair for light and shade in the human drama, and in order to keep his friends up to scratch he would accuse each of meanness to the others. Ross, Harris and Douglas helped him whenever they could; and after Queensberry's death in '99 Douglas gave him over £400 at different times. He never borrowed from the prominent people he had known in his prosperous days, French or English, leaving it to them to help him unsolicited if they cared to do so.

Several well-known stage folk came to his assistance in a diplomatic manner by giving him money in advance for plays which they felt certain he would never write. In this way they were able to help him without humiliating him, as he said of Dal Young's payment. Mrs. Brown-Potter and Ada Rehan were among them, and Charles Frohman was another. The latter handed Seymour Hicks, who was visiting Paris, a cheque for £200 payable to Wilde with the words: "Give him this if you can find him and say it is on account of a new play I want him to write for me. Of course I know he'll never send me anything, but—well, he was a great man and I expect he's in a pretty bad way—and that's all there is to it." Hicks came upon Wilde one evening at a small restaurant in Montmartre, explained his errand, and received this message: "*Tell* Mr. Frohman he shall have a very *beautiful* play with a *wonderful* plot, and *wonderful* lines and *wonderful* characters in it. And I am sure he will have a *wonderful* success." Hicks hastily bade him good-bye, "for he had as his companions two creatures of the kind who had been his ruin." William Rothenstein had a similar experience. He and his wife took Wilde to an open-air restaurant where a mauve Hungarian band was playing what Wilde once described as "mauve Hungarian music." Oscar chose a table close to the musicians, saying he liked being near the music; but during dinner, says Rothenstein, it became plain that he was less interested in the music than in one of the musicians.

The two actors who had been most closely associated with his triumphs also behaved well. Herbert Beerbohm Tree sent him something and in a letter dated Feb. 17, 1900, said: "No one did such distinguished work as you . . . I do most sincerely hope . . . that your splendid talents may shine forth again. I have a lively remembrance of your many acts of kindness and courtesy and was one of those who devoutly hoped that misfortune would not submerge you." George Alexander, who told Ross long afterwards that he had been ashamed of his behaviour at La Napoule, made up for it by getting out of his cab one day in Paris and speaking to Wilde who was strolling along the pavement. This was in July, 1900, and from a letter that Wilde wrote to Alexander we learn that an arrangement was made whereby the actor should pay the author £20 a month, probably because Alexander had bought for next to nothing the acting rights of *Lady Windermere's Fan* and *The Importance of Being Earnest* when Wilde went bankrupt, and he wanted to make some return for the bargain. In justice to the memory of Alexander, who was a kindly if cautious man, it must be stated that he paid royalties to Wilde's estate on both the plays when they were revived, though he need not have done so, and on his death left them to Wilde's son.

The only man who took Wilde's promise of writing or collaborating in a play seriously was Frank Harris, who heard Wilde tell the story of the drama which he had sketched out for Alexander at Worthing in the autumn of '94, and suggested a collaboration, Wilde to provide the scenario and write Act 1, Harris to write Acts 2, 3 and 4. Wilde agreed, but nothing more was done about it until Harris's hotel speculation failed and he was in need of money. He then wrote the whole play, using Wilde's plot and characters, and entitled it *Mr. and Mrs. Daventry*. On its acceptance by Mrs. Patrick Campbell, he went over to Paris in the autumn of 1900 to discuss terms with Wilde. On September 26th he signed an agreement to pay Wilde £175, with more to come if the play were successful. He said that he had left his cheque book in London and could only give Wilde £25 on the nail, but that he would send the balance of £150 "within a week." Wilde never got another penny out of him, though the play, produced in October, was successful; and Wilde's last illness was exacerbated, his end hastened, by Harris's behaviour. Needless to say, Harris's account of what took place does not agree with the foregoing, for which there is documentary evidence. The one truthful part of his statement is that, immediately it became known he had written a play with the help of Wilde, several people who had advanced money for a play with a similar plot were annoyed because someone else had jumped their claims. Which also provided Wilde with another cause for complaint: "Frank has deprived me of my only source of income by taking a play on which I could always have raised £100."

Wilde's behaviour after his downfall has been sharply criticised by those who have had the good fortune not to fall down; but whatever he did is a comment on what was done to him. The conditions in which his peculiar genius could flower were denied him; and if he was, as Bernard Shaw called him (on the evidence of Frank Harris) a swindler, we must not forget that he had been swindled by society; for not only had he been ruined by the action of the law, but every avenue of rehabilitation had been closed to him after he had purged his offence. However, as no one except Harris took his "swindles" seriously, no one but Harris could have been swindled; and in the case of *Mr. and Mrs. Daventry* Harris did the swindling. Shaw also described Wilde as "an unproductive drunkard." Yet no one has ever called Christ or Socrates unproductive because each of them spoke his thoughts instead of writing them down. In fact the use of the word "unproductive" in connection with Wilde is unimaginative: to put the thing at its lowest level, he earned his living every time he opened his lips. As to being a drunkard, the capacity of human beings varies: what is one man's drink makes another man drunk. Wilde, as we know, could drink Colorado miners under the table, and he was seldom seen the worse for liquor by his friends. On the other hand, there is no doubt that in his last days he drank more than was good for him. But he did not drink for the sake of his health. He drank in order to forget, and absinthe, as he said, brings forgetfulness, only demanding repayment with a bad headache. He was lonely, and he could not endure loneliness; so he went to cafés and bars to seek company. There was a little bar on the Boulevard des Italiens called "Calisaya" where he could talk to journalists, or, failing them, the barman; and there was a place in the *Quartier Latin*, frequented by artists of all sorts, where he was treated as a "master" and where he did not have to pay for his drinks, the young men being only too eager to supply liquid refreshment in exchange for the spiritual sustenance which he provided. After one such enjoyable night, he announced with an air of great solemnity: "I have made an important discovery . . . that alcohol, taken in sufficient quantities, produces all the effects of intoxication."

He spent the summer of 1900 in Paris and visited the Exhibition several times. He was often to be seen at the Grand Café, 14 Boulevard des Capucines, where he dined with Douglas in August. All through dinner he was in the highest spirits, keeping Douglas continually amused; but just before they separated he became depressed, saying he had a presentiment that he would not live for long. Douglas tried to laugh it off, but he went on seriously: "Somehow I don't think I shall live to see the new century." He paused impressively before adding: "If another century began and I was still alive, it would really be more than the English could stand." His presentiment did not mislead him: Douglas never saw him again.

The feeling that his time was short drove him into extravagances of speech which sometimes suggested hysteria. Parables and paradoxes, humorous stories and tragic dramas, reminiscences and fantasies, poured from him, as if he wished to give form to every idea that entered his head, every thought that flashed through his brain, before the final darkness. Sometimes he left a tale half-finished because another had to be caught as it flickered on the screen of his imagination; and that too might be dismissed half-told if a fleeting third tempted pursuit. Meeting him on a steamer going up the Seine to St. Cloud, the Comtesse de Brémont asked him why he no longer wrote. "Because I have written all there was to write," he replied. "I wrote when I did not know life; now that I do know the meaning of life, I have no more to write. Life cannot be written; life can only be lived. I have lived." Everyone who knew him agreed that he was not only fully alive himself but that he made others live more abundantly. When three *apaches* waylaid him one night, he turned the hold-up into a joke and took them to a café, where they paid for his drinks and laughed for two hours at his impromptus, a more liberal way of spending the time than if they had been committing robbery with violence.

Sherard called at the Hôtel d'Alsace one September day, and took note of Wilde's dingy apartment. His little bedroom was on the first floor, facing the courtyard. The bed looked small, and was in fact some inches too short for him. The hangings of the bed, the window-curtains, the upholstery of the furniture, were the same colour as the lees of wine. The other furniture consisted of a rickety table, a faded thread-bare sofa, and a few bookshelves. A soiled and tawdry mirror was above the mantelpiece, on which stood a massive clock of metal and marble supported by a crouching lion.

"You are working, too, I see," said Sherard, pointing to the litter of papers on the table.

"One has to do something. I have no taste for it now. It is a penance to me; but, as was said of torture, it always helps one to pass an hour or two." Sometimes he did a little hack-work for a few francs.

"Come and see me again," said Wilde as Sherard rose to go, "though I hardly like to ask people to see me in this room."

"Why, I had never noticed it," lied Sherard politely. "What does the *mise-en-scène* matter?"

"*Qu'importe le verre, pourvu qu' on ait l'ivresse?*" said Wilde.

Fortunately for him, he was a good sleeper, and in the last months of his life he never awoke before noon, when he breakfasted, getting up at about 3 p.m. unless he had an appointment for lunch. Many of his more active hours towards the end were spent in the yard of the hotel, where he sat for long periods reading and sipping cognac. He re-read the whole of Balzac, no doubt remembering his early days at the Hôtel Voltaire nearby, his favourites being *La Cousine Bette* and *Eugénie Grandet*. He also read a number of books on prison life, including Howard's.

He began to suffer from headaches, and on October 10th he had an operation on the ear that had given him trouble ever since he had fainted in Wandsworth Prison. But the operation did not ease the pain, and Ross went over to Paris in response to an urgent wire, calling at the hotel on the morning of the 16th. Oscar declared that his sufferings were terrible, but as he followed the statement with comical stories about the doctors and himself, accompanied by peals of laughter, Ross did not think him seriously ill. For a month Ross stayed in Paris, seeing Oscar daily. Meals were usually provided by Dupoirier, whose devotion and generosity went so far that he never mentioned to Ross the sums Wilde owed him, and even bought champagne and other luxuries without once revealing the fact that the cost came out of his own pocket. Wilde's rash had returned, and he apologised for scratching himself. "I'm more like a great ape than ever," he said, "but I hope you'll give me a lunch, Robbie, and not a nut." His sister-in-law, who had married Texeira de Mattos, came one day with her husband, and champagne appeared with the lunch. "I am dying, as I have lived, beyond my means," remarked Oscar, who again declared that he would not outlive the century, that he was responsible for the failure of the Exhibition, the English having left when they saw him there so happy and well-dressed, and that this would make the French hate him.

On October 29th he got up at noon for the first time since his operation, and after dinner he and Ross went to a café in the *Quartier Latin*, where he drank absinthe. The following afternoon they went for a drive in the Bois de Boulogne, stopping at nearly every café for an absinthe. Ross warned him that he would kill himself. "And what have I to live for, Robbie?" he asked gravely. Three doctors disagreed about his illness, though naturally none of them knew what was wrong with him. Reginald Turner had come to help, and Oscar said one morning "I have had a dreadful dream. I dreamt that I was dining with the dead." Turner remarked "My dear Oscar, I am sure you were the life and soul of the party." This delighted Oscar, who promptly became the life and soul of the present party. He was much worried about his debts, suffering remorse over some of his creditors, especially Dupoirier, and Ross wrote to Douglas saying that Harris ought to send something, as the doctor had said that Oscar's money troubles were retarding his recovery. Douglas, who was in Scotland, sent £10 at once, but Harris sent nothing. On November 12th Ross went to say good-bye as he was leaving for Nice with his mother. Oscar became hysterical, said he would die before Ross returned, begged him to stay, and broke down, sobbing violently. Ross thought this was merely another of Oscar's moods and left the next day. Turner took his place, attended to Oscar's needs, went out driving with him, nursed him with the help of Dupoirier, and tried to prevent him from drinking alcohol. "You are qualifying for a doctor," said Wilde. "When you can refuse bread to the hungry and drink to the thirsty, you may apply for your diploma." Another friend, Maurice Gilbert, relieved Turner now and again, and Wilde reported to Ross "I've shared all my medicines with him and shown him what little hospitality I can." Every day the doctor came to dress his ear-wound, and Wilde wrote to Ross that his throat was a lime kiln, his brain a furnace, and his nerves a coil of angry adders.

On November 28th Ross heard by wire that Wilde's state was "almost hopeless," and returned to Paris. Frequent injections of morphia had been given to ease the pain, but even in his delirium he had raised his hands to his head in agony, swearing volubly. He was dying from cerebral meningitis, probably complicated by syphilis. When Ross arrived Wilde was conscious but unable to speak. Remembering an old promise, Ross wanted to know whether he should fetch a priest. Wilde signed his consent, and Ross brought one of the English Passionists, Father Cuthbert Dunne, who asked Wilde whether he wished to be received and put the usual questions. Again Wilde gave the necessary signs of affirmation, and Dunne administered Baptism and Extreme Unction, the penitent being unable to take the Eucharist. In explanation of his conduct, Ross told me that he had never encouraged Wilde's leanings towards the Church and never favoured his conversion, "as it wouldn't have suited his constitution, and no priest could possibly have listened to his confessions in a becoming frame of mind. But he made me promise to bring a priest when he was no longer in a fit condition to shock one, which I did." We may say of his reception into the Church that, being unable to speak, it was the best exit he could devise, and, like all his gestures, perfectly sincere at the moment it was made.

Ross, Turner and Dupoirier were in the dying man's room at 1 o'clock on November 30th. At a quarter to two he seemed to be struggling for breath, and Dupoirier lifted him slightly and held him so. Five minutes later he sighed deeply; the pain left him, and he was at peace.

Douglas came to the funeral, the expenses of which he paid, and the chief mourners were himself, Ross, Turner and Dupoirier, the last of whom contributed a wreath made of beads with the inscription "*A Mon Locataire*." Part of the service was held at the church of St. Germain des Prés, and the burial took place at Bagneux on December 3rd, 1900.

In July, 1909, Wilde's body was removed to the cemetery of Père Lachaise, where, a generation after his death, ten people asked to see his grave to every one who showed an interest in that of Balzac or de Musset or Bizet or Chopin or any other of the immortals lying there.

Lapidary inscriptions have a depressing sameness which makes one wish that greater care were taken to provide epitaphs more suitable to the personalities they commemorate. In a light-hearted discussion with Ross concerning his own epitaph, Wilde had unconsciously spoken the fittest for himself; one that captures his charm, his humour and his boyishness; but it is not on his monument:

"When the Last Trumpet sounds, and we are couched in our porphyry tombs, I shall turn and whisper to you 'Robbie, Robbie, let us pretend we do not hear it.'"

AUTHORITIES
(*Selected*)

The Works of Oscar Wilde, Collected Edition, 1908.
Bibliography of Oscar Wilde, by Stuart Mason (Christopher Millard), 1914.
The Life of Oscar Wilde, by Robert Harborough Sherard, 1906.
Oscar Wilde: His Life and Confessions, by Frank Harris, 1930. (This work is
    nowhere reliable, but it contains letters by Wilde, and contributions by
    Robert Ross, Alfred Douglas, and Bernard Shaw.)
The Autobiography of Lord Alfred Douglas, 1929.
Oscar Wilde: A Summing Up, by Lord Alfred Douglas, 1940.
Aspects of Wilde, by Vincent O'Sullivan, 1936.
Recollections of Oscar Wilde, by Charles Ricketts, 1932.
Oscar Wilde: The Man—The Artist, by Boris Brasol, 1938.
Victorian Doctor, being the Life of Sir William Wilde, by T. G. Wilson, 1942.
Oscar Wilde Discovers America, by Lloyd Lewis and Henry Justin Smith, 1936.
Oscar Wilde: The Story of an Unhappy Friendship, by Robert H. Sherard, 1908.
Oscar Wilde: A Study, by André Gide, 1905.
Sir George Alexander and the St. James's Theatre, by A. E. W. Mason, 1935.
Men and Memories, Recollections of William Rothenstein, 1872-1900, Vol. I, 1931.
My Diaries, by Wilfred Scawen Blunt, 1932.
Self Portrait, taken from the Letters and Journals of Charles Ricketts, R. A. Col-
    lected and Compiled by T. Sturge Moore, edited by Cecil Lewis, 1939.
Time Was, by W. Graham Robertson, 1938.
The Trembling of the Veil, by W. B. Yeats, 1926.
As We Were, by E. F. Benson, 1930.
The Life of Sir Edward Clarke, by Derek Walker-Smith and Edward Clarke, 1939.
The Romantic '90s, by Richard Le Gallienne, 1926.
Oscar Wilde and His Mother, by Anna, Comtesse de Brémont, 1911.
Oscar Wilde and the Yellow Nineties, by Frances Winwar, 1940.
Oscar Wilde, by G. J. Renier, 1933.
Oscar Wilde, Fragments and Memories, by Martin Birnbaum, 1920.
Echo de Paris, by Laurence Housman, 1923.
Impressions of America by Oscar Wilde, edited by Stuart Mason, 1906.
Art and Morality, by Stuart Mason, 1912.
Oscar Wilde: Three Times Tried, compiled by Stuart Mason, 1912.
After Reading, Letters from Oscar Wilde to Robert Ross, 1921.

After Berneval, Letters from Oscar Wilde to Robert Ross, 1922.

The Real Oscar Wilde, by Robert H. Sherard, 1915.

Letters to the Sphinx from Oscar Wilde, with Reminiscences of the Author, by Ada Leverson, 1930.

Oscar Wilde: Some Reminiscences, by Leonard Cresswell Ingleby.

I Have Been Young, by H. M. Swanwick, 1935.

All That I Have Met, by Mrs. Claude Beddington, 1929.

In Good Company, by Coulson Kernahan, 1917.

In Victorian Days, and Other Papers, by the Right Rev. Sir David Hunter Blair, Bart., 1939.

Stewart Headlam, by F. G. Bettany, 1926.

A Collection of Original Manuscripts, Letters and Books of Oscar Wilde. (Catalogue issued by Messrs. Dulau & Co. Ltd.).

Frank Harris, by Hugh Kingsmill, 1932.

Works and Days from the Journal of Michael Field, edited by T. and D. C. Sturge Moore, 1933.

The Green Carnation, by Robert Hichens, 1894.

Patience, by W. S. Gilbert (The Savoy Operas, 1932).

Twenty-five Years in Paris, by Robert H. Sherard, 1905.

Sixteen Letters from Oscar Wilde to William Rothenstein, edited by John Rothenstein, 1930.

Oscar Wilde, by Louis Wilkinson (*The New Statesman*, Jan. 3, 1914).

Oscar Wilde Twice Defended, by Robert H. Sherard, 1934.

Oscar Wilde, by Desmond MacCarthy (*English Wits*, edited by Leonard Russell, 1940).

The Romance of the Oxford Colleges, by Francis Gribble, 1910.

The Gentle Art of Making Enemies, by J. McNeill Whistler, 1904.

Whistler, by James Laver, 1930.

Without Apology, by Lord Alfred Douglas, 1938.

My Fill of Days, by Sir Peter Chalmers Mitchell, 1937.

Without Prejudice, by Sir Chartres Biron, 1936.

Recollections of a Savage, by Edwin A. Ward, 1923.

Memories of a Misspent Youth, by Grant Richards, 1932.

This Life I've Loved, by Isobel Field, 1937.

Social and Diplomatic Memories, 1884-93, by the Right Hon. Sir James Rennell Rodd, G.C.B., 1922.

My World as in My Time, Memoirs of Sir Henry Newbolt, 1932.

Both Sides of the Curtain, by Elizabeth Robins, 1940.

Ellen Terry's Memoirs, 1933.

The Days I Knew, by Lily Langtry, 1925.

My Memoirs, by Sir Frank Benson, 1930.

Time Gathered, by W. B. Maxwell, 1937.

Herbert Beerbohm Tree, Some Memories collected by Max Beerbohm, 1920.

Memories and Adventures, by Sir Arthur Conan Doyle, 1924.

This For Remembrance, by Julia Neilson, 1940.

Melodies and Memories, by Nellie Melba, 1925.

Self and Partners, by C. J. Holmes, 1936.

Twenty Years of My Life, by Douglas Sladen, 1915.

Twenty-five Years: Reminiscences by Katherine Tynan, 1913.

Jimmy Glover His Book, by James M. Glover, 1911.

Mrs. J. Comyns Carr's Reminiscences, edited by Eve Adam, 1926.

Twenty Years of My Life, by Louise Jopling, 1925.

Horizon, a Review of Literature and Art, edited by Cyril Connolly, April, May, October, 1941. (Articles by A. J. Symons.)

Memories of a Victorian, by Edgar Jepson, vol. I, 1933.

Me and My Missus, by Seymour Hicks, 1939.

Not Guilty, M'Lord, by Seymour Hicks, 1939.

The Life and Death of Conder, by John Rothenstein, 1938.

Sir Evelyn Ruggles-Brise, compiled by Shane Leslie, 1938.

Victorians, Edwardians and Georgians, by John Boon, vol. I, 1928.

The Journals of Arnold Bennett, 1911-21, edited by Newman Flower, 1932.

The Life of Lord Carson, by Edward Marjoribanks, 1932.

A Bookseller Looks Back, by J. S. Bain, 1940.

The Wild Geese, by Gerald Griffin, 1938.

Both Sides of the Curtain, by Genevieve Ward and Richard Whiteing, 1918.

Everyman Remembers, by Ernest Rhys, 1931.

Wales England Wed, by Ernest Rhys, 1940.

Adventures of a Novelist, by Gertrude Atherton, 1932.

Mainly Players, by Constance Benson, 1926.

The Bancrofts, by Sir Squire and Lady Bancroft, 1909.

Empty Chairs, by Squire Bancroft, 1925.

A Player under Three Reigns, by Sir Johnston Forbes-Robertson, 1925.

Portraits of the Eighties, by Horace G. Hutchinson, 1920.

William Heinemann, by Frederic Whyte, 1928.

Portraits of a Lifetime, by Jacques-Emile Blanche, 1937.

My Reminiscences, by Lord Ronald Gower, 1884.

John Lane and the '90s, by J. Lewis May, 1936.

The Eighteen Nineties, by Holbrook Jackson, 1927.

A Playgoer's Memories, by H. G. Hibbert, 1920.

Fifty Years of a Londoner's Life, by H. G. Hibbert, 1916.

Memoirs of Marie Corelli, by Bertha Vyver, 1930.

As I Was Going Down Sackville Street, by Oliver St. J. Gogarty, 1937.

Seventy Years Among Savages, by Henry S. Salt, 1921.

Last Letters of Aubrey Beardsley, 1904.

Letters from Aubrey Beardsley to Leonard Smithers, 1937.

W. E. Henley, by Kennedy Williamson, 1930.

William Sharp, by Elizabeth A. Sharp, 1910.

The Reminiscences of Lady Dorothy Nevill, edited by Ralph Nevill, 1906.

The Life and Letters of Henry Arthur Jones, by Doris Arthur Jones, 1930.

The Life and Letters of Sir Edmund Gosse, by the Hon. Evan Charteris, 1931.

Oscar Wilde, by R. Thurston Hopkins, 1913.

Life of Sarah Bernhardt, 1907.

Autobiography of R. B. Haldane, 1929.

A Writer's Recollections, by Mrs. Humphry Ward, 1918.

Through the Box-Office Window, by W. H. Leverton, 1932.

The Aesthetic Movement in England, by Walter Hamilton, 1882.

Resurgam, Unpublished Letters by Oscar Wilde, privately printed by Clement Shorter, 1917.

A Book of Famous Wits, by Walter Jerrold, 1912.

Various Periodicals.

INDEX